# CONVERGENCE

Jonathan Dixon

Gregg Owen

Published by 26th Street Books

Copyright © 2025  26th Street Books

All rights reserved. No part of this publication may be reproduced, distributed, or transmitted in any form or by any means, including photocopying, recording, or other electronic or mechanical methods, without the prior written permission of the publisher, except in the case of brief quotations embodied in critical reviews and certain other noncommercial uses permitted by copyright law.

ISBN 979-8-218-55668-6

*Some names and identifying details have been changed to protect the privacy of individuals.*

Front cover concept by Jonathan Dixon.

Book design by Darko Marceta and LTL.MTN.

Printed in the United States of America.

First printing edition 2025
26th Street Books
Chicago · New York
editors@26thstreetbooks.com

# Dedications

This book is the first in a series. *Convergence*, and each book to follow, recounts events during my career as a prosecutor in Cook County, Illinois. I wanted to capture a portrait of a time and place, and illustrate some of the wild, incredible, almost unbelievable things that happened not just to me, but to my partners, mentors, friends, and colleagues—all of us together. Every word is true, even if it feels stranger than fiction.

This dedication is deeply personal. It reflects not only my journey but also the people who shaped it.

To my mother, who pleaded with me to not drop out of law school when touring with my band made studying almost impossible. Thanks, Mom.

To my children, Gregg and Kristen, who love their dad and could not have made me prouder, and to Marilyn, their mother and one of my closest friends.

To my beloved grandchildren, Christian, Gianna, and Kennedy—this is for you. Four years ago, when Christian was born, followed by Gianna and Kennedy, I began to wonder how old each of you would need to be to remember your Grandpa. My life has been anything but ordinary, and I wanted to leave behind a part of who I am, something that would help you know me even after I'm gone.

To my wife, Kelin, my love, my life, my cheerleader. Thank you, Bunny.

To Tom Breen, Bill Kunkle, and Ted O'Connor—dear friends whose honor and commitment to justice made the story of *Convergence* what it is. Your unwavering integrity has left an indelible mark, and I am grateful to have shared this journey with you.

To Andy, my surrogate father and the Godfather of my son—thank you for 35 years of mentorship, friendship, and resilience. You embraced life fully, even when it delivered its worst. I am forever grateful for the example you set.

To Cedric and Mickey, for doing the right thing.

And finally, to my dearest friend and trial partner, Mike Goggin—without you, this book would never have come to life. Thank you for your partnership, support, and friendship.

**--Gregg Owen**

This is for my son, Beckett, hands-down, far and away the best thing that's ever happened to me. You have no idea how proud I am.

For Brooke Thomas, who's a close second.

And in memory of John Jacob Singer.

**--Jonathan Dixon**

*At the request of families involved, some names have been changed*

# Chapter 1
*March 3, 1976, morning*

Tony Messina could feel it.

Even before opening the door to his son's room that morning, he knew he'd find that Gio hadn't slept there last night, and he was dreading it.

That was two nights running, and Tony could only account for one. It didn't feel right at all.

Going down to the basement, Tony heard Maria's voice somewhere in the house, and the footfall of their daughters, Lisa and Gina, rushing to leave for work. He couldn't hear what Maria was saying, but her voice sounded ragged and underslept. The two of them had gone to bed, exhausted, just a few hours before they got up, but it wasn't because of Gio.

Tony had gotten in late, just as the heavy rain started falling. He didn't pay much attention, but after talking to Maria for a while, Tony noticed the rain hadn't let up.

"Wow. It's really coming down," he'd said to Maria. She agreed and they made a few more remarks about the rain. They were dancing around the matter of Tony's phone call from earlier.

Calling from the car phone, Tony had told Maria he was on his way back. He asked if Gio was home, and then if she'd heard from him at all. When she said no, he asked if she could do him a favor: go down to Gio's room, look in the bottom drawer of the bureau, and see if Gio's 9mm was there. Maria didn't ask why, for which Tony felt grateful. He had tried sounding casual but didn't know if Maria could hear in his voice that he'd started calling her from the car three times, hanging up each call before he finished dialing. Or that he'd been trying to get ahold of Gio all day.

Over the next hour, the rain kept falling in a torrent. At around eleven, Tony had been standing near the basement door and felt compelled to open it, turn the light on, and take a look. When he did, he saw water pooling up in the far corners and a few trickles down the wall near the boiler.

"Oh, shit. Shit."

Maria, coming from around the corner, asked, "What is it?"

"Goddamn rain coming into the basement, and it's starting to puddle up."

The rain stopped before midnight, but the two of them had the wet vac going, pushed water toward the drain with a broom, and piled up towels in a couple of hard-to-reach spots until two o'clock. The flooding allowed Tony to put Gio out of his mind for a little while. When he and Maria went to bed, they both fell asleep right away.

Tony Messina's success grew out of accidents, catastrophes, and bad luck. After years of making friends, building trust, and doing good work, when property owners filed claims for fire or water damage, construction accidents, high winds, or acts of God, the insurance companies often told Tony about the claim first. This let Tony approach the owners with offers to repair and rebuild before anyone else. Timing and friendship gave him the advantage, and charisma carried him the rest of the way.

Tony was long on charm. He was a good talker who remembered clients' wives and kids and asked after them by name. He had an appealing face, a handsome voice, and it had all done well for him. He worked constantly because he'd been a Depression-era kid, with a fear of privation he never lost. He had a family to provide for—Maria, Lisa, Christina, Gina, and Gio, the oldest, twenty-four years old and often at home, something Tony thought of as a success.

They'd had some trouble with Gio years ago, at the start of high school. His grades dipped. Teachers who had thought highly of him were beginning to think differently. He began having discipline problems. Threats and incentives from his parents came to nothing. But eventually, it came to light that school bored Gio out of his mind. He was not, the school psychologist told them, being challenged. During one conversation, without really being serious, Tony floated the idea of sending Gio to military school. Tony was shocked when Gio thought it was a good idea. After a number of late-night talks, Tony and Maria agreed to it.

Gio thrived at the new school, and three years later graduated first in his class.

From there Gio studied economics at the University of Colorado, then earned a master's degree at a nearby college. He started working for Tony, and he thrived there, too.

Tony had decided to make Gio the company's vice president and had the business cards printed up. He had planned on telling Gio the next time they saw each other.

Gio was a good son, a good friend. Tony had renovated the basement into a separate living space with a bedroom and a rec room in order to keep Gio close.

That was the bedroom Tony had gone to the basement to check. And when he opened the door and saw the laundry Maria had left folded for Gio, that it hadn't been touched since she'd put it there on his bed two days earlier, he understood he couldn't avoid it any longer: something was very wrong.

"Actually, I wasn't overly worried. New girl. Serious infatuation, you know? It all had him distracted, doing careless stuff he wouldn't do ordinarily," Tony told the cops later. Then as an afterthought, "I don't blame him, if you want to know the truth, even if I didn't think she was the best girl for him. She was a little wilder than he needed."

It wasn't true that Tony wasn't worried because Gio had never— not once—forgotten to call and let them know he wouldn't be home. Tony knew Gio wouldn't consciously concern his parents like that.

When the insurance companies gave him leads, Tony was effusive with his thanks. The insurers returned the sentiment with more business and an occasional tip-off, like the Arlington Heights company moving to smaller offices, who had to let the bulk of their office furniture go for a song. Tony put a bid in for the desks, chairs, and cabinets, intending for Gio to take and resell them somewhere, a potentially nice supplement to the salary Tony paid him every week.

Tony made a plan to meet Gio there yesterday. It wasn't a vague plan. It was definite, specific. But his son never showed up.

*Okay. Fine. Whatever*, Tony had been thinking. *It's alright that he's taking time to enjoy himself.*

Tony kept repeating that to himself until he almost believed it really was alright.

The truth was that lately Gio was taking a lot of time to enjoy himself. And the more time Gio spent with his new friends, the more often he was coming late to work. A few times when Gio arrived at the office, Tony could smell last night's scotch on him. Tony started hearing about Gio's expensive nights out at restaurants and clubs. Taken together, it made Tony concerned.

But right now he was feeling more than concerned. Gio had given Tony a phone number two nights before and asked for a wake-up call. Tony called, but no one answered. No answer on the next call, a little later, or the call after that, or any of the calls Tony made throughout the day.

"No, there wasn't any sign anything had happened," he'd tell the detectives. "Just a sense. I knew he wasn't down there. It's hard to explain. It felt really, really empty. And all the lights were out. I didn't even need to open the door to know Gio wasn't in his room."

But he'd turned on the light at the bottom of the stairs, went the rest of the way to Gio's room, knocked, got no answer, opened the door. He didn't open it fast. It was even darker in there, and a little chilly. Tony noticed those clothes—the socks and shirts, T-shirts and pants, a pile of underwear. Everything folded and neatly stacked. The room smelled like Gio, but the scent was almost old, faded. Tony pulled the door shut and stood for a moment, turning a few possible explanations over in his head. None of them worked.

Upstairs, Tony found Maria in their bedroom and asked, as casually as he could, "You didn't happen to hear Gio at all last night, did you?"

She was sorting through a drawer in the bureau and didn't look up. "No, I didn't. Not this morning. I was trying to think when I saw him ... yesterday? No—it was Sunday. Sunday afternoon. I heard him come in, then he passed me going out two minutes later."

"All right. I just had a question about scheduling. I'll ask him at the office."

When she looked at him, he could see she knew it had nothing to do with scheduling. Or anything beyond where Gio had been, where he was right then.

Tony's stomach was tightening up.

He was on his way back toward the basement and saw Gina putting on her coat, leaving for work. Tony stopped her before she opened the front door. He spoke to her in a muted, conspiratorial voice. "You talk with your brother at all?"

Gina leaned back a little, sizing her father up, trying to gauge why he was asking.

"I spoke with him Monday night, maybe nine thirty, ten," she said. She didn't mention how dazed Gio had sounded on the phone. "He was at Tinker's. I could hear Cedric, too, in the background. Gio wanted someone's number, but I had no idea who the person was."

Tony had met Tinker, also known as Delphine Moore a few times, not at great length, but enough to know she had some spark. Maybe, Tony thought, a little more spark than Gio needed. She was smart, lively. He liked her well enough, at least at first, though he knew Gio's sisters felt differently. Cedric Sberna, who Gio had met relatively recently—well, the guy was something else. Self-absorbed, arrogant. But he was Gio's friend, and that meant he was welcome at the house anytime.

"And that was the last time you talked to him?" He could see Gina tensing, starting to wonder. She nodded. "Do you have Tinker's number? Okay. And Cedric's? So, could you get them for me, please? Quietly, okay?"

As soon as he'd told her to do it quietly, he wished he hadn't. She'd begun pivoting away to go get the numbers but stopped. She started speaking but he held up a hand and cut her off. "It's nothing. He didn't come to work yesterday, and I need him to drag his ass out of Tinker's place and get to the office. Work problems should stay at work. I don't want to bring them home to your mother. So ... "

Tony could always tell when one of the kids was lying if they overexplained. He'd pointed it out enough times that he worried now about giving himself away, so he was trying to keep it simple. The truth was, he wanted to unburden himself. Siblings had their shared confidences, knew things about each other their parents didn't, and maybe Gina could clarify a few uncertainties. But he wasn't there yet.

His stomach hurt worse than it had a few minutes ago. His hands didn't feel steady, and he put them in his pockets.

"Okay. They're upstairs. I'll get them."

Gina came back after a couple of minutes and handed him the numbers, looking him right in his eyes, trying to read him.

He forced a smile. "Seriously—don't worry. Okay? Go, get out of here, beat it. I'll see you tonight."

Tony watched his daughter leave, and when the front door closed, he listened for Maria, then retreated to Gio's room.

The number Gio had given him matched Tinker's. He turned a light on, sat on the bed, and picked up the phone. Dialing Tinker's number, Tony somehow knew no one would answer but wanted to be wrong so badly he considered praying for it. The relief he'd feel if she picked up ...

It rang five, six times, and he sat holding the handset tight against his ear. At the tenth and eleventh ring, his hope plunged, and he felt a first, fast jolt of panic. He reached over, pressed the receiver down, let it back up, and when he heard the dial tone called Cedric Sberna.

A woman answered and Tony asked for Cedric, and she told him to hold on. He heard movement, footsteps, a voice shouting in the background, a pause, then the voice shouting again. After a long time, a sleep-slurred voice said, "Hello?"

When Tony identified himself and explained he was looking for Gio, Cedric's voice was suddenly clear and alert, even a little stiff, formal.

Cedric said, "I was going to call you as well. I've been looking for him since Sunday, and I can't pin him down."

Tony thought he'd just heard Gina saying Cedric had been there when Gio had called from Tinker's but figured Cedric might have just misspoken, and then Tony's worry trampled right over the thought altogether.

He said, "Can you give me Tinker's address?"

Cedric started talking but stopped. A second passed, another followed, and then several seconds more. Then he told Tony he didn't know what it was.

Tony weighed this for a moment. "You've never been to her apartment?"

Cedric didn't hesitate. "No, no—I've been there. I just don't know where it is, though."

There was another pause. "Okay," Tony said. "Okay, thank you."

Cedric said, "Will you ask him to give me a ring when you get ahold of him?"

"I was about to ask you to do the same thing."

Tony hung the phone up and sat on the edge of Gio's bed. After a while he heard Maria walking around upstairs, and at that, Tony finally stood, turned the light off, and pulled the door shut behind him as he left.

He'd called the operator and given her the phone number, and after a minute the operator came back with Tinker's address. If it's a listed number, the address is available. It was that simple.

Driving to Tinker's neighborhood, Tony had missed the worst of the commuter traffic, but it was still slow going. He tuned into radio stations up and down the dial, back and forth, again and again, but couldn't have told anyone a single thing he'd heard. He wished he could turn around, or skip forward another hour, to sometime after he'd arrived and, Tony fantasized, yelled at Gio and Tinker for giving him this much of a scare. If he'd been this uneasy and unsettled at any time since Omaha Beach, he'd blotted it out.

He had a general idea where the building was—near a hospital, right off Lake Shore—and a need to get there turning urgent. Driving the fastest that traffic allowed, cutting into spaces between the cars that opened up, using his signal when he remembered it, plunging the accelerator, slamming the brakes, feeling the urgency warp into something else, something fiercer that cut him loose from good sense. Drivers cursed behind their windows, Tony cursed back, everyone making gestures at each other. He wasn't like this, and he'd have known he was acting insane if he could have gotten a sudden sense of perspective on what he was doing and causing others to do.

The fantasy of turning around or jumping forward—that had been abandoned a couple of exits back, and now he just wanted to get there and confront whatever was waiting. Crash into it head-on, get it over with. It was going to be bad—he had heard the voice of instinct muttering in the same way it had told him Gio wasn't in his room and hadn't been there for a while—and he was keen on knowing just how bad. Hospital bad, certainly. EMT bad.

Tony argued back at himself, saying he couldn't know for sure, and he considered that for a moment, and as he did—as he thought that maybe Gio had messed up, plain and simple, nothing worse than getting too caught up in a new girlfriend to act in a courteous kind of manner, and Tony wasn't unempathetic to being that sort of oblivious—he experienced an anger toward his son that also wasn't like him. Not because of the discourtesy, Tony thought, but instead, remembering Brando chewing out James Caan in *The Godfather*, "Your brain is going soft from all the comedy you're playing with that young girl ... "

And after a couple of beats, thinking, *Comedy? There's nothing comic going on here. Nothing even remotely funny.*

Tony reached the exit. He took a turn and took another, had to wait at the first light but sailed through a second, and he was almost there. Parked cars lined both sides of the street, packed in tightly, almost bumper to bumper, and as Tony slowed looking for whatever space could accommodate him, he saw Gio's Lincoln Continental—knew it by the blue color. Yes, the city was full of Lincolns, but the odds of this year's model, in the same color as Gio's, parked steps from Gio's girlfriend's apartment were small. Tony might thrill to a long-odds bet, but he wouldn't lay a dime on this one.

A little farther up, just past the building, he saw an empty spot in front of a hydrant and drove for it, parking his car at an angle, not caring whether he got towed. He stepped out of his car onto unsteady feet, and he reeled slightly, then put his hand against the car door, got his balance back, and turned to look at the building. The street number he'd gotten from the operator matched the number on the complex's front door. There were two attached structures, equally tall, equally wide, flanking the main building, and two-thirds of the concrete walkway was in shadow, a narrow causeway into a steep canyon.

In the vestibule, he pushed the buzzer for 131, held it, stepped back. Twenty seconds passed and he reached to press it again but dropped his hand.

*Give them a little time to get themselves together before answering.*

When a minute passed, he buzzed again, holding twice as long this time, and he waited, and no one answered.

When the third try got him nothing, he studied the buzzer to see if there was any way to tell whether consecutive numbered apartments were adjacent or faced each other, but there wasn't, so he contorted his fingers and pressed a few of the buttons at once, letting up and pressing down again several times. No answer. For no reasons that made any sense, and remembering back to his military days, he pressed them again in a pattern—three short taps, three long taps, three more short taps. Again, no one answered, and Tony leaned back and slumped a little against the wall opposite the buzzer, and his frustration wanted any outlet it could find. He thought about pounding all the buzzers, kicking the glass doors in, crying. It occurred to him that pressing as many of the buttons as he saw was the best option, maybe using both arms and his shoulder, but just as he was reaching for them caught sight of movement inside.

The building's super, probably. The guy was dressed like one, at least, pushing a yellow bucket across the floor by a mop handle. Tony thumped the glass with the edge of his hand but thought it might not be loud enough to get the guy's attention, so he rapped as hard as he could stand with his knuckles. The guy looked up, and Tony leaned in to make sure he was in the super's line of sight.

For a moment Tony thought the guy was ignoring him, so he rapped hard on the glass again to make his point. The guy abandoned the mop and bucket and made his way toward the door. When he was close, Tony noticed the super wore a gold band on his ring finger and judged he was old enough to have kids. Actually, as he got right up close, Tony thought the guy might even have grandkids. Maybe he could play on that.

The door opened, the guy waited, and Tony had no idea where to start. Finally, he said, "Good morning. No one has heard from my son or his girlfriend for a few days. She lives in Apartment 131. My son's car is parked on the street, right nearby. Please—I just want to check on them."

The super looked over his shoulder at what Tony assumed was the direction of the apartment.

"Which number?" he asked.

"One-thirty-one."

"Wait. She's his girlfriend?" There was a faint smirk around the guy's mouth. Or disbelief. Or maybe Tony was imagining it.

He ignored the guy. "It's been days. Please."

The super looked at the floor, considering, then stepped back and let Tony in. He pointed the way, and the two men walked together toward Apartment 131.

Tony thought the super looked uncomfortable, looked caught out between the decent thing to do and the thing that might become a big hassle. Tony figured he almost certainly had kids. He'd take that bet. The super hadn't offered more than token resistance.

The super was saying, "I know she gets a good number of visitors. Ms. Moore. But I haven't seen anyone the past day or two. I was off this weekend, though."

Tony tuned him out. The guy wasn't saying anything he needed to know. This was just filling up dead air. There probably wasn't any standard protocol to fall back on when a frantic parent comes knocking. The guy probably didn't deal with frantic parents at all.

Tony felt it again—that sense of things in bad disarray, that he'd be greeted by something terrible. It was just as clear as before but louder now, more insistent. Before he even knocked, he knew his life was changing.

When he did knock, no one answered. Tony and the super both leaned in, ears cocked, listening carefully. Nothing—a deep quiet. Knowing it was pointless, Tony knocked again, long and loud enough that the super turned and stared. The silence was stubborn and held itself, and Tony understood it would outlast their efforts to break it.

The super was still looking at him, the expression on his face asking, *What now?*

"You've got to let me in there," Tony said.

The super's whole posture changed. "No, no. No, sir. I can't. I'll get fired; I just can't do that." He crossed his arms over his chest in protest.

"I know this is asking a lot. I know it. But man, please, I'm begging you here. As a father. One father to another." Tony was putting it out there, and the super didn't correct him. "I need to know what's going on. My son is missing. His mother's going out of her mind."

The super dug in. "I'm not permitted to enter anyone's apartment without express permission. And I don't have it."

After a moment, Tony reached into his pocket and got his money clip. He pulled it out and held a fistful of bills toward the super, trying to do a quick mental count. "There's four, five hundred dollars here. Take it. It's yours. Just let me in there."

The guy wasn't going for it. "I can't do it. You need to get in, call the cops. I can't help you here."

When personality failed him, Tony sometimes caught fire. He reached over, put a light hand on the guy's upper arm, looked directly into his face.

"Open that goddamn door. Open it up or I swear to Christ I'll kick this fucking door down."

Tony hadn't considered that the super might be the tougher, more dangerous of the two of them, but the way the guy looked back at him made Tony think about it now.

A long ten seconds passed, wordless. Then the super reached and pulled a heavy, jangling key ring out of his pocket. It was on a retractable cord. "Move," he said.

The super held the knob with one hand and stretched the keys toward the top lock but stopped midway. He turned the knob back and forth. "It's unlocked," he told Tony. Then he pushed the door open.

## CHAPTER 2
*March 3, 1976, morning*

That same morning, at the same time, and ten blocks away, Gregg Owen's bus inched toward DePaul University. It had been eleven months since a bullet meant to kill him hit his wall instead, and two months since he sat in at show at Mother's. He had finished doing six months as a courtroom intern a while ago, arguing cases against hookers and shoplifters in front of the Honorable J. J. McDonnell. And now he was about to sit for the second half of the Illinois Bar Exam.

Owen had months of preparation behind him. He'd studied constantly since autumn, every day, for twelve hours at least, until Sunday afternoon when he knew, finally, there wasn't anything more he could do. He'd closed his books, rubbed his eyes, and spent the rest of the day lying low. The test would be given on Tuesday and Wednesday. He was ready or he wasn't.

Last night—Tuesday night—he'd had a tough time staying asleep. This morning, he was out of bed and getting ready long before he needed to leave. He left the house and boarded the bus while it was still dark, the street lights dim in the fog, the sidewalks wet from the drizzle. It was chilly and raw outside, and the heat from the floor vents on the bus felt good against his feet.

Now Owen didn't even want to look at his watch.

He was amped up. Expectant, nervous, alert. But being wired wasn't enough to successfully carry him all the way through the exam. He wished he'd gotten just a little more sleep.

And pass or fail, this time tomorrow he'd be on a flight to L.A. to join his bandmates.

Owen already worried that once he left the band for good, he'd never stop regretting it.

He snapped back to the present, on the bus. It was still stuck at the same red light, and horns honked from all directions. The man across from him yelled at the bus driver—as if that would help.

The registration papers for the exam had said that if anyone arrived late, they'd be allowed in at the discretion of the administrators. At this rate it looked like he'd be past dealing with discretion pretty soon and relying on mercy. Owen had spent most of his life trying not to be at the mercy of people carrying clipboards.

A small, unfamiliar panic ambushed him: a thin wire coiled around his spine, conducting cold, unpleasant electricity. Was it even possible something this small, some tiny thing like a late bus, would keep him out of the world of law he was angling his way into? And what if the doors back into the world he'd left were locked tight, leaving him in limbo because his fuckups had deeper roots and further-reaching echoes than he knew. His naivete had already gotten him in trouble. How had he been the only person in the whole courthouse who didn't know that Judge McConnell was a bad apple?

The bus reached DePaul. Owen was out of his seat and at the door before it stopped. His watch said he had four minutes until the test started. He stepped off and walked into the law school lobby. His heart was still racing. It was as crowded, noisy, and humid as it had been the day before.

Owen looked over the crowd the way he might have once scanned an audience. The same crowd as yesterday: a lot of puka shells and pearls. Immense glasses. Sweater dresses and denim suits. Lots of rust and camel colors. Apple greens and baby blue. Stripe block patterns. Plaids and macrame. Turbans, scarves.

He recognized almost all of them. He nodded hello to a few guys he remembered from the courthouse, waved at the handful of other people he knew, and took another look at some familiar faces.

Over by the staircase, he recognized two people from his Constitutional law class: a young woman in a military jacket and red turtleneck, with painfully straight hair hanging to the top of her hips, who told him one time she was angling towards civil rights law. And, he remembered, the guy she was talking with, in a wrinkled plaid blazer and a mustard shirt, only twenty-four or twenty-five, and already with William Kunstler's hair, had said the same thing. Or maybe he'd said he was interested in labor law. Either way, good for them both.

Owen began maneuvering through the people standing alone or in groups, watching how they stood and gestured, and listening to what they told each other. Opposite the girl in the olive drab and red, on the other side of the staircase, there were two men and a woman standing together, with ill-fitting clothes and petulant faces. They'd been in his property law classes. He didn't have good associations—they were always talking about money.

Owen recognized another guy from his second semester but couldn't recall the class. He was grimly serious, standing alone in a military dress uniform. Owen imagined that after the bar exam, the guy might be off to prosecute war crimes or maybe send some of the grunts supposedly smuggling heroin home from Vietnam in body bags to long stretches at Leavenworth. Ever since the war ended, those sorts of stories were more and more common.

And then, Owen thought, there was this bunch. His eyes and focus landed on a boisterous group of four who seemed as if they took that infamous line from *The Godfather* as some sort of affirmation—the one where Brando tells Tom Hagen that a lawyer with a briefcase could steal more than a hundred men with guns. They were bumping chests, high-fiving—just being really loud—on and on about the Bulls losing to Portland last night, the Blazers probably sorry they traded the Rubber Band Man to Chicago last year, busting their asses studying for no reason because the exam was that easy. On and on. The wannabe fixers, big-money litigators, profit-concealing corporate counselors. The ones who think a juris doctor is like a Kevlar vest.

Owen decided what needled him most wasn't that anyone could see how eagerly these guys would embrace dishonesty. And it wasn't the noise, per se. It was that they were shitty performers.

Owen had once seen The Who at a teen club in Arlington Heights. At the end of the twenty-minute set, they started trashing the stage. Pete Townshend rammed the neck of his guitar through his amp, which started to pour out black smoke. Everyone scrambled for the exits. Afterward, people said it was reckless and dangerous, and Owen didn't entirely disagree, but at the same time the mayhem seemed legitimate, even inevitable—where else do you take music after that kind of crescendo?

He understood that, sure, a good lawyer knew the law. But great lawyers also knew how to perform. They were keyed into the power of perception and persuasion. That was how you won a jury over.

These four guys hadn't earned the right to smash their instruments.

The bell rang. The crowd broke apart, all at once, and moved to the bank of registration tables for the day's room assignment.

He'd been making music since the age of fifteen. He'd never known anything else.

*You've lived half the time in front of others*, he reflected, *half for yourself. Take away one half and there's a big void to fill. A lot of questions about yourself that you can't answer anymore. A lot of experience you don't know what to do with. A lot of things you don't know, period.*

But right then, he felt good. The pressure of time was gone, and he felt good. Assured. Confident. Good.

The room was just about full when Owen got inside, but he saw a table toward the back and walked for it. The administrator was closing the door when one last straggler rushed in.

Everyone looked. She wore a red ankle-length winter coat that was brighter and louder than anything else in the room, so it was hard to keep from looking. She scanned the seating and walked toward the back, toward the table where Owen sat, taking her in as she got closer. Dark hair, tight turtleneck, jeans like a second skin, high black boots with small spurs at the heels.

*There is absolutely nothing wrong with her*, Owen thought. His mind jumped away from the test. As she sat down, she met his eyes, seemed to assess him unfavorably, then looked away.

"Those are really beautiful boots," Owen said. "But I have to say, you do a lot more for them than they do for you."

She let out a harried sigh, turned away, pulled her chair in, and took out her pencils. Sometimes Owen forgot he was a civilian. He didn't remember he'd cut his hair short, gotten rid of the eagle feather and earrings. He could have been any other guy in the room. The administrator walked table to table, handing out tests, doing a quick recap of rules and timing, and told everyone to get started.

Today was the essay portion of the test. There was a rustle of papers, pens scratching when everyone wrote their names, and then a silence. It was quiet enough to hear the lights buzzing, and the hush held for a moment, until a few people let out muted groans.

From the front, the administrator said, "Quiet, please."

Owen waited a second before doing anything. He sat getting his head straight, reminding himself he'd sail through this.

He put his eyes on the paper and got to work. He forced all his focus onto the test, and on not smelling the scent of the woman's shampoo—a scent like herbs and sweet incense that he absolutely didn't notice.

All the study and diligence, all the work was paying big dividends. The answers were right there in his mind, hanging like fruit on branches. Owen couldn't pluck them fast enough. It was a good feeling. Nothing dragged him. No doubts, no worries. He knew he'd do well.

The administrator called out that they should lay their pencils down and turn their tests over. It was time for the lunch break. Everyone needed to leave the room.

Owen clocked a few grave expressions right then—grave and irritated—and a couple of despondent faces, a lot of angry hands snatching at coats and scarves, and at different places in the room, a few looking satisfied, assured. For his part, he was close to exhilarated. Owen put his coat on, walked from the room, maneuvered through the crowded lobby, walked out of the building. It wasn't much warmer than it had been earlier, but after a nervous morning and the dry stifle of the rooms inside, the wind and the drizzle came as a relief. He glanced at his watch: a little less than an hour before he had to be back.

After a few minutes of walking, he heard sirens, and he watched as several police cruisers, lights spinning, approached the intersection and barreled through, with an ambulance lagging a few lengths behind. Whenever he saw police making a commotion like that, Owen thought, *Someone's day just went right off the rails.* He turned and watched them.

## Chapter 3
### *March 3, 1976, morning*

Ted O'Connor was at his desk before 8:00 AM. He skimmed a few status reports, looked over some APBs. When he finished reading, it was 8:37.

O'Connor could see Lt. Jules Gallet getting ready for roll call and watched the other detectives start coming in: Philbin, Morask, Skelly, Toenings, Adorjan. They hung up coats, checked their desks for messages, lit cigarettes, made small talk, went to the machine and poured themselves coffee. They all clustered around Adorjan, who was showing them something in his hand. All the detectives were laughing, and O'Connor wanted in on the fun.

Adorjan held a small badly printed pamphlet, with a reaper's skull, hooded, in the style of old woodcuts, dominating most of the cover. Above the skull, it read *Welcome to Fear City*. Under the skull, it explained it was *A survival guide for visitors to the city of New York* and credited to the NYPD. They leafed through its few pages. Among other things, the pamphlet warned never to go out after six o'clock. *If you do need to go out*, it said, *don't even think about taking the subway, and under no circumstances walk anywhere. Do not go to any other boroughs*, it went on, *and never carry anything valuable on your person. With that said, don't trust a hotel safe, and if you try and stow something in your car, assume you've been surveilled and will have it stolen.*

O'Connor thought it was almost pathetic and considered that if anyone in Chicago had written it, Daley would have had them exiled.

Someone said, "So you're saying—just coming right out and saying—that you, the cops, can't do your job. The bad guys win. Don't even bother coming here. You're signing your death warrant. We need a slogan: 'The Second City—in our morgues, there's always room for one more.'"

Everyone, including Gallet, was laughing. Gallet shook his head, saying, "I don't want to hear this, man. I'm superstitious."

Right then his phone rang. Everyone laughed harder.

He answered, listened, and sat down heavily. He looked and met everyone's eyes, then grimaced, and picked up the pencil nub again.

"Okay. Repeat the address," he said. "Uh-huh. Uh-huh. Okay. Okay. Tech is going to be my next call. Thank you, Officer."

Gallet gave Ted O'Connor the lead on this one. When Gallet said two bodies, O'Connor's mind went right to Cabrini-Green, just out of instinct. The North Sheridan address surprised him: 2970 North Sheridan. O'Connor could envision, if not the specific block, a general picture of the neighborhood. Bungalows, greystones, a few high-rise apartment buildings. Nice but not so nice as to be prohibitive. If you were upper-middle class, it was a place you'd aspire to be. That the victims were young said to him they'd either lucked into an affordable place or came from a little money. It didn't sound like they were students, from the description Gallet gave him of the scene and victims. If they were students, probably law or premed. It was possible it was a starter apartment for someone recently hired as an associate at a firm or beginning a residency at a hospital.

Gallet had called the mobile crime unit right off, and officers Jackson and Brown were probably just arriving. O'Connor sent Morask and Skelly over to get the preliminaries rolling, telling them clearly, several times, to make sure no one who wasn't Jackson, Brown, or the two of them was allowed inside—at all, or again if it was too late. This held especially true if any plainclothes officers from general crimes showed up—which was likely. The uniform who'd called it in told Gallet that the victim's father was at the scene.

O'Connor wished he wasn't. Grief and crime scenes usually worked to each other's disadvantage.

He got his coat, went downstairs, and signed for a supervisor's car. The one he got must have just been returned: the gas tank was full and the car interior pleasantly warm. On a raw morning, headed over to see two bodies and a grieving father, the day owed you warm Naugahyde under your ass, at the minimum.

The ashtray, though, was spilling over with crushed Pall Mall butts and mounds of gray ash, and he found this irritating.

One of his peers had said of him, "Teddy's a deep, complex, extensive thinker. The thing is, he tends to think out loud."

O'Connor knew about the comment, just as he knew he was sometimes referred to as Dr. O'Connor. He assumed this was in reference to the master's degree in criminal justice he'd earned at Joliet.

Screw 'em, whatever they said. He didn't particularly care. More often than not, his insights into a case were right. And if not, at least they weren't completely wrong.

The first face he recognized made him furious. O'Connor was almost in front of the apartment, and when he scanned the crowd out front—a dozen at least, sizable already, and not even half an hour into it—he saw Bulldog Drummond, a famous and well-loved reporter from the CBS News, edging his way through to the sidewalk. Right behind Drummond was a television reporter from ABC, whose name he didn't recall. He was incredulous that the press had arrived before him. O'Connor knew one of the beat cops, possibly even someone from Area 6, had called and let the media know what was going on. He wondered how contaminated the crime scene was with all these people walking around.

Skelly met him at the door when O'Connor walked up and led him down the hallway to Apartment 131. The door was ajar, and O'Connor heard voices inside and caught sight of some motion. This was all a good sign, in a way. When a scene was really bad, when it edged beyond the pale, the cops involved stood outside the crime scene and away from the center of it.

It wasn't a particularly well-lit apartment, but the shades were up, and the room was bright enough to see. The forensics guys had set up extra lights and they were busy taking photographs. O'Connor saw a pair of plainclothes from the Special Operations Group. They had probably heard about a double homicide on the scanner and decided to check it out. If SOG was here, O'Connor figured, complications weren't far behind.

SOG had the freedom to respond to anything that caught their interest. Some investigators welcomed them as a resource, a few extra hands and eyes—but others saw them as something like a localized FBI: walking uninvited into the middle of a scene, causing problems, bailing out when things went badly, pinching the credit if things went well.

From all the tape, measures, lights—there were a number of areas of interest. He could see the photographer leaning over … something on the floor, the SOG guy and Brown standing too close. The guy was pressing his lips together in irritation, making them bloodless. He closed his eyes, bowed his head, then looked up and snapped that everyone needed to move back. They all did, and when the photographer angled himself to take the shot, they all stepped in again. "Goddammit, please. Move back," he said.

"Guys, come on," O'Connor said. "Give him room."

Brown and the officer from the Special Operations Group backed up to give the photographer more space.

One of the SOG guys was staring, and O'Connor, thinking maybe the guy did look familiar, tried placing him but couldn't do it.

Flashbulbs popped. The other tech was at the photog's elbow with a pad and drawing pencil, sketching quickly but with a controlled, deliberate hand. The SOG guy's expression bordered on hostile.

O'Connor was standing in the doorway. He saw Morask inside the apartment, talking with one of the techs. Morask broke off and walked over.

O'Connor said, "What do we know now that we didn't know half an hour ago?"

"This belonged to Gio Messina." Morask held up a plastic envelope with a gold watch in it. O'Connor took the envelope from him. The watch looked expensive, and O'Connor saw it used a gold coin as a base.

"Messina? He's the victim?"

"Right. Gio Messina—"

O'Connor jerked his thumb back toward the lobby. "That's the father? The older guy I saw when I came in?"

"Yes. Tony Messina."

O'Connor thought he knew the name. "Messina. Is he a builder?"

"I think so. I think that's what he told Skelly. I'll find out for sure. This also belonged to Gio Messina." Morask held up another envelope with money in it, a small stack of bills folded over in half. "Seven hundred dollars. Seven hundred-dollar bills, nonconsecutive numbers. And then there's this … "

Morask held out a third envelope with smaller packets inside containing something white. "We haven't weighed it yet."

O'Connor stood looking at it for a moment. "Is that all there is? What you've got there?"

Morask knew what O'Connor was getting at. He shook his head. "No, there's more. Not a lot, but it's obvious."

Sometimes if there were drugs involved—if the amounts were negligible—the investigators might drop them down a drain, flush them down the toilet. If it looked pretty clear that drugs were not a motive, then losing them actually made things easier. Drugs sapped everyone's zeal—cops and higher-ups both. The guys at the top figured, Fuck around with that stuff, and you deserve whatever you get. Tell your supervisor you found coke at a crime scene, and you could watch the guy's fire going out.

Morask could read what O'Connor was thinking.

"Not so much that it was the reason anyone got killed. In other words, we don't have to harp on it. You want to go inside?" Morask touched O'Connor's arm. "Before we go in, Gio Messina was in the bathroom; we had to move him. CSU got him documented before we did. You just missed it. He was up against the radiator, so in addition to the stab wounds he's got some significant burns on his upper legs. I got his dad out of here before he was moved."

"Okay. Good to know." He walked inside.

Even in a big space, the nexus of a crime scene is small, and everything orbits around one, or two, or several compact areas. Everyone involved calibrates their attention to the minute and easily missed. Apartment 131 wasn't a big space—O'Connor guessed it was around seven hundred square feet, all told, including the bathroom, living room, kitchen area, and what looked, even from across the apartment, like a pretty small bedroom.

Once inside the living room, O'Connor reflected that after you get a good dose of that smell, you never mistake it for anything else and recognize it, no problem. In fact, he sometimes wondered whether the smell—like today's—was all that bad, or if you just knew what it was, and once you knew you couldn't forget. Like a pebble in the shoe or the slow and regular drip from a faucet, you couldn't ignore it once you were aware of it.

If he was pressed, O'Connor could have come up with a few reasons why he didn't mitigate the smell, but nothing definitive. Some guys worked cigarette filters into their nostrils, or wet a handkerchief with cologne or deodorant, or smeared some Vick's across their top lip—but O'Connor never did. It might have had something to do with solidarity. This was the state of the victim, and O'Connor wanted to make sure he understood that state fully.

Maybe something to do with not creating a buffer between the victim and the pursuit of the killer, keeping the stench present so you couldn't pretend it was something other than what it was. From time to time, some of the guys smoked cigars to try to mask the smell.

The problem was none of that stuff really worked.

O'Connor took one step, then a second, then stood looking for a place to plant his left foot. There was visual litter all over the floor—lengths of tape describing squares, more tape and a few measures around larger and smaller, dried and blackened puddles of blood that, O'Connor noticed, flowed from where the girl was lying dead.

It seemed almost like she was asleep, but as if sleep had made her skin a mottled, soiled white, with the faintest blue undertone. He saw cuts on her back—one rather large, with black blood dried around the rim of the wound, the flesh drying into a bright berry-red, nearly orange color.

He saw Jackson waiting for him across the room, in the bathroom doorway. O'Connor planted his foot, checked the ground around him, took another step, reaching Jackson eventually.

"We'll start in here," Jackson said.

"Christ," O'Connor said after sticking his head in. "There's a lot of blood in here."

A third of the bathroom floor was covered with it, reddish black, still tacky in places.

Jackson gestured toward the ceiling. When O'Connor looked up, he saw black spatters trailing across the painted white ceiling, like strange constellations in negative.

"Go ahead in," Jackson said. "Meet Mr. Gio Messina."

O'Connor stepped in. Starting from the radiator and letting his eyes sweep in arcs over the linoleum, O'Connor took a long and careful look.

"For the amount of blood," O'Connor said, "there's not a lot of spatter, and what there is—"

"Is pretty broad and thick. Drops, not spray."

"Yeah, that's what I was thinking. So, how many times was he stabbed? Not many, right? The killer got a lucky shot in?"

"More or less. Four wounds to the chest, contusions on the right side of the neck, contusions on the neck posterior. Abrasions on both. Let me show you." Jackson pivoted back toward the body, walked over, crouched down. O'Connor did the same. Jackson pulled the sheet down. Gio's skin had the same dirty-sallow tone as the girl's. His eyes were open. He had an expression something like shock on his face.

Or maybe not shock—more like pain and dismay.

"Some of the bruises," Jackson was saying, "Are definitely older. These are probably ten days old or so."

He pointed at an area near Gio's shoulder. O'Connor saw several bruises colored semi-violet and semi-green.

Jackson continued. "But these, here—" He angled Gio's neck to show a few long, narrow bruises, dark blue, with the edges clearly defined. "—these are definitely perimortem. He got knocked against the door or the edge of something. Really hard."

"These sliding abrasions—" Jackson pointed to some scrapes. "I'm thinking there was a fierce struggle. This guy fought. So the perp is going to be a big guy, because our victim isn't exactly puny. I bet they wrestled around for a while."

Both of them stood back up. O'Connor gestured toward the other body.

"What do we have there?"

"Delphine Moore, twenty-four or so, according to the Gio's dad. Originally from Florida. Actress. Ran the name. No priors. She has a brother, a musician, here in the city. We're tracking him down."

"I'm assuming you didn't find weapons?"

"No. Nothing. We did find the cocaine, though. Traces all over that table over there. I found a little glassine packet in his pocket with something powdery and white. I'm positive that's coke. The kid had $700, too, in his wallet. He was wearing a very fancy gold watch. We also found a couple pills loose on that table. The code on the tablets—seven-one-four—translates to quaalude. See those drinking glasses? You can smell liquor in all of them, probably the Johnny Walker from the bottle on the kitchen counter. It's uncapped."

"What's in the brandy glass there?" O'Connor indicated a glass filled with something clear, sitting in the middle of the detritus on the table. "Is it water?"

"Seems to be." Neither of them said anything further because they both knew what it meant: people possessing coke in any significant quantity kept a container of water on hand, and if trouble came busting in, they could dump the stuff in the water, and it would disappear in an instant.

O'Connor walked over to the girl, knelt down, took a long look at her face. She showed cuts or scrapes on her chin and ugly wounds on her chest. Her expression seemed like it signaled terror and pain, contorted in an effort not to cry. Like she wished her mother had been there. It was an otherwise very pretty, verging on beautiful face. Working homicide, O'Connor and others like him had learned to see through even the most savagely wrecked features.

It had occurred to him a long time ago that cops working homicide had a more intimate relationship with a victim than anyone did when the victim was alive. They found out spots, lesions, scars, and other indices of health and illness that even physicians might not know. The victim lies there in a state of so much vulnerability that it's almost embarrassing—helpless, in full indignity, frozen in a moment of panic so extreme they probably hadn't experienced anything like it since childhood, back when the world was a terrifying place, illogical, full of unknowns. And they'd died having that view of the world confirmed.

The sympathetic voiding of the bowels and bladder—hard not to feel humiliated on the victim's behalf, even as you felt a reflexive disgust.

And with a little probing into the way the victim lived their life, you might find out secrets that were spoken only in the confessional, or maybe to a shrink, and sometimes not even there.

There was always the moment, too, when the victim lost their name and was just a body, and you might find yourself amazed for the tenth, fiftieth, hundredth time how much blood the body contained, how much damage a body could overcome, yet how little it took to shut the whole system down for good. One blow, one stab, one shot to the right place …

O'Connor stood up. He said, "You know, obviously we've all seen a hell of a lot worse than this. Still, it's a little strange."

"Things don't quite gel?" Jackson said.

"No, they don't. If this is about money, the killer didn't look all that carefully. If it's about drugs, then basically it's still about money, and they didn't look very carefully. I mean, someone left a fucking month's salary lying around. And crime of passion? Pretty lethargic passion."

O'Connor went back toward the front door to talk with Skelly, and as he reached it, he heard a noise.

He stopped, listened, and heard it again, low and constant. He held up a hand and said, "Everyone quiet down for one second, please."

The room went mute. From outside he heard clearly the squawk of police radios in the squad cars, and the sounds of engines and tires creeping along in front of the building as the drivers slowed to look at the commotion out front. That wasn't what it was. After another second, he realized he'd heard a television, the sound of it coming through the wall of the adjacent apartment.

He turned to Skelly. "Are we at the point of talking to whoever that is?"

Skelly told him, "Not yet. We're still getting a handle on everything."

O'Connor looked around. "I mean, we've probably got it locked down. How about we give a knock on the door? Find out what they might have heard?"

Skelly stepped into the hallway. He gently influenced the others away from the door and then knocked. No answer. The volume remained steady. Skelly turned to one of the cops and asked, "How long have you been here?"

"About the same as everyone else. Maybe thirty minutes."

"Has the occupant opened this door?"

"No. Someone looked out through the peephole, but no one's come out."

Skelly turned back and hit the door harder, with the edge of his palm. The TV sounds went mute and after a moment, he heard the latch over the peephole slide and then slide closed.

The door opened. A woman, middle-aged, wan, bland, almost immediately forgettable, looked up at Skelly with an inquisitive face.

Skelly ID'd himself and asked, "Over the past day or so, maybe two, possibly three days, have you heard anything unusual? Any shouting, any noise, anything like that?"

From the length of the pause and the way she looked down at the ground for a moment, Skelly knew she had.

"Well, yes. Yes, I did hear something. Night before last." She stopped there.

Trying not to let his irritation show, Skelly asked, "What did you hear?"

"I heard voices. Loud voices."

"Loud voices saying what, exactly?"

"The young woman who lives there, I heard her shouting, 'Stop. Stop. Stop it, you crazy son of a bitch.'"

"What time was this?"

"I think it was …" She thought about it for a moment. "Probably about 10:30. Around there."

Skelly knew how she was going to answer the next question, but he wanted to hear how she explained herself.

"What time did you call the police?" he asked. She looked at him but said nothing. He kept waiting.

O'Connor turned when he saw Skelly had walked back into 131. "Anything?"

"As a matter of fact, yeah." Skelly's tone was tart, contemptuous. "She said she heard someone she identified as the young woman living here yell, 'Stop. Stop. Stop it, you son of a bitch.' Then she heard some clattering, maybe, something being knocked over, falling over. I ask her what time she called the police—and, goddamn, I knew the answer before she said it—and she tells me she never did call them."

"You're fucking kidding me." O'Conner was incredulous. He shook his head, gave out a single soft and humorless laugh.

"No, no—hold on. It gets worse. I ask, why didn't you call the cops? And she says, 'I didn't want to get involved in someone else's trouble.' I knocked on the other doors nearest this one. No one home. They're at work."

"She doesn't work?"

"She's sick. Under the weather. Now I probably am too." Skelly was quiet for a moment, then he seemed to remember something. "Mr. Messina is sitting out there, he's been here for a few hours already, and maybe we should …"

"Yeah, yeah, of course," O'Connor said.

Skelly and O'Connor walked down the hallway to the lobby and found Tony Messina on the same love seat he'd been sitting on for a few hours, right by the big glass doors of the entryway. He sat resting his arms on his knees, staring at his hands, head bent, shoulders contorted with tension.

Both detectives watched him for a second, reading for a few different things—clues to his state of mind, how close he might be to losing his shit, whether he might know more than they did about what happened, might have a darker involvement.

From where they stood, they could see his eyes were red and glassy and swollen. He'd been crying. They had to look hard, but they saw his hands trembling. Tony seemed to notice it too and pressed his hands, palms down, onto his knees. He squinted his eyes shut, raised his face to the ceiling, and then let his head drop back down, bowing toward the floor.

O'Connor thought it looked like Tony had been about to pray but then given up.

When Tony raised his eyes, they saw the whole story right in front of them: anger, outrage, distress, horror, stupefaction, fear, repulsion, affliction, lament, the dull and disconsolate half-light in his eyes—all of it there at once. The face of grief.

"Sorry for your trouble," O'Connor said.

Tony looked like he might say something back but then nodded instead and offered a grim, very faint smile.

Then he sobbed. He recovered himself, opened his mouth to speak, then sobbed again. Finally, he said, "I'm sorry."

"No, no, not at all," Skelly said.

"Don't be sorry," O'Connor said. One of the hardest things to watch was someone who was stricken but trying to hold it together. "I'm sorry. I hate asking questions while you're in the middle of this. But understand, I wouldn't do it if it wasn't crucial. The more we know, and the earlier we know it, the better it is for the investigation."

"And the sooner we catch this guy," Skelly said.

Tony's eyes moved back and forth between them. There was a pause, then he nodded slowly.

Skelly said, "We want to get you home to your family as soon as we can. And let me ask, is there anyone you need us to notify? Any calls we can make on your behalf?"

Tony looked at each of them again in turn but this time shook his head no. Then he said, "No, I've spoken to my wife already. I've told her everything. But I do want to get back to her and the girls."

"And we will," Skelly said.

Tony broke in. "But I know you need me here now, so… "

O'Connor asked him, "Will you tell us again about the last time you saw Gio?"

The way he shifted in his chair, dropped his head, sat back up straight, exhaled, looked at them again before answering—O'Connor could tell Tony was struggling.

Tony took a deep breath, let it out. Then he told them the story.

## Chapter 4

He recognized the odor right away, Tony said. It only took part of a second: thick, sour, rotten, hot, wrong. Without thinking, he stepped back and started pulling the door shut, but realized he had no other option than going in.

At Omaha Beach, close to a thousand had fallen and died around him. Bullets, shells, men blown apart. The bodies of the soldiers breaking down, out of control, bleeding out, and the scent of it all mixed in the air. A year later he was at the edge of Berlin, right after Zhukov led his Russians through, and in their wake limitless dead spoiling under the summer sun. From the beach to Berlin, that smell was everywhere, pervading everything, and it was vile. The worst thing you could imagine. The worst thing you could remember. Tony stood in the doorway, almost against the super's back, smelling it again.

Over the super's shoulder, Tony saw black paint splashed and pooled and streaked all over. In a particularly thick puddle that looked as if it might still be tacky to the touch, Tony saw someone small and fragile asleep in the middle of it. It took a second, but his eyes finally read it right: it was a woman's body. She wasn't asleep. And Tony knew immediately it wasn't paint.

Whatever hope he'd held was gone, and now he felt resigned, maybe, but grim too, and duty-bound to go inside. Tony angled himself and started sliding past, but the super blocked him, saying, "Don't."

It wasn't an order. The super's voice was humane, sad.

Tony put his hand on the super's shoulders. "You need to call the police right now."

The super turned and took a deep breath, then shuddered and nodded. "My God." He walked away in a hurry.

Against his better judgment—he knew he shouldn't walk across the scene of a homicide—Tony stepped in and looked around. He saw more and more blood dried all over everything. The door to the bedroom was open, but the bathroom door had been pulled almost shut.

Tony knelt down next to Tinker and put his hand on her shoulder, thinking in a vague way he might shake her awake, but when he felt her skin, it was cold and hard. He jerked his hand away and stood up.

He picked his way carefully across the floor, trying to step only on bare spots. He nudged the bathroom door ajar. A body lay underneath the sink basin, and without having to think about it, he saw it was Gio crumpled in a pool of blood.

He was aware enough not to touch the doorknob as he pushed it open a little wider.

Not a pool of blood—a lake of it. Gio's head haloed by blood, like saints in paintings or stained-glass pictures in churches. Gio's pants and shirt, saturated, dyed purple and black with blood. Bigger and smaller drops of blood spattered in arcs and curves across the walls, across the sink, even up onto the ceiling. Blood splattered on the mirror. A stark, dark contrast of blood dried against the white porcelain of the toilet. Footprints tracked through blood on the floor.

A towel rack had been ripped from the wall and lay on the floor. The shower curtain sat crumpled next to Gio, all the eyelets torn.

When he was a green recruit, he'd heard experienced soldiers talk about how the dead looked almost pathetic, even sometimes tragicomical, and Tony had thought it was outrageous. Yet after a very short while he understood what they'd meant. It was a neat trick of the mind to see the dead that way because if you didn't—if you accepted the full weight of what was in front of you, or surrounding you, if you thought in terms of who and not what—you'd be overwhelmed and fall apart completely.

Gio was the furthest thing from pathetic Tony had ever seen, but Tony wouldn't accept the enormity of the moment. He didn't want to. He couldn't allow himself to. He'd shatter and collapse later, but in the moment, Tony felt like everything hinged on holding himself together.

Gio's body wounds were hard to see, but those on his face and throat were obvious.

From where he lay, Gio seemed to stare up at Tony. Over the years Tony had looked into those eyes and seen them full of love, awe, anger, confusion, joy, patience, sadness—full of life—and now he saw only an absence.

He hoped there hadn't been time for Gio to be afraid, to wish that Tony had been there to help him.

Tony's hand reached out to touch his son, but he pulled it back.

He wouldn't ever describe this to Maria. He'd never let her look at a picture of the scene. He didn't want her seeing Gio this way. He wouldn't want her even imagining Gio this way.

Tony stood in the doorway and stared at his son for a long time. Then he turned and walked back to the living room and was standing in the center of it when the phone rang.

It rang a second time, and then a third, and when it rang a fourth time, Tony stepped to it and answered. He never understood why he did it, he'd say later on.

"Hello?" He heard his own voice as flat and airless.

There was a pause, then, hesitant: "Is Tinker there?"

Tony turned toward where Tinker lay on the floor. "Yes, she's right in front of me."

The pause went on and on. The caller was about to speak, but Tony cut in. "Actually, she's not here. May I tell her who called?" The caller said, "No, that's okay. This is just a friend of hers." Then they hung up.

After a moment, Tony hung up too and then turned to go back out to the hallway and wait for the police.

When he was done recounting this to the detectives, Tony bent his head. O'Connor waited a beat, then said, "Just to clarify something: your oldest daughter, Gina? Is that right? She told you afterward that Gio had called later that night?"

Tony cupped his hands over his face, nodded.

"I wish I'd been the one to answer," he said.

O'Connor said, "It was just a call, Mr. Messina, like every other call. You didn't know; he didn't know. It's significant only because of what came afterward. And even then... " He trailed off.

Tony didn't know how to take it, whether O'Connor was being empathetic or trying to set him straight or what. He looked at O'Connor's face, saw it was serious, concerned, determined, and figured he was being both.

Tony said, "Yeah, she said that Gio called around 10:30. She told him that a friend of his had called earlier, looking for him."

"Who was the friend, again?"

"Cedric Sberna. *S-b-e-r-n-a.*"

O'Connor said, "And you talked to him too, this morning?"

"Right. I called him. He told me he'd been trying to find Gio too." Something popped into Tony's head. He looked at the ceiling, trying to figure it out.

Skelly said, "You look like something just occurred to you... "

"Yeah. Yeah. I feel like Gina said ... No, I'm pretty positive she said she told Gio that Cedric was looking for him. And that Gio said he'd either spoken to him or he was there, at Tinker's."

O'Connor and Skelly exchanged a look.

Skelly said, "Did he tell her how long he'd been looking for Gio? Did he say—"

"Apparently, Cedric told her he was about to call me to ask if I'd seen Gio."

O'Connor had gotten Skelly's point. He said, "I'm just thinking aloud here, but if he was going to call you, the parent of a friend, a parent he really didn't know all that well, it was something so important he was willing to risk alarming you. But he called you, not the police, so it wasn't a physical emergency. I wonder what made Cedric get to that point after one day. Maybe something dire happened, but wouldn't he have given you a sense of that?"

"Well… " Tony gathered his thoughts. His brow was furrowed. "I think I see what you're getting at. But … no, that can't be right. There's nothing about Cedric that would make me … I mean, there's no reason to think he's involved."

O'Connor saw that after Tony finished answering, his brow was still furrowed. Tony was thinking, looking at the floor. O'Connor looked over at Skelly and gave a slight nod. Skelly stood, smoothed his pants, walked off. O'Connor said, "Just a few last questions …"

## CHAPTER 5
*March 3, 1976, afternoon*

Owen knocked on the door of the Rush Over. He wanted to take Don Lolly up on his offer of lunch.

After letting Owen into the club and shaking hands, Don Lolly was able to hold it in for about a minute's worth of small talk. He pulled a barstool over and sat down. Then, "Gregg, I gotta ask. What the fuck? I'm not being an asshole. This is just ... It's unique."

"No argument there. Look, man, it's a great life, but ... " Owen searched for words.

"And you're a great keyboardist."

Owen shook his head. "No. No. I might be good, but ... I'm not great, you know? Won't ever be as good as the other guys in the band. I didn't want to be holding them back. And it's not just a technique thing. I knew I was meant to be doing something else. All the signs were there."

In the Rush Over, the heat wasn't up yet. A couple of barbacks carried cardboard boxes of scotch and gin up and down the cellar stairs, in and out of the storeroom. The glass bottles knocked and clattered when they lifted the boxes or put them down.

There had been a bound stack of *The Scene* right outside the door when Owen arrived and knocked. Lolly dragged them in, cut the binding, and each of them took a copy. Owen's picture was an inset on the cover, the interview running over a few pages inside. There were a few then-and-now pictures, from the Shady Daze, American Breed, and Jerico eras, side by side with recent pictures—hair cut to courtroom-respectable length, jewelry-free, white-collar weekend-casual outfit. No rock-star pout, just a wide, silent-majority-friendly smile.

Don Lolly had known Owen for more than a decade, had always liked Owen's company and conversation, had long been a friend to his bands.

Lolly had heard a thousand bands, met ten thousand musicians. His hearing testified to as much. He had a faint but shrill drone resonating constantly in his ears. Sometimes he didn't notice it, but if he did, he couldn't hear anything else. It often kept him awake.

Most of the bands he booked were—if not terrible—middling and instantly forgettable. Having his hearing damaged by mediocre noise galled him, but it was a by-product of the job. He had a warmer view of the good groups, thinking maybe it would be worth it all to have been around when the best of them were getting started. Styx, for example. A big hit a few years back, and now a new singer, about to release a new record. Or Cheap Trick, who he knew were destined for big things.

Lolly had thought Jerico would be one of them, so he'd been surprised to hear about Owen quitting. Quitting just like that, cold, out of the blue. He was more surprised—and a little dubious—when he was told Owen was not only studying law but interning for the State's Attorney's Office. He'd heard, too, that Owen had quit because of a girl and that the girl had tried to kill him. That was a bit much to believe. But there was a girl involved and some third party from another band. It was hard keeping track of all the scene's petty feuds and rumors, and Lolly wasn't inclined to try.

Besides, Owen never talked about that sort of shit with him. It was a key reason Lolly liked him so much in the first place.

Lolly thought the myth of the brain-dead rock musician was bullshit. He'd heard an interview on the radio with Mick Jagger recently, and you didn't get to where he was by being stupid. On the contrary. It took some serious smarts to succeed on that level. But most musicians didn't set their sights that high, didn't concern themselves with much more than intragroup rivalries, idle gossip about possible record deals, other musicians' drug problems. Owen was one of those few who could talk politics and give you the averages for every player in the major leagues. Most of the guys in Jerico were the same way. Smart people tend to keep company with smart people.

"Plus," Owen added, "I can't sing. And that's a liability." Owen hesitated. "Hey, Don. Can I use your phone?"

Lolly said, "Of course. Yeah, go ahead."

"I'm calling L.A."

"That's fine. I don't care."

Owen said, "I'll keep it short. Just want to see how everyone's doing out there."

"Someone told me you guys were out there recording?" Lolly winced inwardly. *You guys*. Slip of the tongue.

Owen didn't seem to notice. "They are. I'm flying out tomorrow. I'm the 'Under Assistant West Coast Promotion Man.'"

"What studio?"

"The Record Plant."

"Really?" Lolly was impressed. "How? I mean, that must cost…"

He trailed off. It wasn't his business.

Owen grinned a little. "Check this out. The Eagles are there recording, and when they're not in the studio, Jerico gets to use it for free."

"Goddamn, man. How'd that get hooked up?"

Owen grimaced. "Sheri. She hooked it up."

"No way. Shit." Lolly smiled, shook his head. "You dog. Don't you always land on your feet. Amazing. How'd that happen?"

"Last Christmas. She was home. I just went over and asked. I mean, she wasn't thrilled to see me, let alone have me ask for a favor. Since I'm not in the band anymore, I guess she was willing to help them out."

A few quiet seconds passed. "Okay. Excuse me," Owen said. He went back to Lolly's office. Lolly laid the paper open on the bar top and went back to reading the interview.

He thought it was a little disorienting, looking at the pictures, seeing the transformation of someone he'd known so long. Owen had been a kid when they'd first met.

It was funny, too, he thought, looking at the outlandish outfits—body-hugging and glittery—what people chose to wear to make themselves stand out. But everyone wore their uniforms. Still, if Owen had walked into any backstage room dressed as he was today, everyone would have figured it was a bust. But Lolly figured, too, that showing up at the State's Attorney's Office looking like a member of T. Rex would get you precisely nowhere.

After a few minutes, Owen came back. He looked as if he was in serious contemplation.

Lolly waited for him to speak, and when he didn't, asked, "How's it going out there?"

Owen grinned, but it didn't seem genuine. "He sounded a little out of it. A lot out of it, actually."

"It's pretty early, no?"

"Or pretty late. And I heard laughing in the background from what sounded like two different chicks. "

"That's what you're giving up?"

Owen kept grinning, but Lolly had seen something ripple over his face. "Don, man, you have to grow up sometime."

Back at DePaul, Owen was one of the last few stragglers rushing toward their test rooms. Once he reclaimed his seat, Owen planned on ignoring the woman with the red coat.

She was in her seat, head bent over a copy of *The Scene*.

He draped his coat over the chair, a few drops of water running down the fabric onto the linoleum. The woman looked up, staring for a moment.

"Is this you?" She pointed at the pictures accompanying the article.

He said, "Sure is."

He watched her fingers twisting and untwisting cables of her hair. She was smiling, shaking her head, and writing on a piece of paper.

"I liked your interview." She handed him the paper. Her phone number. He folded it into quarters, tucked it into his back pocket.

He nodded. "I'm so glad to hear that."

"You can begin, starting now," the proctor said. He got his pencils ready.

## CHAPTER 6
*March 3, 1976, afternoon*

A little later, O'Connor was alone at the apartment. Tony Messina was gone. Gio's body, Tinker's body, the other cops, the spectators were all gone. O'Connor was about to seal the apartment up for the rest of the day and head back to Area 6.

Earlier, there had been a knot of onlookers out front, watching nothing: just the blue lights strobing; yellow tape stretched in front of the windows, periodically snapping in the wind; one cop walking in, another walking out. They'd watch for a while, then a few drifted away, replaced a moment later by a few new sets of eyes, everyone quietly speculating about what had happened.

O'Connor had one officer step outside through the front door to distract reporters and onlookers while the bodies were wheeled on gurneys out of a side door, both of them covered with sheets.

Quite frankly, the onlookers annoyed the living shit out of O'Connor. Cops went to inhuman lengths trying to unsee things they'd witnessed, and these ghouls contorted themselves trying to get a look.

When the crowd peaked, O'Connor asked the super to stand by the door and ID people trying to get in. They'd been able to ferret a couple of reporters out that way.

He hadn't gotten a chance to take much of a look at the apartment earlier. This was one thing that always hit him hard: looking at the emblems of a life. The things people valued, that they used to express themselves. The things they believed made their lives prettier.

Out of habit he used a pen on the light switch, and the apartment was suddenly bright. The smell of blood and shit still in the air, actual blood still on the floor. He heard knocking noise in the pipes running out of the floor and through the ceiling, then a quavering whistle that gave way to a prolonged hiss of steam.

After a moment, it was noticeably warmer. The heat made the smell come more alive.

The bright light came from an enormous orange pendant lamp. He saw décor on the wall he hadn't noticed earlier.

There were a few wall hangings, in beige, black, and yellow, embroidered with elaborate circles that struck him as Far Eastern. On one wall, they'd hung an *Easy Rider* movie poster. Dennis Hopper, Peter Fonda, both on bikes, the tag line reading, *One man went looking for America and couldn't find it anywhere.*

As a cop he'd crossed paths with a few bikers over the years, the type of guys, he suspected, who'd probably root for the rednecks who blew Hopper and Fonda off their cycles.

His eyes fixed on another wall hanging, a folksy thing with flowers and letters cut from felt. The letters had been glued on to read, *Go get the butter*. It took him a moment, but then he remembered: in *Life* or *Time*, maybe an issue of *Cosmopolitan* he'd idly leafed through in a doctor's waiting room … Marlon Brando … *Last Tango in Paris*.

O'Connor wasn't a prude, didn't care one way or another if someone enjoyed that kind of thing, but it irritated him that people considered themselves sophisticates for watching *Last Tango* or *Behind the Green Door* or *Deep Throat*. Only someone who'd never had it believed that's the way sex was, and only a moron would want it to be.

He took a slow walk through the rest of the place.

The colors were ugly. A large throw rug in orange shag. The sofa upholstered with a mess of psychedelic colors. A couple of beanbag chairs—more orange and brown. Pink-and-rust-colored crocheted blankets on the arms of the sofa.

He walked to the TV—a big Motorola the size of an oven door—and saw a *TV Guide* on top, with a charcoal sketch of Bob Hope on the cover. Next to it were a few 8-tracks: Elvis, Merle Haggard, the Rolling Stones. He read the spines of the few books on the shelf above the TV: *Jonathan Livingston Seagull*, *Salem's Lot*, *Terms of Endearment*, *The Philosophy of Andy Warhol*.

It was a young person's apartment, an ad hoc starter place. He picked the *TV Guide* up and flipped through it. He saw someone had circled *Chico and the Man*, *Baretta*, and *The Waltons*. The circles seemed somehow childish to him, and for some reason, he started thinking of Tony and the way he'd looked up from where he sat on the love seat, like he was begging O'Connor to reach out, take his hand, and pull him out of the void.

*Christ*, O'Connor thought. *It makes you want to weep.*

## Chapter 7
*March 3, 1976, evening*

After Tony Messina hung up, something about Cedric's phone call—about the timing, the tone—kept insisting itself.

Tony tried pushing his thoughts past it. There were matters of immediate concern: relatives and friends to notify, a memorial to plan, business arrangements he couldn't ignore, a dozen different things he'd told himself not to forget. He was at his desk in his study. He thought he might make a list.

He'd been forcing himself all day to push past the knowledge that Gio was dead. Gio was dead, and Tony had seen his lifeless body, and if he stopped to consider it in any way, he'd fall apart completely.

Tomorrow, he'd have to get someone in accounts to put in a bid on the fire-damaged apartments on Ashland, the flooded place in Elgin. He had a small but heavy cut-glass tumbler on the desktop, with a few ice cubes floating in white rum. He watched the condensation forming and running down the sides. Cedric's voice on the phone had sounded frightened, petulant. What he said had sounded rote, rehearsed.

Tony picked the tumbler up, sipped, swallowed. His throat convulsed. He never drank ordinarily, but the moment seemed to demand it. He'd need to be careful. Each sip so far had undermined him, left him more inclined to let things go undone, but the idea of being in his study, without alcohol, trying to get priorities straight was unbearable.

He couldn't recall who he'd agreed to have lunch with tomorrow. No one could come watch the games Saturday or Sunday, so four or five more calls to make right there.

Cedric had sounded like a kid speaking in a young man's voice, almost whining, and his condolences came off as empty.

Tony had an urgent thought that Gio's car would have to be moved but then recalled Morask telling him they'd be taking it into the crime lab, going over every single inch, looking for evidence.

His shattered family was upstairs, reeling. It was quieter now, everyone nearly sobbed out. The sound of footsteps, faucets. Tony had come down to the study so he could think, but the call had come in.

On the first two rings he hadn't even considered answering. Speaking intelligibly or even speaking at all felt beyond him.

On the third and fourth rings, he felt the force of reflex again, tugging his hand toward the receiver.

Tony's eyes felt stung. His head ached.

The phone rang a fifth time.

It was dusk outside, even more dim inside, everything in lighter or darker shades of gray, and the edges of things getting vague. He turned the lights back on.

He answered on the sixth ring.

"Hello?"

"Mr. Messina?"

"Speaking." Tony couldn't place the voice but knew he'd heard it before, and recently. That he couldn't recall it was getting him agitated.

"Uhhhh ... I just ... "

"Yes?" He was gripping the phone so hard the skin over his knuckles was bloodless, shining and white.

"It's Cedric Sberna. Gio's friend. We talked earlier."

*And you've been at the house. You've eaten here.*

Tony said, "Yeah, of course. I remember you, Cedric." Tony picked the tumbler up and drank twice.

"I just heard about Gio and ... " However long it actually was, the pause seemed as if it stretched over minutes. "I'm so sorry. I can't even tell you."

Tony wondered if Sberna was all that sorry because he sounded flat more than anything else.

"Thank you. Thank you for that. I appreciate your condolences."

Tony was curious how Cedric Sberna knew. Did word really travel that fast? Did a newspaper get it this quick?

"You're welcome." Another pause. "Mr. Messina ... I need to ask you something."

"Okay." *You're welcome?* From a room upstairs he heard Maria cry out, and then there was Gina's voice, then Lisa's, then it was quiet.

"The police called me, and they asked me to come in because they had some questions about Gio."

Incredibly, it sounded as if that was what Cedric found distressing.

"Well ... Cedric, you were his good friend. Of course, they want to speak with you." Tony couldn't understand why they were having this conversation or why Cedric spoke as if they might have known each other only by name.

"But why do they want me to come in?"

It boiled over him quickly, but Tony fought a compulsion to snarl at him, ask if it was such a big imposition, given that his good friend was dead and all. Instead:

"It's how they do it, Cedric. That's the way it's done." He wished he hadn't picked up.

"The way they asked, it was like … It was like they think I had something to do with it."

Tony paused. He wasn't sure what Cedric wanted him to say or why Cedric kept pressing the point. "Cedric, why would they think that?"

"I don't know. I have no idea, really, but I think they might."

"Cedric … come on, man, if you weren't involved then you've got nothing to be worried about." Tony pushed the tumbler back. His tongue felt heavy and numbed.

"Did you tell the cops that there was no way that I could be involved?"

The question surprised him. "No. No one asked me anything like that. I told them we'd spoken this morning. That's it."

"That's all? You're sure?"

"Yeah, Cedric. Yeah, I'm sure."

He'd stared at the phone after he hung it up, then sat back and tried to think about his obligations, but then he thought about the call instead, and he kept thinking about it.

Finally, Tony reached for his wallet and took out a card he'd been given by one of the detectives that morning. He picked up the phone and dialed.

## Chapter 8
### *March 3, 1976, afternoon – evening*

*"You're not a real lawyer. You're never going to be a real lawyer."* That's what that asshole Goggin had said. *"You're not shit."* But now Owen was certain he would be a lawyer. A good one. And a great prosecutor.

Owen finished the exam in an hour. He looked around. All the others were still bent over their papers. Owen stood, pushing his chair across the tiles, put his coat on, and picked up the exam—and everyone in the room, administrator included, looked up at him with what seemed like alarm. The woman seated next to him looked too, a soft smile on her lips. Owen winked, turned, and left.

It was still drizzling outside, still foggy and raw, but he didn't want to go home yet. He knew he'd just done well—fairly certain he'd done really well—and he was happy about it, happy to be done. But he thought he should be feeling something more, something deeper than happy. After the earlier rush, he now felt strangely empty.

He turned onto Jackson and went under the tracks, crossed South Michigan, then walked farther up Jackson on the other side, through the fog, until he could see the lake, or at least where he knew the lake was. A lot of students were coming and going around him, alone, paired, in groups. He made eye contact with one girl or another while he walked, but it seemed pointless, dreary.

*Leave it for now*, he thought. *Save it for LA.*

He couldn't see anything of Grant Park through the fog ahead of him, and it was thick enough that he couldn't see the clouded afternoon sky either. He stopped and stood for a moment thinking that a person might step off the curb and into the path of a car, never see it coming.

He suddenly wished he was on his way to Los Angeles, right that moment. He didn't want to start his next phase of life without resolving the one he was leaving. He didn't want to keep regretting any more than he had to. A number of people had told Owen it wasn't wise to have regrets. Anyone who said that was obviously not a deep thinker.

He pushed forward through the fog. Without regrets, how did anyone learn anything?

Owen figured it might be time to go home, pack for the flight. He began scanning the street for a cab.

Thirty minutes later, he got out of his cab. While he waited for the driver to count out his change, Owen watched a delivery van pull up next to a *Tribune* newspaper box. The van idled as the driver leapt out, opened the box, and shoved a new stack of papers in.

Owen walked over and looked through the box window. He could still smell the exhaust in the air. The headline read, *Contractor, Actress Slain.* And the subhead: *Sheridan Rd. Flat Scene of Stabbing.* In the right column was a picture of a woman—presumably the actress. She was pretty, dark-haired, with something knowing and impish in her eyes.

He started reading the article through the glass. *An aspiring actress and her boyfriend, a wealthy contractor, were found stabbed to death in the woman's blood-spattered apartment* … He read a few more lines, but a strong, cold gust of wind bit at him. He straightened up and walked into his building.

He heard the phone ring while he unlocked the front door, and he fumbled the keys and slapped at the lights, rushing to answer the phone in the bedroom. He wasn't feeling anxious at anything specific; it was just that given the shape of things over the past months, his mind went for the shadows when the phone rang. It might have been someone calling with a problem in California or news concerning his ex, Melissa, with whom things had ended badly—really badly—or even Melissa herself, with another stoned apology or, like the last call, more venom. He felt glad, hearing his brother on the other end.

"What's happening?" Holding the receiver against his ear, Owen stood, trying to get his coat off. "What's good?"

"I've been calling," Jay said. Owen heard something off in his brother's voice.

"I was taking the bar exam." He'd filled Jay in two days ago and a few times before that too.

Jay went on. "Oh, right. I remember now." He still sounded strained. "How was it?"

"It was … " Owen searched for the right word. "Rigorous."

"Jesus," Jay said. "I'd hope so. I need to talk to you."

"Right now? I'm packing." It was cold in the house. Owen walked over to the thermostat. "I'm flying to LA in the morning. I may have told you, but I got Sheri to do us a solid, and—"

"Did you see the news today?"

"She's giving Jerico studio time overnights—"

"Did you see the *Tribune*? About a murder?"

Owen considered this for a second. His suitcase lay open on the bed. He had to bring clothing that didn't brand him as a prosecutor but didn't look like an also-ran rocker's costume. On Jay's end, he heard the sound of a chair scraping across the floor, then a long exhale.

Then it came back.

"Yes," Owen said. "I did. I saw that thing in the *Tribune* on the way home. The contractor and the actress. On Sheridan. The 'blood-spattered apartment.' I only got to read the first paragraph."

"They were my friends, Gregg." From Jay's end, the scrape of the chair again, then footfalls. He was pacing. "They were both my friends."

And on Owen's end, an immediate but unrooted concern. He wanted to ask, *You're not in any danger, are you?*

Instead, he sat on the bed and said, "How well did you know them?"

"I knew Gio Messina pretty well. I never told you about him?" The pacing stopped, then after a second picked up again.

"Not that I can recall. Tell me now."

"I was just about done fixing the Cadillac—this is last year—and I went to Elgin one Saturday, trying to find the last parts I needed." Jay had bought a Cadillac at a police auction. It was a '74—brand new, almost—but a bit busted up, a stolen car the cops had recovered. "I'm there, I find what I need, I'm getting ready to leave, and a guy driving a nice, brand-new baby-blue Continental pulls in. It's Gio Messina. He gets out of his car, comes over to mine, and he's admiring it; I'm admiring his.

"We start talking shop about rebuilding cars, then we get onto guns, and it turns out he's got a nice collection. And that was it."

"You found your gun-car buddy."

Owen heard Jay open his fridge, then a ring tab pulled off a can, then the sound of the chair again. "Well, I found someone who was seriously fun to hang out with. Really free-spirited guy. Spirited in a way we were never allowed to be, you know? And a pretty smart guy, too. Really smart. I enjoyed his company, and I always wanted to see what kind of wildness he'd pull next."

Owen got up, opened the drawers in the bureau, pulled out socks, underwear, a few T-shirts, and kept packing. He wasn't paying much attention to the suitcase. "Wildness meaning?"

Jay hesitated. "Let me put it this way. When I was checking his car out, I got into the driver's seat. I happened to look down, and between the seats, he had an automatic. Just sitting there, right out in the open."

"It's stupid," Owen said. "Stupid but maybe not really *wild*."

"I'm getting to that. He tells me he'd started collecting guns, but it took me two seconds to realize he didn't have the faintest idea how to use them. He's carrying these things around, but when we went to a range, he almost shot me when he was trying to load one."

"What did you say his last name was?"

"Messina. As in the construction company."

Owen recognized the name but couldn't give it context.

Jay continued. "I'll tell you, though, he had a pretty nicer set up there at home."

Owen walked to the bedroom doorway, looking out at the living room. Two big bullet holes, not particularly close to each other, skewed and uneven, looking like two empty sockets. The drywall pulverized, a rough circle of paint chipped off around each hole. Owen didn't want to cover them over.

Jay said, "If someone built an apartment for you in the basement, with its own entrance and a rec room, I don't know that I'd ever leave."

"You went to the house?"

"All the time. All the time. I was an honorary Greek princeling. They were great. His dad was great, his mom was great. His sisters. Gio was great. If I called him and said I was in a jail in Juarez, he'd leave that second and drive down and bail me out." Gregg heard Jay sit and let out a long full-body exhale. "I was going to ask a favor, but now that I know you're leaving tomorrow, never mind."

"Jaybird, tell me what I can do for you?"

"Tomorrow, I was going to go to Gio's parents' place, just tell them how awful I feel about what happened, what they're going through. I was going to ask if you'd come along. But now that I'm saying it aloud, it doesn't sound right. Forget about it. This isn't your concern."

Owen walked back into the bedroom, sat down on the bed. The suitcase was still almost empty. His ticket was on the nightstand. "I would. You know I'd do this for you, right? But I've got a ticket already, and the band is expecting me to be at the studio and to record a few overdubs—"

"I know. I know you would. And I appreciate that. And I appreciate your situation. You going to be gone long?"

"It takes about two months to get the bar exam results, so I'm going to hang with the band until I find out if I'm going to be a 'real' lawyer."

## Chapter 9
*March 3, 1976, evening*

Lieutenant Jules Gallet stood leaning against his desk, surrounded by the Area Six detectives he'd assigned to the Messina-Moore murders. "Okay. So, let's figure out how to move ahead with this one. Several canvases a day, all right? Until we find someone who heard or saw something. By *someone*, I mean someone who isn't one of those two fucking neighbors. I still can't believe no one called emergency with that much yelling going on. I almost refuse to believe it." He shook his head. "Dredge the sewers and drains nearby, see if any knives turn up. We're calling all the other Areas, right? I doubt it'll come to anything, but maybe someone's got an unsolved case that looks the same. What are we thinking about the super? Anything? Messina senior? Okay, but let's triple-check those alibis.

"Ted, you mentioned the super told you—how do we put it?—that Delphine Moore entertained a decent number of 'gentlemen callers.' Let's find some numbers from that address book, maybe have someone dig a little."

Skelly spoke up. "Messina mentioned a friend of his son called looking for him and that he seemed a little concerned. Cedric Sberna, S-b-e-r-n-a, lives in Lake Forest, with his parents. What got our attention was the timing here: why call someone's father—and according to Messina, he didn't know Sberna very well—so, why call someone's father, all concerned, after a day, day and a half, unless you had some idea something wasn't right?"

"Any reason that name rings a bell?"

"Probably not the right bell. The guy's father is one Carmine Sberna. I've got a friend, Kapuscinzsky, used to be in the organized crime unit, but moved to narcotics, and I bumped into him in the elevator. I figured I'd save a phone call, so I mentioned the coke we found and asked if the name Messina ever came across his radar. He said no, but when I asked about Sberna, he said maybe. He called a little later, says there was a Carmine Sberna—importer/exporter—whose name came up a couple times in some tariff investigation. Maybe lightly connected but definitely not a player and probably not looking to be one."

"The kid?"

"No priors. A few traffic violations. Two speeding tickets. But still, we're bringing him down to see if he knows anything useful. Actually, he's supposed to be in pretty soon."

Gallet made some notes. Then he said, "Another long shot, but see if any hospitals had anyone with bad cuts on the hands coming in. From a psych perspective, what are we thinking?" He addressed it to everyone, but he meant O'Connor.

O'Connor cleared his throat. "I'm trying to figure out who the intended victim is. It was her place, but ... there's zero evidence the killer was attacking her and that Gio Messina interrupted. There'd be all manner of shit pushed out of place, knocked over. Stopping someone from being stabbed—it isn't delicate work. And if he's getting attacked first, why was she even still there? Why didn't she run? Would you stand there yelling 'Stop it! Stop it!?' No, you'd fucking book on out of there.

"So, I don't know who was meant to get it," O'Connor said. "Now, the other thing—and I was saying this to Tommy and Rich—something simply does not compute here. It sort of dovetails off of the intended victim thing: nothing jumps out as a motive.

"We've got two bodies, a healthy measure of cocaine, stab wounds, a lot of blood. A dope deal gone wrong usually ends with a shooting. If a problem comes up, a bullet eliminates it immediately. A knife, though—a stabbing victim probably won't go quietly, and I'm betting most dealers figure that the successful transactions are the quiet ones."

Skelly said, "From what I could see, and I think Ted will back me on this, there wasn't enough cocaine here to make a business-minded dealer murder anyone. Plus, stabbing someone is close, personal. It's hard to stab someone to death. And most people don't have it in them."

O'Connor said, "I do agree with that. Stabbing two people over and over requires a lot of anger or hatred. Or serious mental illness. When I was in Area 1, we nailed a dealer who had executed a few people in the course of business. Used a gun each time. He did, however, stab his girlfriend multiple times until she died, but he was known as a kook, and stabbing her was a function of his being completely out of his mind. I'd also venture that efficient drug dealers don't tend toward mental illness.

"So, chances are everyone in the apartment knew each other. And I kept thinking of two cases I worked a while back.

"There was this woman in Cabrini-Green. Her husband's a piece of shit who'd leave work on payday, drink until he could barely walk, and then go home and demand she have sex with him. He'd beat her to the floor if she refused. On one payday, he comes back wasted and finds her in the kitchen, standing at the sink with her back to him. He lets her know it's time for her to do her duty. When she ignores him and doesn't move from where she's standing, he steps to her, says, 'I'm talking to you, bitch!' and then spins her around to face him. She sticks the butcher's knife she's been holding right through his chest, into his heart, and he falls to the floor and dies. She knocks on a neighbor's door a few minutes later and asks them to call the police because she just killed her husband.

"Then—stay with me here—there was the Rourke case … "

Someone said, "The cop … "

"Right," O'Connor said. "The amazing, wonderful Officer Rourke of Area 2. The asshole beats the living crap out of Mrs. Rourke like he's on a schedule. And she's no shrinking violet. She gets pissed about something? She goes ahead and tells him what's the problem. One evening, the guy is watching TV in the basement. *Friday Night Fights*, I think it was. She's all riled up about something or other, so she goes down and tells him. He just sits there and says to her, 'Bitch, when this show's over, I'm coming upstairs and I'm going to kick your fucking ass.' She turns and goes upstairs, goes to where she keeps a gun—a .25 automatic—then goes back to the basement. She walks up behind him, raises the gun, and puts a bullet through the back of his head.

"So, you're asking yourselves, 'What's the difference?'—"

A phone rang on a nearby desk, and everyone turned.

"Mine," Morask said. He walked over to the phone and answered.

"The difference," Skelly said, "is this: one is on-the-fly, and the other's deliberate."

"Yes. Right," O'Connor said. "And one other thing too: in a situation where your killer isn't an outright psychopath, a knife tends to be defensive. And unpredictable. A single stab wound might kill someone, like the Cabrini-Green woman standing at the sink did, but there's no guarantee that you'll even be able to slow someone down if you stab them, let alone incapacitate them. That woman must've been terrified, choking with rage, utterly desperate, and she lashed out with the thing that was closest at hand.

"But a gun—that's for when you want the right tool for the job. That woman understood that the gun gave her the element of surprise.

She's holding that gun, and she's more powerful than the guy who beat her up again and again, and if she wanted to put a stop to the abuse, she had to put a stop to him. The gun guaranteed she'd come out on top of the situation."

Gallet said, "Mass murderers—serial killers—they stab victims in a not-insignificant number of cases. And those are planned. Carefully planned. They're deliberate."

"True," O'Connor said. "But I'll bet you this: a psychiatrist would say that a serial killer plans out opportunities to give their rage some sort of … uncontrolled release.

"I think stabbings tend to be unplanned—psychos and prison inmates excepted. And they're not always meant to be lethal. Slashing at someone can be like … ramping up a fistfight. Either way, it's messy. There's a lot of blood in the human body, and a blade lets it out quick."

"Like sex," Skelly said.

"What do you mean?"

"Release. A quick release."

After a few minutes, Morask walked back from his desk over to where everyone was standing. He said, "Two things. I just got off the phone with Tony Messina. He says Cedric Sberna called him last night, told Tony that Area 6 Homicide wanted him to come in-person for some questions. Messina says Sberna tried a few different ways of asking what Tony might have told the cops. Tony tells him he didn't give us anything. But then Tony told me that Sberna didn't ask how he was doing, didn't mention the Moore girl at all."

"Well. All right." Gallet stood, considering. He smiled, shrugged. "Second thing?"

"Sberna's here. Just arrived. Philbin brought him to the interview room. His lawyer was waiting here when Sberna came in."

O'Connor said, "Who's the lawyer?"

Morask looked at his notes. "Jeremy Keller."

Everyone looked at each other. Gallet shrugged.

"I have no idea who he is," Morask said.

A row of filing cabinets stood nearby, with stacks of phone books and directories on top. O'Connor rummaged through them, pulled out the *Illinois Legal Directory*, opened it toward the middle, and started flipping the pages. After a minute, he said, "I don't know. Slip, fall, sue-your-ass-off type. At least that's what it looks like. Can't really tell. What's your read on him?"

"Squirrelly. Half thrilled, half petrified. Are you asking if he's going to be a problem?"

O'Connor shrugged. "More or less. It doesn't matter. Listen, let's do it this way: maybe you and Philbin do the talking. I'll drift in and out and look pissed off."

## Chapter 10
*March 3, 1976, evening*

There was a printed sign on the wall with the words to the Miranda rights. Otherwise, the interview room was drab, bare, badly lit. It was all by design, giving an interviewee nothing to focus on, nothing to give attention to other than the immediate situation. When it got quiet—no voices, no shuffling in the chair, no sobbing or gasping for breath—the lights buzzed at a pitch that made them sound frantic, pressurized. That wasn't by design. It was just a nice coincidence.

When Skelly and Philbin came in, Sberna was at the table, Jeremy Keller next to him. Cigarette smoke hung in a blue-gray haze by the ceiling. Sberna had one of the department's cheap aluminum ashtrays in front of him, four or five crushed butts in it, a crumpled box of Marlboro cigarettes next to that. He had the pack's last cigarette between the fingers in one hand. His other hand was absently bending an empty pack of matches.

The detectives sat so Sberna was across from both of them, with Keller off to the side, almost excluded.

O'Connor stepped to the two-way to look in, and he thought Morask was right. Keller looked like the kid at the birthday party who won the treasure hunt but at the same time like he had absolutely no idea what to do with it. He also had the air of someone used to being disliked. O'Connor figured Keller would be easy to step on, that he'd be less of a problem, more of a minor inconvenience.

He had a more intense reaction to Sberna—not quite revulsion but getting there. Good-looking to the point of absurdity, like he was straight from a Brut cologne photo shoot, but at the same time had the vacant expression of a golden retriever or other overbred show dog. Wherever he'd gotten in life was a factor of money and genetics, but his head was reaming his own ass so completely, it never occurred to him that was the case.

Philbin began, his voice low, serious. "Mr. Sberna, I want to thank you for coming in. I just want to say, we're going to be deeply grateful for any help you might be able to offer. And on behalf of the department, we're sorry for the loss of your friend."

Sberna shrugged. He went back to keeping his hands busy.

"I guess we all grieve in different ways," Philbin said. He looked over at Skelly, who rolled his eyes slightly. "Can we get you anything? A Coke? Coffee? Water? Slice of pizza? Hot dog?"

Sberna turned to Keller, who made a faint gesture that seemed to say, *They're asking you; why the fuck are you looking at me?* Sberna said to Philbin, "Do you have any matches?"

"Matches? Sure. And you look like you might need more cigarettes? We'll get right on that." He didn't move. Philbin looked at the two-way mirror against the wall, knowing O'Connor, Gallet, and Morask were watching. There was an intercom in the ceiling above the table, so Philbin knew they could hear too. He didn't say anything more. They all watched Sberna, watched what he did with his hands, how he had them planted flat against the tabletop, then curled his fingers to stare at his cuticles for a few seconds, then drummed a quick, erratic rhythm with his fingertips. They watched to see if there was anything to read in what he did, if he was giving anything away.

At least a minute passed. Keller was looking increasingly anxious and starting to fidget, glancing at Sberna, who kept tapping his fingers. Finally, Sberna seemed to notice he was being observed. He put the cigarette between his lips, looked back and forth between Skelly and Philbin, gave Keller a faintly quizzical side glance, then asked, "Who has a match?"

Skelly said, "I don't smoke." There was a pack of cigarettes just visible in his shirt pocket. Sberna looked like he was about to say something concerning Skelly's cigarettes but thought better of it and returned to beating out his rhythms.

Skelly said, "You were friends with Gio Messina and Delphine Moore, correct?"

Sberna looked at Keller, who just stared at the table.

"Is that correct, Cedric?"

"They were all right. I liked them well enough." He shrugged again.

Behind the mirror, O'Connor said, "What a prick."

"How long had you known them for?"

Sberna took the cigarette from his lips. "I've known Gio a couple months. Tinker I've known about the same time."

"*Tinker?*"

"We just called her that. Delphine, I mean. We called her Tinker."

"So, not long," Philbin asked.

"Long enough."

O'Connor said, "What the fuck does that mean?"

"How did she get 'Tinker' for a nickname?" Philbin asked.

Skelly said, "When was the last time you saw them?"

Without hesitating, Sberna answered, "February 29. Sunday. We had brunch together at the Sheridan Northbrook."

"Who is *we*?" Philbin, poised with his pen over his legal pad.

"Gio, Tinker, me, and Mickey." He looked down and watched his hand as he rolled the cigarette back and forth between his fingers. A few moments passed.

"Is Mickey famous?" Skelly asked.

Sberna looked confused. "No?"

"Then how would I know who Mickey is?" He gave Sberna a smile that was utterly without warmth.

Keller made a throat-clearing sound. "I don't think—"

"Shhh." Skelly cut him off, laying his index finger across his lips. Both Skelly and Philbin were surprised that Keller obeyed.

"A friend, I guess. Someone I know from around. Her real name is Mary Carlyle."

"What does this *Mickey* do?"

"She's a waitress."

"Okay. A waitress meaning … ?"

Sberna gave a little snort. "A waitress meaning, people order stuff from her, and she brings it to them."

Skelly looked over at Philbin. "This is going to take all night." Then he said to Sberna, "Where is she a waitress?"

"At a bar … "

Philbin threw his pencil down, Skelly pressed the heel of his hands against his eyes.

"I don't know which bar." Sberna blurted it out. Keller was looking at him.

"Brunch was the last time you saw them?"

"Yes."

"Did you see either of them any time after that?"

Keller interjected. "Don't answer that."

Skelly, puzzled, asked, "Why not?"

"We won't be answering questions about anything after the date of February 29."

"Again, why?"

No response. O'Connor said to Gallet, "I'll be right back."

He walked out from the observation room to where the interview was taking place, opened the door and stepped inside. He closed it behind him and leaned against it with his arms folded across his chest. Everyone looked over at him.

"Detective," Skelly and Philbin said, nodding.

"Gentlemen. How's it going? Mr. Keller? Mr. Sberna, how are you?"

Sberna started speaking. "Well, I'm—"

O'Connor waved him off. "It was just a rhetorical question."

Philbin took his pen up again. "Were you at Delphine Moore's apartment at any time prior to February 29?"

"Sure," Sberna said. "Quite a few times."

Keller shifted in his seat.

Sberna asked, "May I have a match?"

"Sure," Skelly said. He didn't produce one. "Just to clarify, you were at the apartment on the twenty-ninth but not afterward?"

"Don't answer." Keller put his hand up. "We won't answer any questions about anything subsequent to the twenty-ninth as far as Mr. Messina and Ms. Moore are concerned."

Skelly saw Keller looking toward the door, then down at the table, then taking a deep breath, seeming uneasy. When Skelly looked toward the door, he saw O'Connor, lips pressed tight, faintly shaking his head, glowering at Keller and Sberna. Skelly wanted to laugh.

He said, "All we're trying to get at here is whether they might have mentioned any plans they had, whether they were going to meet someone, go somewhere. We're not saying you're involved in any way. No one's even hinting at that. I'll admit, though, it's hard to keep an open mind when we're asking for your help and you won't even answer some really basic questions. So—and this is just us trying to pin down where they were and when—did you happen to see them on the first of March?"

"Don't answer."

"Did you go to the apartment on the first of March?"

"Again, we won't answer any—"

"You're drawing a little suspicion here. You understand? It's … strange." Skelly was speaking to Sberna. He paused. "Okay, can you tell me this: was Gio or Delphine involved in anything illegal?"

Keller and Sberna spoke at the same time.

"Don't answer that," Keller said.

Sberna said, "No, not that I was aware of. Listen, did anyone call the police whenever this happened? Two people killed in a tiny apartment that has walls that are paper thin, and Gio and Tinker were always playing their music loud, and the neighbors would either knock on the wall or pound on their door and tell them to shut the music down. Someone must have heard something?"

O'Connor pulled the door open, walked Sberna and Keller out, and then told everyone that the next day, first thing in the morning, he was driving down to Eleventh and State, the Chicago Police Headquarters building but also the 911 Communications Center, to see if he could find any call that had anything to do with the evening of March 1 or the early morning of March 2. Morask said he'd ride along.

## Chapter 11
*March 4, 1976, Morning*

As they drove over, O'Connor was saying, "People of a certain age, people our age, we hit sixteen, eighteen—boom. We get dropped into life. I think our parents figured there are only so many ways to live. 'You've seen us raise you, how much more do you need to know? You've got the idea.' Then it's the military, marriage, college. Maybe not in that order, but … "

Morask said, "When we bought furniture, right after getting married, the first thing I looked at was a sofa almost exactly like the one my parents had when I was growing up."

"Right. Exactly. When we were there this morning, at the North Sheridan address, there was this sense I got of being someplace where people played at being adults. Like they got some idea of how sophisticated grown-ups conducted themselves from a movie or TV show they watched. 'We've got our absurd clothes that you don't want to wear near open flame; we've got our cocaine. We go to this kind of—' I'm not articulating this very well. I feel that the way a lot of us came up, there was a sort of immigrant mentality. 'Me and my family. Me and my neighborhood. We do for ourselves. We close the ranks.' With these people, it's like there's no 'me and … '; there's just 'me.'"

They hit a little traffic, and O'Connor fought the urge to hit the flashing red lights, turn the siren on.

Morask said, "You're fairly certain the coke isn't a big factor here?"

"If we find out Gio Messina sold a little coke, I won't be all that shocked. That water bowl trick? If you've got a gram you're planning on sharing with your sophisticated friends, you don't have water to dump coke into just in case the cops burst in. Why would anyone burst in to begin with? But there wasn't enough evidence to make me think someone was worried about Gio Messina cutting into business.

"According to his dad, the kid lives rent-free, gets a company car, gets fed, draws a weekly salary for … what, being the owner's son? I don't know that anyone in that position is going to need to sell cocaine in any real quantity. It's probably just adventure. He sells to some of his friends. Exciting, has a little surface-level danger to it, but really? It's risk-free risk.

"Now, let's say the guy who killed him, maybe he's an adventurer too. Maybe he sold a little coke to people, doing it at the same level, same social circles. That guy thinks, 'Well, what does a drug dealer do in a situation like this? Oh, I guess I kill him?' And it goes down like two kids in a shitty high-school play, using real weapons because, why not? They weren't really going to do anything to each other. Just playing. But real life? In real life, drug disputes get settled with guns. But if the guy's a novice, maybe he thinks, 'Gun? Knife? What's the difference?' Then he discovers how hard it is to actually kill someone with a knife, and he bails out. Which he did. There weren't that many wounds."

"No. Uh-uh," Morask said. "He didn't bail out … He left two dead bodies. You're overthinking. How much rational logic do you look for in a fundamentally irrational act? I've always thought, when someone commits suicide and people are like, 'How could he have done that?' or, 'Didn't she know what it would do to her kids?' it's the wrong set of questions. You don't look for presence of mind in those cases. You don't start asking the body why it gets a fever."

They drove quietly for a moment.

O'Connor said, "Overthinking?"

"Yes."

"My gut says drugs are just color here. They're the easy narrative. Easy solution to a hard detection problem. That's what'll get pushed. And that's when no one will give a shit anymore."

O'Connor and Morask arrived at Chicago Police Headquarters a little after 8:30, signed in, and went directly to the Communications Section in the basement. It was a very large room, holding around sixty desks. There was an operator wearing headphones at each one, answering a constant stream of emergency calls.

The noise was overwhelming. O'Connor found himself amazed at the volume of calls coming in this early. He'd been here a few times before but always later in the day. He tried imagining what it would be like late on a Saturday night in the summer, how much of a frenzy all the operators would be in, and that certainly some of those calls would ultimately involve him and the rest of the homicide squad. It was an oppressive thought, and he let it go.

When Morask and O'Connor saw one of the operators get up from behind her desk and walk in their direction, they intercepted her to ask where the lieutenant's office was. She pointed to a glass cubicle at the far end of the room.

The lieutenant offered a tepid, slightly irritated greeting. It was clear they were an unwelcome interruption, but all O'Connor could see in front of the lieutenant was a faintly steaming cup of black coffee and a copy of *The Ring*. The guy had his hands spread over a picture of what looked like Joe Frazier.

O'Connor thought, *Lazy asshole*.

He introduced himself and Morask and told him they needed to hear any or all calls that came in overnight on the first and involved anything in the vicinity of 2970 North Sheridan Road, from 10:00 p.m. on March 1 to 4:00 a.m. March 2.

The lieutenant slowly picked up the phone and dialed. He said, "Sergeant? I've got two Hollywood Division guys who want to hear some calls from the other night. Can you accommodate these important visitors?"

The guy looked up as he said it, checking for a reaction. Neither detective gave him one.

O'Connor and Morask were led to another room, given a set of headphones each, and started listening.

*It's exactly what you'd expect,* O'Connor thought, listening to the recorded calls. Hysteria. Tears. Some incoherent, slurred pleas for help or indignant accusations of this neighbor or that man. A couple of obvious hoaxes. Almost an hour passed, and O'Connor despaired of the time this was going to take.

"Got it," Morask said. He pulled the headphones off. "We got it. Listen to this."

O'Connor took the headphones, and Morask played the call back. O'Connor scrawled *Call 17* and *12:36 a.m.* on his pad and asked Morask to play it again. When he heard the call end the second time, O'Connor left the room, found the sergeant who'd brought them in, and requested three cassette copies.

"We'll wait," O'Connor said.

They arrived back at Area 6 at around one o'clock. They were headed toward Gallet's office when one of the secretaries called O'Connor's name. She handed him two message slips. O'Connor saw one was from Gina Messina, asking him to call her back as soon as he could. The other came from the Communications Center but not from either the sergeant or the lieutenant they'd dealt with. It was from a dispatcher.

O'Connor was curious why a dispatcher would call him shortly after he had left the center. It didn't seem right. He decided to return that call first. As he dialed, he wondered what Gina Messina wanted. To tell him something? Ask a question? He didn't know. After a few rings, he got the dispatcher on the line.

"Detective, I just want to say in advance that I realize this was a big error," the dispatcher said. "I'm not supposed to be starting my shift until tonight, but I was watching the news, besides which I saw the *Tribune*, and I realized I needed to do the right thing here and call ... Look, the only excuse I have is ... I didn't believe it. I didn't believe it was real."

O'Connor listened, thinking, *If the guy isn't even trying to pass the blame for whatever it is he's talking about, if he's calling homicide with it, it's going to be something I really, really don't want to hear.* O'Connor closed his eyes, bowed his head. "What are we talking about, Officer?"

"At about 12:30 early on the second, I got a call. Male caller. Said that he was on a phone at the bar in the Ritz-Carlton—"

O'Connor started protesting silently. *No. No. No. Do not tell me what you're about to tell me. Goddammit. No. No. No.*

"The caller told me ... the caller indicated—"

*Indicated.* O'Connor caught the change in diction, which he took to be further proof he was being told something bad. He began grinding his teeth.

"—that he had witnessed the murder of two victims in an apartment on North Sheridan Avenue and that both victims had been stabbed to death."

"That's what you thought wasn't real?"

"Correct."

"Meaning you didn't dispatch anyone, and that's why the victims weren't found for *two goddamned days*?" His voice got thick, and the volume of it rose. He wasn't even trying to maintain an even keel.

"That's correct. More or less. I need you to understand. It sounded like a prank. Just a joke. I mean, we get them. A lot. You wouldn't believe the number of fake calls that come in."

Trying to stay steady, keep his voice down, figure out a way to salvage something from this, O'Connor said, "Listen. Here's what we're going to do. I'm going to need to have you write down exactly what you just told me. Exactly. Do not leave a single thing out. And if anything occurs to you that maybe you forgot to mention? Well, feel fucking free to include it. Please have it ready when I arrive. I don't give a shit if you're there or not. Maybe it would be better, actually, if I didn't see you. But I'll be there in an hour."

He hung up and signaled Morask, then Philbin and Skelly. He walked into Gallet's office with the tapes and waited until the others were all there.

"You need to hear this. Listen, tell me if it's Sberna's voice, and then tell me how bad we land on this dispatcher." He pressed *Play*.

When Detectives Philbin and Toenings arrived at the Ritz-Carlton, they saw there was a single pay phone by the front desk and close enough to the desk so any conversation would be audible. No one in their right mind would make the call from there. They spoke to the manager on duty, who confirmed that he was working the other night and that no one had used the phone at all. Then he told them there was a huge bank of pay phones on the twelfth floor next to the hotel's bar.

They rode the elevator to the twelfth floor and when the doors opened saw at least ten pay-phone booths located a few feet from the entrance to the bar. They stood at the pay phones for a moment. They could see the entire bar from that vantage. Except for one older man in a blue suit, seated at the farthest end of the bar, the place was empty of customers. A waitress busied herself around some tables. The bartender was wiping the bar top with a cloth.

They walked over to the bar, identified themselves to the bartender, and asked to see the manager. The manager appeared within a minute.

Philbin said, "I'm Detective Philbin and this is Detective Toenings. We are investigating a case, and we think you might be able to help us out. May I have your name, sir?"

"Nick," the manager said, "Nick Ranelli. What kind of a case?"

"Mr. Ranelli, we apologize but we can't disclose the nature of our investigation right now," Philbin said. "But if you don't mind, we do have a couple of questions we'd like to ask. Is that okay? Good. Thank you. Okay. Were you working Monday night and early Tuesday morning?"

Ranelli said, "Yes, I was. I worked from 5:00 p.m. to 2:00 a.m."

Philbin scrawled on his notepad. Toenings asked, "Did you notice or see anything unusual occur here, say, after midnight on Tuesday?"

"Could you explain what you mean by 'unusual'?"

"Anything that caught your notice. Anything that made you pause for a second and think, *Huh, that's odd.*"

Ranelli was quiet for a moment. Then he breathed in deeply, shrugged, and said, "As a matter of fact, I did. You see that waitress over there?"

He gestured toward a waitress arranging a tabletop. Even from a distance, it was clear she was a beautiful woman.

Ranelli continued. "That's Mickey—I mean, Mary—Carlyle. Her boyfriend came in around 12:30 early Tuesday morning. He was … shaky. Actually, he seemed freaked out. Mary walked over to him at the bar. He had a couple of drinks. They talked awhile and then she asked me if she could get off early. She said she had a family emergency. The place was empty, and we had two waitresses on, so I figured, why not?

"She went into the staff room, changed her clothes, and came back to her boyfriend at the bar. While she was gone, he couldn't sit still. He kept fidgeting, shifting around." Ranelli did an exaggerated, jerky impression of someone fidgeting. "He kept looking all over the place, like he thought someone was watching him. Anyway, she came back, they talked for a second, and then they both went out by the pay phones. I got busy but I happened to look a few minutes later, and they were both gone."

Philbin said, "Mr. Ranelli? We appreciate it very much. This has been very helpful. We just need to ask Miss…"

"Carlyle."

"Miss Carlyle a few questions."

Mary Carlyle, uniformed and groomed, was moving from table to table in her assigned sections. The top of every table had to be pristine, as if no one had ever sat there before. It needed to be set, ashtrays positioned, matches arranged, candles lit. She was twenty minutes behind. Her hands trembled. Back in the storeroom she'd dropped a nearly full box of tea candle holders on the concrete, and the glass had gone everywhere. She had to scan the floor carefully for shards, and when she thought she'd seen one glinting under the wire racks, she tried sweeping it out in the open. It stabbed right into her finger, and when she extracted the splinter, she saw she was bleeding. She put a Band-Aid on, though she wouldn't leave it there for long. Regulations prohibited Band-Aids when serving food or beverages.

It was a vain hope that the other waitresses would pitch in and start getting her tables ready for the predinner rush. Carlyle sensed correctly that they didn't care for her. She got bigger tips, more compliments, and no one ever grabbed her ass. She was too beautiful to be profaned like that. At least, most men acted as if they thought so. At some point she'd started believing it was true.

Something bad was happening. Cedric Sberna and Jeremy Keller had both called the bar looking for her, and both left messages saying it was crucial she call back. She called but hadn't gotten either of them on the line.

Whatever the trouble was, she knew it involved what had happened two nights ago.

She was trying to gauge how heavy a situation her boyfriend had just dropped on her, how it could play out, whether it would resolve in a way that kept Cedric safe and herself uninvolved. She didn't know if she could help or even if she wanted to. She intuited she had to protect herself, had to be in a position of strength before she thought about helping anyone else.

Carlyle had been smitten hard when she and Sberna met, and she'd let herself go all in right away, without wondering overmuch if it was a grand romantic leap or a grandiose, reckless one. He had a rawhide masculinity, but his clothes were perfect, immaculate. Perfect in the same way his hair was and his polished, manicured fingernails. A lot of the evidence of his charm was in the details. His personality came through on a when-he-wanted-to-be basis. He was kind, when he wanted to be. Funny, when he wanted to be. Considerate, thoughtful, attentive when he wanted to be. She'd immediately moved him to a central position in her life. The majority of her thoughts and choices took him into account. She believed she was succeeding in turning *when he wanted to be* into *most of the time*. Carlyle was willing to be patient.

Because of her looks, her sense of herself as a woman was shaped by the way people, usually men, reacted to her. The energy and electricity those interactions catalyzed were immediate and of the moment, in real time. As a result, she wasn't particularly forward-thinking or future oriented. But now, with everything going on, she had to be.

She considered telling everyone she felt sick and had to leave. Carlyle had pulled that move twice in February, and she thought she could get away with it again tonight. But it would be better to wait until her shift got further underway.

She lit a candle, positioned it, arranged some cocktail napkins, placed the drink menu where it belonged.

Carlyle looked up and saw two men standing just outside the bar. She thought they might be deciding whether to come in, but after a few seconds, it was clear they were looking at her.

She looked away, moved to the next table. She lit a candle. When she looked again, they had stepped just inside the entrance and were talking to the bartender, a new guy whose name she'd already forgotten. He walked from behind the bar into the back room. Carlyle heard the bar phone ringing and watched the bartender wipe his hands on a towel before answering. She couldn't hear what he was saying, but she saw he was looking at her while he talked.

Nick Ranelli, her manager, emerged from his office and spoke with the two men for a minute. At one point, Ranelli had gestured toward her. She felt a tremor of genuine fear.

A moment later, the men began coming over. They were both tall, both well dressed—the suits were sharp, a little flashier than most of the business suits she saw in here—and when they were close, she could see they both had guns.

They looked affable but she knew they weren't. One of them showed her a badge. He said, "Miss Carlyle? I'm Detective Philbin, this is Detective Toenings. We're with the Chicago Police Department. Were you working this past Monday night and early Tuesday morning?

She looked from one man to the other. Finally, she said, "Yes."

"And you have a boyfriend? Named Cedric Sberna?"

They saw her freeze. After a second, she nodded.

"We'd like you to come with us and answer a few questions. Help us get some information sorted out."

Carlyle said, "What's this about?"

"We just need to ask you some questions about your boyfriend."

"I don't know anything about Cedric or whatever you're trying to hassle me about." Carlyle's voice was wavering. She sounded near tears.

Philbin said, "Ma'am, would you please come with us?"

"Are you arresting me for something?"

Philbin affected shock. "I hope not. But please, would you come with us?"

"I'm working." Even as she said it, she could tell how feeble she sounded.

"Someone will cover for you."

"I need to know what this is about," the fear in her voice sounding like anger, giving the words a little more force.

Toenings gave her a wide, warm smile. "We need to ask some questions about Mr. Sberna that may help us with an investigation we're conducting."

"I need you to tell me more about what you want. I don't know *anything* about—"

"We're done playing." Toenings was still smiling. "Are you coming with us, or are we taking you with us?"

Carlyle shifted from foot to foot and when she did so saw the detectives tense up. "May I go change?"

The men looked at each other. Philbin said, "Sure, but you need to be quick."

They followed her right to the employee locker room and stood outside, waiting. It took her a long time. While they waited, both men thought they heard her voice, speaking in what might have been a furious whisper.

They knocked and said her name, and they heard the talking stop. A moment later, looking small and defeated, verging on sobs, she came out. They escorted her down and outside.

They sat her in the back, and both men got in front. For the first five minutes, no one said anything. Finally, Carlyle broke the silence. "About Cedric. I don't know that I'd call him—"

"Shhhh," Philbin said. "Just wait. Let's have a quiet ride back."

Back at Area 6, Philbin helped Carlyle out of the car, keeping a hand behind her shoulder. Toenings walked a few steps behind. Inside, they walked up the long flight of stairs. Waiting at the top was the same person—the squirrelly attorney—who'd been with Sberna earlier. It was clear he was waiting for them.

"Jeremy! Jeremy!" Carlyle called out. Keller waved to her.

Carlyle said to Philbin—a little desperately, he thought, "That's my attorney. I need to speak with my attorney."

When they were closer, Toenings said, "Mr. Keller, I guess we'll be enjoying your company a while longer?" and whisked her past him.

He followed Carlyle. He called out, "Detective, I need a minute with my client.

Carlyle was in the interview room for about ten minutes, then walked out, eyes full of tears, next to Keller, who had his arm around her shoulder.

Ted O'Connor walked over to the stairway leading to the first floor and the building's exit and was fuming. Once Keller and Carlyle had walked outside, he did a vicious mimic of Keller: "'Don't answer that! We won't answer any questions pertaining to any events after the twenty-ninth of February.' We got her name. We got her address. We got her place of employment. That's it."

He'd been carrying a notepad, and he threw it against the wall. "Good Christ, has anyone ever held these people accountable for a single fucking thing in their lives?"

## CHAPTER 12
*March 5, 1976, morning*

By 8:00 on the morning of the fifth, O'Connor had been at his desk for about an hour or so. He'd arrived when it was quiet and still pretty calm in the squad room, but Gallet would do roll call soon and the phones were sounding, the air turning opaque with smoke. The case was only twenty-four hours old.

The tech guys had sent the photos of the North Sheridan crime scene over, and so far, O'Connor had spent his time staring at them. He'd numbered each one in the order they'd been sent, then went through them several times in sequence. They'd taken wide shots of the area around each body and moved in closer for each subsequent shot.

When he felt satisfied he'd gotten a good sense of the photographs and how they related to each victim, he paired photos of both bodies according to the distance from which they'd been taken.

He couldn't stop fixating on the blood. It was everywhere, all over the apartment, but in the bathroom, where Gio had been killed, there was far more spatter and a much smaller puddle. It was difficult to make any judgment about blood spatter with Delphine Moore because she'd been killed in a more open space. But the pool of blood surrounding her was enormous.

Eventually O'Connor started thinking he'd want to check and see if any stab-happy home invaders had been paroled recently, someone who'd maybe picked up old habits but taken things too far. That was seriously unlikely but not impossible. There was some precedent for home invasions, but in this case, with cash and cocaine left lying around, the theory didn't resonate at all.

Sooner or later someone would start wondering aloud about Black Power militants, this or that Liberation Front, acid-freak Manson types, Process Church people, thrill killers, all manner of lurid possibilities, none of it worth entertaining.

Every homicide detective's maxim was to get a solid investigation going before forty-eight hours passed. Some of the best evidence at a scene had a short shelf life and needed processing before it degraded. And if it was the sort of case where the papers and local networks took an interest—and this case was certainly one of those—the real coverage became public on the second day, and then the killer would get spooked, run, or hide, becoming exponentially harder to find.

The medical examiner called O'Connor around 11:00 to let him know that they'd found a small foil-wrapped packet containing several grams of cocaine inside Delphine Moore. The ME said he wanted to let O'Connor know before Joseph DiLeonardi, the chief of police, made the info public at the press conference he was planning for the early afternoon.

*Inside.* O'Connor sat for a second trying to take that in, thinking maybe he misheard the ME.

Then he asked, "What does 'found inside' mean?"

"She put the packet in her vagina." The ME sounded clinical, matter-of-fact, like it was routine.

If there was an appropriate response, O'Connor didn't know what it was. He went with a question, changing the subject. "Let me ask you something. Let's say you have two victims, both of them stabbed to death, basically equal as far as the number of wounds and the amount of violence. Both of them are found lying on the floor. But one has a huge puddle of blood around them, and the other has a much smaller puddle. What would that mean? I have a hunch, but I want you to weigh in."

"Tell me your hunch."

"Blood stops pumping when you die. So the person with the smaller puddle died sooner—before the one with a bigger puddle."

"Yeah, that would be my hunch too."

O'Connor thanked him and was about to hang up, but the ME cut in and said, "It's really a shame, you know. Young, pretty. She had a beautiful vagina too. I've seen a lot of them and this one was a genuinely beautiful vagina."

O'Connor shut his eyes and willed himself not to exclaim or register disgust or react at all. He said thank you a second time, then went ahead and hung up.

Counting what they extracted from Delphine's genitalia, the amount of coke found at the scene totaled about eight grams.

O'Connor was willing to consider that Morask was right, and he was overthinking, but he still knew on a gut level drugs hadn't directed these murders.

He was coming back from DiLeonardi's press conference downstairs and saw he had two messages. One, from CPD dispatch, asking him to return the call. The other was from Gina Messina.

Tony Messina had mentioned his daughter Gina several times yesterday. Gina and her sister, Lisa, both.

O'Connor took his jacket off and hung it on the back of his chair, thinking that his prediction—the one he'd made to Morask the previous evening—was true. In the few minutes he spent talking to the press, the chief had mentioned cocaine a handful of times.

O'Connor understood the logic: if the drug angle got any sort of traction, concern about the case would dwindle pretty quickly, and everyone was almost off the hook if the investigation failed to turn anything up. He understood, but it didn't piss him off any less.

## Chapter 13

Thirty minutes later, with a start, Ted O'Connor remembered: he needed to call Gina Messina.

He reached across his desk for the phone and dialed the number, hoping that Tony wouldn't answer because he liked the man very much and felt enormous empathy for him, so it couldn't be a short conversation. He was relieved hearing a young woman's voice answer.

He made his own voice as soft and low as he could. "Am I speaking with Gina? This is Detective O'Connor, and I hate the fact that I'm calling while you're all in the middle of this, but I did get your message from this morning, and given what you're dealing with, I figured it had to be very important."

"Well, thank you, Detective. That's very considerate of you to say. My dad said nice things about you and … Detective…?"

"Morask. He was working with me yesterday."

"Right. Morask. I do need to get back to my parents, but I was calling because of Cedric Sberna?" She put an interrogative lilt on the name, as if double-checking that O'Connor knew who she was talking about.

"Sure. Your brother's friend."

"Right. I guess." Something in her voice had turned a little dark. "I'm not sure if you know this, but he called looking for Gio on Monday night?"

"Yes. We did know that. But my understanding is they didn't connect."

"That's not true. My dad got the impression from Cedric that he didn't see Gio after Saturday, when they were in Arlington Heights."

O'Connor weighed how much to give away. Better to keep it vague. "Okay. I had a different impression, but can you tell me yours?"

"Yes, but it's not an impression. Cedric called looking for Gio on Monday night. He called twice, actually—early in the evening and then at maybe nine thirty. But I talked to Gio at eleven, and he said Cedric was there with him."

"There?"

"At Tinker's place."

"And you're sure about the timing? It was definitely eleven o'clock or right around then?"

"Absolutely. I was worried the phone ringing had woken my parents up."

O'Connor felt the first blush of excitement. "Gina, seriously—thank you. That's really helpful. I know you need to go, but if there is anything you need, or that I can help you with, will you let me know?"

He thought he heard her say "Uh-huh," but then she ended the call.

O'Connor thought for a moment, then reached for the file with the typed report of Cedric's interview from the previous night. He found Cedric's number in Lake Forest and called it.

"Hello?" The voice was blurred with sleep, but he was pretty sure it was Cedric's. O'Connor didn't say anything, just covered the mouthpiece with his hand.

"Hello?" When he heard the voice again, O'Connor was positive, and he hung up the phone. He beckoned Philbin, Skelly, and Morask over. "Anyone know who's watching Sberna's house in Lake Forest? We need Sberna brought in. It's got to be right now."

Skelly said he'd call dispatch, then asked, "Bring him in or arrest him?"

"Just bring him in. But don't give him a choice, don't let him drag his feet, and don't let him call anyone. If he insists, make sure they do the dialing for him. But he doesn't call anyone but his lawyer. No one else."

"I can't help feeling this is just simple intimidation," Keller was telling O'Connor, Morask, and Philbin. Sberna had arrived about thirty minutes earlier, and right after he came in, Morask had dialed Keller's number for him. "I told you yesterday, and nothing has changed since then: we won't answer any questions about anything pertaining to Gio Messina and Delphine Moore, subsequent to February 29."

"I think you will today." O'Connor made a point of keeping his voice neutral but looked hard at Keller. Sberna sat in the same place as yesterday, quietly smoking a Marlboro. Keller had gotten a smarmy, pissy expression going—like he thought he was showing everyone who was in charge—and O'Connor wanted to slap it off his face. He pictured the look of shock and panic that Keller would get if O'Connor clocked him hard and open-handed.

"Then you'd be wrong," Keller said.

O'Connor turned. "Mr. Sberna, is that the case? No answers?"

Sberna looked from O'Connor to Keller, said, "Yes, that's right," and went back to smoking.

O'Connor nodded to Morask.

"Mr. Keller, may I speak to you privately?" Morask gestured toward the hallway.

Keller rose and turned to Sberna. "Don't say anything."

In the hallway, Keller was hostile, asking Morask, "What is it? You're trying to separate me from my client, but trust me—"

"We have a piece of evidence."

There was a pause. Then Keller's lips seemed to tremble, very faintly, and his eyes had gotten wide.

Morask continued. "It's your client's voice, on tape, phoning Emergency to let them know there had been a stabbing. Now, for one thing, we figure maybe someone guilty of something terrible wouldn't be enough of a moron to call the cops, tell them about his own handiwork. The second thing is, we can put your client in the apartment on the night of the murders. This is his chance because, everything being equal, he is definitely an attractive suspect. So, tell me, do you still want to decline to answer?"

"My client is, I think, concerned he's going to get hassled about recreational cocaine use."

"None of us gives one cheek of a rat's ass about whether he snorted some coke or not."

"Can I have that in writing?"

"No. Now, what do you want to do?"

Keller walked back into the interview room. "I'd like to speak to my client alone."

O'Connor waved at the doorway, and Sberna and Keller walked out of the room together, huddling out of earshot, Keller doing most of the talking, speaking right into Sberna's ear. Everyone in the interview room watched silently, intently. After another minute, Keller and Sberna walked back, and both men sat down.

"Okay," Sberna said. He stared at the table, gathering his thoughts, then lit a cigarette, dragged on it, exhaled, tapped it on the rim of the ashtray. He looked right at O'Connor. "I'll tell you everything you want to know about that night."

## CHAPTER 14
*March 5, 1976, evening*

Gregg Owen was getting ready to go over to the Record Plant. Just the notion of walking in was difficult to handle. He wanted to put off seeing Sheri as much as he wanted to just get it over with. At the same time, he very much wanted to see the band. He still loved them all. They'd been there for the worst event of his life. And this was the Record Plant, after all. This was the big time. It didn't get much bigger.

Rupp greeted him at the door with a bear hug.

"I've missed you, man," he said and led him down the hall. Signed photos of B. B. King, Frank Zappa, Lynyrd Skynyrd, Billy Joel, Fleetwood Mac, and dozens of others lined the walls. Owen's heart was racing, and when he saw Sheri from afar, he reflexively got ready for the confrontation. But coming face-to-face with Sheri was a nonevent. She'd been on the phone in the control room. She looked at him and then looked away. He stopped and watched her.

She really was done with him. She was okay on her own.

For a split second, he flashed on the first time he'd met her, at her sixteenth birthday party, when Owen was eighteen. She'd begged her father to hire Shady Daze to play, and he'd given her what she wanted.

When she saw he was still looking, she pushed the door shut with her foot.

Approaching the studio, Owen saw a dark-haired man in a red T-shirt, obsessively positioning, adjusting, and repositioning a battery of nine or ten microphones. Another man stood nearby, arms crossed over his chest, looking astonished and exasperated under a brown, bristling halo of hair. It was Don Henley, the drummer for the Eagles.

Standing in the doorway, he saw Bill Jordan talking with Joey Vaccaro, a longtime friend of Owen's and Jordan's and the roadie for Shady Daze. Now, he worked as a road manager for the Eagles. Jordan and Vaccaro broke off and greeted Owen warmly.

"Joey was just filling me in on how the Eagles sessions are going," Jordan said. "Tell Gregg about Florida."

Vaccaro laughed and said, "Oh, yeah. So, we were in Miami, at Criteria Studios. Black Sabbath had the studio next door to us. They were so loud, you could hear it through the walls. We were trying to get a song down, and every take got wrecked because the sound leaked through."

Cold Chicago felt like a distant world. The testing room at DePaul felt like a different planet. For a second—just a second—Owen let himself pretend he was a full member of the band, standing around killing time until the work started. He leapt from the fantasy and got hit by a pang of sadness about what he'd given up. And then a thin, wild current of anger that it hadn't really been under his control.

He bellowed to himself that he needed to knock it off. He'd made the right decision. The coming years would bear him out.

"How'd you end up in Florida?" Owen asked.

Vaccaro pointed to the man in the red T-shirt.

"Selznick didn't want to produce it if we were in LA." Selznick was the chief engineer at the Record Plant. "I guess his house is on a fault line, and there were a few tremors. Scared him shitless. So, we compromised: half the record in Florida, half here at home."

"Between us," Jordan said to Vaccaro, "how's the music? What do you think?"

"I mean, at this point, they're still laying down basic tracks." Vaccaro dropped his voice. "But it's good stuff. Really good stuff. *One of These Nights* is about to go gold, and I bet they get close with this one. Two of the songs ... okay, Joe Walsh? He brought in one tune called 'Life in the Fast Lane' that I think is going to be a big fucking deal. And Felder brought in something him, Henley, and Frey have been reworking for months. That one—let me tell you—is going to be huge."

"What's it called?" Owen asked.

"The working title was 'Mexican Reggae,' but I think they just changed it to 'Hotel California.'"

They all watched Selznick, still addressing himself to the microphones.

Owen said, "Man, when Shady Daze recorded, the drum had one mic and a few baffles."

"Shit," Vaccaro said. "You have no idea. Selznick had them harmonizing one line for ninety minutes. Ninety fucking minutes. No exaggeration. Over and over and over. It was so surreal they couldn't even get pissed."

They watched Selznick again.

"Remember being at the Chess Records Studio?" Vaccaro said.

"Of course," Jordan said.

Owen said, "I'll never forget that."

He recalled the feeling of awe and elation when he'd walked up the long, steep stairway for the first time. He'd been seventeen years old, and from the cigarette-scorched floor to the oblong RCA Ribbon mics, it had seemed like just standing there—belonging there—was the greatest success anyone could ever know. It was where Chuck Berry recorded. Bo Diddley. The Rolling Stones had recorded "Time Is on My Side" and "Satisfaction" there. The name alone had the power of a talisman.

Vaccaro continued. "So, you guys are free to use the studio any time it's empty. We've got it booked for three months. When we're not here, it's just going to waste." He indicated the intricate setup of equipment and instruments. "Stay away from that, though. Any of that gets moved, Selznick's liable to kill. See you around."

Selznick came up to them a moment later. "I worked it out with Sheri, and it's fine if you guys are here. Just, please—do not get near the equipment."

He rushed off. Henley walked by them without looking.

Jordan said quietly, "Come here. I've got to show you something."

He led Owen farther into the studio toward a Bosendorf grand piano and pointed at the lid. "Look at that—can you believe that shit?"

Fine white powder like a light snowfall was spread across the corner of the lid. Owen followed Jordan's finger to the floor. The powder saturated the carpet around the piano leg, as if there had been a heavy frost during a frigid night.

Jordan sounded incredulous. "There's got to be three grand worth in that shag."

Owen shook his head, laughed, shrugged. He said, "God, I hope no one is going to try and put a couple bullets in my head again."

## Chapter 15
*March 5, 1976, evening*

Hours later, as Sberna was just about done, O'Connor stepped out of the room and walked back to his desk. He lifted the phone and called Carlyle's number first, figuring it was more likely she was at the bar. But she answered on the second ring.

O'Connor hung up.

He opened the door to the interview room and motioned to Skelly and Morask. Philbin stayed with Keller and Sberna. O'Connor said, "I need you guys to go and pick Carlyle up. Except I want you to bring her to Twenty-Sixth and California. Take her up to homicide, right near the grand jury room. Ask her if Keller is still her lawyer, and if she says yes, then I'll make sure he gets over there. I'll be joining you too."

Morask grinned. "What are we up to here?"

O'Connor said, "From time to time, you just have to break someone down."

Mary Carlyle sat alone at a table, immediately outside the doors of the grand jury room. It was getting late in the day, and only a few minutes ago she'd watched the jurors filing out, looking worn and depleted, a few on the verge of tears.

When the jurors walked by, Carlyle saw Morask and Skelly, standing by the exit, avert their eyes and look at the floor. It gave gravity to whatever had been underway in the room.

Something weighty, something having to do with someone's fate, Carlyle guessed.

The thought wrenched a small, queasy spasm in her stomach. The sense she'd had last night that something bad was happening was still with her, had, in fact, grown more acute and left her sure she'd stepped right into it this time. She knew it when the men who'd picked her up at her apartment—she recognized Morask as one of the men who'd come for her earlier, but couldn't remember his name. She didn't feel remembering most men's names was particularly important—she knew it when those men had been utterly, completely indifferent to her.

Carlyle had tried her breathy, vaguely British ingenue's voice but it got her nothing. She thought she'd seen Morask roll his eyes. She arched her back to make her breasts press outward, and no one looked.

Things didn't go this way, usually.

Walking to the room where she sat now, she'd tried giving her hips a little more swing, and not one of them noticed. When they brought her in the room, one of them pointed to the chair and said—coldly, she thought—"Sit there." Then they disappeared.

She watched cops and clerks coming in, going out, saw people conferring, arguing, and no one looked at her. And when a woman she thought was a receptionist of some kind did look at her, Carlyle was surprised to see the woman had sadistic eyes.

So she knew she was in deep and was getting more scared she hadn't even suspected the extent of it.

She found herself aware of every sound, every motion going on around her.

She knew the detectives were going to step through the door before they actually appeared, and she guessed they'd be terrible to her.

She tensed, but then the tension slid away when Skelly said, "Can we get you anything? There's coffee, Seven-Up, I think, tea, Coke. Would you like an ashtray?"

"May I have a Coke, please?"

"Of course. And we were about to get something to eat—some takeout—and if you're hungry, we'd be happy to bring something back."

"I don't ... uhhh ... what are you getting?"

"Burgers. Some fries. Detective Morask is a big fan of the peach pie they have at this place."

"A burger, please."

"You got it." Skelly put a hand on her shoulder, smiled, and turned to go.

"Officer?"

"Detective," Skelly said.

"Detective. Thank you for not being mean to me."

Skelly affected an aggrieved expression. "No, no—we're asking for your help."

"The other detective, the one who, who ... " She trailed off.

"Detective Morask? Detective Philbin? Ted? Ted O'Connor?"

"Maybe. I don't know. He was mean. Very mean."

Skelly nodded, as if he knew who she meant. "Well, he's very dedicated. But just the same, we thought it might be better to have a conversation with you here rather than the station. Detective O'Connor, I think, doesn't know we're talking with you. Hopefully he doesn't find out." He winked, reassuring her, then walked off, calling out over his shoulder, "I'll be back with that Coke."

Skelly stepped out of sight and joined Morask, who handed him a Coke. He pulled the tab off and took a sip. Right then, O'Connor came through the doors.

"Good?" he asked.

Skelly took the Coke back to Carlyle, who accepted it with a look of such gratitude that he felt embarrassed for her.

"We've put the order in at the diner. Just one other thing I wanted to—oh, shit," he said, sounding pained, looking down the hall.

Carlyle turned to look too. "What is it?"

"Ted's here."

Skelly turned and stepped quickly out of the room, and then O'Connor was in the doorway, drawing himself up, breathing slowly, deliberately. He had the posture of someone on the verge of detonating.

When Carlyle saw him, she froze holding the Coke can in midair. Then she heard Keller's voice, down the hall, saying "Excuse me, excuse me, I want to talk with my client alone."

"I'm going to give you one chance right now," O'Connor said. "One chance to answer some questions, and then I'm done with this kid gloves shit. Okay? You understand? So, what do you think?"

Carlyle decided she resented being made to feel afraid. She thought maybe the thing to do was stand up to him as much as she could, and maybe he'd ease up.

She put the can down on the tabletop and struck a pose she thought signaled determination. "I'm afraid I can't discuss anything without my lawyer here."

O'Connor covered the ground between the doorway and the table in two steps. He reached out and smacked the Coke can off the table. It hit the wall and fell to the floor. Several brown fizzy trails ran down the wall.

"Do you know where we are?" He was shouting at her. Her expression was immediately disbelieving, shocked. He pulled the table away from her, and it teetered, almost going over. "This is where the grand jury meets. This is where we decide who gets charged with felonies. Does that sink in with you? Do you understand that? That's why you're here—look at me, you sad, pathetic waste of a thing. Look at me. You're here because we are one fucking hair away from charging you with a felony. Someone is going to answer for these two dead kids. You fucking obstruct us? We will put you away. We will put you right away."

His voice got even louder. His face was purpling.

"Someone's going to answer, and if it's you, then you better goddamn believe I am A-OK with that. Now, I'm asking you one final time. One final fucking time."

Carlyle was weeping soundlessly, eyes squinched shut, shoulders shaking. "Please. Stop it. Send Jeremy in. Tell him I want to talk to you."

O'Connor pivoted and walked out. He pointed to Keller. "Your client. She wants to talk to you, then she wants to talk to us."

Keller angled himself carefully and sidled past. O'Connor stepped out of sight and joined Morask and Skelly. They were silently applauding. O'Connor bowed. "God, my throat," he said. He started laughing. "Oh, man, that really hurts. I'm going to be hoarse for a week."

Keller and Carlyle started speaking in the adjacent room. They kept their voices low, but from where the detectives stood, it was still easy to hear them.

Keller was saying, "As your attorney, I am strenuously telling you not to talk. Cedric talked with them for an hour—"

"What?" Carlyle spoke sharply, sounded pained. "What exactly did he say to them?"

"You know I can't tell you that. All I can tell you is he spoke with them for an hour. But listen. Seriously. Listen to me: I can't represent you both. So if you do want to speak with them, I will stay here with you, I will stay the whole time, but then that's it. So think about this really hard."

"Can they charge me with a felony?"

Keller paused. Finally, "No."

"Are you sure?"

Another pause. "No."

"Tell them I want to talk."

Outside the room, standing with the other detectives, O'Connor was beaming.

Ninety minutes later, he had both Carlyle's and Sberna's stories.

What they told O'Connor was this:

Believing he'd been affronted, Cedric Sberna had spent most of a day calling everyone he could think of and then calling them again, indignant and increasingly single-minded about speaking to Gio Messina.

Sberna knew he should feel slighted, and he did in fact feel slighted but felt as much wounded as he did angry and was more pissed that Gio made him feel impotent than at Gio treating Cedric like a lightweight.

A week ago, for reasons lost to scotch and cocaine, Sberna loaned Gio $3,000, with the understanding that he'd need the money repaid by Sunday, February 29.

Gio thumbed through the wad of bills Cedric had handed him, making a mental tally, then smiled and promised he'd make good. Then Cedric watched Gio start spending recklessly. Gio spent big money one night at an Italian place where Sinatra had been eating at the same time. He made some bets. He indulged his vices.

Sberna understood better than most the need to spend in order to impress others as being a successful player. If, for example, you were at a bar where the drinks were less than $1.50, you were drinking in the wrong place. An apartment should rent for a cost commensurate to its location. Cedric himself drove a maroon Porsche 911, which indicated to him that everything was as it should be.

Sberna had no idea what an apartment rented for because he lived at home with his parents, and he didn't know what a Porsche cost since his father had provided that too. Not that he'd never heard the amounts, just that big or little money, money right or wrong, had little traction on the way his life unfurled. Money simply *was*, as foundational as the ground under his feet. The specifics had no more resonance than being told the temperature that morning in Tulsa. Gio was the same way. The two of them had that much in common.

Sberna finally got ahold of Gio at Tinker's apartment, and Gio told him to come over.

It was a forty-five, fifty-minute drive, and when Sberna arrived, Gio was on the phone, ending a call to his sister Gina. During the conversation, Gio told Gina he was really high. Cedric watched Gio restlessly moving across the living room and then back, all around, from one end of the room to the other, smiling broadly. From Cedric's perspective, Gio seemed to be in an especially good mood.

On Tinker's living room table, there was a gun—a 9mm pistol—a mirror, a small glass vial, an uncapped bottle of Johnny Walker Black, a large tumbler of water, and a bag of cocaine. Cedric knew the pistol to be Gio's. He'd seen Gio with it several times before that night.

Cedric pointed to the glass of water. "What's that for?"

"If the cops bust in on you," Gio told him, "You dump the coke into the water. It dissolves instantly, and that way they can't do shit."

Sberna got back to being pissed off. "Listen, man. I'm dead serious. You have got to calm the fuck down. The parties, the restaurants, the bets. Calm down and stop acting so fucking crazy. You owe me a lot of money."

"You're going to get your money," Gio said.

"When? How?"

Gio made a gesture toward the coke with one hand and picked up the phone with the other.

"I know a guy."

Mitchell Weinger knocked on Tinker's door just before midnight, and conversation left off midsentence. Gio and Tinker stood up. Gio moved from the sofa to the center of the carpet and stood with his hands thrust in his pockets. Tinker stepped to the door, put a hand on the knob, and turned to look at Gio. Sberna stayed where he was.

Gio's posture looked slack, aslant, haphazard. He was trying to get it together. He rolled his shoulders, lolled his head—a stoned effort at alignment. He drew himself up and gave Tinker a half-nod. She pulled the door open.

"Hell-oooooo!" She spoke in the loud, protracted locution of hospitality. "Come in, come in."

"Heyyyyyyyy." Gio affected a similar tone as Weinger stepped in. Tinker looked from Weinger and back at Gio, waiting for Gio to introduce them. When he didn't, she said, "I'm Tinker. You must be Mitchell." She extended a hand. After a moment Mitchell slowly reached, took her hand, and shook.

He ran all his words together. "Howareya? Howyadoin? Good." Weinger didn't look at her, spoke past her. He pulled his hand away.

Tinker feigned not noticing. Cedric saw something lightly vexed ripple across her face. She inclined her head toward Cedric. "That's our friend Cedric Sberna."

"Hey, man." Cedric wanted to sound casual. He gave Weinger a half-wave. Weinger looked over briefly, didn't say anything, and then turned to Gio. Cedric was incredulous—he thought Weinger might have actually just been smirking. *You motherfucker*, he thought.

"What's up, Gio?" Weinger said. His voice was flat and detached, seemingly affected to a degree Cedric found a little outrageous. "What's up? What's good? What's shaking?"

Weinger stepped farther in, forcing Tinker to step back. He was wearing an enormous parka with bushy fur trim around the hood. His movements inside it were careful and deliberate, as if he was trying to keep the material off especially tender skin on his back or side. He'd tucked his white T-shirt into his jeans to show off a belt buckle of hand-worked turquoise with a faint Navajo look to it. He had a beaded necklace of similar style and color.

"Let me take your coat." Tinker had recomposed herself. Weinger ignored her and pushed past.

*They know each other*, Cedric suddenly thought. He wondered why they pretended not to.

When Weinger settled onto the sofa, the parka rode up and seemed to draw him in. He sat, nodding, looking around the room. For all the attention he paid them, he might have been in a public space, seated among strangers. Gio hadn't said anything more, and he stood in a way that indicated he was uncertain what to do. Seeing Gio—Gio, who usually vacillated between loyalty when he liked you and antagonism when he didn't—seeing him irresolute signaled to Cedric that the flow of things was warping. He noticed Weinger wore a pair of driving gloves and hadn't taken them off.

Weinger's arrival had given a weird charge to the room. It made more obvious all the different currents moving at cross-purposes—Tinker's forced graciousness, Gio's uncertainty, the acrid cigarette smell Cedric had helped make but found suddenly overwhelming, the rootless uneasiness he felt, the barely liminal hostility arcing between Weinger and Tinker.

Cedric wondered if the two of them had slept together. At any other time, he would have found it perversely funny, but right now he was desperately hoping nothing had happened. He didn't want to be caught in a situation where everything came to a head, that might demand something from him he couldn't deliver.

If he had to describe the attitude everyone there had towards him, Cedric would have said indifferent.

Indifferent, at best.

He hated it. He did not believe he should be made to feel like he was becoming a ghost presence in the eyes of others, as he was feeling now. It made him confused, unmoored, and because his emotional lexicon was so limited, he tended to translate complex feelings into anger. If he ever perceived himself as cornered or threatened, an instinct for self-preservation took over. It braked any significant, meaningful friendships. At a table with others, he was the guy who served himself first, took the biggest portion, and claimed the last serving without any thought.

Right then, Tinker stepped in with a small mirror and placed it very carefully onto the coffee table in front of Weinger. She'd cut several lines of coke. Weinger reached for his wallet, opened it, took out a bill—a twenty, Cedric noticed—rolled it into a tube with deft fingers, still wearing the driving gloves, bent his head toward the mirror, and snorted sharply. Weinger shot up again in his seat, squinting his eyes shut.

Sberna thought, *People always shut their eyes tight, or open them widely.* Either way, the moment belonged to the drug. Cocaine overwhelms everything.

Then he wondered, why did she offer him, Weinger, the mirror first? He was half surprised when Weinger handed him the mirror and the bill. Cedric snorted a line, felt his mind start screaming itself alive, and handed the mirror back to Tinker. She turned and held it out to Gio, but he waved her away.

"Hey, Mitchell—you want to step into the office?" Gio had found his voice again. He gestured toward the bathroom.

"Yeah, let's do that," Weinger said. He stood and readjusted the parka with a few delicate tugs on the sleeves and shoulders. Cedric thought that coming from someone of Mitchell's size and bearing, the delicacy seemed a little mincing, almost comic.

But then it seemed like Weinger noticed something. He moved to the where Tinker had her dining table, with the glass full of water and the scotch. Cedric thought Weinger was going to take a slug straight from the bottle, but he reached behind it instead, moved a newspaper out of the way, and then held up Gio's pistol.

Cedric recalled Gio telling him he'd bought the gun because he figured he might need to use it for "protection." Or at least wave it around. Cedric conceded—not without some envy—that Gio was right, and it was a smart thing for Gio to own. Gio lived a life of greater risk, Cedric thought. Neither of them considered that the people buying the tiny quantities that Gio sold were not the type to rip him off or otherwise try to burn him.

"Awww, shit!" Weinger hefted the gun in his hand. The excitement on his face was like a kid's. He spun in one direction and pointed the pistol at some phantasm of a target. "Freeze!" he called out. He spun again. "I said 'freeze' motherfucker!" Then he spun toward Cedric and sited him. "Boom!" Weinger shouted. He turned and sited Tinker. "Boom!" Weinger started cackling in a demented way.

Cedric went breathless, felt like his legs might fail. He saw Tinker and she looked terrified, stunned.

Weinger bellowed, "What? What? You got something you want to say?" Then he laughed again and laid the gun down. The whole thing had happened so fast that no one had gotten it together to yell at him to stop. Cedric looked at Gio, who stood watching as if nothing had just happened.

Weinger walked into the bathroom, and after a beat of hesitation, Gio followed him in and shut the door. Tinker sat down and stared at her hands.

From the bathroom, Cedric heard the voices of Gio and Mitchell but couldn't make out any words. Neither Tinker nor Cedric said anything. Tinker got up, turned a radio on, and stopped on a station playing the Rolling Stones. She came back and sat down, not looking at Cedric.

Another minute passed and Gio stepped out of the bathroom, closing the door behind him. He was grinning. He started doing an exaggerated set of dance steps, as if he was ecstatic. He put some money on the table and picked up the two small packets of cocaine he'd portioned out earlier. He tossed the rest of the cocaine to Sberna and said quietly, "Hold this, okay? Hold on to it because I know if I have it, I'm going to do it. Remember—if the cops burst through that door, dump this shit in the water glass."

Gio turned and walked back to the bathroom. Tinker went into the kitchen and returned with a small piece of foil. She wrapped the packet, pulled out the waist of her leotards, and shoved the bag down her front. After manipulating it for a moment, she withdrew her hand and let the leotards snap back into placed.

"Does he really think the cops have ever even heard his name?" Cedric asked Tinker. She didn't bother answering.

A loud thump sounded from the bathroom, followed immediately by an equally loud raspy coughing noise. Tinker and Cedric stood up. The noise continued, raw and labored, then came a quieter thump, then silence. Cedric thought the rasp had the same qualities as Gio's voice.

"Gio?" Tinker called, but Gio didn't answer, and she said it again loudly. "Gio!"

She and Cedric looked at each other, and he saw Tinker was frightened past having any idea what to do next. She had one arm laid across her stomach with her fist clenched. The other arm hung by her side, and Cedric saw her hand trembling.

What he did next wasn't for her. It was to try to reset the evening, blunt the sharp edge of tension. He walked to the bathroom door and knocked lightly. "Gio?"

There was no answer. Cedric was about to knock and call for Gio again when he heard Weinger say, "We're just having an argument. It's okay. No one's hurt. Just an argument. We'll be out in a second."

There was no precedent for this in Cedric's experience. He looked again at Tinker and by the terrified, bewildered expression saw she had none either.

A very long minute passed.

"Gio?" Cedric called again. Then he stepped quietly to the door, reached for the knob, turned it gently rightward, and slowly pushed the door open.

The door was slammed shut again almost instantly, but Cedric had seen the whole of the situation: Gio's hand against the side of his throat, blood spurting through the fingers; a wide, thick slick of blood puddling on the floor; Weinger, panting, holding an enormous butcher's knife.

Cedric stood with his hand still on the knob and considered this.

He turned to Tinker.

*Give me that gun*, he mouthed.

"What?"

"Give me that gun." He said it louder than he meant to.

"No, don't do that," Weinger told them from behind the door.

"Oh my God," Tinker said. "Oh my God. Oh my God." She picked up the gun and carried it over to Cedric. He thought she looked shocked, horrified, enraged, about to lose her shit.

Weinger called out. "We had an accident. We're both fine. We'll be out in a second."

Cedric felt making any sense of the situation was impossible, and he didn't have the first idea what to do next. He said, "Mitchell, come out of there. Now."

"Ummm ... no."

"What the fuck? I said, come out of there. Now."

"Right. And I said no. Not if you have a gun. Put the gun down."

"Call the cops," Cedric said to Tinker.

"No, don't call the cops," Weinger advised.

"I'll call the cops." Tinker reached and picked the phone up.

"Tinker, are you calling the cops? Listen, you do not want to call the police. I'm a federal narcotics agent."

"Bullshit," Cedric said.

Tinker yelled. "Mitchell! Come out now! We need to take care of Gio." She was holding the phone but hadn't dialed.

"No, it's not bullshit. I'm a narcotics agent. And there are three agents outside the building. If the cops come, it's going to blow our cover. And that is going to really, really piss me off."

Tinker's voice was verging on out of control. "Goddamn it, Mitchell. Get out of the fucking apartment. Get out. Let us take care of Gio. Get out now."

"Is he really a fucking agent?" Cedric was incredulous.

"He's not a fucking agent, you idiot."

Mitchell corrected them. "Yes, I am."

Cedric was shifting from foot to foot, unable to contain a rising panic. "Listen. Tinker—let's go. Now. Let's get out of here. Right fucking now."

"I'm not going anywhere, Cedric. Mitchell, you motherfucker, come out right now!" She finally broke and started sobbing. "I need to take care of Gio. Let me take care of Gio."

"I need to go," Cedric said. He was starting to shake. He threw the packet of cocaine at Tinker, who caught it and cupped it in her hands. "I'll call you later to make sure you're okay."

Tinker stared at him as if he'd just spoken in tongues. Then she hooked a thumb into the waistband of her leotards, pulled it out, and with her other hand crammed the packet of cocaine down as far as she could.

"Are you leaving, Cedric?" Weinger called from the bathroom. "That's it—you've definitely got the right idea. Go. Get out of here."

Cedric thought he heard Weinger moving behind the door. It was time to go. Right now. He looked at Tinker. She was disbelieving, forlorn. He said, "I promise I'll call you."

With that, Cedric walked quickly to the front door and out of the apartment. He was still holding the gun.

Whatever Sberna may have told family, lawyers, friends, and cops later on about going for help, or doing the best he could for Tinker, or finding himself with no other choice, it was adrenaline and a pounding heart and panic that propelled him out of the apartment—a stronger, more raw version of that animal instinct for self-preservation.

And it was a certain intuitive cunning that kept him from slamming the door behind him, sprinting down the hallway, or shouting for police or an ambulance.

He was aware that behind every door someone might be taking a long, thorough look at him through the peephole. It was late. It was quiet. The hallway seemed overbright, so his face would be spotlit.

Someone might be able to describe it later. The building's super might be floating around. Someone might be coming home. If there were narcotics agents waiting outside like Weinger had threatened, and he looked too jumpy as he left or moved too fast, they'd see in half a second that he was smoldering in a haze of coke and murder, and they'd be all over him.

His hands and feet felt cold. The fluttering feeling in his gut started hardening into nausea. There was sweat suddenly on his forehead, under his arms, running down his back.

There was a lot competing for Sberna's attention. But nothing nagged as much as the compulsion to get outside. He noticed there was a fire exit just next to Tinker's door. It wasn't alarmed. He stepped through, turned, saw a second door, and went through that one too.

Then he was outside, in the cold, alone. No cars, no cops, no pedestrians, nothing else. And coming on just as sharp and sudden as the cocaine he'd done a short while earlier, relief broke open and rolled all through him.

The city was perfect, everything was fine, he was going to be all right. He stood there for a moment and savored the feeling of a miraculous rescue.

But then he became aware of weight in his hand, and when he glanced down to account for it saw he still held Gio's 9mm. He felt the world tilt.

Sberna would have dropped the pistol, but his palm was pressed against the back strap, and his and fingers were locked around the grip, and it was impossible to make them relax.

Where was Weinger? *Why isn't he chasing me down?*

Sberna felt a little emboldened by the gun. If Weinger was suddenly there and came at him, if Weinger did start chasing him down, he could blast Mitchell's brains out of the back of his skull. There was, briefly, some solace in that thought. But then it would only be Tinker's word against his that Sberna had only been present, that he wasn't a dealer, let alone that he hadn't hurt anyone.

Sberna risked a look back down the courtyard of the building and didn't see anything.

He didn't see anything either in the small inside area visible behind the glass door. Two wings of the complex were perpendicular to the central structure where the entrance was, and they rose up over the courtyard. Almost all the windows were dark. He stared at the entrance again for a moment. His hands shook and his shoulders trembled, but nothing else moved, other than flickers and flashes of gray-violet television light from a couple of windows on the upper floors.

Something moved. He'd seen it off to the left, from the corner of his eye. Sberna didn't question whether the vague glint was anything actual or a product of his senses shorting out. He just started running.

His Porsche was parked on the corner, half a block up, on West Oakdale, and he dug into his pockets with his free hand for his keys. Now his fingers cooperated. He laid the gun on the roof, held his coat under his arm, and put his key into the door lock. His reflection showed against the window glass. The streetlight nearby highlighted the sweat on his forehead, and he wiped it away, then rubbed some of the sweat out of his hair, which had gotten matted down. He used his fingers to claw it back into place. He looked at the front and sleeves of his shirt. There wasn't any blood, just dark patches from perspiration. His shirttail was out, and he tucked it back in. He didn't find anything on his pants either. The cuff of one pant leg was caught on the tongue of his shoe, and he fixed it and then looked himself over again. He tossed his coat in, put the pistol on top of it. He rolled his window down, started the Porsche, and drove away.

After a single block, he rammed his foot against the brake, and without looking, cut toward the curb. He'd noticed a phone booth a short way ahead and also heard—distant, faint—a siren. It had to be the police, and there was only one place they could possibly be going. It caused him almost to wail out loud. After a moment, he recalled he was right near a hospital, and then it became clear the siren belonged to an ambulance. He realized why he'd noticed the phone booth in the first place—Tinker. Cedric had promised he'd call to check up on her.

He'd told her to come with him—twice—and she'd refused both times. Then he said he had to get out of there.

The expression on her face when he'd said it ...

He wasn't sure that the look she gave him was as complex a mix of despair, betrayal, disbelief as he remembered. It couldn't have been because he'd offered to help her. If she was that shit-scared, she wouldn't have stayed. So, no, definitely not. He was misremembering.

Sberna also squandered a moment considering whether saying *I promise* was an actual promise or a figure of speech. He decided on the latter.

But spilled blood negated any promise he could possibly make.

But he liked Tinker.

He didn't want her hurt. And if she was okay, she'd be able to tell people what his role there had been. If she wasn't, he needed to know that too because it could mean a lot of trouble, and he wanted a head start getting out from under it.

He couldn't understand: Why did she choose to stay and keep screaming *Mitchell! Mitchell!* and *Hang on, Gio!! I'll get help!?* It was just so stupid. So fucking stupid.

He got a dime from his pocket, found her number in his wallet, and walked to the booth. He dialed and let it ring for a long time. The longer it rang, the less likely it seemed that anyone would pick up. He considered one reason the call was going unanswered but immediately tried to hold the thought at a distance, not just out of his mind's eye but out of its peripheral vision altogether.

He was imagining the phone's bell cracking the silence of the living room, then—he couldn't hold it off—an image came, unwelcomed: Tinker reaching for the phone from where she was sprawled on the floor, bloodied and helpless. If there was enough life left in her. Or any life left.

The pool of blood that had started forming around Gio … it defied belief there was so much blood inside us straining to get out.

Tinker would probably have much less blood since she was so small, he thought.

The phone kept ringing.

Sberna was thinking Mitchell must have had that knife hidden inside his coat. He must have planned it. That's why he was moving like that—because he was maneuvering around a massive butcher's knife in his coat.

He was certain now that no one was going to answer, and he hung up the phone, returned to his car.

He started it, pulled out, and reversed direction.

If the cops had been alerted, he had to know. Not knowing—that was something he simply couldn't stomach.

He turned onto West Oakdale and drove the length of the block, then onto North Pine Grove, a right onto West Wellington, and another right on North Sheridan, back where he'd started.

He didn't see anything. No flashing lights, no ambulances, no cars, no cops, no EMTs, no one at all. Just the building, sleeping, early on a Monday morning. He looped around again, this time going farther up to North Broadway before turning. As remote as the possibility was, those agents of Weinger's could be waiting for Sberna to walk out and away from the building, right into a snare. Still nothing.

As he drove, he analyzed his relationship to the situation, specifically whether the police might try to prove he had any culpability and whether any accusations might stick.

He concluded he was blameless.

It was bad timing and worse luck to have been there, but as far as it concerned him, Tinker and Gio had invited Mitchell Weinger, and if they'd had any notion things could go bad, then it was on them. If they'd had no idea, then it was on God, or fate, or whatever, and it was fortunate that Sberna hadn't been harmed. Neither Gio nor Tinker would want that.

Satisfied after a third loop, Sberna took a left, onto North Sheridan this time, then onto Belmont, and then Lake Shore, steering toward the Ritz-Carlton, where Mary would be working for another hour or so.

It dawned on Sberna that of course there were no narcotics agents involved with this, and there never had been.

The way Weinger was walking around wall-eyed, barely coherent, picking up the pistol and waving it all over the place. Weinger was as much a narcotics agent as Sberna's mother was best friends with Patty Hearst.

The realization wasn't entirely welcome. He ran—escaped, he corrected himself—because narcotics agents were about to burst in. That was the only reason. It was cops, not cowardice.

It took very little thought before he saw how ridiculous it was to believe Weinger was an agent. In fact, he probably even knew it in the moment. But if he knew that and ran, everyone could say Sberna was a pussy. If he believed Weinger, then there was an argument to be made that Sberna was an idiot.

In the end, he elevated himself above the argument entirely.

At that exact moment, he figured, under those precise circumstances, with all that chaos, it was reasonable to believe Weinger's claim. The smart move was obvious: get the fuck out of there. He could even argue that given the urgency, taking the time for a back-and-forth with Tinker was an act of courage.

All it took was the single flash of red from a distant car tapping its brake, which Sberna's terrified paranoia read as the initial flash of a police light. He held that notion for less than a second, but the safe haven of rationales and contingencies he'd built for himself collapsed into pieces. He came close to tears. He mastered a spasm of nausea in his gut.

He considered Mary for a moment. She was the most beautiful woman he'd ever seen in person. He was eager to get to the bar. It would be empty, and he could get a drink and tell Mary what had happened, and she would have some idea of what to do.

When Sberna got to the twelfth floor, it was just as empty as he'd expected. One or two customers sunk into couches, a waitress he didn't recognize, and Mary.

She looked up when Sberna came in and motioned him closer. He asked her if he could have a brandy, and she went to get it. As she walked away, he watched her ass, but when she moved out of his line of sight, Tinker's face came back to him—contorted, tragic—and he felt certain that the thing to do was go back again and see if the situation had changed, if it was a crime scene now, crawling with police. Somehow, it seemed he'd be able to get a better sense of whether or not he was okay.

He was doing his best to hold it together, but when Mary came back with his brandy and asked if everything was all right, if anything was wrong, it all got away from him, and he crumpled.

"Gio got stabbed." He tried keeping his voice even and steady but heard himself quaver.

Mary said nothing, gave nothing away. It was impossible to read her face.

He said it again, without any strength: "Gio got stabbed. And I don't know what to do."

Sberna told her what had happened, in detail, at length, then said it again. "I don't know what to do."

"And you think I know what to do?" She sounded incredulous, mildly panicked. "Oh, God. Cedric. What are you—"

"I need help here. Someone's help. You know people. You must know someone who might have some idea of what I need to do."

Mary appeared to contemplate this at length. Finally, she said she might have an idea and then led him toward the phone booth.

A few minutes later, Mary held the phone out to Sberna, explaining she had called a friend of hers, a medical student. From what Sberna could tell from Mary's end of the exchange, the call had woken the guy up. "He said he'd talk to you."

Sberna took the phone. "Hello. This is—"

"Yeah. Okay." The medical student sounded exasperated, a little confused. "All right. I have no idea what's going on. Now, Mary says someone got stabbed, or you stabbed yourself, or … or what?"

"A friend of mine got stabbed. Like, really stabbed. With a knife. A big one. A butcher's knife."

The guy didn't answer at first. Then, "I don't know what you're asking me."

"Okay, you're a medical student. In your opinion, if a guy gets stabbed and he loses blood—"

"How much blood?"

"I'm not sure. I'm guessing a lot of it. So if a guy loses—"

"Why the fuck are you asking me anything? What the fuck, man? You don't want to talk to me. You want to be talking to 911. Fucking call them. Right now." The medical student hung up.

"What did he say?" Mary asked.

"He says I should call 911. Immediately." They looked at each other for the span of a couple of heartbeats. Mary let out a long, weary sigh.

"I guess you better call them, then."

A little after 12:30 a.m., a dispatcher with the Chicago Police Department answered an emergency call from a clearly distraught adult male. The call lasted about two minutes, and the caller wouldn't give his name but said he'd witnessed a murder or maybe an attempted murder. A man with a knife—a knife with an long, long blade—had attacked his (the caller's) friend and left the friend lying on the blood-covered bathroom floor of Apartment 131 on North Sheridan Road.

"I don't know what the hell is going on here," the caller said, "but the guy is nuts. He is nuts."

"So, you're not in the apartment now? Where are you?"

The caller seemed to not hear the question. "I don't know the chick who leased the place."

"So, this isn't your apartment?"

"Mine? No. It's listed under D. Moore. Delphine. Delphine Moore."

The dispatcher said later that he wrote and wrote on a sheet in the call log. "Can you tell me the name of the person who stabbed your friend?"

"I had to get out of there because I was going to get killed too, if I stayed." As if the dispatcher, again, hadn't asked him anything.

"Sir, can you tell me your name and your location?" It had taken a couple of seconds to realize that the caller told him he didn't know who lived there and then within a second gave her full name. The dispatcher leaned over and just managed to get a finger grip on the spine of the Chicago telephone directory. It was the 1975 edition, the latest one. He pulled it across the desk and opened it, almost to exactly the right spot.

The dispatcher asked again. "Can you tell me your name and your location, sir?"

He looked at the listings and in the fifth column saw a few *Moore*. Chas. Moore lived on North Sheridan, but at 6325, which was four, four and a half miles away. There was an D. Moore on North Lake Shore—using just the initials signaled it was probably a woman.

"I'm calling from the Ritz-Carlton," the caller said and then hung up. The dispatcher listened to a few seconds of the hum and faint pops of dead air and then he hung up too. He'd heard some ambient sounds of people in the background of the call, so whoever placed the call was phoning from either the lobby with its ridiculous fountain with the big brass birds or the club on one of the higher floors—the hotel had just opened, and the papers had run a few stories about it. He'd read about the club one early morning when his shift was over.

Also, it was possible the guy wasn't at the Ritz at all. Probable, actually. There were a few red flags waving, and he figured the semaphore was beginning to spell out *fake*. There was no way this wasn't a prank, he decided. He ripped the sheet he'd been filling out from the binder, crumpled it with his right hand, tossed it in the bin. The phone rang again, and he answered.

Sberna felt the call to 911 had put him in the clear. Carlyle said she'd assumed the same thing. What did he know that anyone would want to hear? What had he seen that made any difference to whatever happened next? When the police arrived, the scene should be self-explanatory. There was nothing he could add, and there was nothing to refute or clarify. What could he tell anyone about Gio or Tinker or even Weinger that someone else who knew them better couldn't? At the very least, he'd be much less interesting to the cops now. Making the call declared as much; it said that the person making it wasn't hiding anything, or at least anything crucial. Declining to give his name—that was just playing it safe.

The worst of the night lay behind him. He tried letting himself relax into that idea. But then new thoughts occurred, or old thoughts reoccurred, and he'd suspect he was wrong, that the night might get worse still.

He'd drunk half of a second brandy, and Carlyle was finishing her shift, riffling through receipts, counting tips, almost ready to leave for the night. She was breezing through inconsequential small talk—a little desperately, Sberna thought—as she organized herself. It was no sooner spoken than forgotten. He made some noncommittal noises in return. She didn't notice.

The two of them were going through the motions of being a couple sitting together for whom nothing was wrong, but the real action of the moment was in their thinking.

It dawned on Carlyle that even if things hadn't gone exactly like Cedric had said, if he believed what he told her was true and conducted himself like it were true, then he was going to act like a fugitive and might be irrational. That would create problems for her.

In a very real way, she didn't want to know much about what happened, only wanted to know if the blowback was going to hit her. But in another sense, the more she knew, the better she could discern what her options were. What *their* options were.

Carlyle entertained a fleeting wish that Gio and Tinker were more than acquaintances. If she knew them, they'd be more real. And that would help her think more carefully, with greater focus.

The ambiguities had Sberna and Carlyle dizzy. In the end they agreed on driving back to the apartment building to see what was going on. There was too much uncertainty not to.

Sberna drove fast and they covered the distance in just a few minutes. Neither of them said much. The rattling, hysterical-sounding torque of the Porsche engine expressed the moment perfectly.

Right after taking the exit, Sberna slowed into low gear, pulled up to the curb, and they sat idling across from Tinker's building. The narrow courtyard leading to the entryway was empty, and there was no sign at all of any activity beyond it. Most of the windows were dark. In a couple of them, they saw the flickering gray electric light of televisions.

Something was off. Neither of them could make any sense of it.

Sberna had called 911 almost an hour earlier, and he'd been convinced they'd arrive and find a night-shattering riot of sirens, and red and blue lights, and every kind of emergency and law enforcement personnel making a commotion. Cedric watched for a while, unable to understand, even dimly, why the scene ran so contrary to what he'd expected.

The silence spooked him deeply. He had a sense of things unspooling beyond his understanding, and his stomach felt filled with hardening concrete. He pulled the car forward and took a left. He circled the building.

"What the fuck is going on, Cedric? What is this?"

Carlyle, too, had figured they'd arrive and see a frenzy of EMTs and cops, trying to restore everything to the silence and peace she and Sberna found when they arrived. Their 911 call should have set it in motion. Even if Sberna had fabricated the whole narrative, there should still be cops at the building. Carlyle had no idea a world existed where the authorities wouldn't bother with a body. She felt outraged.

But she did sense an upside: a world that let dead bodies go neglected, right here in a nice part of Chicago, was a world that had no right to—that couldn't—involve her in a situation like this.

Assured but shaken that there was no one around, Sberna drove up just past the building, pulled over, and turned off his lights. He left the car running, then thought better of it and killed the ignition, putting the keys in his pocket.

"If anything happens … " He trailed off. He didn't know what anything might be. "If anything happens? Then go ahead and … "

"And what, Cedric?" Her voice was thick with panic.

He had no idea. "Go ahead and do what you need to, whatever that is."

He shut the door and trotted off into the dark before she said anything else.

As Sberna approached Tinker's window, the concrete in his gut felt heavier and hotter, and his mouth had turned watery, forcing him to keep spitting it empty. Sweat broke out on his forehead, and he felt his stomach sobbing. All these tics of the body drew most of his attention and kept Sberna from thinking of almost anything other than relieving his sickness. The ground was cold and solid under his shoe soles, and the area running along under Tinker's window was still neat and manicured from when it was last tended in the autumn. His stomach made it known it intended to throw up, but Sberna willed otherwise.

He thought, *These people. These fucking people.* Whatever they got was what they deserved.

Sberna took a few deep breaths and squared his shoulders, then he stepped to the windows looking into Tinker's living room. He saw her there lying on the floor, ripped apart.

It took some time to sync the easygoing, laughing, living person he knew with the dead girl, there, sprawled in her own blood, right in front of him, behind a barrier of glass, but the moment he did, Sberna pivoted away and threw up with a violence that nearly knocked him down. When he was done, he found that he was too wracked to run and remain upright, so he staggered his way back to the car, one freighted step after another, as fast as his body allowed.

Carlyle was incredulous. From the car, she could clearly see Cedric at the windows, looking in like a pervert. He'd be that much more visible to anyone inside any of the apartments who happened to look out the window when he crept by like the Midnight Rambler. She wanted to shout to him, tell him how it looked.

If a car came down the street, its lights would catch him. She closed her eyes, bowed her head. When she looked again, there he was, reeling grotesquely by the windows, like someone loaded to the point of alcohol poisoning, or hit with a massive blow to the head.

He told her, "Tinker. Tinker got it. Oh my God. He fucking killed her. Oh, no. Oh, my God. We're in so much trouble. We're so fucked."

He got in the car and sat for a moment. She reached over and put her hand on his, startled at how cold he was to the touch.

"We need to go back to my place, okay?" Sberna was moaning as she spoke. "Listen. Cedric. Listen to me. Drive to my place. I think I know who we can call."

## Chapter 16

The person Carlyle wanted to call was a lawyer she'd hired last fall to help her with a few documents. She'd come to believe Jeremy Keller, practicing for two years at that point, wasn't particularly good at what he did. Another lawyer might recognize Keller as someone with a loose grasp of the law, out of his depth and adrift if at any point he'd been required to discuss, say, standards of care with any nuance or get into the finer points of comparative negligence or proximate causes.

Other lawyers would see Keller as someone who generally knew the language and when to use it appropriately but didn't know much about making the law work for him or how to fulfill his attorney's oath in spirit and not just letter. He was the sort of lawyer who'd hit on a client when he found her attractive, which he'd done to Carlyle on several occasions. He'd been living with his girlfriend the whole time she'd known him, a few blocks from Carlyle's apartment.

As for Carlyle, she found him unpleasant, and as an advocate, uninspiring. But he was always available to her, as most men tended to be.

That night was no exception. After she and Cedric got back to her place, Carlyle called Keller at around 1:30; he showed up within a few minutes. His T-shirt was frayed around the collar, his sweatpants were ragged.

"I was in the middle of doing laundry," he explained.

Carlyle told Keller what had happened. As she talked, Keller nodded and looked over at Sberna from time to time with bloodless, appraising eyes. She leaned on certain points of the story and rephrased them a few times to make clear she had a late and limited involvement. Keller posed an occasional question and—a good, attentive listener—kept nodding as Carlyle answered. From time to time, it looked as if he'd cringed inwardly and had to stop himself from shaking his head. When she told him about the call to 911, it was obvious to her he fought to hide his dismay.

When Keller arrived, Sberna reacted inwardly with a pitiful, cloying gratitude. At a moment when any kind of good ending seemed out of the question, someone might come and deliver you out of it. He was lucky that way and had been so his whole life. Lucky to the point where he believed it was simply part of his birthright.

A thought glittered briefly that this was proof he'd done the right thing leaving Tinker behind. He'd begged her to leave with him, and she'd refused, and Weinger would have killed them both. It would have been an outrageous fucking waste if two had been murdered when only one was necessary.

But within a couple of minutes, Sberna decided Keller was a repellent asshole. It wasn't about anything he'd said to them, at least so far, or even that he was conducting himself like a prick. Some people just have shittiness at their core. Sberna couldn't think too hard about it. He was disconsolate again, and it had come back with a force stronger than the worst cocaine crash he could remember. Desperation had him on the brink of prayer. But he had to accept that Keller was the only one presently positioned to keep him out of serious trouble. Even panic-stricken, Sberna understood a lot would hinge on what they all did next.

When Carlyle finished, Keller didn't say anything. He looked at Carlyle, then Sberna, and then off at nothing while he thought.

Carlyle tried imagining what was going on in his head. Maybe listening to her had given him an idea of how deeply she was or wasn't involved and what advice he might offer, and now he almost certainly wanted to hear what Sberna said. That would make things clear. She assumed Sberna wouldn't say anything significantly different. And she knew he'd want to speak with Sberna privately. This was a small apartment, and the only place with a door to close was the bathroom. Carlyle suggested the two of them speak there.

Once the door was closed, Sberna saw Keller notice his disarray up close. He glanced at himself in the mirror. Distress had made his pallor dull, his eyes glassy. He knew he smelled of alcohol, and he probably had a sour-bitter scent Keller would recognize as puke. There wasn't anywhere he could step that got him a comfortable distance away.

It turned out Sberna's account didn't diverge much from Carlyle's. But then Keller had a question.

"What did you do with the gun? Where is it?"

Sberna looked a little baffled. Then he touched his coat pocket. "It's right here."

This didn't sit well with Keller. "Man, what the fuck? What the *fuck*? I can't have a conversation with you when you've got a loaded gun."

Sberna didn't appear to need an explanation. "But what do I do with it?"

"You get rid of the fucking thing."

"Should I give it to you?"

"No! No, you shouldn't give it to me. Listen, here's what we need to do. You're going to give me a ride home. I need to get my laundry out of the dryer. While we're out, you're going to get rid of the gun. You understand me?"

Sberna didn't say anything. Keller pressed the point. "Do you understand me?"

Sberna nodded finally and the two of them left the bathroom.

Sberna pulled the Porsche up in front of Keller's place, and Keller stepped out. "I need about fifteen minutes. So you meet me back here in no more than that."

As soon as Keller got in the front doorway, Sberna raced off and looked for the right place to abandon the gun. It would be found if he dropped it in a garbage can. He wouldn't get enough distance if he tried to throw it in the lake—the pistol would land too close to shore. If he threw it into a drain in the gutter, it would just sit there and probably be visible. His eye kept on seizing at possibilities, and then his mind let him know why each option was reckless. A paralysis of thought was setting in.

Until he saw a manhole cover in the center of a street. Age and elements had made the asphalt uneven, and one edge of the manhole angled up so part of the lip tilted higher than its opposite side. Sberna got out and rooted around for the kit he carried in case the tires needed changing. Once he'd found it, he saw one end of the big lug wrench was broad and flat like a screwdriver. Sberna yanked the wrench free, threw the kit back into the car.

He didn't see anyone else out, not a single car or pedestrian coming from either direction.

Sberna pried the cover up, arms aching from the effort, until it came free. He maneuvered it until he'd given himself enough of a gap to accommodate the gun. When he dropped it into the darkness, a full second passed before he heard it clatter against what sounded like concrete. He moved to the other side and forced the cover back into place.

Sberna threw the wrench behind the seat, and it banged against the kit. He drove off way too fast. Arriving at Keller's, he pulled up and sat idling. Keller appeared moments later, shaved and dressed. Sberna was curious why, at this hour, anyone would bother but forgot about it when Keller came around by the driver's side door and stopped.

Sberna rolled the window down. "What are you doing?"

"I need to check to see if you ditched the gun."

"I did."

"I think I need to not trust you right now. Step out of the car. Do it. Now."

Sberna stepped from the car and raised his arms without being asked. Keller leaned in and ran his hands flush against Sberna's shirt, up the ribs and under the armpits, down to the hips, around the small of his back. Then, he reached a hand between Sberna's legs and patted his inner thighs, then cupped Sberna's balls. He stood up again. "Okay, let's get back."

## CHAPTER 17
*March 6, 1976, midnight*

O'Connor, Skelly, and Morask had sat at a table in the interrogation room all morning, sifting through her account, figuring out how much of it was bullshit.

"For the most part, I believe her," O'Connor told them. His tone said he wished he didn't, that if he hadn't found holes in her story, it meant he wasn't looking hard enough. But he did believe her. "Their stories meshed. I was hoping she'd get spooked, knowing that Sberna gave everything up, and she'd be pissed at the lawyer for telling her to fuck off. Maybe she'd do a little implicating."

Morask said, "I think she did feel those things. But there was no one to implicate."

"Who's Mitchell?" Skelly asked.

"A decent candidate for our killer, if Sberna's not full of it," Morask said.

O'Connor said, "He doesn't have guts enough to lie and be that bold about it. Too much potential for the whole goddamn thing to collapse on him."

"I don't know he's smart enough to recognize that potential," Skelly said.

"Instinct and smarts aren't the same thing," O'Connor said. "I do believe him. Or I believe him 90 percent. As soon as cocaine was off the table, he was singing like a choir."

Skelly said, "He doesn't know coke isn't off the table. We didn't promise him anything. If that's his assumption, that's his problem."

"If all we get out of this investigation is some piddling little coke deal, then we are going to look like the biggest jagoffs on the force. And rightly so," O'Connor said. "As far as Sberna goes, I couldn't possibly care less about a few grams of cocaine. But we pretty much told him he was off the hook for this whole mess. We made sure to let him know that phone call to dispatch was his get-out-of-jail-free card, and since no one's stupid enough to call the cops on themselves and then go back to the scene, it actually is his get-out-of-jail card."

"I mean, there's the possibility—remote, granted—that he's a smart enough crook to make that call and deflect suspicion," Morask said. "Smart, with a set of big brass balls."

"Really, really remote. I'm not sure he's crafty enough not to implicate himself," O'Connor said. "If he was the guy, he would have slipped up. Plus, he got so damn nervous when he finally understood we weren't playing chicken with him. He wanted to talk after that. Guilt doesn't sit so well for a Catholic kid with little balls."

"We know he's Catholic?"

"I mean, no—he didn't say it. But he didn't fight us. He didn't question our legitimacy. He took our authority for granted. The guy wanted to avoid trouble, not challenge anyone. He's not enough of an independent thinker for that. We were like priests to him, he wanted to 'fess up. First opportunity, he was telling us the whole story. He didn't begrudge it. He gave us a lot of detail. He wanted a clean slate, and he was going to spill it all to get it. That's a Catholic kid impulse."

"And Carlyle?"

"I don't know. Is she guilty of anything more than stupid choices? Probably not. She wasn't even all that useful. All she did was corroborate what Sberna said. We weren't giving much thought to her being involved anyway. She had an alibi. Maybe accessory after the fact, but not enough time's passed to even make that stick. Plus, she was in on that call. However—Keller? What a piece of work. Telling Sberna to ditch that gun? Unbelievable."

Skelly said, "The question remains: who the fuck is Mitchell?"

Something about Richard Morask had seemed to make Tony Messina think harder and dig deeper when asked a question, so O'Connor had Morask make the call to ask if Tony knew anyone named Mitchell.

"Mitchell? God, I don't know. Let me think. Mitchell. Mitchell."

"Mitchell, possibly Mitch." Morask happened to look at his watch. Tony's thinking stretched for a long fifteen seconds, then into thirty, the second hand finally passing the one-minute mark before Tony answered.

"I'm sorry. I can't think of anyone. I'll ask the girls."

"It would be a big help. And you'll ring me back right away if they do know anything?"

Later that evening, O'Connor signed Gio's address book out of evidence, returned to his desk, and took it out of its protective plastic. There were traces of fingerprint powder on the spine and bottom edge. He rubbed it off, then wiped his fingers clean on a napkin he found under his coffee mug.

He opened the book, reading through it carefully, page by page.

In pencil and several different inks, Gio had filled in the entries by first name and sometimes using just the first few letters. In a number of places—the *C*'s for example—Gio had scrawled random names, so *Cedric*, *Chris*, *Connie*, and *Conrad* were next to *Edward* and *Tim*.

On some pages, O'Connor could see indentations, and he figured Gio had written on another piece of paper and bore down with his pen or pencil. O'Connor angled the pages into the light, but the dents didn't seem to reflect any numbers. If he needed to, he could find some tracing paper and do a light rubbing, the way he'd seen people do rubbings on old headstones, but he suspected he wasn't going to find much. He might try it if he got desperate enough, but for now, he just kept turning pages.

Someone had spilled what looked like coffee on a big section of pages, starting with the letter *J*. The ink had blurred; the paper had dried and warped. The damage stopped right where the *M*'s began, which is where O'Connor saw the name *Mitchell*, underlined, and sitting above the numbers *708-3060*.

The name leapt from the page with the force of revelation, like something coiled and waiting to be found and put to use, calling out, *Finally, I've got your attention.*

There was another name nearby. Gio had written *Matty* close to—some of it on top of—the entry for *Mitchell*, and he'd done it quickly. He'd scrawled the letters—two uneven humps for the *M*, double *T*'s with a slash that barely grazed the verticals. But Mitchell was written neatly, everything proportional, flush against the entry line. He'd probably copied it off of something else. At least that's what the neat, deliberate penmanship seemed to say. And if he'd painstakingly copied the info, it was someone Gio knew. And if another name had been written almost over Mitchell's, it implied Gio had known Mitchell for a little bit. Certainly, longer than Matty, although who could say by how much?

If he wanted the address, he could do it the time-intensive way and serve the phone company with a warrant, or he could take a not-quite-by-the-book shortcut. O'Connor had a friend, a former cop, who currently worked at Illinois Bell security. He decided to give his friend a call.

Ten minutes later, O'Connor had a last name and address for the phone number in Gio's book: Mitchell Weinger, at 6033 North Sheridan Road, Chicago.

O'Connor scanned the squad room.

Who was still here?

It was well into the second shift. Jimmy Nolan and his partner, Paul Roppell, were both at their desks, and John Toenings was at his, all of them bent over piles of paper and manila folders.

"Jimmy, Paul, John—" Everyone looked up. "Feel like taking a break to go pick up a killer?"

## Chapter 18

O'Connor and Roppell rode together, with Toenings and Nolan following.

O'Connor liked Roppell, thought they shared an outlook and methodology: careful, thorough, fully considered. Roppell had taken the detective's test almost immediately after the academy, making him the youngest homicide cop in Chicago's history. He had a pile of notebooks on his desk that he'd filled on the job, a practice O'Connor respected.

A lot of cops would have watched Roppell's quick rise with resentful eyes, but O'Connor was never that insecure.

He liked Nolan too, but Nolan was perpetually joking, and the quips and wit sometimes sat uncomfortably on O'Connor's nerves. Also, the guy drove like Steve McQueen racing through San Francisco in *Bullitt*.

O'Connor was concerned about making a wrong move. No, not a wrong move—he was worried about making a premature move. Taking Weinger in—it was all on Sberna's say-so, with Carlyle backing the story up. A wannabe dealer of cocaine and a woman who wanted a cocaine-dealing boyfriend.

He had a bit more contempt for Carlyle than he did for Sberna, which surprised him because when Sberna called the cops, it had been at Carlyle's urging. But he'd gotten a sense of Carlyle as a grinning voyeur, and the two dead bodies might be bits of exotica in the knowing, worldly life she wanted to cultivate.

It came down to whether or not Sberna was reliable. O'Connor thought he was, mostly because of that call. Add to that Sberna's admission about the gun—that he'd had it, ditched it, and told them where he'd ditched it. Plus, he put himself back at the scene a second time. A decent canvas could almost definitely produce an eyewitness to that. And he was open about using cocaine. O'Connor assumed Sberna was hedging about the coke, but he was being honest when he told Sberna earlier he didn't give a shit what the full story was.

Roppell said, "So you're saying you've got it solid enough in your mind to drive over and get him."

"I'm close to 95 percent that he's the guy."

"Is it between 'bring him in' and 'arrest him'?"

"I'm closer to arrest. Sberna witnessed—well, he says he didn't see it—he saw this Weinger guy go into the bathroom with Gio Messina. He hears a scuffle. He runs. When he goes back, Messina is dead, Moore is dead."

Roppell looked out the window, thinking. It was past midnight, the traffic pretty thin. When he looked into the side-view, he could see Nolan's car behind them, following too close.

He said, "I'd say that's plenty for an arrest. Plus, you bring him in without arresting him, and say he gets released. How much you want to bet you're going to have to search for him after that?"

O'Connor said, "No bet. But if I wasn't reasonably sure I'm not going to be releasing him … " He trailed off. "Here's my plan: bring him in, do some talking, drag Sberna in to ID him, get a warrant."

"Of his apartment? You don't actually think you're going to find the knife, do you?"

"No, that knife is in the lake or the river. But who knows? I doubt I'll find any clothes with blood from either Messina or Moore on them, but weirder things have happened. Sberna mentioned some type of necklace—a turquoise Indian thing—and a matching belt buckle. And let's say we don't get his clothing—I wouldn't be surprised if we got his coat. Sberna said he kept it on. Weinger will be more likely to try and clean it than to ditch it. Coats are expensive. I'll be happy with anything that connects everyone to everybody else—another address book, whatever."

"Let me ask you," Roppell said. "Is it true about the porn?"

O'Connor turned and looked at him. "What the hell are you talking about?"

"It was in the *Tribune*. Moore did a skin flick."

The police radio came suddenly alive—an assault and robbery in Old Town. Suspect fleeing on foot. For a moment, voices chattered back and forth.

"Come on. Bullshit," O'Connor said. "She was an actress, but she did theater stuff, as far as I know." He made a mental note to check that. After a moment he said, "What are we talking? Porn as in *Deep Throat*? Here, in Chicago?"

Roppell said, "No, it didn't seem that hardcore. Daley'd be all over that. Someone from the hall would be demanding an investigation. I think it's probably more like *Hair*."

O'Connor signaled and pulled up a ways past the front entrance of Weinger's building. It was a boxy, modern-looking thing. Pricey, alienating. A place for people without enduring roots.

The four cops stepped from their cars and walked to the entrance.

A doorman came out as they got close. O'Connor said in a low voice, "Jimmy, when we go up, can you sit with this guy? I don't want him giving Weinger any sort of warning."

"Yeah, absolutely."

At the door, O'Connor showed his badge and asked after Weinger. The doorman told them the apartment number, adding, "I can't say if he's here or not."

"Can't or won't?"

Nolan reached and put a hand on the doorman's arm.

"Why don't you come wait over here with me?" He influenced the doorman away from the buzzer and desk.

The doorman suddenly wanted to make himself clear. "It's not that I won't. I've only been on duty for thirty minutes. I don't know who's up there and who isn't."

When they got off the elevator, they walked carefully down the hall, quiet enough so there were only a couple of whispered squeaks from someone's shoe leather.

At Weinger's door, O'Connor took his badge out and knocked, then let his hand move by reflex to the butt of his pistol. Roppell and Toenings positioned themselves on either side of the doorway.

No answer. O'Connor knocked again; still no answer. He leaned in so his ear almost touched the door but couldn't hear any movement. No TV, no radio, no talking. He knocked a third time, listened again, didn't hear a thing. He said, "All right. Let's head back down."

Toenings said, "Do we get him when he parks or when he's walking in?"

"When he parks. If he gets a look inside and sees us in the lobby, he might run. It's late and I can't say I'm all that keen on a chase right now."

The elevator went all the way down to the garage, but they stopped on the first floor, and while Roppell held the door, O'Connor took Nolan aside to explain what was going on. He got back on, and they rode down.

The door opened on the valet station, and the sound and echo made the attendant look up. O'Connor stepped out holding his badge. The attendant didn't seem surprised or alarmed, just curious.

O'Connor asked, "Is everyone here assigned a parking space?"

The attendant nodded.

"And Mitchell Weinger, he has his own space?"

The attendant nodded again.

"Is he parked there now?"

The attendant craned his neck. "No, his car isn't there."

"Do you know when he left, or where he was going?"

"No, sir. I just came on. I don't know when he left, but—" He looked over at the entrance ramp, at the headlights and source of the engine noise beginning to echo off the concrete. "Here he is now."

A long red Continental was just coming to a stop. The engine cut and the lights went off. Its door opened and a man stepped out. He was medium height and didn't appear very heavy, not of intimidating size. He was putting his coat on and hadn't seen them yet.

As O'Connor watched, he paid attention to what Weinger did with the keys, thinking for no reason, *Every time I do valet, I take the keys with me. I never remember.* Weinger appeared to leave the keys in the ignition. Then he stepped forward.

O'Connor said, "Mitchell Weinger?" He had his badge out again, his free hand moving back toward the gun. Weinger watched him coming.

"Yes. I'm Mitchell Weinger," he said when O'Connor was a few feet away. O'Connor was waiting for him to ask why they were there, but he didn't. Weinger kept looking at O'Connor.

O'Connor said, "Mitchell Weinger, you are under arrest for the murders of Gio Messina and Delphine Moore," then recited the rest of Weinger's rights. "Do you understand your rights as I've read them to you?"

"Okay," Weinger said.

"I'm not asking if it's okay. I'm asking if you understand these rights as I've read them to you."

After a few seconds, Weinger finally said he did.

"Do you understand why I'm arresting you?"

"Yes. For murder."

"Do you understand you need to come with me to the Area 6 police station?"

"Sure."

O'Connor thought he heard Toenings laugh softly, sounding incredulous. He said to Weinger, "Okay, turn around, and place your hands behind your head. All the way around. Okay. Good."

O'Connor stepped in and pulled back on Weinger's interlaced fingers. He hooked his leg around Weinger's, prodding Weinger's ankle until he stood in a wide straddle. He patted Weinger at the armpits, ran his hand over his ribs and back. O'Connor squatted and pressed against Weinger's pockets, felt the front and back of his groin, slid his hands down the length of Weinger's legs.

This was the vulnerable moment of a pat-down. You ran the same sort of risk as you would standing behind an agitated horse.

When Weinger shifted—and it was nothing more than that, just someone recalibrating his balance—all four cops recoiled, reaching to draw their guns and poised to make a tackle.

Not for anything close to the first time, O'Connor recognized just how mistakes got made.

But not that night. Weinger had his eyes locked on something distant. He didn't move again until O'Connor closed the handcuffs around Weinger's wrists, and Roppell helped ease Weinger into the back seat. Before O'Connor settled behind the wheel, he'd taken out a card with the Miranda warning on it, and he read it to Weinger again. He knew it by heart, but he wouldn't risk having to cut someone loose because he'd dropped a few words by accident.

As they drove, O'Connor had to fight an impulse to stare at Weinger in the rearview. Weinger didn't look troubled, nor did he look relaxed. He just seemed a little perplexed. He sat behind the passenger's seat, looking out the window, calm and reflective. At one point he cleared his throat, and O'Connor thought he might be on the verge of speaking, but he remained quiet.

Finally, Weinger broke the silence. "Why do you think I murdered someone?"

"Shhh," O'Connor said. Anything Weinger told him wouldn't be on the record if he said it here in the back of the car. The light just ahead blinked from green to yellow, and O'Connor sped up and cruised through it. He looked in the mirror again but past Weinger this time, trying to see if Nolan and Toenings were still tailing them. They were, and still too close.

"I just want to understand why I'm being brought in."

"This is a quiet car. Please respect the rules." He looked at Weinger, saw something ripple under his calm.

Weinger said, "So you're really not—"

"Did you not hear me say shut up?"

The car was a couple of turns from Area 6, and O'Connor saw Weinger's mien lose some of its fight. Some but not all of it. Not even most of it. In fact, as they made the first turn and streetlights shone full on Weinger's face, O'Connor thought Weinger looked like he wanted to explode, but he considered, too, that maybe that's what he wanted to see. O'Connor was always struck when the violence of a crime and the demeanor of the criminal were at odds. That was usually how it went. Bullets through the brain, a blade stabbed into something vital, bruises around a neck from a strangler's fingers—you expected to find a demon but wound up with someone sad and deplorable.

When the abused killed the abuser, or someone was threatened beyond rationality or tormented past the breaking point—O'Connor had some empathy there. The throughline connecting motive and act was pretty clear. But Weinger had nothing of that going on. Nothing visible, no obvious disturbances, no flickers of craziness, nothing hinted at, nothing that said his right hand didn't know what his left hand was doing. More than psychos, kingpins, mob bosses, almost anyone else, the people who gave O'Connor chills were the ones who killed but couldn't explain why with anything better than a shrug.

Weinger, though, couldn't keep quiet. "Before we go in, I want to let you know I have hepatitis."

O'Connor decided he'd try out his best bull-roar. "SHUT THE FUCK UP!"

## Chapter 19

O'Connor always found that the symmetries, the echoes, the neat parallels were what gave policing some its most reliable, enduring satisfactions. Just a few hours earlier they'd had Sberna first, and then Carlyle, sitting in the same room, at the same table where Weinger was sitting now—Sberna giving it up so easily once he realized they liked him quite a bit for primary suspect, Carlyle sobbing her way free of what she believed were going to be felony charges—and O'Connor had been cautious not to even allude to what those charges might be—and now Weinger had his wrist cuffed to the restraining bar running the length of the wall, sitting in front of an ashtray still holding a few of the butts Sberna and Carlyle had smoked right down to the filter.

He'd sensed right off Carlyle was a nonentity in all this, and it took very little for him to realize homicide wasn't going to have much interest in Sberna. But Weinger grabbed his attention from the second Carlyle backed up Sberna's account, and each moment since turned interest to certainty. O'Connor was becoming more attuned to the small evidences that Weinger was a killer who'd probably never guessed he had it in him, who was sitting there keeping company with recollections of what he'd done just a few nights ago and not surprised by it, not especially remorseful. Probably not remorseful at all.

O'Connor would have bet a month's pay that they'd clear this case solely on evidence, that any consideration of motive wouldn't avail them of much. The guy hadn't betrayed even a hint of someone driven to kill. O'Connor guessed Weinger didn't even know why he'd done it—why he picked up a weapon and used it—only that he had done it and by some distorted logic was justified in doing it.

First thing, O'Connor asked Morask to get Sberna back in. Then he asked Toenings to scare up some other cops, or any civilians on premises who were average height, well built, and wore a mustache, and get them ready for a lineup.

Next, O'Connor found Philbin and asked him to get ready for a sprint over to night court with a request for a search warrant and to have the paperwork all set.

Then O'Connor went in and sat down across from Weinger.

As he got his pen and papers ready, he felt Weinger staring, but he took his time and didn't look up. When he did, O'Connor and

Weinger's eyes met and they held the look for ten, fifteen seconds, which felt closer to an hour's worth of time in a freighted, dead-air moment like this one.

Weinger broke eye contact first.

It wasn't in a way that made him seem spooked. It was more as if he'd seen all that was interesting in O'Connor and wanted to fix his attention on something better.

O'Connor felt an urge to show Weinger that right now, O'Connor was the most interesting thing around. Then he thought that someone like Weinger should never be allowed to make anyone—especially someone like O'Connor—feel the need to justify himself. In a way, that was at the root of the problem that ultimately brought them together in the room: the instinct to prove or justify yourself gave Weinger the sort of power and status that let him believe it was okay to be the person—the killer—he was.

O'Connor pointed to the sign bearing the Miranda rights. "I'm going to read you your rights again."

"I understand my rights."

"Fantastic. Then we'll consider this a quick review."

"I know what my—"

O'Connor talked right over him. "You have the right to remain silent—"

"I told you I was aware—"

"Anything you say can and will be used against you in a court of law. You have the right to speak to an attorney and to have an attorney present during any questioning."

"Okay, okay."

"If you cannot afford an attorney, one will be provided for you."

"I assure you I can afford—"

One final time, loud: "Do you understand your rights as I've read them to you?"

Weinger, sounding weary. "Yes. I understand."

O'Connor waited, then said, "So what do you say—you willing to help us out here? Answer a few questions for me?"

Weinger closed his eyes and gave his head a slight, incredulous shake. "Sure. That's fine."

"Great. Thank you. Question one. This is easy. Do you know Gio Messina?"

"Yes, I know him."

"I guess we should say *knew*, right?" Weinger stared at him, coming off as slightly shocked. O'Connor continued. "Was he a friend of yours?"

"Yeah. I mean, he wasn't...yes, he was my friend. Not a close, close friend. But..."

"He wasn't just some guy you knew."

"Right. He was a little more than that."

O'Connor nodded, and pretended to scratch a few words on his pad. "What about Delphine Moore?"

"No. Never heard of her."

O'Connor sat, pen poised, as if waiting for Weinger to finish his answer. A few moments passed. Then a few more. The weight of the quiet got difficult. Finally, Weinger said, "What I mean to say is that I never heard that name until tonight."

O'Connor feigned more writing. "Tell me about Cedric Sberna."

"No—"

"What do you mean, 'no'?"

"That's not what...I mean I can't. I don't know anyone by that name."

"When did you last see Gio?" O'Connor watched Weinger fix his eyes on the table, like someone who didn't have an immediate answer but was trying to find one as fast as he could.

Weinger finally looked up. "Sunday, I guess. Sunday the twenty-ninth of February."

"How good a guess are we making?"

"It was the twenty-ninth."

"Where?"

"At the apartment on Sheridan."

"Delphine's apartment?"

"Right, but I only learned later whose apartment it was."

"And you're sure it was Sunday? It wasn't Monday, the first of March?"

"Yes, I'm sure."

O'Connor put his pen down, cracked his knuckles, then drummed his fingers on the table. He reached and took up the pen again. "You know what, Mitchell? Honestly? I think you were there on the first."

Weinger pretended to consider this. "Maybe you're right. Maybe I was there on Monday the first. Monday the first of never."

"That's clever." O'Connor affected a quiet chuckle. "Okay. So, you were there the twenty-ninth. Did you go anywhere on the first or the morning of the second?"

O'Connor heard Weinger take a slight inhale and hold it, like he was doing something that required effort, and it seemed to O'Connor that he could almost see the engine revving in Weinger's head. Twice over the next four or so seconds, Weinger looked on the verge of an answer, but then he didn't offer one.

"You're hesitating," O'Connor said.

"I'm thinking. I mean, do you want an answer?" Weinger's tone didn't sound sharp or steely, but O'Connor thought he heard him making an effort not to sound short, impatient.

"I do want an answer, but I want a true answer." O'Connor hadn't really thought saying that would prod Weinger one way or the other, but as he watched, he saw something interesting: it was like Weinger was seeing that if he answered now after that sort of prompt, it would sound like he'd been withholding, but if he kept quiet, it might look like he was groping to find an answer.

Weinger shrugged, held his hands up, like he was at a loss but needed to pick something. "Yes. I went out around, maybe seven o'clock."

Weinger looking at O'Connor then, and O'Connor seeing a little activity in the eyes, some second-guessing: *Good answer or bad answer? The lady or the tiger?*

"Really?" O'Connor laid his pen down, scrutinizing Weinger, messing with him just a little bit. His scrutiny got him a glimpse of something pissed-off around the lips, up at the eyebrows. Just a half-strobe of something, there and gone.

"Really. I went to a friend's place. To play cards."

"Okay. We'll get to that. I need to know why you went to see Gio the night of the twenty-ninth."

"What do you mean?"

"What do I mean? You can't possibly need me to explain what *why* means."

Weinger was staring at the tabletop and kept gnawing at his moustache with his bottom teeth. O'Connor put a broad smile on for whenever Weinger concocted an answer and looked up to give it. After another few seconds he finally lifted his eyes.

"I owed Gio money."

O'Connor gestured with his hand indicating, *Give me a little more.*

Weinger said, "I lost a bet with him. We had a bet on the Bulls game, for $40 and a steak dinner."

"What was the score?" O'Connor asked.

"The Knicks won by twenty points. Eighty-one to a hundred-and-one."

The score was actually eighty-five to ninety-three. O'Connor had watched the game and lost $5 to Gallet. It wasn't clear if Weinger was just making an innocent mistake or not. O'Connor asked, "And you were definitely giving Gio money? Paying him? This wasn't an exchange?"

Weinger seemed puzzled. "Exchange of what?"

"Exchange of money for coke."

"Coke?"

"Coke. Blow. Flake. Nose Candy. Cocaine. What did you think I meant?"

Weinger laughed, despite himself. "You've got it wrong. I don't do cocaine."

O'Connor waved his hand to indicate he wasn't concerned and dropped his voice to a conspirator's level. "Mitchell, between you and me, I'm trying to solve a murder here. A double murder. And I couldn't give a fuck if you do a little coke. You can tell me. I feel like we trust each other here, right? Isn't that right? I just need to get a picture of the whole scene. Rule a couple things out. You guys snorted a little, right?"

Sounding defeated, Weinger said, "We snorted a little cocaine, yeah."

"I'm fascinated, Mitchell. Tell me more."

Weinger sighed, shrugged. "I gave Gio his money. He asked if I wanted a little cocaine. I said no, but then his girlfriend comes over and she's got a mirror and a razor and a glass of water—"

"A glass of water?"

"A…a…what do you call them? You drink brandy or cognac out of them."

"A snifter."

"A snifter. Right. And Gio brought some coke out—"

"Why a snifter of water?"

"Honestly, I'm not really sure," Weinger said. He sounded genuinely puzzled. "If you have a little extra on your razor blade or whatever, you tap it into the water."

"Is this some kind of superstition?"

"No. I think eventually you can drink the water and get high. You tell me—you're the cop."

"Did you do that?"

"Drink it? No. I tapped my razor blade on the rim, but I didn't drink it."

O'Connor pointed a finger as if he'd suddenly remembered something. "Hey, let me ask you: where did Gio keep his coke?"

Weinger waved a hand in irritation. "I don't know—in a little medicine bottle. Anyway, his girlfriend came over and Gio brought the coke out, and they insisted. So I felt obligated."

"Because you didn't want to be impolite?"

"Yeah. Exactly."

O'Connor folded his hands on the table. "Man, I wish the world had more people as…" He pretended he was searching for the word. "As *courteous* as you."

"It would be a more beautiful place, wouldn't it?"

"You said there was someone else there."

"No, I didn't."

"My mistake. Sorry. Was there anyone else in the apartment?"

"As a matter of fact, yes. I didn't catch his name. I don't know if we were actually introduced. He had longish black hair and a moustache. Some guy. He didn't have anything to say."

"Longish black hair…oh, you must mean Cedric Sberna?"

"I just told you I have no idea who that is."

"Hey—did you touch the glass?"

"What?"

"Sorry. Did you touch the snifter?"

"I don't…I don't know." Weinger grew suddenly uneasy. "Maybe. Maybe not. It was a while ago."

"It was four days ago."

Weinger shifted in his seat. "The bracelets are really uncomfortable."

"The what? Did you say 'bracelets'?"

"The bracelets." Weinger shook his hand, rattled the metal.

"The handcuffs?"

"Yes. The handcuffs. Obviously."

"I wasn't sure what you meant. I mean, you could have been telling me about some jewelry you have. See what I mean when I say I need to hear it from you? And 'hearing it from you' means 'be specific'. If you mean 'handcuffs,' then you need to tell me 'handcuffs.' Being ambiguous doesn't help us."

"Help us do what?"

"Help us clear this mess up. But while we're on the subject, are you into jewelry?"

"What do you mean?"

"I mean, are you, say, an aficionado of jewelry?"

Weinger shrugged. Then he seemed to be weighing an answer. He shrugged again. "I appreciate jewelry."

"Do you appreciate gold jewelry?"

Weinger slumped, waved his hand, as if indicating he'd indulge O'Connor. "Sure. I appreciate gold."

"What about diamonds?"

Weinger, looking amused. "Not for everyday wear, maybe, but sure. Why not?"

"Platinum? What about platinum? I love it. What about you? Do you like platinum?"

"I sure do."

"Do you own any platinum jewelry?"

Hesitation. "No, not at the moment. Someday maybe."

"Just to jump back, you told us that you went out on the evening of the … "

"The first."

"At six o'clock?"

"Yes. No. No. I thought we were talking about…No. It was later than that. On the first."

"Where did you say you went?"

"To a friend's place. My buddy Steve's. We were playing cards."

"What time?"

"Nine, maybe. Nine thirty. Around then."

O'Connor let that hang. "Was anyone else at your buddy Steve's apartment?"

"No. Just the two of us."

"Okay. Just to jump back, do you like turquoise jewelry?"

Weinger looked very faintly stricken. "Turquoise? No. I don't really like that stuff."

"You don't own any?"

"Turquoise jewelry? No."

O'Connor made it plain he was peering over the table's edge. Weinger followed his eyes, then touched his fingers to his belt buckle. "This? It was a gift. My wife gave it to me. It's not really jewelry, though, right?"

"Your wife gave it to you?"

"Yes."

"Wouldn't she know you're not partial to turquoise?"

Weinger shrugged.

"And you weren't at Delphine Moore's apartment on March 1, am I right?"

"Nope."

"Nope, as in I'm not right and you actually *were* at the apartment?"

"I wasn't at that apartment you're talking about." Weinger's voice was rising a couple of degrees louder, and as he spoke, he gave each *t*-sound a little snap.

"You were at Steve's—"

"On the first of March I was at Steve's. Until maybe ... I don't know—two thirty."

"In the morning? And after that? Home? You went back home to your wife, and she can vouch for you? What's Steve's last name?"

"Glassman. And yes, my wife would be happy to vouch for me."

"Oh, I have no doubt of that."

"And you can ask Steve to vouch for me. We were playing cards until—"

"Two-thirty?"

"I don't know, man. Maybe later than two thirty. Actually, definitely later. The sun was just rising."

"What game were you playing?"

"Poker. And before you ask, it was draw poker."

"Just the two of you? That must have been a seriously exciting game. How'd you do?"

"Not too well."

"Are you a decent player, ordinarily?"

"I'm not bad."

"I'm terrible. People who are good at poker? They're really good at bluffing. I don't bluff very well. I'm angry? I can't hide it. Sad? Happy? I'm a terrible liar. If I tell you something, you can pretty much absolutely guarantee I'm on the level. What about you, Mitchell? Are you a good bluffer?"

Weinger was looking at his free hand resting on the table. He didn't like the question, O'Connor could tell.

"Listen, Mitchell. I'm going to need Steve Glassman's number and address. I'd love it if you didn't waste time bullshitting, telling me you don't have the number."

The big grin Weinger flashed, the enthusiasm with which he reached for his wallet with his free hand and pulled a folded scrap of paper out, told O'Connor he was about to get snowed.

Weinger said, "I don't need to bullshit you. Here—this is his number. I'll give you his address if you want to write it down. I'd write it down for you, but—" He shook his right hand, the one in cuffs. "I'm right-handed."

Weinger gave him the address aloud, and O'Connor wrote it down. Without looking up, still writing, O'Connor said, "Here's the thing, Mitchell. I don't believe you. I think you're full of shit."

"What are you talking about?" He sounded like he couldn't understand what he'd just heard. "I'm full of shit? Damn, man. I don't know what to—I don't what to tell you."

"You could tell me the fucking truth about where you were on the first." O'Connor slapped his pen onto the table and stood so abruptly his chair slid a few feet. The volume of his voice shot up. "How about that? How about you tell me something that isn't a fucking goddamned lie?"

Weinger exhaled, then looked at O'Connor. He tilted back in his chair. He said, "You know what? I think I'd like to talk to that lawyer now."

Philbin and Toenings would have followed through on their threat to kick the door down, but the super on duty at Weinger's building finally lost his reluctance to leave his spot in the basement and opened the apartment door for them.

"Do I need to wait here?" the doorman asked.

Philbin said, "Why? Are you going to help?"

The apartment was better appointed, if less neat, than most of the places they went into. A lot of loose piles of envelopes and what looked like opened bills. In the kitchen, on the table, there were crumbs, a sticky smear of what Philbin decided was jelly or jam, and an empty coffee mug with a dried ring around the bottom.

Philbin thought he caught a faint, skunky smell of marijuana under the more forward scents of old grease and cigarettes. He went into the bedroom while Toenings tossed the living room.

When the judge signed the warrant, he'd said the same thing as Roppell when Philbin told him where he was going. Both men had observed, "You don't think you're going to find that knife, do you?"

*Probably not*, Philbin thought. The room had the close funk of sleeping bodies. The bed was unmade, the floor covered with little hillocks of dirty clothes. Most of it was women's clothing, but he separated out the few men's shirts, put them into an evidence bag.

The closet didn't yield anything. Philbin went through it, garment by garment, feeling into each shirt, jacket, and pants pocket. He opened all the shoeboxes on the floor, and they all contained shoes. He checked in those too. He pulled at the carpet on the floor of the closet, but it was tacked down tight.

Philbin lay on the floor, torso fully under the bed, where there was nothing but dust and a dusty tube sock with red and blue stripes at the top of the cuff. When he emerged and stood up, he spent a good half-minute ridding his shirt and jacket of dust clumps.

"How's it going?" Toenings yelled from the living room. "I'm coming up empty."

Philbin called back, "You're being thorough, right? Inside the cushions? In every record jacket? Combing your fingers through the shag in the carpet? Maybe check the dirt in the plants?"

"Maybe go fuck yourself?"

Philbin walked to the dresser, turned the light on, stopped short. Right on top, a piece of paper, under a small handful of loose change. It looked like—Philbin swept the change away—it was Gio Messina's name written on it, with a phone number underneath. He called out, "Here we go."

Toenings walked into the bedroom, and Philbin saw dirt on the fingers of his gloves. Philbin asked, "Did you seriously check the dirt in the flowerpots?"

"What have we got?" Toenings said.

"Can you open one of those evidence bags for me? Thank you. What we've got is Gio Messina's name and phone number." Philbin tugged the top drawer open. He said, "Oh, man. Look at this. It's an Easter miracle. What's this? A turquoise necklace? Yes, indeed. And what have we here? A news story clipped from the *Tribune*, dated March 3, 1976? That's right. Three guesses as to what the story's about?"

"Could it be a story about a double homicide? I'm right? I guessed right? Now, let's go for drawer number two."

Steve Glassman looked pissed-off. It was coming on 3:00 a.m. He was wearing sweats and a Buffalo Bills T-shirt, and his hair was sticking out. Roppell had woken him up.

Glassman insisted several times he had to be up in a few hours and wondered why it couldn't wait but finally got cooperative after a little browbeating from O'Connor.

O'Connor said, "I can't apologize enough for waking you up, but we needed you here to get your statement on the record. And, you know, this is a goddamned homicide. We can't wait with this. So, can you confirm Mitchell Weinger was there with you on Monday night March 1?"

At the word *homicide*, Glassman stiffened, and his expression looked confused, then incredulous. "What homicide? This is about a homicide?"

"Was Mr. Weinger with you on the evening of the first?"

The length of the pause before Glassman answered bordered on painful. "Yes. Mitchell Weinger was with me."

"What time was he with you? Between which hours?"

"From ten, ten thirty until … " He looked like he was searching. "Until … I don't know. Maybe midnight? Maybe a little later."

"What did you do while he was there?"

"We played cards."

"What cards?"

"Poker."

"What kind of poker?"

"The kind you play with cards, and you make bets."

O'Connor said lightly, "Don't treat me like I'm some kind of dumb asshole. Got it? Who won?"

"He cleaned me out."

The door to the interview room had been open, but now O'Connor crossed the floor to close it. He turned back to Glassman, tried to give his voice a metal-cold tone. "Listen to me. I mean it. Listen to me and listen carefully. You're full of shit. No, no—don't tell me different. You are full of shit. I'm going to tell you once: this is a fucking murder we're talking about. Two murders. This isn't just a goddamned homicide, it's a double goddamned homicide. So, you wanna bullshit me? That's gonna be making you an accessory. You want to go play poker with Weinger up in Menard? No problem. I don't give a shit. So. Don't. Fuck. A-round. Do you understand me?"

Glassman looked more than pissed-off now. "That mother…that *bastard*. He told me … Okay. He asked me, if anyone wanted to know where he was that night? Tell them he was with me, playing cards. I figured he was off screwing someone who wasn't his wife. He'd done it before, he's asked me to cover for him before, but no one ever actually asked me if he'd been with me. But I resent him dragging me into this. I mean, *really* resent it."

"So he wasn't with you on the first?"

"No, he wasn't."

"When did he call and ask you to cover for him?"

"On the second. He called on the second at around dinner time."

"Seriously, I promise he can't see you." Skelly was at Sberna's elbow on the see-through side of the two-way, looking at six men on the other side, everyone around the same height, every face with a mustache.

Sberna had a disheveled look around the eyes, and the eyes themselves were glassy and darting back and forth across the row of men. His breathing was shallow and ratty, and his arms were tight across his chest.

"Cedric, man, it's almost three in the morning."

Sberna, taking a long, careful look at each face, excessively long, Skelly thought. A little late for good citizenship. He was sure Sberna had recognized someone within a few seconds but hesitated now. Sberna probably knew, if unconsciously, that picking a killer out of a lineup was a move into new territory. He was committed now. Not just some bystander but someone who'd landed right in the middle of a situation, on the wrong side of things, and had to save his own ass. Given the family he came from, this was probably verging on unforgivable.

Finally, Cedric said, "It's that one. Number four."

"You positive? Absolutely, 100 percent?"

"Yeah. Absolutely. Number four."

"Number four? Please step forward. Everyone else is free to go."

Mitchell Weinger took a step forward, stood staring at the mirrored glass, expressionless, as the other men around him turned and walked for the door.

## CHAPTER 20
*March 6, 1976, early morning*

It was late enough after O'Connor finished charging Weinger that he toyed with the idea of not going home at all. He'd be back in the morning to bring Weinger to bond court. He felt obligated to come to the station to make sure nothing went bad.

But it had been a long few days, mostly sleepless, except for whatever short, sporadic catnaps he could manage. He was tired to the point where just at the edge of his vision he was seeing small lightly colored things flashing along the floor. Nothing was there when he turned to look. Plus, he felt soiled. Like he had a thin film of smoke particles and lies all over his skin.

He decided to go home. He drove back and showered and penciled a note for his wife, asking that she wake him up at seven forty-five. He left it on the kitchen table and went to the couch in the living room. He got his shoes off and lay down. He was trying to remind himself of a couple of matters he'd want to address in the morning, but he lost the thread to voices whispering from the edge of sleep, and a pileup of images from the last couple of days, and then he was gone. He came back awake under his wife's hand, which was on his shoulder and gently shaking him.

The idea of getting up and going back to Area 6 was, briefly, unbearable and required tremendous will to sit up, stand, and engage the morning. Soon, his thoughts went to Weinger and Sberna and, most importantly, a motive for killing Gio Messina and Tinker Moore.

It was too soon to shower again. He brushed his teeth, splashed his face with cold water, and thought about how he couldn't assign a motive. Yesterday it'd had him baffled, but this morning, after dreaming something vaguely related to the case, he felt surprisingly angry about it. And if he was honest, there was very small anxiety chiming out from under the anger.

He was uneasy with the evidence. Not with Weinger's guilt—of that he was certain to 96 or 97 percent. But the points of contact between the different pieces of evidence felt brittle, like even negligible pressure might make them fall to dust.

No. That wasn't right. There was stronger evidence than that. Maybe not steel-clad strong but still strong enough to resist easy arguments from the defense table.

As O'Connor drove back to Area 6, he put the evidence through possible lines of attack and defense. He argued and counterargued and probed for flaws and failings, and he was increasingly sure he had it locked, that he could satisfy any reasonable doubts.

The officer on duty at the Area 6 holding cells said, "I hope you don't mind me saying this." He gestured toward Weinger's cell. "That guy is a real asshole."

"No, I don't mind," O'Connor said. He signed and dated a logbook. "What was it that made him such an asshole?"

The officer shook his head, curled his lip. "Fucking guy called me 'faggot.' He had some nasty shit to say about my mother, who is actually a very nice woman."

O'Connor thought he caught a faint whiff of schnapps. He didn't care—he instinctively liked the guy. "He insulted your mother?"

"Yes. Then ... " The officer worked himself into a pique. "Then, he demanded breakfast like he was Henry Kissinger or something."

*Kissinger?* O'Connor thought it was an admirably strange choice of comparison. "Did you feed him?"

"I gave him a Snickers bar from the machine and a cup of very burnt, very weak coffee. I figured the Snickers had peanuts in it."

"Peanuts are nutritious," O'Connor agreed. He thought for a moment. "Hey, what time does the next guy come on?"

The officer sighed. "I'm pulling a double."

"Can you stand a few more hours with him?"

"No," the officer said. "Absolutely not."

O'Connor was laughing. "Come on—just a few? Listen. Hear me out. What if, when I get back to deal with that scumbag, I happened to be a little too late for bond court. I got held up or something. What do you think might happen then?"

The officer affected a serious, contemplative nod. "I'd hate to see it happen, but our friend would have to go to county and get processed. They'd have to print him, all that stuff. So, he'd probably—just a best guess—have to spend the night and a good part of tomorrow there."

"He'd have to go to holiday court, I bet."

Holiday court referred to courtrooms in session over weekends and holidays. The young and inexperienced judges, the state's attorneys who screwed up evidence or bent the truth on a report were assigned to holiday court. They'd deny Weinger's bond, send him back to county for the weekend.

"Yeah, I bet he would."

O'Connor slapped a palm lightly on the counter. "Okay, my good man, I'll be back later."

The officer gave a curt nod. "I'll see you then, Detective."

## Chapter 21

Working homicide, O'Connor understood that some experiences couldn't coexist peacefully with others, and they refused to simply be woven into the fabric of a person's memory. Certain experiences were like foreign objects trapped in the body. The body would try to function around them, then try rejecting them, and then infection would set in, and the body marshaled all its resources to fight it.

Seeing a dead, brutalized child, hearing the remorseless confession of the father who did it, encountering the whole spectrum of cruelties people inflict on each other, finding dismembered or gutted corpses or victims who'd had every drop of blood spilled onto the floor—those were the sorts of experiences that became infections, and in order to fight them off, O'Connor had watched other cops hit the bottle, go to Mass every morning or at the end of every shift, beat their wives and kids, narcotize themselves, take their own lives.

For his own experiences, O'Connor made use of a safe. Not a real safe—it was purely mental yet vividly detailed: painted black with a steel handle, brass hinges, and a brass dial, standing on four brass feet, the whole thing trimmed with gold. All the nastiness he encountered in his day-to-day working life, all sorts of awful images and sense impressions got banished into the safe and then forgotten. Whole case files disappeared into it, not just the cold facts but all the frustrations and torments associated with them.

When Weinger was charged with the murders, O'Connor moved on to the next case. Weinger was the business of the state's attorneys now and not his.

After the night of the arrest, there was no news for a couple of days, until word came that Weinger's counsel was requesting a psychological evaluation.

He thought, *That's it. We've got you now, motherfucker.*

O'Connor was elated when he heard. It meant, simply put, the defense knew it was screwed. With no chance of acquittal, the only option to mitigate the penalties was to claim insanity. He figured the defense would dick around and ask for postponements, try to stall for time, and the judge would probably shoot them down. He hadn't expected the request for an evaluation.

And he didn't expect to hear that Weinger had two lawyers acting on his behalf and that they were Patrick Tuite and Herbert Barsy. Both of them were prominent and they defended people charged as crime syndicate figures, venal and corrupt city officials, and others who were roughly on par.

And he didn't expect to hear that Weinger's arraignment would occur at the Daley Center. That's where the scofflaws, petty crooks, maybe a john or two, got their wrists slapped by judges and prosecutors who couldn't be gotten rid of but couldn't be allowed to supervise proceedings of any importance.

O'Connor didn't expect to hear that the arraignment was scheduled for the Saturday of a long holiday weekend, which meant it was happening out of sight, that it was getting buried. It was happening in bond court. It was outrageous. This was never done.

And he didn't expect to hear Weinger would be released on a million-dollar bond. A double murderer out on bond. He couldn't believe it. And who could afford it? Who could afford to pay a million bucks?

When he heard all that, O'Connor closed his eyes and pictured the safe, and he gathered up everything he saw and heard and discovered while investigating the murders of Gio Messina and Delphine Moore, everything about arresting Mitchell Weinger for committing the murders, and he opened the safe, put it inside, closed the door, and locked it up again.

## Chapter 22
*April 28, 1976, morning*

The phone rang at 6:30 in the morning, California time, dragging Owen out of sleep.

He rubbed his eyes with his thumb and forefinger. The phone rang four more times before he answered.

"Why did it take you so long to answer? Is there some floozy there with you? Some groupie? Are you trying to get yourself shot at again? You're disgusting."

"Mom?" he said.

He thought, *Oh, no—this is really not going to be good.*

He said, "Mom, what happened? Did something happen?"

"I tried calling yesterday. I bet you were with some tramp then too." She sounded furious.

"There's no tramp. No floozy. It's two hours earlier here, Mom. Is something wrong?"

A long pause. When she finally spoke, her voice was cooler. "I have some mail here for you. I opened it in case it was important."

He sat up in bed, gulped from the glass of water on the nightstand.

"Are you interested in what it says?"

"Of course I am. What is it?" His mother had an unmatched talent for high drama.

"The first letter is from the ... hold on, let me get the envelope ... from the Illinois Bar Examiners—"

He had a quick flash of nerves. "Is the envelope thick or thin?"

He'd heard from old classmates that a thick envelope was a bad omen, that it included paperwork to sign up and take the test again..

"What?" She sounded impatient. "It's not thick at all."

Owen's stomach relaxed.

"Thank God," he said aloud. His confidence those days in March had been warranted.

His mother cleared her throat and read in a stately voice, "Dear Mr. Owen, we are pleased to inform you that you have successfully passed the Illinois Bar Exam, and you are invited to attend the swearing in ceremony on May 3, 1976, at the Daley Center, 50 West Washington at 10:00 a.m."

"Then, there's the second letter. This one is from the Cook County State's Attorney's Office. Should I read that too?"

"Please."

This time her voice contained a touch of Katherine Hepburn. "'Dear Mr. Owen, having received notice from the Illinois Board of Bar Examiners that you have passed the Illinois Bar Exam, we are pleased to offer you the position of assistant state's attorney.' There are four or five paragraphs more, but that's the long and short of it."

*Wow. Holy shit*, Owen thought. *This is actually happening.*

"Well?" She sounded frustrated.

"'Well' what?"

"Well, how do you feel?"

*How do I feel? Relieved. Assured. Gratified. Really good.* But he knew better than to share his elation with her.

"I feel like studying sixteen hours a day for three months paid off," he said. "And I'm happy to have a job."

Four days later, a little too early in the morning, Owen boarded a TWA 727 back to Chicago.

He was thinking about finalities and endings and the start of a new life that a little over a year ago would have seemed improbable. More than improbable. Actually, it wouldn't have seemed any way at all. It wasn't something he ever would have pictured.

He looked out the window. Los Angeles never changed. There were seasons in Chicago, each with its own mood, each with a passage from grief to possibility. LA had only one season. The view he was gazing at now, with its palm trees, gray tarmac, and flat blue sky, was identical to the view he'd had the last time he left this city, more than a year ago. The sameness made time accordion, and he was pressed into the memory of that day. The day he'd abandoned his band. The thought of it still made him feel queasy and unmoored. He'd abandoned so much for Melissa, and all that had come of it was violence.

When he met Melissa, Sheri had been his girlfriend for years. Sheri was attractive, smart, socially graceful, and talented. Her dream of a career as a studio engineer had been becoming real for her, and she'd felt emboldened enough to tell Owen to shit or get off the pot. He could either make space for her as an important piece of his life, or he could go away.

He refused for the sake of refusing. Their conversations went round and round. He told himself he was too busy to put a woman, even Sheri, at the center of his world. But into the middle of their endless talks and negotiations walked Melissa Black.

A young woman showed up one night to see Jerico. The spotlights were on the band, but she snaked through the audience as if they shone on her. She walked right up to the stage, focused on Owen only—he could feel her looking at him with her sharp blue eyes. She was ethereally beautiful. She dressed like Stevie Nicks—a shawl, black flowing skirt, a ring on every finger. But she had the angelic face of Isabelle Adjani. When he looked up from his keyboard and saw her staring, he felt that she didn't only want him, she *needed* him. Later that night, she knocked at the dressing room door a few minutes after the band finished their set and suggested to Owen that they take a drive together. His favorite song was "Sweet Melissa," and this woman had that name written in glitter across the heels of her platform clogs. She reached for his hand and pulled him outside to her Mercedes. She made him feel as if she couldn't live without him, and that feeling was more intoxicating than any drug he'd sampled. This was how Melissa entered his life.

He cut things off with Sheri abruptly. Three weeks later, Melissa was living with him. They bought a Doberman puppy and named him Dagon, made meals together, took long walks, and spent a lot of time in bed. She came to every gig he played with Jerico. While he studied for Tort Law or Constitutional Law class, sometimes she'd go out and spend time with her friends.

If Melissa gave overt signals of being off or malign, Owen missed them. She was gorgeous and soft—and she always looked straight into his eyes like nobody ever had, had him hexed in a way he thought nobody ever would again. Then their relationship dissolved like a mirage. After a year of living with Melissa, Owen found out that she'd been sleeping with Sherwin Spector behind his back. The man was a talented singer with a repugnant personality. And he dealt cocaine. Apparently, Melissa couldn't get enough of the stuff. Later it would never cease to amaze him that he hadn't noticed. She was good at deception when she wanted to be.

Owen was in LA with the band when a friend from Chicago called to break all of it to him. Even as his brain struggled to absorb the information, Owen immediately decided to go home.

It was the worst timing imaginable. Mercury Records was sending one of their A&R guys—a recruiter—to the Starwood club in West Hollywood to watch Jerico play. As he paced around his hotel room grabbing a jacket from the end of the bed and his wallet off the desk, he kept thinking he shouldn't be leaving—he knew he shouldn't even consider leaving—but he was tormented by the humiliations he knew he'd have to endure. He was certain that every friend, peer, audience member would never see him as anything more than ridiculous—a ridiculous figure, hoaxed and betrayed by Melissa. And something told him that the truth would be even worse than what he was imagining.

He crammed the last of his things into a suitcase and forced the latches closed.

*Walking out on these guys is more wrong than what Melissa did,* he thought. He stood there for a minute. He moved to undo the latches and unpack, but even a gesture toward staying felt false and compromising, and he left the latches done.

It would be necessary to tell the band in person, but there was little he wanted to do less than look them in the face and explain, while possibly running the risk of being talked out of leaving.

Eventually he convinced himself of the wisdom of a letter. He took a pen and some stationery and began writing.

*Dear Bill, Joe, Glen, and Gavin,*

*I hope you all can accept my apologies for more or less screwing things up. I tried to think of a way that I could play my best under the circumstances, but today I found out that Melissa has been cheating for a long time, with Sherwin Spector. I have to go home. There are things I need to take care of, or go crazy. Please try to understand and forgive me. I love the band, but I'm worried for my sanity. One more day of thought might be too much for me to take. Don't let anyone know where I've gone. Maybe I'll surprise them in my bed—that's just what I need. Whatever I can do to repay this I will. Please understand and help me. I love you all. Gregg.*

Voices and laughter and music came from some of the rooms, but when he pressed his ear against Bill Jordan's door and listened, there was only silence. He shoved the note under the door before he could second-guess himself. He listened again but heard nothing.

Now a stewardess was giving the passengers safety instructions. Shortly after that, the plane began to taxi down the runway, and then it took off into the cloudless sky.

But when he'd gotten back to Chicago last year, everything seemed to have dissolved overnight. Melissa acted like he was an inconvenience when he reached her at a friend's house—she said she loved Sherwin, not him.

He didn't have it in him to confront them together the way he'd fantasized about. It was just him and Dagon, wind, gray skies, classes, and tests.

Owen slept for a while to the whooshing of the jets, then the pilot announced there was a bit of light turbulence coming up. Owen opened his eyes and looked at his watch. He'd land in Chicago in a little over an hour.

He started remembering how, in the midst of believing himself utterly hopeless, things had simply changed. Instantly, completely. It was on February 26th of 1975.

He'd been in class—if he remembered right, it was probably Contracts—trying, but mostly failing, to stay focused. He fell asleep at some point, and when he snapped back, his professor was standing over him.

"I just asked you, Mr. Owen, if you agreed with the Court's interpretation?"

When Owen didn't answer, the professor offered a snide semi-smile and returned to the front of the classroom.

He'd spent the rest of the time in class sitting in his chair, gripping a pen, listening as hard as he could, getting outflanked by thoughts he'd rather not be thinking.

Owen had never been a drinker at all—nasty-tasting stuff that sparked even nastier behavior.

He'd never been more than a dabbler, drug-wise. Keeping a general distance from drugs was a deliberate choice.

Sure, the way weed skewed the world brighter, louder, and more interesting; the way quaaludes got you soothed, loose-limbed, and horny; the way cocaine sent you surging—the end of one high got him craving another. But chasing that compulsion very far would knock law school right off the tracks. He wasn't much for splitting his focus.

Owen also had a couple of people in his circle, and a few adjacent to it, whose drug use had graduated from regular and routine to intravenous. The switch had them looking messed up and haunted already.

He'd known this much: if he made a practice of getting stoned, he'd wind up in their company eventually. His obsessive bent wouldn't let him stay away.

As the professor wound down, Owen thought of the Emerson, Lake, and Palmer show at the Coliseum and how his spirits wilted during "Jerusalem" and "Toccata," through the long improv coming out of "Lucky Man," through the rest of the show until the lights came up and how he knew as he walked out he'd never be a great keyboardist.

He thought about Jerico—best friends, brothers—and how much upheaval he'd caused everyone by walking out and quitting. About how he'd pretty much shot the band's career right between the fucking eyes.

What he'd gotten wasn't anything less than what he deserved. A lot of infidelities. Acting in bad faith with Sheri. More than once. Many more times than once. This was Karma. He belonged exactly where he was.

From the hallway, the footfalls and voices of classes letting out.

In the classroom, a last insight, a few closing words, then the professor brought class to an end. Owen got into his coat, gathered his things, walked out the door.

The crowd bottlenecked at the head of the staircase, and Owen joined the knot of people taking one step, then another, slowly down the steps. Halfway to the bottom, he found he couldn't take his eyes off the bulletin board hanging in the lobby. He'd seen it before but wasn't ever really aware of it.

He stared at it the whole way down.

When he got to the first floor, he stepped out of the fray and in front of the board. The thing was papered with notices from what seemed like every law firm in Chicago.

Owen let his eyes play over the board, and nothing grabbed him. All the different notices, in varied fonts and a range of light colors, that all offered the same basic opportunity.

But then he looked up: a card tacked to the topmost part of the right corner. White, four by six, the lettering in black. It was poorly placed, if the intention was that it actually get read. Owen saw the date—tomorrow—and a room number in the same building he was in now. He didn't read more than that.

He looked away, skimmed the notices again: paid internships, opportunities to do litigation on a contingency basis, what was probably a barely salaried job advocating for the wrongfully incarcerated. He gave the most thought to that one, but in the context of the white-shoe firms and personal injury mills, he suspected a lot of its appeal lay in what it wasn't.

Owen found his eyes on the card again, and this time he read the whole thing: "The Cook County State's Attorney's Office will be conducting interviews for assistant state's attorney positions. Thursday, 1:00 – 3:30, Room 406."

He had never believed in anything spiritual before, but he did today—but wouldn't ever ignore his instincts again—within a few seconds he heard voiceless speech telling him three times: *You need to change your life, or it will kill you.* He wasn't sure where the voice was coming from, whether it was being literal or figurative. Wherever it might have originated, it spoke with unshakable authority and conviction, and two things were suddenly obvious: a life in music with only limited prospects was too trite and trivial to think about and that he'd be at the interview tomorrow.

He had no real idea what a state's attorney did, but Owen knew he was supposed to be one.

But then he knew another thing: there was one obstacle, and he needed to address it right away.

He went to the small bank of pay phones mounted on the wall a few feet away and picked a dime from the change in his pocket. His mother would be home by now. He dialed and she picked up on the third ring.

Owen said, "I need to ask you a favor. It's really important. Will you please call the guy who does your hair? Is it Dino? I need to get my hair cut tonight. It has to be tonight. And after that, I need your help finding something decent to wear. Could you do that for me?"

The interview in Room 406 went well. A pleasant, if uncomfortable, recruiter from the State's Attorney's Office asked him a lot of questions about how he did in different classes, why he'd chosen law school, why he'd come to this interview today. It went well enough that the recruiter made Owen an appointment for the coming Monday morning, at 11:30, to go to the police station at Eleventh and State, to the seventh floor, and meet with Supervisor Bill Kunkle.

On Monday morning, March 3rd Owen stepped into Bill Kunkle's suite.

The only thing in the waiting area—there were no chairs, no people, no other candidates for the job—was a Harley-Davidson motorcycle, resting on its kickstand. It was polished and in pristine shape.

A door opened. A man stepped out—linebacker-size, broad and impenetrable.

He said, "Are you Gregg Owen? I'm Bill Kunkle. Come on into my office."

This was the state's attorney? The motorcycle was Kunkle's: there were photos scattered around the office of Kunkle leaning against a bike with the Chicago skyline behind him, another with mountain peaks, another taken in the desert, several shots of Kunkle riding. He'd hung framed sketches done by court artists of himself, in front of a judge, alone, questioning a witness, addressing the jury. What an insanely cool thing to have.

"Let's skip the bullshit." Kunkle moved back behind his desk and sat heavily in his chair. "Here's the thing: The State's Attorney's Office has a backlog of cases that could take us into the twenty-first century before we even make a dent. We're understaffed. And that's putting it mildly. For obvious reasons, then, we need to do something about that backlog.

"So, our idea was, why not bring in the best students we can find—students in their senior year of law school—and assign them to misdemeanor courts, working with prosecutors who've been around for a bit. Graffiti, drunk and disorderly—violations on that order—paying a hooker for a blow job, driving like an asshole. Just people doing stupid stuff. Misdemeanors move through the system pretty quickly, and there are a shit ton of them.

"Anyway, we got the go-ahead from the Illinois Supreme Court. And here you are. So, you'd be assigned to a courtroom. You'd be working in there, prosecuting the backlogged misdemeanor cases. Every courtroom has a lead prosecutor, so that guy will be supervising. How does that sound? Think you're up for something like that?"

"I..." For half a second, Owen felt dazed. Then he resolved himself. "Yes. I think I can. Absolutely. Just so you know, I've never worked in a courtroom before."

"Yeah, I know. Don't worry about it. You'll do fine. So, how about starting today?"

Owen wasn't expecting that. Today? His first thought was to beg off, take a day or so, go home and (do what?), get used to the idea.

"Sure. I'm happy to start today, if you'd like me to," Owen replied.

"Great." Kunkle laid his palms on the desk. He closed his eyes and exhaled. He seemed relieved. He sat up and started writing something on a legal pad. Then he ripped the page away and handed it to Owen. "If you leave now, you can make it over there in about fifteen or twenty minutes. If you haven't eaten, grab a sandwich to on the way. When you get there, you're going to look for Judge J. J. O'Donnell's courtroom. When you find it, ask for Ron Santiago. He'll get you started. I'll call over, let everyone know you're coming."

On the way over, Owen imagined different pictures of misdemeanor court and what it would look and sound like, what it would *feel* like standing in the center of its action. It would be busy. Fast-paced—minor offenses, quick proceedings. Not quite like an assembly line, but probably not all that far from it. Charges read, pleas entered, penalties given. The gavel coming down. The next case called.

Maybe someone gets belligerent, maybe someone even gets tackled, cuffed, dragged out. That was doubtful, though. The only time drama and intrigue happen is when they're scripted for the screen. No, it would be orderly and humming along, not much talking out of turn—maybe the judge once or twice telling people to be quiet when they murmured past the threshold.

Charges, pleas, penalties, gavel. Next.

After a fifteen-minute ride, the bus stopped near the big, brick municipal building. Owen, along with nine or ten others, rose and shuffled to the bus doors and stepped down onto the sidewalk, right near the entrance.

He couldn't tell how many people were crowding the turnstile door. Probably dozens.

He stood and watched. People came out and a few went in, replaced by others who came down the sidewalk from both directions, working their way to the end of the line. The crowd swelled and thinned and swelled again in a slow, nearly steady rhythm, like a pulse.

There were far more people going in than there were leaving. Owen took a deep breath and a few hesitant steps and got in line.

It was relatively quiet in the queue by the doors and silent when he stepped into the enclosure and pushed, and when he emerged into the lobby, the cigarette haze, and the scents of sweat and bodies, the noise of a few hundred conversations counterpointed with shouting and yelling hit him in the face like an open hand.

People having angry words with suited men clutching briefcases and shifting impatiently from foot to foot, looking again and again at their wrist watches.

People slowly shouldering their way through knots and streams of other people.

People dressed up and dressed down, looking tired, pissed off, important, crooked, bereft, official, dazed. Cops and security guards standing ineffectually among them.

Owen saw a few signs with arrows pointing to different courtrooms, and he moved around looking for a sign that pointed to Branch 46. Several custodians were standing together and talking, hot dogs in one hand and steaming Styrofoam coffee cups in the other, and when one of them moved, Owen saw the guy had been blocking the sign for Branch 46.

Owen followed the arrow on the sign toward another hallway. A packed line of people stretched all along the length of it, around a corner, far down the next hallway, all the way to a door with a sign beside it announcing this was Branch 46.

Half the line looked resigned; the other half looked hostile. Everyone looked unhappy.

Owen couldn't figure out why the line was so long or why there was a line at all.

He was at the door and reaching for the handle when it flew open hard enough to make him have to rear back. A very angry guy with a red face and cheap suit came out talking to another very angry guy in a denim jacket with a black-and-white Led Zeppelin patch and an orange T-shirt with the graphic of a car and the words *Corvette Summer*.

The one in the T-shirt had greasy hair falling to his nipples. He looked a little too old for the pimples covering his cheeks.

"Everyone's mother is sick. Everyone's mother is always sick," the man in the suit was saying. "We agreed that I'd represent you for $300. And $300 is what you're going to pay me. Not sixty dollars. Not one hundred dollars. Not $200. *Three* hundred."

"Whaddya you want me to do? She needs her inhaler—"

"*I* don't give two shits. *I* need $300—"

"You know I'm good for it."

"No, I don't, which is why you got till end of day today to come up with the rest, or I'm withdrawing from the case—"

The two men kept it up as they disappeared around the corner. The tone, the words put Owen off.

*Incredible. This is the law? That's being a lawyer?*

He reached for the door again, pulled it open, and the noise in Branch 46 was even worse than the lobby. Every seat was taken. People stood two and three deep at the walls. The smoke was more a smog than a haze. The air was thick and damp, and it smelled terrible. Owen entertained a feeling—brief, half formed, but nonetheless deep—that he'd made a serious mistake. Not coming to this courtroom, and not going to law school—no missteps there—but in believing that court and practicing the law were wildly different from what they actually were. He felt naïve, even a little self-deluded. Had he ever really believed court was like on television, like *The D.A.* or *Hawkins*? He wouldn't have thought so. Maybe some part of him wished things were like that.

The feeling came suddenly and disappeared just as fast. Owen found himself watching the hum of activity far up in front of the room, where the judge sat hearing a case, and a court sergeant standing a few feet from the bench bellowed out different first and last names. Each time he did, a uniformed cop came from among the crowd pressed along the walls or rose from the benches and made their way toward the bench.

At the same time, on the opposite side of the room, a young Latino man shouted out his own set of names, trying to make himself heard above the sergeant. He had a thick stack of files in his hand. He stood next to a cart piled with stacks of more files.

This had to be the Ron Santiago who Kunkle had mentioned. Owen started picking his way to the front of the room.

Just a few nights ago, Owen had joined Jerico onstage, playing for an audience of over a thousand. Being in Branch 46 felt like he'd been carried away from something familiar and pleasant and dropped—under-equipped—into a war zone.

When Owen approached, the guy wheeled on him and looked like he was about to start yelling some kind of reprimand until he noticed Owen wore a tie and carried a leather briefcase.

The guy said, "What is it?"

Owen said, "I'm here on the 711 program. Bill Kunkle sent me over."

The guy thought about that. "What's your name?"

"Gregg Owen."

"Yeah. Okay. Bill said you'd be coming down. I'm Ron Santiago." Santiago moved his arm, and Owen held his hand up to shake, but instead Santiago reached for a stack of files that had been lying on the table. He picked them up and gave them to Owen. "Okay. Here. Start calling names."

Owen felt something crucial had been left out. He said, "I don't understand what you mean."

Santiago seemed faintly irritated. "There's nothing to understand. Call the names."

Owen held the files, read the first couple—last name, first name, charges—hoping something else in them would make it clear what he was being ordered to do. They didn't. Then, he read the next few. Nothing. He looked around the room.

The clerk started shouting for a Mariah West. While the clerk called the name, the judge was lecturing a young man standing in front of the bench. The man looked impassive; the judge looked angry.

When Owen still wasn't calling names, Santiago closed his eyes. He wasn't just faintly irritated anymore. Then, "All right. Call the names, and when they come over tell them to stand over there. Then, just watch. Just pay attention to what I do. It's going to be pretty obvious after five minutes."

Owen picked up a file, flipped through the couple of pages inside, then called out, "McGarry. Joseph McGarry." He waited, scanning the room.

Santiago stepped back to him. "No, no, no. No one's ever going to hear you. Like this." The attorney shouted for McGarry again, loud enough to make the cords on his neck tight and his face red. Then he said to Owen, "There you go. Do it like that."

No one named McGarry responded.

Owen saw a woman making her way toward the front, calling out, "I'm here, I'm here" as she came. She was scowling. Her lips were thin and tight.

She stopped and stood next to a defense lawyer, in front of the Judge O'Donnell.

Santiago announced, "Mariah West, arrested on January 28 and charged with petty larceny. Shoplifting a scarf from Wieboldt's, valued at five dollars. Detained by store security. Security observed her removing the scarf from a rack and placing it in the pocket of her overcoat."

The judge looked at West. "Mrs. West, how do you plead to the charge of petty larceny?"

"Not guilty."

"Mr. Santiago—the gentleman to your right, is that the security guard?"

"No, Judge. This is Gregg Owen. He's one of the 711 people, and thanks to Bill Kunkle, he'll be here for a while helping us out."

The judge beamed at Owen. "Welcome, Mr. Owen. Mr. Santiago, you'll be showing him the ropes?"

Owen thought he saw Santiago's jaw pulse.

Santiago said, "I will indeed. May I have one moment, Judge?"

He beckoned at the bailiff, who came over, and Santiago said something in his ear. The bailiff whispered back and shook his head *no*.

Santiago looked disgusted. He said, "Judge, I'm afraid Joseph McGarry, the security guard, won't be appearing today."

"Really? Not at all? All right, that simplifies things. Mrs. West? The charges are dropped. The case is dismissed. You are free to go. Next case?"

The clerk bellowed again. "Richard Robertson. Richard Robertson."

Richard Robertson came down the aisle, a too-thin man with his shoulders hunched tight and a generally unwell look about him. He stood next to the defense. The clerk called out for an Officer Lerner, who stepped out of the crowd and crossed in front of the bench to stand by Santiago and Owen. Santiago explained that Robertson was found in possession of brass knuckles during a pat-down by Lerner and was here today answering charges of possession of a dangerous weapon.

The defense stepped in before the judge had a chance to speak. "It was a bad search, Your Honor. Officer Lerner had no probable cause to stop Mr. Robertson, did not explain to Mr. Robertson why he was being stopped, and physically detained—with some force—Mr. Robertson from leaving the scene."

The judge asked, "Officer Lerner? The defense is claiming a bad search."

"It was a bad search," Lerner said. "I felt there was probable cause, but in hindsight, I don't think I was right."

"Why did you stop him?"

"The way he was walking. He was leaning to one side, like he had something heavy in his pocket. I thought that was reasonably suspicious. But I realize it was a ... a bad search."

Owen saw Santiago look hard at the floor.

Richardson was on his way out a few moments later.

Santiago turned to Owen. "You getting the idea?"

"How many of these cases get done in a day?"

"That's the wrong question. You don't ask that. You don't think about it. You just go until the docket's clear or the judge tells you to stop, whichever comes first. Got it?"

Owen didn't answer.

Santiago leaned in and spoke louder. "You got it?"

"Yeah," Owen said. "I got it."

"Good." Santiago turned and looked down at a file. "Stolarchuk? Larissa Stolarchuk?"

## Saturday, May 1, 1976

Once Owen got back to Chicago after abruptly leaving L.A., Melissa started calling—not to talk but to demand Owen give her the things she'd left. He told her he didn't want her things there, and she could come get them anytime.

She'd keep on demanding, in a rabid, rending tone, like she hadn't heard what Owen just said.

She invariably ended with, "And I want the fucking dog too." If she cut the conversation short before bringing the dog up, she'd call back. Owen held firm on that one. No chance, he told her. No chance. Then she'd call him all kinds of obscene names and announce she planned to put a hex on him. Owen could often hear Sherwin stifling laughter in the background.

Sherwin had probably waited his whole life to lord it over someone, to put them in their place like this. He was almost certainly living this moment to its fullest. Melissa wouldn't have ever looked at Sherwin if he wasn't pushing cocaine. Owen wondered how many dollars of the stuff they did each day. He wondered what Sherwin would do to keep Melissa with him.

Bill Jordan called Owen on a Saturday and let him know the whole band would be dropping by late the next morning. Owen knew right away, from the tone of Jordan's voice, that they wanted to check on him, make sure he was holding everything together. They'd seen Melissa haunting the gigs. They'd noticed how quickly he'd been slipping away after, even once she stopped. He tried putting Jordan off—between court and studies, the time pressure was significant—but he didn't listen.

The next day, a little before ten, Owen sat marking time until the band arrived. Late morning probably meant 11:30. Possibly earlier, if they were feeling ambitious. Which they probably weren't.

Owen expected a call from Jordan soon, saying they got a late start, they'd be there in the early afternoon. When the phone rang at 10:00, Owen answered on the second ring.

No one responded. No voice. Just quiet, ambient noise on the caller's end—the hum of phone lines, the sound of a quiet room. Then, clearly holding the handset away from her, Melissa giggling. "Hello," she said, laughing. "Stop! Stop it! I'm on the—stop! You're such a creep." She laughed again and followed it with a soft grunt of pleasure. "No, you're going to have to wait five minutes!"

Now her voice was bright. "Hi, Gregg. Sorry about that. Sherwin keeps putting his finger—"

Owen hung up. He stood there, fighting an impulse to punch the wall. He pressed his palm flat against it instead and waited for Melissa's next call. It came within a few minutes.

Her voice was low, the words constricted. "That was really rude. *Really* rude."

Owen didn't respond.

"You have nothing to say? Nothing? Listen, to me, you fucking motherfucker, I want my shit."

Owen exploded. "Then come and get your shit. It's waiting for you."

He heard loud sniffing and knew exactly what it was.

"Did you pack it?"

She said it like an accusation. He heard sniffing again. Fucking Sherwin.

"I put everything in trash bags, and I'll leave them at the end of the driveway." He was thunderstruck that he'd ever loved her.

"You just dumped it in trash bags? Just … just … willy-nilly?"

He laughed at the absurdity of the phrase.

"You better have Dagon's shit ready too. The bowls, the leash—everything."

Owen hung up. He reeled to the sofa and sat down, pressing his fingers against the dense spots of pain that had just begun throbbing above his eyes. It felt like hornets were stinging the bone.

He was being punished. Clearly. But for what? Where to start …

For Sherri? For bringing her so low she fled to LA?

For derailing the band?

For every time he wished a heart attack or deadly wreck on his stepfather?

Never mind *where to start?* The real question was *where to end?*

He'd really stepped in some shit this time.

Dagon came across the room, stopped in front of the couch, and prodded Owen's hand. Owen rubbed behind Dagon's ears. A moment later, the dog turned, barked, and trotted toward the front door.

Owen heard car doors slamming in the driveway, then voices, then a knock.

"Come on in." Owen stood up and went to greet them. There were hands extended, arms crisscrossing, hands taken, a few quick clumsy hugs. Owen led the way to the living room.

After a few minutes of small talk, Joe made a show of appraising Owen and then nodded.

"You look good. You look like you're doing all right." Joe's voice was mock-dire. "Thank God. I mean, we were starting to think ... Well, never mind."

"Starting to think what?" Owen asked. "Did you hear something?"

"We didn't hear anything. At least not from you. It's been a while since we heard from you."

Owen shook his head. "No, come on. It hasn't been that long."

"It's been three weeks," Joe said.

*Shit*, Owen thought. *Has it been that long?*

Jordan broke in. "Kidding aside, we just wanted to see what was up. We've got the gig in a week. Probably time to do some rehearsing, no?"

"Yeah. Of course I'm still doing it." Owen had forgotten the gig. He also felt he had to explain himself. "Sorry to be incommunicado. I'm in court every day now. Between that and studying ... "

Steve, one of the roadies, asked, "What's that like? Court, I mean."

Owen thought about it. "Generally pretty interesting. It can get a little repetitive, but it's nonstop so time goes quick. I mean, mostly it's just processing shit as fast as you can."

He felt strange saying it that way, as if he was downplaying it. One of them might say, *You bailed on us for that?*

Jordan said, "What's the worst thing you've seen?"

"Worst? Like the most fucked-up? Nothing, really. It's all misdemeanors—fighting, vandalism. It would be in a different court if the case was that bad. No drugs, no guns, no murder, no attempted murder, no bank robberies." He thought the band looked a little disappointed. "But let me tell you about what goes on at Branch 34 on Monday mornings ... "

"What about Monday mornings?" Jordan said.

"*Whore court*, as they call it. All the hookers are arraigned. All of them who got arrested over the weekend. A dozen, fifteen, twenty prostitutes, plus the johns who were caught getting serviced. But some of those ladies might have been locked up since that Friday. No one's at their best or freshest."

"What happens to them?" Gavin said.

"They get cut loose. Time served."

Owen noticed Jordan casually scanning the living room and kitchen. Probably looking for signs of self-neglect. Dereliction. They wouldn't find any. Owen had always been neat, and over the past few months he kept things pristine. Disorder wouldn't serve him very well. It was an easy slide from disorder back to despair. He'd had a hard climb out, and he knew he couldn't do it twice.

Eventually conversation drifted to the future, weighing Jerico's options and possibilities, how the search for a new keyboardist might proceed, whether any part of the prospective Mercury deal could be salvaged.

Steve had perched himself on the windowsill. He asked Owen, "Is it okay if I smoke in here?"

"Yeah. Sure." It was a strange question since Rupp and Jordan had cigarettes going. "Go ahead."

Dagon wandered in, looked around, and walked back out.

Steve got an orange packet of ZigZag rolling papers from his shoulder bag and then a baggie with a nugget of pale-green pot. He took a paper from the packet and a little pot from the bag.

Owen stiffened.

"Wait a sec. Hold on." Owen was genuinely shocked. "I thought you meant a cigarette. I … I can't … I'm a prosecutor, man. If we got caught, that would be … That would end my career real fast."

It sounded ridiculous to his own ears. He'd been around so much pot that he stopped noticing long ago. So much speed. Acid. Coke.

He noticed now.

"Okay," Steve said. "No problem, man." He dropped the pot back in the bag, crumpled the paper into a ball, and dropped that in too.

Things got quiet. From the way they were looking at him, or away from him, Owen *knew* they were trying to figure out exactly who he was to them now. And he knew without a doubt their thoughts had moved to that night in Los Angeles. That's where *his* thoughts had gone. Leaving that way had declared his priorities. He hadn't *really* addressed it with them, though. Not fully.

He'd apologized right afterward, and at the time, he saw they were conflicted—concerned, empathetic, resentful, pissed. He'd been forgiven—he'd counted on that, felt his history with them earned forgiveness—but the immediacy of what happened, its lingering, near-physical presence, would be a long time fading. The broken bone, reset and healed. Never quite the same. Different. Telling Steve to put the pot away was proving the point.

It was clear to Owen the burden of the moment was his. He'd rehearsed possible things to say before now, but as he saw their faces looking up expectant, demanding, maybe even confrontational in a way he'd never recognized before, he threw the script away.

"I'm sorry," he said, finally. His voice had a quaver. "I'm so sorry. I don't know what I can even say. I lost my shit. I came undone. Every time I think of what this did to you guys—what I did to you guys, it just makes me sick to my stomach."

Dagon wandered over, and Owen crouched down to pet him. Dagon leaned into Owen's torso. The dog's brown hair was sleek under Owen's hand. Stroking him, scratching him behind the ears—these were comforting, always. When Owen stood up again, the dog trotted a few feet to the front door, pressed his nose against it, then went back to the kitchen.

There was more he wanted to say. He tried getting his thoughts in order. The guys exchanged charged looks.

"You apologized to us, man." Rupp broke the quiet. "You apologized *already*. You don't have to keep feeling this bad. You did what you needed to do. The heart gives some weird instructions sometimes."

Rupp sounded sincere, but how could he be?

Jordan picked it up. "Look, man, right now, we're not the band. We're your brothers. Did I kind of want to kill you at the time? Sure. But the only important thing right now is making sure you're doing all right. And you *are* doing all right. Not with us, maybe, but that's okay. We were friends before Jerico. We're still friends now. It's not like you're dead to us." He laughed to himself. "And it's not your fault, man. This is Melissa's fault."

Owen couldn't quite bring himself to believe Jordan meant it. What would he be saying to Jordan, or Rupp, or Gavin if the situation was reversed?

And then there was the heavy torque of an engine, some ways off but loud, and after a moment really loud, rattling like it was right outside. The noise stopped abruptly. Two car doors slammed.

Rupp stood, looked out the window. "Holy shit. Holy shit. What amazing timing."

The front door flew open, and there was Melissa, filling the whole living room with her coke-deranged static. From a distance she looked as she always had. But as she came closer, Owen saw her face wasn't the same at all. It was subtly, slyly ravaged. The skin was shabby and tired and textured with a colorless rash. She had a few scattered lesions, like tiny crusted islands, on her forehead and cheeks. Her makeup was smeared around her eyes and mouth. Her eyebrows were patchy. Her deep-blue skirt—Owen remembered her coming home from her favorite boutique with it—was hanging below her jutting hip bones.

This couldn't possibly be Melissa, he thought for a split second.

She stomped toward Owen.

"I'm here for the dog. I want the dog, and I don't want any of your bullshit." She was shouting at Owen and waving her hands around. It looked as if she might start squaring off with him. Owen glanced behind him. Everyone else was watching. They looked dumbstruck. No one moved.

Owen almost laughed. "Where exactly do you think you're going to take him?"

"None of your goddamn, fucking business. Get the fucking dog."

"Fuck you if you think the dog's going anyplace."

She turned her head back toward the front door and might have been shouting *no* or *now*, or something else entirely, but she loaded whatever she'd said with so much anger, it distorted into a shriek. Sherwin Spector, the singer, the cocaine dealer, the man who had ruined her, stepped out of the shadows behind her.

And then Sherwin pointed his arm at Owen, and an explosion came out of his hand with a white-orange flash and a billow of gray smoke. Owen heard a sharp snapping above his head. Another flash and billow, another *snap*, a thick cordite smell, and the sound reverberating again and again off the walls.

Steve rolled himself out of the open window and sprinted up the street, going for help, screaming over and over that someone had just killed his friend.

"What about now, fucker?" Sherwin's eyes looked like they hadn't been shut in days. He looked surprised that Owen was still standing in front of him. The hand holding the gun was shaking. "You going to give her what she wants now?"

"Where's my shit?" Melissa shouted it over and over, moving out of the living room, in and out of the bedrooms, coming back to the living room, passing into the kitchen, and through the door into the garage. "Where's my shit, you motherfucker!"

She slammed the door behind her. Owen looked at Sherwin.

"Do whatever you need to." Owen hadn't realized his hands were up. Terror had come on so sudden and thorough that he didn't even recognize it for what it was. "Do whatever you want. Take whatever you want. Just don't hurt my friends."

"Your friends," Sherwin said. "These are your friends?"

It didn't seem like he was faking.

They'd all known each other for years—Sherwin and Jerico—and Sherwin's failure to recognize them struck Owen as a terrible sign. Sherwin was out of his head, and anything might happen. Everything was possible. Sherwin pointed the gun at Jordan.

"Is he your friend? Huh? Is this your friend?" Sherwin shook his head as if he was trying to clear it. He laughed to himself. His lips were very wet.

"Why are you pointing that at me?" Jordan said.

Sherwin steadied his gun hand. He laughed again, then licked the spit from his lips.

Melissa came back from the garage, holding all four bulging bags in her hands. She was facing Owen, but he couldn't tell if she was actually seeing him. "Dagon! Come! Dagon!"

The dog didn't come. Later, Owen would find Dagon hiding under the bed, and even later than that, they would fall asleep together.

Very faintly, there was the sound of a siren. It wailed louder and louder by the second. Neither Melissa nor Sherwin seemed to hear it. But then they did.

Melissa shrieked again and cursed and dropped the garbage bags. She and Sherwin were almost knocking each other down, trying to get out of the house as fast as they could. Owen, cold, trembling, moved to the front door and watched. In the driveway, Sherwin called Melissa's name and tossed his gun. She caught it. They didn't even touch their car doors before the first cops pulled up and blocked the driveway, jumping out, rushing the two of them. Things moved a beat faster than Owen could take in. Somehow, Sherwin was on the ground, one cop kneeling on him, pushing a gun against the back of his head. And he saw that during all this, Melissa had wound up prone too, the other cop suddenly materializing over her, warning her not to move, not to even blink. Owen could hear her crying, begging the cop not to hurt her. For a brief, irrational moment, Owen had the urge to comfort her.

As the rest of the guys crowded around the door, watching the driveway, speechless, Owen turned and walked back into the living room. Owen reached his fingers up and touched the bullet holes. They were warm to the touch. The room still smelled of cordite.

The gunshots made Owen's ears ring for days

# PART II

## CHAPTER 23

On November 19, 1979, a little before seven in the morning, Gregg Owen was at home, getting ready for work. Owen wasn't doing a trial, but he had a crucial appointment at his office. He was meeting with Carol Lumpp, the twenty-four-year-old daughter of a well-liked, widely respected lieutenant in the Chicago Police Department, to discuss her role in the contract killing of Richard Bernoski.

Bernoski was the fake archbishop of the fake Old Holy Roman Catholic Church. The church wasn't recognized by the Vatican. Bernoski had made it up out of whole cloth. He'd appointed himself archbishop, and named his boyfriend, John Percic, as vice-archbishop. Percic had paid Lumpp and her boyfriend—also her pimp, according to some stories—$500 to murder Bernoski.

Lumpp's lawyer had called Owen the previous Friday, saying that Lumpp wanted to "flip" and help the prosecution in exchange for leniency. Owen had made it clear immunity wasn't on the table, but agreed to meet with Lumpp.

He needed to find out if she had anything valuable to tell him. He doubted it.

Owen buttoned his shirt to the top, flipped his collar up, and draped a tie over his neck. He wrapped the wide end twice around the narrow end, then up and over into a four-in-hand-knot. His phone rang as he pulled it tight.

He figured it was Goggin or his mother, one of the two, but it was neither. When he answered, Owen was a little surprised to hear his brother's voice.

"Jay? Shit. What's up, my man? Everything good?" Owen didn't think Jay had ever called this early. There was a pause and then a long exhale. It sounded weary.

"Hey—do you remember that murder?"

"You might need to narrow it down a little."

"Gio Messina. That one."

Owen remembered. "Your buddy, right? Yeah, of course. I do remember that. Why?"

"As a prosecutor, can you tell me why the hell a case would just get dropped? I mean, if someone gets arrested and charged with a murder, why would it just go away?"

Jay sounded angry. Owen sat down at his kitchen table. "It could be a lot of reasons, Jay. Insufficient evidence. The cops did something wrong. Witnesses disappeared or changed their testimony. Why? What's going on?"

"The asshole they arrested for Gio Messina's murder isn't getting tried. He gets to walk away."

"So, they caught the guy who did it? When did this all happen?"

"Oh, yeah, they caught him. He was arrested four years ago but he never got tried. Honestly, brother, it sounds like someone on your side of things might have blown it. His lawyer has kept asking for delays—for *years*—and all of a sudden, it's at a point where the case is just going away. I've stayed in touch with his family since he got killed, and they heard about this a couple days ago, and, man, they are wrecked. Gio's dad said something about lost evidence? Something like that. I'm sorry if I spoke too soon, but I said I'd ask you to just take a look and see what's what. Is that possible? Would you be able to find out what's going on? I really don't like asking. I mean, I know you're busy as shit, and I don't want you thinking that—"

"Jay, it's fine. I'm happy to check it out. Do you happen to remember who the lawyer is?"

"God, I've heard the name but ... I can't remember. His dad said he knew about the guy. A quote-unquote *notorious* lawyer."

"That's a really big pool of candidates. Look, I've got to get into work now. But this afternoon, I'll ask around." He sighed to himself. Time that afternoon was pretty tight already. "And listen—his dad probably misunderstood. I'm sure no one lost all the evidence. We'll talk later, okay?"

"Big brother, I'm eternally grateful. Thanks, man. I owe you one."

Later, after the meeting with Lumpp had proved pointless, Owen asked around. The murders of Gio Messina and Tinker Moore had been assigned to the Daley Center.

That surprised him. Actually, it astonished him. How a double homicide wound up at the Daley Center was beyond his understanding. The center housed a dozen or so civil courts, and ten felony courtrooms, but the only criminal cases tried there were for prisoners on bond, and most cases were low-key and low stakes.

It made even less sense that someone accused of killing two people was out on bond at all.

Owen got to the Daley Center around 2:00 that afternoon, and took an elevator to the eighth floor, where all the assistant state's attorneys assigned to the center's courtrooms had their offices. He'd never been to the eighth floor before.

Owen found the whole floor was nearly silent. Along the main hallway were ten offices for prosecutors, and as Owen looked inside each office, he was surprised to find them empty.

The distant sound of a typewriter came from down the hall and around the corner and Owen followed it to the steno pool. Usually it was a noisy room with fifteen or so typists, typing up motions, letters, jury instructions, or whatever documents the prosecutors needed. Today there was a single young woman at work. Owen called out "Excuse me" two times before she started and looked up.

"I'm sorry to interrupt, but I was looking for … actually, I was looking for … anybody." He gestured toward the prosecutors' offices. "No one's there."

"Oh. Well, they all went home, I think." The woman appeared uncomfortable.

Owen glanced at the clock hanging on the wall behind the woman's desk. He felt a spark of frustration. "It's barely two o'clock. They went home? Really?"

The woman looked pained. "I'm afraid so. Can I help you with anything?"

It was clear she hoped he'd say no. Before he could answer, he saw one of the ASAs he knew come from around the corner, looking at some documents as he walked.

"Sandy," Owen called out. Sandy was an exception to the Daley Center's caliber of lawyer. He'd been at Twenty-Sixth and California but had suffered dire heart trouble. His doctor ordered an easy convalescence, and so Sandy transferred over as deputy supervisor. Owen respected him and thought Sandy should be running things here rather than the current supervisor, David Pierce. Pierce had a reputation for being singularly unambitious.

Sandy seemed pleased to see him.

"Owen. Shit, man, what's up? What's so dire you'd be over here slumming it?"

They shook hands. Sandy said, "What do you need?"

"Where is everyone?"

"What do you mean?"

"I mean no one is here."

Sandy offered a rueful smile. "No, of course not. Everyone went home."

"Why? Is it a half-day or something? Who's in the courtrooms, then?"

"No one's in the courtrooms. Not since Monday."

"You guys don't have any cases?"

"We've got a shit ton of cases. That's why I'm here a little late. I didn't get a chance to meet with the defense for a few of my cases, so, you know, I've got—" Sandy counted through the files he was carrying. "I've still got eleven to plead out."

"And Pierce isn't up everyone's ass?"

"I haven't seen him since Tuesday. Okay, so what can I do for you?"

"I'm trying to get some info on a double murder case you guys have here. My brother knew one of the victims, and he was curious about the status of the case."

"Double murder? You must mean Weinger."

Owen hadn't expected to hear that name.

"How'd you know that?"

Sandy shrugged, shook his head.

"You think we get many double homicides here? I wish I could tell your brother differently, but there's no status to report. It's going away by the new year. It's a shit case."

"What do you mean?"

Sandy put his hands in his pocket and leaned back against the filing cabinet.

"I mean, no one wants to get near that case. Pierce made it pretty clear he doesn't want to touch it with a ten-foot fucking pole. We've got a rich kid perp. We've got a single eyeball. The eyeball won't testify. We brought the guy in a little while ago—couple of months, maybe—and the asshole said if we tried making him talk, he'd take the Fifth."

"Why? On what grounds?"

"From our perspective, it looks like a coke deal gone bad, and we think the eyeball was in on it. He's scared that if he testifies and he admits to any cocaine being involved, then we'll have enough on him to send him way for possession to deliver."

Owen started to say something, but Sandy cut him off.

"Hold on. It gets worse. You know Ted O'Connor, right?"

"Yeah, of course. I know Teddy."

"He was the lead on the murder. He was the one who made an arrest. Teddy and his guys recovered a bunch of evidence from the perp's apartment, and lo and behold, we go to take a look a month or so back, and it's all vanished. The defense had filed a motion to suppress all the evidence anyway—"

"What was their argument?"

Sandy grinned without humor and shook his head slowly. "I can't even remember—bad search, beyond the scope of the warrant. Whatever it was, they got it—motion granted The judge just gave it to them. It was pretty kinky because no way Teddy O'Connor didn't play exactly by the book."

Owen whistled, incredulous. "I'm assuming you appealed."

"Of course we did. The Appellate Court reversed the judge's ruling, but when the case file and physical evidence came back to sheriff's inventory, everything but two pieces was gone."

"Shit," Owen marveled. He was at a loss. He kept thinking he'd moved beyond being surprised and was always proved wrong.

"Look, everyone's relieved, to tell you the truth. You know who Weinger's dad is?"

"No. No idea. Who is Weinger's dad?"

"Some kind of metal baron. Makes metal? Treats metal? Something involving metal, anyway. Worth, like, a trillion dollars. Rich enough so his kid wasn't getting a guilty verdict. And since a not-guilty would've made state's look bad, and it's an election year, so ... you get it."

"Can I take a look?" Owen said. "Just so I can tell my brother."

Sandy shrugged. "Of course. Careful, though. It's obviously cursed. You don't want the taint rubbing off on you. Wash your hands afterward. Come on, I'll get it out for you."

Sandy led Owen into a big, open room, banked all around with filing cabinets. There were a few haphazardly placed tables and desks. On one wall, there was a TV mounted near the ceiling. The floor was covered wall-to-wall with dark gray carpet. There were two people in there, standing near the television, talking quietly.

Sandy turned and looked at the cabinets, found the *Wa-Wi* drawer, opened and flipped through it, then flipped through it again, and then again, moving his fingers up and down through the tabs of all the files in the drawer.

"It's not there." He sounded perplexed and irritated. "Okay, let's try over here ... "

Sandy walked to the *M*'s and slid a drawer open. After some searching, he said, "Not here either."

He slammed it shut so the cabinet shook.

"You guys are geniuses of organization," Owen offered.

"No shit." Sandy stood, thinking. "Hold on."

He walked to a desk in the far corner of the room, got down on his hands and knees, and came up a minute later holding a box.

"Here you go, *People v Weinger*-Double Murder 76-1287. Enjoy yourself."

It was a very light box.

"Sandy, thanks man. I appreciate the help."

Owen found a chair at an empty desk and opened the box. It was a lot less full than he'd expected. He lifted a few of the folders out.

The radio began that day's news stories. A bunch of militants publicly beheaded in Saudi Arabia. The first shipment of arms to Afghanistan. Chrysler had issued a statement thanking President Carter for a billion-dollar bailout.

Owen heard it but wasn't listening closely. He pulled out several thin manila files and one large file.

World and national news finished, and the broadcaster began reading the lead local story.

"*Senator Richard M. Daley, son of late Chicago mayor Richard J. Daley, announced his candidacy for Cook County state's attorney earlier this morning. Daley is hoping to unseat the two-term Republican incumbent, Bernard Carey.*"

Owen stopped to listen. The two others in the room stopped too.

"*Addressing rumors of his intention to run and whether or not Senator Daley saw the state's attorney position as a path toward the Attorney General's Office, Daley aide Frank Kruesi declined a direct answer but gave some indication about where Daley's ambitions might lie.*"

"*'If you look at statewide offices, the only one that matters is the governor's. You can be elected attorney general, comptroller, whatever, but you're still working for the governor, and the governor calls the shots. Like here in Chicago. If you plan on staying around, the only job that matters is mayor.'*"

"*State's Attorney Bernard Carey was dismissive when asked whether Daley's campaign posed any significant threat.*"

"*'I can't help thinking that if the people of Cook's County are going to entrust someone with the serious responsibilities that go with the office, they deserve someone who managed to pass the bar exam the first time around.'*"

"Ouch," someone said nearby. "There you go, Rich."

"*Mayor Jane Byrne, who has long had an antagonistic relationship with Daley, has not yet commented.*"

Owen thought he'd rarely heard Carey lash out that harshly. Carey must have been nervous. It was inevitable that every case the office tried from here on out would be subject to intense scrutiny. Owen liked Daley and also held Carey in high regard.

When Owen opened the large manila folder, Mitchell Weinger's mug shot was right on top.

Owen appraised him. A good-looking guy, probably around Owen's age, a wide mustache thick on the upper lip. Eyes nearly looking right into the camera but not precisely.

Owen started putting the photo elsewhere but stopped and looked at it again. Owen found himself lightly disturbed by the expression on Weinger's face. It was odd—an empty, absent look, almost a void at first glance, but after a few seconds: attention showing a different sort of nothingness. The impression Owen got was of someone preparing to give the photographer the mien of a person wrongly accused.

Owen removed the picture and laid it face down on the desktop next to the box. He lifted a few folders from the box and began paging through.

Transcripts. Interview notes.

A memo in Johnny Philbin's terrible handwriting.

What seemed to be an impressively thorough typed report by— Owen took a guess and turned to the last page and saw he'd guessed correctly—Detective Ted O'Connor.

A thick stack of photographs.

Owen sorted through those, recoiled a little at a few of the more gruesome shots. They were taken close enough so the stab wounds looked just as brutal as they actually were, but far enough away to give them proximal context. The glassy, shocked expression around the dead eyes of both victims was visible in quite a few of the photos.

He'd seen a lot of crime scene photos, and many had been worse. But something about them bothered Owen more deeply than usual.

He knew people just like them. He knew people that age. He knew people who dressed this way. He went to parties and mingled with people like this.

Owen was a person like this. If it were him lying dead, and if Gio and Tinker were looking at a photo of the death scene, they'd say the same things.

He felt a vague spasm in his stomach. He'd come close to being the subject of a death scene photo. Very close. If he'd been one step to the right, Sherwin Spector's bullet would have bored through Owen's skull.

If Sherwin had paused for an extra half a second and taken better aim, some ASA might be looking at a photo of him—Owen—with the back of his head blown apart.

He looked at Weinger's photo again for a long time. In his mind he saw some paunchy, gray, expensively dressed, arrogant defense lawyer sliding a thick envelope to a piece-of-shit judge, just like Fischer. He had a vision of all the evidence against Sherwin disappearing.

The thought made him outraged. Then he had an invented image of Melissa, coked up, grinning triumphantly as Owen's blood pooled on the floor. The outrage grew worse.

After Melissa and Sherwin were arrested in his driveway, Owen had waited for a call from the State's Attorney's Office telling him that a trial date had been set and they wanted him for a witness. The call never came. Then more than a year later, Owen heard that the two of them had been tried already. They must have had good lawyers because they were found guilty of illegally discharging a weapon—a misdemeanor—and paid a fine.

He thought about that for a moment there in the Daley Center. His whole life had been upturned, and the memory of the sound of the bullets passing a few inches from his head was something that still got his mind rioting.

Owen was so angry right then his fingers shook.

He put the photos back, shut the folder, shut his eyes.

After a moment, Owen opened his eyes and looked for the small pieces of evidence listed on an inventory sheet—a turquoise necklace, a few pages from Weinger's phone book in his writing, a collection of newspaper clippings that betrayed an abnormal interest in the murders—but none of it was there. He couldn't find a voucher or any other indication of where the evidence went.

He looked through more of the file. He saw Pat Tuite's name—the lawyer Jay had referenced. Tuite had served as Weinger's defense right after he was arrested four years ago. Tuite had been there when Weinger was arraigned. Owen wondered again at how the case made its way from Twenty-Sixth and California to the Daley Center.

Owen was starting to remember Jay's call four years ago, and the article in the paper, a little more clearly.

He still couldn't figure how Weinger had gotten bail on a double murder. Not with crime scene photos like these. He found that baffling.

The million-dollar bail had been paid in cash. He found that amazing.

Owen read a request from Tuite that Weinger be given a psych evaluation. There had been something about an evaluation request in O'Connor's report that Owen had only half noticed. He picked the report up again and found what he was looking for right away: O'Connor had mentioned the evaluation and in a handwritten footnote explained that he thought this was a damning move on Tuite's part. If his client wasn't guilty—hadn't admitted guilt—why lay any groundwork at all for an insanity plea?

Owen went back to the police files. He paged through. Nothing about motive.

He paged through again. Not a word. No mention anywhere.

The locale, the personnel involved, the bond, the shrinks—there were all sorts of incongruities. And there was the picture of Weinger too, which had hovered as a sort of phantom afterimage the whole time Owen had been reading. There was something very slightly uncalibrated in the man's face.

"Gregg."

Owen turned. Sandy was back, leaning through the doorway. He said, "I'm heading out. When you're done, just put it under a desk. Anywhere is fine. I'll keep it around if you want to see it again."

"Thanks, Sandy."

"Tell Goggin and Kunkle I said hello."

Owen returned to the files. There was something off here. None of the elements were fitting together. But he figured it was probably easy to account for. Like a stereoscopic picture, where you had to look at it in just the right way to see the entire image, he wasn't seeing correctly because he wasn't looking properly. Which raised the question, what would the correct view look like?

He pondered that for a few minutes as he looked at the material spread out in front of him. Whoever had let the case take this shape was either dumb or dirty. Maybe both.

He replaced the papers in the file and began asking himself how it happened to be that in a series of incremental moves—bold but incremental—a killer could kill and put his murders behind him and just walk away. Who put the money up; who looked the other way? Who didn't give enough of a shit to try to stop it?

Then he picked it up again.

Here was the face of a kid who had everything and wanted for nothing. He'd never known two seconds of deprivation. He'd never had to fight for what he had. He'd never had to think in terms of surviving.

Weinger wasn't a Cabrini-Green kid. He was white. He was from the North Shore. His family was richer than God. And it wasn't that Weinger had every opportunity in life. It was more than that. His entire life was an opportunity.

## Chapter 24

There wasn't much decision involved: one moment, he was just walking into the empty office for a glance on Jay's behalf; the next moment, he was dialing the phone at an empty desk nearby and calling Mike Goggin to ask for Goggin's help pursuing the case. He knew Goggin wouldn't say no. He knew he could trust Goggin completely, implicitly.

It hadn't always been that way.

Goggin and Owen had a storied relationship.

It began when Owen was assigned as a law clerk in the courtroom of J. J. McDonnell, back in the late winter of 1975, after his interview with an ASA recruiter.

Everyone knew McDonnell was a dirty judge.

Except Owen. Owen had no idea. He was new. Bill Kunkle had placed Owen there. Owen couldn't have known.

When McDonnell wanted to offer Owen advice, Owen would sit in McDonnell's chambers and listen. McDonnell would light a cigar, lean back, and pontificate. The advice was usually pretty good.

Owen was often in McDonnell's chambers. A lot of people noticed. Especially Mike Goggin.

Goggin suspected Owen of ethical violations because of the time he was spending with McDonnell. More than suspected: Owen would find out later that Goggin was convinced of it—the evidence showed the violations as a foregone fact. Owen was spending serious time with a crooked judge. Which meant he was running contrary to the only ethics that mattered: be blameless, keep your hands clean, stay way beyond reproach. In Goggin's mind it couldn't be clearer, couldn't be starker. The line between right and wrong was black and white and too thin for anything gray.

And Goggin understood that when "moths and rust doth corrupt," the first compromise is small and seems inconsequential.

One morning, around 8:45, Owen came out of McDonnell's chambers and face-to-face with a man he hadn't met or even seen before. The man was belligerent, almost enraged, and went on the offense immediately. He moved to within a few inches of Owen's face and asked, "Who the fuck are you?"

While Owen tried figuring out the nature of the moment, the stranger answered his own question.

"You're the new guy, right? Owen? That's your last name?"

"Yeah, that's right. Gregg Owen."

"And you spell it funny, right?" He grinned at Owen. "Well, let me ask you something, Greg-guh-guh. What were you doing in the judge's chambers?"

"What do you think I was doing? I was in the judge's chambers. Talking. With the judge."

"About what?"

"About none of your fucking business."

A lupine grin broke across the guy's face. He poked Owen in the chest. "Oh, it's very much my fucking business, Greg-guh-guh. What did McDonnell give you in there?"

"Who are you?"

"How much was it? How much was it he gave you? It's okay. You can tell me."

After a half-second, the guy continued. "You don't want to tell me? Well, I'm going to tell you something, Greg-guh-guh. I want you to listen." His voice dropped. "Are you listening? You are not to ever go in those chambers again. You understand that? You heard me, Gregg-guh-guh? Under no circumstances are you to go in there again. Not without one of us. And you don't touch a single case file without one of us looking at it first. Am I clear?"

It dawned on Owen that the guy had more standing than he did. He knew how he spelled his name. He was aware Owen had been in McDonnell's chambers that morning because he knew where and when to wait for him. He seemed to know Owen had been in the chambers before. He was ordering Owen around. He was hinting at threats. He implied he'd be watching Owen at close range. Unreasonably close. Owen wasn't sure who "us" was.

*How much was wha*t? he wondered. Then, aloud, calmer now, a little more deferent, cautious: "Who are you?"

"I'm really glad you asked, Gregg-guh-guh." That same razor wolf-grin. His voice swelling with false good humor. "I'm Mr. Goggin." He emphasized the *Mr.* "I'm a lawyer. Oh, wait. Let me clarify. I'm a real lawyer. A real lawyer. You're not shit. However you used to do things? Forget it. We'll be explaining the new way to do them."

"Ron didn't—"

Goggin cut him off. "Santiago is gone. Santiago isn't here anymore." He stared until Owen felt deeply uncomfortable. From around the corner, they heard the noise of a door closing, keys jingling, and the sound of McDonnell walking away down the hall. "I think we might be too late, trying to intervene on this one. I just don't feel quite right about it, you know what I mean? I don't know if I'll ever feel right about it."

Goggin shook his head ruefully. Goggin's voice was magnanimous. "Go ahead, man. Go on home. Have a great weekend, Gregg-guh-guh."

A couple of years later, in 1977, long after Owen had passed the bar and started working in the different courthouses, he met Goggin for the second time.

He'd been working with Tom Breen for a while, but that was about to end.

Owen wasn't ever quite sure what he'd done to piss off Mike Ficaro, but it was enough to get him pulled from working with Breen and exiled to Judge John Moran's courtroom. No one volunteered a convincing explanation.

Everything fit into a small cardboard box that Gregg Owen was in no hurry to fill. Without enthusiasm, he packed an assortment of ballpoints that always felt right in his hand; his 1958 ebony-colored Executive model Swingline; an unused coffee mug he'd been given, embossed with the Cook County State's Attorney seal; his pads and notebooks; and the job offer letter the State's Attorney's Office mailed him back in 1976, which his mother had framed.

He felt like ten times the lawyer he'd been when Kunkle assigned him to Judge Frank Wilson's courtroom, where he shared an office with Tom Breen and Ray Garza. Prior to that he'd known all the elements necessary for arguing a case, but Breen gave him a deeper, more nuanced education. Breen taught him how to win.

Now, Owen had been assigned to Judge Moran's courtroom. Owen had seen this guy in action. Moran dithered endlessly back and forth when pressed for a decision and was missing the part of the brain a person needed to come up with anything other than nonsense. Maybe that would teach Owen something about patient endurance. There wasn't much else he'd come away with. How had some of these people even become judges? Well, Owen knew how.

He carried his few possessions, and a weighty sense of dread, over to his new office—the one attached to Courtroom 602. He opened the door and felt even worse.

It was narrow and constricted, too tight and absurdly compact—inadequate for one body but meant to accommodate three. There, a chain of several desks lined one side, and file cabinets banked all along the other. Only the farthest desk in the row was empty. Overhead fluorescent lights—each end glowing a faint, dull orange—dimmed and flickered, and five or ten or six seconds later brightened again.

"Mr. Angarola, would you believe our new colleague found his new office all by himself?"

The voice was sudden and loud and booming in his ear. Owen started. He knew exactly who it was. It had been a while, but he knew. He turned and looked. He was right.

"Hi, there, Greguhguh. How's it going? You remember me, right?" Mike Goggin said. He gave Owen a wolf's grin. "Welcome to Judge Moran's courtroom. I know Tommy Breen has been holding your hand for a while back there, but that's over, Greguhguh."

"Oh, come on." Owen closed his eyes, made a slight, derisive wave with his hand. "Are we still doing that?"

"Doing what, Greguhguh?" Goggin's voice was wildly, falsely earnest.

"That. That moronic 'Greguhguh' shit. I'm a prosecutor, same as you. So, enough, got it? Let it go."

Owen immediately regretted saying anything at all. Now, Goggin had to keep at him.

Goggin's smile widened, getting bloodier, more feral.

He said, "So sorry, hippie boy. My deepest apologies. I was about to explain how things were different over here in Judge Moran's courtroom. Now, this—" he indicated the man standing at his shoulder "—is Michael Angarola. Let me tell you something about him, okay? Mr. Angarola used to be Sergeant Angarola of the United States Marine Corps. He fought in Vietnam, so he's not used to working with a freak. He's the first chair in our courtroom. Mr. Angarola is the man in charge. You might remember that I'm Mr. Goggin. I'm second chair. And when Mr. Angarola isn't here, I'm first chair. No matter who's here, we're your bosses. You're the third chair. Which is only a quarter step up—maybe—from an intern."

Goggin's eyes were lightly deranged. His voice had coarsened. A pink flush rose from under his collar and up his neck.

Briefly, Owen considered telling Goggin to fuck himself but thought that the guy was so wound up, he might throw a punch without much provocation.

Mike Angarola stood his ground, grinning. Goggin wasn't done.

He said, "I want you to think of this office as a hill. Can you do that? Can you picture a hill, Greguhguh? Mr. Angarola handles the very important stuff. He's at the top of the hill. I—that's Mr. Goggin, remember—I'm a little lower, in the middle. I handle the rest of the important cases. You? You're *allllll* the way at the bottom."

Goggin feigned deep consideration. "You know what they say about shit?"

Owen shrugged. He didn't bother saying anything.

Goggin said, "Shit rolls downhill. You understand? I'll say it again: shit rolls downhill. All the shit cases? All the shit work? It's all rolled down to you. It's all yours now."

Angarola snorted. Goggin turned and smiled appreciatively at him.

"So, if I was you? I'd remember that shit work was all I'd ever be good for, and I wouldn't take the trouble getting ambitious."

Owen gave back a bitter whisper of a grin. "You rehearsed that, didn't you?"

Goggin pretended to consider it. Finally, he said, "No. I didn't rehearse that. It's just something I've had to say—over and over—to a lot of people who don't know their place."

Michael Angarola, recruited to the State's Attorney's Office by Mike Ficaro, the Twenty-Sixth Street Felony Trial Court boss, was working a special case that would keep him out of the office for three weeks at least. Possibly—probably—more than that. Whether or not the crime was significant or especially severe, every trial required a team, so Goggin brought Owen with him to court out of necessity. Goggin had a routine where he wheeled a cart to the office door, loaded it with files and evidence, and then walked away. Owen was supposed to push the cart to the courtroom.

The sixth or seventh time, Owen broke.

"You think I'm your fucking water boy?" he said to Goggin.

Goggin wheeled on him. "I wouldn't trust you to carry my water."

During trials, Goggin handled opening statements, closing arguments, and all the rebuttals. When he had to, Goggin let Owen cross-examine a witness, usually someone inconsequential, who couldn't and wouldn't damage a case. Before a trial, when they selected a jury, Goggin made it clear he didn't give a shit what Owen thought concerning one juror or another. Despite himself, Owen felt a little awed that Goggin's spite never flagged.

The months dragged on and on.

But one morning, Goggin rode in from Oak Park with his boyhood friend and colleague at Twenty-Sixth Street, Joe Claps. At the end of the day, Claps was stuck at his desk and couldn't leave, so Goggin found himself stranded. He needed to get home in time because his wife had an obligation somewhere, and Owen heard Goggin asking around whether anyone could give him a lift to Oak Park.

Owen, indulging a small, sadistic impulse, listened for a time until finally signaling Goggin and telling him, "Hey, Mike, I drive home on the Eisenhower. I'll give you a lift."

"Don't worry about it," Goggin said, barely looking at him. Goggin pulled a torn and frayed Yellow Pages out of his desk drawer and dialed a few cab companies but had no luck. He put the directory back in his drawer, cursed, and slammed it shut.

"I can give you a ride," Owen reminded him.

"I told you, don't worry about it." He looked at his watch. "Goddammit."

Owen threw his hands up. "Just let me give you a ride!"

Goggin took another look at his watch. "Okay. That would be great," he said. His tone said otherwise.

They drove out of the city in Owen's yellow VW Bug, and neither one spoke to the other. After a little while, it got oppressive. The traffic was dense. They hadn't moved very far in the last five or so minutes.

Owen had the radio tuned to WXRT. When the Doors' "Five to One" came on, Goggin tapped along to the rhythm of the vocals. It was clear Goggin knew the song well. Finally, the lack of talk was too much.

"When I was seventeen," Owen offered, "the band I was in opened for them at the Coliseum. It was ... pretty terrifying."

"Your band opened for the Doors?" Goggin studied him. "Really? No shit?"

"No shit. May 1968. Their second record had just come out."

"Which was their second one?"

"*Strange Days*. The one with "Love Me Two Times" and "When the Music's Over." So, when we first started playing, everyone booed."

Goggin considered this, then turned and looked out the window. Owen was getting sick of Goggin being so dismissive. He felt his anger mounting.

Then Goggin spoke. "That must have freaked you out."

"I was so nervous, my leg was shaking. I mean, really shaking. I couldn't make it stop. It was just humiliating."

"Were they booing at you the whole time?"

"No. We got a little applause after the second song. By the third song, though, we'd started cooking. At the end of thirty minutes, everyone had gotten into it, so they wound up clapping, making a lot of noise. That was a rush."

Goggin asked with genuine interest, "Did you meet Morrison?"

"Yeah, I met him. Absolutely. I don't know what they usually did for dressing rooms, but for that show, all the bands had to share this cinder block room that was partly a storeroom and partly a lunchroom for the staff. It reeked. I mean, it just stank."

"Of pot?"

"No, of piss. I'm almost positive someone took a leak in the corner. Anyway, we figured we probably weren't going to meet the Doors. We were pretty happy we'd get to watch from the wings, though. But we finish our set, thrilled that we didn't get bum-rushed off the stage. We walk into that dressing room, and there they are—all four of the Doors."

"That had to have been intimidating."

Owen laughed. "Oh, man. Of course it was. Those guys were older, they were famous, they toured all over the place. But they turned out to be really cool. They said hello, kept their stuff out of our space. So, we walk in, and there's Jim Morrison, holding court."

"Draw the Line" by Aerosmith came on. Goggin reached and turned it down.

"He's sitting in this big upholstered easy chair. He's up on top of the back of the chair, with his feet on the cushion. Next to the chair, there's a table with a case of Budweiser on it, and every bottle is open.

"In front of the chair, there's this twenty-, twenty-one-year-old woman, sitting on the footstool. She's a writer for *16* magazine. Blonde, hair in a ponytail, silk scarf, conservative dress. She's interviewing Morrison, and he's just going on and on, mumbling one second, almost yelling the next. Not making a ton of sense.

"The poor girl is writing as fast as she can—"

"Was he wearing the leather pants?"

"Yes. He was wearing the leather pants, and he didn't have a shirt on. Anyway, she's trying to write down whatever the hell he's talking about, and in between answers, he keeps leaning over and picking the bottles up with his mouth. No hands. Then he'd tilt his head back and drink it. He was really good at getting the bottle up to his mouth, but when he started drinking, it spilled all over him.

"So, you've got to remember this is around the time when everyone's doing free concerts, giving away free clothes, free food, free drugs. Money was not cool. No one wanted to be seen as a sellout.

"I'm trying not to be too obvious about it, but I really want to hear what the reporter's asking and what Morrison's saying, so I get as close as I can. He goes down to get another beer, but when he comes back up, it falls out of his mouth, spills beer all over the reporter. She looks half pissed off, half terrified.

"This, I'm never going to forget. She asks him, 'Mr. Morrison, what would you say sets you apart from other rock-'n'-roll singers today?'

"He downs the rest of the beer and leans in really close to her and says, 'Darling, it's the size of my pocketbook.' I had to run out of the room. It was great. She didn't how to react.'"

It was quiet for a moment. Then Goggin said, "I bet there were a lot of groupies, right? Like, you've probably lost count of how many girls?"

"No, it wasn't like that," Owen protested. It was a subject where he tended toward modesty. "I mean, maybe there were a couple here and there."

"Just a couple here and there? Come on."

"You play in a band, you meet women. It was part of the job."

"And you were seventeen? Must have been hard to control yourself."

Owen leaned on the horn.

"I'm not sure I did. But I heard you say once you played football, basketball—you didn't get a lot of cheerleaders throwing themselves at you?"

"I went to an Irish Catholic boys school. Fenwick. The powerhouse of the Catholic football league. I'm sure you've heard of Fenwick."

Owen said, "Of course. Great reputation."

He'd never heard of Fenwick.

Goggin continued.

"So, no. There weren't cheerleaders throwing themselves at me. There were a lot of beers getting thrown down my throat, though." Goggin reflected for a bit. "Oh, well. Doesn't matter what I missed out on. If I missed out on anything. I can't imagine not being married. I love my family. I love my wife, both kids. Were you married?"

"No. Someday."

"No kids?"

"I just said, I never got married. I was too busy being a musician."

"So, no kids that you know about."

Owen laughed.

Goggin said, "Do yourself a favor. Have kids. It's like nothing else. It's amazing."

"Honestly, I want to. I really do. I know everyone has a rough childhood, but mine was … "

"Yours was really rough?"

Owen didn't answer for a moment. "I'd treat my kids very differently than I was treated. Let's put it that way."

"You'd right some wrongs, in other words?"

"Exactly."

"There are a lot worse reasons than that to have a kid."

The drive to Oak Park took about an hour. When they pulled into the driveway, Goggin held his hand out and said, "Thank you. I really appreciate the ride. This was a lifesaver."

Owen shook Goggin's hand. Goggin had a firm grip.

"Seriously, it was no trouble," Owen said. "It was nice having the company."

Goggin let Owen's hand go. He said, "Well, thanks again. I'll see you tomorrow, man."

Goggin swung the door shut and started walking inside.

## Chapter 25

Owen called Goggin from the Daley Center. "Hey, Mike, there's a case my brother wanted me to take a look at, but it's at the Daley Center. I just took a look at the file, and the case sucks. It's a murder case, and Jay was a really good friend of someone involved."

"Who got murdered?"

"Actually, two people got murdered. It's a double homicide."

"Hold on. It's a double homicide, and it's at the Daley Center. How in the good Lord's name did that happen?"

"There's some weird shit going on with this one."

"What do you mean, 'weird shit'?"

"The defense filed a motion to suppress the evidence. It was on a search warrant. Teddy O'Connor was in charge."

"Who was the defense?"

"Pat Tuite and Harry Busch."

"Jesus. I assume that motion got laughed at?"

"No. The judge granted the motion."

"Who was the fucking judge?" Goggin sounded incredulous, outraged.

"Judge Fischer."

Goggin made a face. "Right. Of course."

Fischer was known for handing down some outrageous rulings. Owen continued.

"But the bottom line is two people stabbed to death. One male, one female. The guy was a friend of my brother's, and his killer is going to walk away. You and I should keep that from happening."

Goggin was quiet for a long time. Then, "Okay. If you're asking me to do it, I'll do it. One condition, though. We're not going to do it if it's at the Daley Center. It'll be a bench trial and a waste of our time. Get it moved over here. Do that, and I'm in."

"How in the hell do I get it moved?"

"I don't know. Figure it out. For starters, if I was you, I'd give Kunkle a ring."

Later, Owen called Bill Kunkle, his boss and the man who'd brought him on and guided him through the first stages of being a prosecutor after Owen had passed the bar. Kunkle had acted as a patron and mentor, helping Owen avoid the pitfalls that made long-term enemies and derailed careers, and negotiate the politics that could be as important as achievement when it came to advancement.

Owen spoke to Anne Hensley, Kunkle's secretary, and waited several minutes until Kunkle picked up. He sounded a little harried..

"Gregg—how are you? What can I do for you? I'm glad you called, man. I need a break—it's eighteen-hour days of John Gacy, John Gacy, John Gacy."

"How's that going?"

"Trial starts February 6. Sam Amirante is a pain in my ass. They're going to go for an insanity plea."

"Of course they are. What else can they do?"

"I know—how do you argue that some stroke who killed thirty-three people isn't insane? And the whole world is watching." Kunkle shifted to a slower gear. When he spoke his voice was calmer. "Anne says you need my okay on something."

"Yes, I do. There's this case at the Daley Center, a double murder—"

"I bet I know which one you're talking about, but go ahead."

"Okay. A double murder, and it's about to go away, and it shouldn't. Goggin and I want to take the case."

"I bet I know the case you're talking about. Is this Caleb Weinger's kid?"

"Yeah. Exactly. How did you know?"

"Everyone knows who Caleb Weinger is. So, if his kid murders someone, of course I'm going to know about the case." Kunkle snorted.

"Well, we've got to get it transferred over here. Mike suggested I go to Fitzgerald's office. But, you know ... it's Fitzgerald. It seems ... "

Richard Fitzgerald was chief judge at Twenty-Sixth Street. Prosecutors, defense lawyers, other judges—all of them revered him as an unparalleled jurist. Owen and Goggin were no exception.

"Fitzgerald? 'Why, man, he doth bestride the narrow world like a colossus.'" Kunkle often wove Shakespeare into conversation. "But don't sweat it—he's a good guy."

Owen didn't react. His palms, however, seemed a little more damp than a moment ago. He wiped them on his pant leg.

"Go see Fitzgerald," Kunkle said. "You'll be fine."

Owen said, "You're okay with my taking the file out of the center?"

"Yeah, of course. Be my guest. Keep me in the loop. I'm sure I don't need to tell you—probably better if you keep this one under the radar."

He couldn't put it off any more. It was 4:45, and everyone would be trying to finish for the day. Owen took the elevator down to the main floor, walked across the foyer, and went to Fitzgerald's office in Room 101. He knocked on the door, heard some movement inside, and it was opened by Mary Catherine O'Rourke, Fitzgerald's older, perpetually benevolent secretary. Every lawyer in the building considered her half holy just by her association with Fitzgerald.

"Oh, hello—I know who you are," she said. Her voice was warm, her demeanor pleasant. "Come in. You're Gregg Owen. Aren't you?"

Owen was surprised. "Yes. How did you know that?"

"I've seen you on the news, and I saw your picture in the *Tribune* several times. Plus, I hear you're doing excellent work."

"I hope I am," Owen said. His modesty wasn't fake. "I was hoping I could make an appointment to have a quick talk with Judge Fitzgerald. There's a case at the Daley Center I've been assigned, and I wanted to ask if there was a possibility of getting it moved."

"Oh, Gregg—an appointment isn't necessary. I think he's free right now."

*Holy shit. Right fucking now?*

Owen shoved his hands in his pockets. There hadn't been any time to rehearse what he'd wanted to say. He said, "No, no—that's okay. I wouldn't want to just drop in. I'll make an appointment."

"Don't be silly," she said. "You're here, he's here. I'll check and be right back. Don't go anywhere."

She walked to Fitzgerald's office door, gave a single knock, and went in. Owen heard a murmur of voices, and after a moment, Mary Catherine O'Rourke opened the door. She stepped out, and gestured inside. "Go ahead in, Gregg. He'll see you now."

Owen walked in, and Fitzgerald rose from behind his desk, extending his hand.

Owen thought, *He really does bestride the world like a colossus* ...

Fitzgerald stood well over six feet, with a thick head of white hair, an athlete's build. When Owen shook his hand, Fitzgerald's grip was almost uncomfortably firm. There were two leather chairs in front of the desk, and Fitzgerald waved at one.

"Have a seat," he said. "So you're Gregg Owen."

The way he said it sounded as if he'd heard the name several times before.

"Yes, sir, I am."

"I've heard your name come up quite a bit. You've got quite a future by all accounts."

"That's really great to hear," Owen wondered who said it.

"I've been told you're doing a great job, and you're easy to work with."

Owen had no idea what that meant.

Fitzgerald continued. "So what can I do for you, Mr. Owen?"

Owen's palms were slick. He really wished he'd had a chance to think about what he wanted to say. He plunged ahead. "Well, Judge, Mike Goggin and I have been assigned a case that is currently in Judge Fischer's courtroom, at the Daley Center."

Owen knew that Mike's father, John Goggin, had known Fitzgerald for years. It seemed a good idea to throw the Goggin name in as quickly as possible. So far, Owen thought, this wasn't going badly.

He continued. "You can probably guess, we are trying cases here at Twenty-Sixth Street pretty much every day, and it would really screw up our court call if we had to travel from here to the Daley Center for hearings, continuances, and the trial itself.

Owen wasn't sure why he'd said "screw up." It seemed a little vulgar in Fitzgerald's company. Then, he hoped Fitzgerald wouldn't ask him how it was that he and Goggin were assigned to the case.

Fitzgerald nodded. "That's not a problem, Gregg. I'll put it on call for ... let's see ... three weeks from today. So I'll see you on December 5. How does that sound?"

"It sounds like what I hoped you'd say. Thank you, Judge. I appreciate it. I'll see you in December."

Back in his office, Owen called Goggin. "Mike—guess what?"

"What?"

"I went to Fitzgerald's office and got sent right in to see the man himself."

Goggin groaned. Owen continued. "The case is out of the Daley Center and coming here, so you and I—we're set to go."

"Shit," Goggin said. "Shit. I didn't think you'd actually pull it off. Here I was figuring it wouldn't happen and I'd still get to look like the good guy. Okay. Screw it. Put it together. I'm in."

## CHAPTER 26
*December 4, 1979*

It was a first for Owen. Most murder trials got underway while the blood was still steaming. He'd never looked into a case this old and never one this skeletal.

Jay had wanted it, though. Jay had asked, and Jay never asked for a thing.

Owen attacked each trial, every time, like a crusader.

Each trial, every time.

But this one … so far, this one was out of duty. The fire hadn't kindled yet. It was still early stages. The tinder had barely even sparked. But he wasn't about to tell his brother no.

Most people wouldn't get involved in a case like this. Void of significant evidence. Absent any motive at all. Toxic, as Sandy put it.

It occurred to Owen that Jay actually hadn't asked for any more than that Owen take a look at the file. No action beyond that. No commitment.

He recalled the crime scene photos. Gio Messina and Tinker Moore sprawled out bloody and dead. The close-up shots of the lifeless eyes.

He was reasonably certain the fire would catch, but it wouldn't be on the scraps and shreds of evidence he had. Nothing but a thin pile of bullshit leavings.

He remembered Melissa's and Sherwin's drug-scorched, demented faces, full of life but the wrong kind.

What he had so far was a little more than nothing and a lot less than necessary. He needed to be careful with what he did have, which meant he needed to be especially smart, and he'd already done the best, smartest thing he could do: bringing Goggin into it.

But before Goggin got set into motion, the first steps were Owen's. And the very first one was calling Tony Messina.

Tony would tell him later that he'd sat in the Lutheran General Hospital parking lot, waiting to meet Owen, who was driving up to Park Ridge from Chicago, and he'd had no idea what to think, what to expect. Tony had gotten there early, around 10:30 a.m. He'd chosen the place because it was right off the highway. He watched an orderly come out and smoke a cigarette, then retreat out of the cold back inside. He watched a couple leaving the hospital with an infant in a bassinet. He remembered driving Maria to the hospital when she had Gio. He drove a thousand miles an hour and considered red lights optional.

He dialed up and down through the radio stations and stopped at Dean Martin singing, "You Belong to Me." A car like the one Owen had described as his pulled in, and Tony flashed his lights.

Owen parked in the closest space, and Tony watched him step from the car. He wore no coat other than his suit jacket. The closer Owen came to Tony's car, the younger and younger he looked. When he got to the passenger side, Tony rolled the window down.

"Are you Mr. Messina?" Owen said.

"I am. But it's Tony. Call me Tony. You must be Gregg. Your brother Jay has had a lot of nice things to say about you. But why don't you get out of the cold?"

Tony unlocked the passenger door. Owen opened it and slid in.

After they shook hands, Tony looked intently at Owen. He said, "Can I ask you something, Gregg?"

Owen shrugged. "Anything you want."

"Please don't take this wrong way. Are you old enough to be a state's attorney?"

Owen laughed, a little ruefully. From Owen's bowed head and slumped shoulders, Tony knew he'd been asked the same thing before. But the kid looked young. Younger than Gio, even though they were probably the same age.

Good-looking, like Gio. Maybe Gio had some height on Owen, but Owen was alive.

"Believe it or not," Owen said, "I'm on my forty-fifth murder trial. I've got a lot of good experience."

He just stated it. There was nothing defensive or aggressive in his tone.

*So much confidence for someone so young,* Tony thought. He was moved. He had a sudden urge to make sure Owen never lost it. He didn't know why.

"You're aware the State of Illinois is set to dismiss the case against Mitchell Weinger, right?" Owen said.

Tony nodded.

Owen said, "I wanted to let you know that after a lot of thought and discussion, we decided that couldn't happen, and we're bringing the case against Mitchell Weinger to trial and putting it in front of a jury."

"Wow. That's … this is really unexpected," Tony said after a moment. "But the last I heard, I mean, as far as I understood it, the case was at the … at the … "

"Daley Center."

"Yes. Thank you. At the Daley Center, and there was no … all the evidence was gone. They said that if it was at the Daley Center, there wasn't going to be a jury trial."

"Yes, that's true," Owen said. "But we got it moved from the Daley Center to Twenty-Sixth and California."

"How the hell did that happen?"

"We made it happen."

"My understanding is, there isn't much chance of winning." Tony saw something flicker across Owen's face. "What I mean to say, there's no evidence, right? It's gone? Vanished?"

"That was never where the strength of the case was."

"Then you've got something else?"

"I do. But I'm not going to lie to you. This is a tough one. There's a lot that has to go right. My partner and I need your help to make it go right."

"Who's your partner?"

"Assistant State's Attorney Mike Goggin. We're a very good team."

Tony considered this. There was a lot he wanted to ask. But he decided not to. Right that second, he was buoyant with a sense of possibility. If he asked, he'd get some hard certainties, and those would probably bring him crashing down.

An ambulance came screaming in and drove straight to the ER entrance. The EMTs jumped out, flung the rear doors open. They removed a stretcher, let the wheels down, and sprinted inside.

"So, what is it you need my help with?" Tony said.

"Remembering. I need to find people that Gio knew, and you might remember things about them. I know this will be painful, but we'll want to go over everything you can remember about the days leading up to Gio's death, the day he died, and the day after he died."

"Everything I can remember? I can remember everything. Everything. A lot of times I wish I couldn't. My daughters ... they spoke to Gio that night. They knew things about him I didn't. They can help you."

"I was trying to figure out a good way to ask if they'd be willing to talk."

Tony sat bolt upright and shook his head no several times. He leveled a finger at Owen. "No. Uh-uh. There's no need to hedge anything. Nothing to figure out. If you want to ask something, just ask it. We buried Gio. I found him. I got to see my son's *body*. I know this won't be pleasant, but by now, we're tougher than that. But there's something no one has been able to give us. Something we've wanted for a long time."

"What is that? I mean, what *do* you want?" Owen asked. "I just want to make sure you don't have ... This isn't a death penalty case. If Mitchell Weinger gets a good lawyer, it's probably not even a life-in-prison case. I want a conviction, you want a conviction, but is that going to leave you feeling cheated?"

After a moment staring through the windshield, Tony said, "I've spent a lot of time thinking about this. In my darker moments? I've wished Mitchell Weinger was dead. Though even at my craziest I know that probably won't happen. But what I really want—what the whole family wants—is peace of mind. No one's been able to offer us that. There's just so much unresolved. And not just for us but that poor girl's family too. Sometimes, I think she's been almost forgotten. Don't you think?"

Owen's response was quick. "Not by me. Her brother still lives in Chicago, but her folks are in Florida. They're very old. This probably sounds bad, but it's easier to focus on Gio. He left a bigger hole. Tinker had her brother but not too many friends. But I haven't forgotten her."

"I didn't mean by you," Tony said absently. He was thinking about wanting Weinger dead and how one night, the urge got the better of him. There was a secret there. He was deeply ashamed of what he'd done. He suspected, briefly, that one day he'd be moved to confess it to Owen. But not today. He didn't want to think any more about it today.

He leapt clear of the memory. "I saw her movie."

"Really? Tinker's movie? The porno?"

"Well, 'porno' might be overstating it. But yeah, Tinker's movie." Tony started laughing. "Her amazing movie. It only got shown in one theater in Chicago. Probably only one theater in the whole country. But

I went. I figured, that movie is the only thing she got to do as an actress. That was her legacy. I figured, Gio loved her. We all thought she was a really nice girl. So, she wanted to act and be seen by people. I wanted to honor that."

"I read a review of it," Owen said.

They were silent for a moment.

Then, Tony asked, "So what's your next move?"

"My next move? I'm going to talk to Cedric Sberna. You know him, right?"

"Not real well," Tony said. "I think I met him two, maybe three times."

"Well, he's saying he won't testify."

Tony scoffed. "Of course he's saying that. Listen, Gregg, I'll be honest. Cedric Sberna … I think he's a real piece of shit."

Owen looked amused. "What makes you say that?"

"Because he lied through his damn teeth to everyone. He was completely uncooperative with us, with the detectives. It was infuriating. Totally uncooperative."

"He's told everyone before that if he had to testify, he would take the Fifth," Owen said.

Tony grew visibly angry. "What the hell for?" He clapped the steering wheel, hard, with his right hand and ran his left hand through his hair.

"If I had to guess, I'd say it's because he's nervous about the cocaine aspect of the case. He thinks he's going to get charged with a drug crime."

"Is he?" Now Tony looked out the window. A pair of nurses got out of a nearby car, chattering.

"No. I couldn't care less about the drugs. Really. I care about murder. That's it. But if he pleads the Fifth, it makes things difficult. From what I can tell, he just doesn't want to admit he had anything to do with drugs."

Tony's tone sharpened. "He better admit it. He was just as involved as Gio was in this cocaine business. And actually, I found out he helped finance this dealing he and Gio did."

You know, Gregg, if the cops had responded to Cedric's 911 call…" Tony's voice caught. He swung his hand toward the picture. Then his voice broke. "If they had responded, there's a good chance my boy would be here now."

Tony turned back to Owen. He steadied himself. "Look, I know you and your partner are going to do a good job. I know you will. I'll just ask you one thing: be straight with me. Don't tell me what you think I want to hear. Don't sugarcoat anything. If there's a problem, if something goes wrong, tell me. I might be—"

Tony looked away. His eyes welled.

"I appreciate what you're doing. Very much. It's not fair of me telling you how much a win or loss is going to matter to me and Maria. But knowing how much effort you're devoting to this ... In the end? We—me, Maria, the girls—we just want some peace of mind. That's what matters."

## CHAPTER 27
*December 12, 1979*

Getting out of Chicago and driving to Lake Forest taxed way more of Gregg Owen's time than he'd wanted to give away on a weeknight. It taxed his time and his patience—over half an hour so far, most of it caught in outbound traffic, another half hour to go, at least, and Owen, fuming, resented every minute. But so far, Cedric Sberna had rebuffed every other effort Owen had made to sit and talk about the trial, and finally, reluctantly, Owen agreed. Driving to Lake Forest like Sberna had demanded was Owen's last civil option. The next step was getting aggressive, and he hoped it wouldn't be required.

Owen had stopped far short of begging and just short of threats, and it was probably his persistence that changed Sberna's mind. Just to stop the calls, if nothing else. Owen had called six times over the past three days, and he'd been making a series of daily calls for a week now.

Owen sat in his living room, legs extended, feet on the coffee table. John Chancellor would be doing the news in ten minutes. He dialed Sberna's number.

This time Sberna answered.

At first, Sberna's tone was indifferent, advanced to irritated, then exasperated, and then back to indifferent. Courteous, at the last, but indifferent nonetheless. Owen thought it was an affect. He thought it sounded as if Sberna had become a little frightened. So, Owen hardened his voice, made it chillier, official, the sound of someone almost out of patience. And at that point, Sberna agreed to meet.

The meeting wasn't actually in Lake Forest but in Lake Bluff, a woodsy, rural-looking village of four square miles, immediately adjacent to Lake Forest.

"I'll be at McCormack's at eight o'clock," Sberna had told Owen but hung up before Owen could ask for directions. Owen had to call the bar and get them from a harried waitress.

Right before eight, Owen came to the intersection of Route 176 and the Skokie Highway and found McCormack's. It was in a converted house, hard against the shoulder of the road, with white aluminum siding and an enormous green shamrock on the street-facing side. A long, narrow parking lot extended down the road with a few cars parked in it. Most of them were big thirsty American vehicles, several years old. Cars like that had been sold, used, for next to nothing when the gas crisis peaked. But it was the Porsche Targa that caught his attention. He didn't have to wonder whose it was.

Owen stepped out of his car. On a leafless tree not far from the door, the wind caused a dozen frayed, faded yellow ribbons tied to the trunk to twist and flap. One of the cars had a bumper sticker reading *Ayatollah Assahola* with a drawing of Khomeini in a style similar to the anti-Semitic caricatures from Nazi propaganda.

He pulled the door open and was hit by a heavy haze of smoke and the smells of stale beer, of something faintly oily, of boiling meat. Owen used to make music in places that reeked just like this. It was redolent of younger days. Potent. Pungent.

The place was empty—maybe thirteen or fourteen others drinking quietly. Van Morrison was playing on the jukebox—a Rock-ola, bright with all the glowing-marquee, neon colors. Moving past it, he glanced through the plastic window at the intricate guts of the machine and thought of car engines, then of the city, then a factory, and as the mechanisms did their work, of pistons, die cuts, stamps, making a noise like gavels.

Then he saw a man sitting alone in a booth, far from the bar. He wore a red, deep v-cut velour shirt, with a couple of chains glittering from his tangle of chest hair. That was Sberna.

Owen was suddenly conscious of his suit. He noticed a few drinkers at the bar watching him. They weren't hostile. They were more curious than anything else. When Sberna noticed Owen, he didn't look much of anything. He stared across the room to Owen, then gestured.

Owen walked back toward the booth. Sberna stood. He was tall, trim, preposterously good-looking.

"You must be Gregg Owen." He extended a hand. When Owen took it, Sberna's handshake was warm and oily, without force.

"Must be," Owen said blandly. He let go of Sberna's hand. "Glad to meet you, Mr. Sberna, and I really appreciate the time."

He sat.

"Just Cedric. Please. Did you have any trouble finding the place? Hope you got here easy." There was nothing meaningful in his tone. He didn't seem much concerned either way.

A waitress approached the table, carrying an enormous tumbler of scotch. She stopped a few feet away and put on a fake, congenial smile. That smile was currency, just like a hundred-dollar bill. She placed the glass in front of Sberna, who got a wolfish look on his face.

"Thanks, honey. Hey, listen—" but she was gone. He turned back to Owen. "Fucking bitch ... She didn't think you might want something?"

"I don't," Owen said.

"Brown Eyed Girl" yielded to "Crazy Love." Sberna drummed his fingertips along with the music.

"I don't come here that often," Sberna volunteered. "I don't like parking my Porsche that close to the street, you know?"

"Sure," Owen said, dismissive. He was resolute—there was no way he was asking about the Porsche.

Owen noticed the rhythm of Sberna's fingers was faster than the rhythm of the song. He watched Sberna a little more closely. After a moment, he noticed a faint, dusty streak of powder on Sberna's mustache, directly under his right nostril. Owen made himself look away.

"So, Gregg Owen. What are we talking about here?" Sberna put a little false bravado into the question. He sat back and pressed his lips into a thin line. His face had an almost idiot serenity, but his eyes were hard and very red.

Owen had already told him on the phone what they were there to discuss. As he drove, he'd been thinking that Sberna's willingness to meet signaled he could be reasonable.

"It's like I said already the other day, Cedric. We're coming to trial soon for the murders of Gio Messina and Tinker Moore." Owen let the names hang there, resonating, but Sberna was looking down at the table, rattling the ice in his glass. "You're the one witness we've got against Weinger. If we want to tag that motherfucker, we need you. We need you on the stand, telling the jury exactly what you told the police."

When Owen said *motherfucker*, Sberna became attentive.

"Are you kidding me? Uh-uh. No. I'm not testifying." He snorted, shook his head. Then, decisive, emphatic: "I can't take the risk."

He looked right at Owen, as if checking for a reaction.

Owen didn't give one. He was trying to figure out what Sberna meant. He had an idea what it might be. Finally, he said, "Risk of what? What possible risk could there be?"

Sberna watched the tabletop but didn't answer. A ring of water on the green Formica had formed from condensation on his glass, and Sberna ran a finger back and forth through it. He stopped and wiped his finger on his pants, then began absently playing with the jewelry on his neck—a tiny gold crucifix and a small spoon, both on chains, that Sberna rubbed between his thumb and forefinger.

"This is just about murder, right? Gio and Tinker's murder?" His eyes were still on the table.

The question seemed nonsensical. Deliberate, goading, Owen asked, "Is there another murder I need to know about?"

"Crazy Love" went off; "Caravan" came on. Sberna brightened when the song started. He dropped the jewelry and slapped the table.

He said, "You like music? You ever see *The Last Waltz*? That part where Van Morrison's doing this tune? Best part of the whole fucking movie. I don't give a shit about The Band—" the words were falling all over each other, "—I mean, they've always sounded kind of brown to me, you know? But my brother wanted to go, so I went. He sent his request in for the ticket lottery when Dylan and The Band toured a couple years back, when they played at the stadium, but he didn't get them. My dad couldn't even get his hands on any. Shit. The movie had me bored out of my mind till then, but my brother had dragged me along … "

Sberna seemed suddenly sapped of a measure of energy. He continued. "But when Van Morrison came out—looking like the Lucky Charms leprechaun in a red suit—goddamn. That part was fucking amazing … " He trailed off.

Owen took advantage of the pause. "Cedric, help me out here. I'm trying to understand this. One of your good friends is murdered, and I mean in a pretty brutal way, and his girlfriend gets killed too—who you were friends with, am I right?—and you don't want to help us nail the piece of shit who did it? We've got to get this case together, stat. We can't waste time."

Sberna became surly. He flapped his hand dismissively and said, "Wasting time? Man, you're lucky I'm even here. And why does everyone keep saying Gio and me were such good friends?"

Owen mastered a nasty reaction. He tried another angle. "Do you know how important you are for this case, Cedric? Let me lay the cards out here. We're really depending on you."

"That's a drag," Sberna said, full of false, morbid sympathy. "I hope you've got more than just me because I'm not getting involved. Like I said."

"You're already involved."

"This is why I didn't even want to come back." He was incensed.

Owen had no idea what he was talking about.

"Come back from where?"

"I loved Sicily, man."

Owen paused and made sure Sberna could tell he was cooling down, changing topics. "That's where you were?"

"Sicily and Milan."

"Lucky ... "

"I guess. Milan was all right. Got some cool clothes there."

Owen found himself irritated all out of proportion by the *I guess*.

"The ones you're wearing?"

Sberna scoffed, and shook his head. "No, I wouldn't wear them to a place like this."

"And then you went to Sicily?"

"Yeah. I was there a while. Great, great place. I loved it." Sberna became animated. "Did you see *The Godfather*? It was exactly like that. I mean, at least when you got out of the city."

"What city were you in? Palermo? Syracuse?"

"Cefalu. But a lot of time up in the mountains, mainly. Seriously, just like *The Godfather*. There were even guys walking around, carrying shotguns."

Sberna watched Owen for a moment. He tipped his glass back and let the last drops of water fall on his tongue. He put the glass back down. He said, "You don't need me."

"We do need you."

"No, you don't. And you're not getting me." Sberna stood up, started putting on his coat.

"Cedric, one second. Just do me this favor. Think about it. No matter what you feel about me, the Courts, the Chicago cops, whoever—Gio and Tinker didn't deserve to die like they did." Owen repeated it, enunciating each word: "They didn't deserve to die like that."

Sberna said, "No one does."

*All right*, Owen thought. *At least we've got that.*

He said, "We have a chance to get the fucker who did it. Who probably would have killed you if you'd still been there—"

Owen was offering this up to Sberna, a pass on running away, leaving Tinker to die. "Just think about it."

"Maybe," Sberna said and walked away, across the floor, stopping near the bar to blow a kiss at the waitress, and then out the door.

Owen watched him go. It didn't look to Owen like Sberna had left enough money on the table to cover his last drink and a tip. He added a couple of dollars.

The jukebox was finishing "Jailbreak," and it started playing "The Boys Are Back in Town." Owen stood up to leave. He'd been there for less than twenty minutes.

As he drove he replayed their conversation in his head and flashed on what had made Sberna reluctant to appear at the trial, what he'd meant when he talked about risk. He had to think it through, but he was pretty sure he might be right. He resolved to test it when they met the next time. Owen wasn't done with Sberna yet.

## Chapter 28

Owen stood next to Sberna a week later around lunchtime, eating sausages at a crowded counter place on Rush Street. It was loud with conversation and shouted food orders. There was a black-and-white television on a shelf above the register, tuned to the news, with the volume all the way down.

The second meeting wasn't going well. Or at least, not much better than their meeting in Lake Bluff. The air around them was quick, terse, a little strained, and Owen was genuinely beginning to despair of getting Sberna in court and talking.

"He's going to go free, Cedric," Owen was saying. "He's going to walk."

Sberna was unresponsive, as if he hadn't heard.

Owen grasped at whatever argument came to him. "What if he does it to someone else? What if he does this again? What if he goes after Mickey?"

Sberna shrugged, utterly indifferent. He took a bite of his sausage. Owen felt the same impulse he'd felt last week to jab Sberna's eye. Maybe this time follow it with a cross to his nose.

With his mouth full, Sberna said, "I don't see Mickey anymore."

Owen could see a mash of bun, meat, and peppers when Sberna spoke. He had to look away.

"Just for argument's sake, what if Weinger goes free and he decides he needs to tie up loose ends?"

Sberna paused, indifferent no longer. Now, he was clearly concerned. It seemed his eyes were trying to look everywhere at once. "What does 'loose ends' mean?"

Owen pointed a finger at him. "What if he comes looking for you?"

Sberna's shoulders got rigid.

He said to Sberna, "Do it for Gio. For your friend. You know Tony Messina. You know the family. You've been to their house, right? You can do a good thing here, man. Help us help them."

Sberna looked pained. He put his paper plate on the countertop. He chewed his mustache. Then, he raised his hands and gripped his head with both hands.

*Come on, man,* Owen thought. He was doing a little psychic screaming. *Come on. Come on. Come on.*

Sberna inhaled, exhaled. Did it again. Ragged. He said, "Only if you give me immunity. I want immunity."

Owen struggled against anger that came strafing up through his ribs. It hurt like he'd been kicked. He shut his eyes. Opened them back up. He said, "You don't want it."

He was thinking, *Immunity from what? What have you done? Are you about to tell me about something you did that's going to mess everything up?* He looked up at the television and saw the opening titles for *The Young and the Restless* on the screen.

He said again, "You don't want it. It makes things worse for everyone. Worse for you. Worse for us."

Sberna turned on him, took a step closer. He had the outraged expression of someone who'd had the rules changed on him just before the end of a game. "What the fuck does that mean? What the fuck? Worse for me? Worse for me how?"

Owen kept his voice low, steady, unwavering. "Think it through, Cedric. You get up there, granted immunity as a witness for the prosecution? Oh, please. Everyone's going to think you're lying. Come on. Give me a break. They're going to think you're either lying for us, trying to save your own ass, or both. They're going to look at Weinger and say, 'Well, if Cedric Sberna is pinning it all on him and he has immunity, then Cedric Sberna must have done something really, really bad.'"

He didn't mention he and Goggin had never offered immunity to anyone. Ever. The question itself—amateur and dumb—could only be asked once someone had decided they very well might do the right thing. When you admit a possibility, you're almost making it a certainty. Plus, he felt he'd been correct the other day about what Cedric had meant by "taking a risk." It was time to test it.

He said, "Look, man, listen when I tell you this: you don't want immunity, but more important, you don't need it."

"Bullshit." Sberna's smile was warped and spiteful. He almost whispered, "You're trying to trick me."

"It's not bullshit. You don't understand how little I give a fuck about cocaine. I couldn't possibly give less of a fuck."

Cedric drew himself up. Trapped and poised to fight his way out through it. "You're lying to me."

"I'm not lying."
"Put it in writing."
"No."
"Why?" Sberna was incredulous.

Owen's mind was moving as fast as he could make it go. "I put it in writing, then you can be damn sure it comes out during the trial. Now, not only will the jury know that you did something, they'll know exactly what it was you did. They're going to say, 'Oh yeah, Cedric Sberna, cocaine dealer—'"

Cedric started. Owen kept going. "And when the *Sun-Times* or the *Tribune* or WGN or the *Reader* report it—and you better believe they will—you're going to be Cedric Sberna, coke-dealing drug freak, forever.

"But one more time: You don't need to worry about cocaine. We don't care about cocaine." He enunciated every word.

Sberna put the last, gnawed bit of sausage and peppers on his plate, slid it away. "I wasn't a drug fiend. I wasn't any fucking dealer either. I didn't even use it much. Swear to God."

"You don't have anything to worry about."

"Gregg, I've got everything to worry about." As if Owen had a notion of what Sberna was talking about, Sberna nodded, deliberate, knowing. He looked objectively sad.

One time, while he was wandering around backstage, someplace in Detroit, Owen thought it was, he watched the girlfriend of someone or other take a massive snort of cocaine. She sat up straight and rigid, the same way everyone does when the coke hits their system. But her face didn't dissolve into elation or something close to ecstatic the way it usually does. Her eyes got wider, her face went ghostly, she gasped. Owen saw it clearly: she was terrified. She'd done too much, almost certainly more than she was used to. The onslaught of the drug might overtake her, or it might burn itself out. It was touch and go. She wore a singular expression—the flash of understanding that you'd made a grave mistake and couldn't do anything to get out of it.

The girl recovered within a few seconds. But Owen remembered that look, too, from when he was a kid and saw another kid on the playground, standing on the very top of the monkey bars, trying to keep his balance but losing it, and as the kid's arms were pinioning, he had that same expression.

And Owen saw that Sberna had it now.

Sberna was clearly terrified. He'd gotten in deep. He knew it. There was no happy ending looming. He could testify, or he could choose otherwise. Either way, Cedric obviously understood it was like being offered a choice of whether you wanted the bamboo splinter hammered under the nail of the left index finger or the finger on the right.

Sberna had to figure out his own best steps to self-preservation, and it was clear he had no confidence in his ability to do so.

Owen watched him, then he said, "We need you, man. I think you'll do great." He spoke as if they'd already agreed. He noticed Sberna wasn't protesting. "It's better this way. Way better, doing it without immunity or without us forcing you."

That might have been a phrase too far.

Sberna recoiled, belligerent again.

Owen was pissed at himself for the misstep.

Sberna was caustic. "You can't force me. I know my rights, Gregg." He spoke like the name was an accusation. "I know you can't force me to talk."

"We can actually." Owen's voice was weary. "We can subpoena you."

"I'll take the Fifth."

Owen heard a slight quaver in Sberna's voice. Between having an ear for music and observing Breen work a witness, he heard what a lot of others might miss.

"And a killer walks away. I'm giving you my word, nothing will come of the coke. We're not going to concern ourselves—at all, in any way—about you and Gio selling cocaine. I don't know if I can make it any clearer."

"Stop saying I was selling cocaine." Sberna considered things for a minute. "You're lying. I know you're lying."

"No, man, I'm doing my job. That's it. That's all I want—to do my job. I've got two murder victims and two families that have been absolutely destroyed. And I've got the son of a bitch who did it. I'm not threatening you. I'm not lying to you. I'm asking you to help us out."

Sberna kept staring at Owen, but his defiance was fading. Owen said, "Weinger did it, right, Cedric? I've got the guy who did it? Weinger was the one?"

"Yeah. It was Weinger." Sberna's eyes were getting wet.

Owen put a hand on Sberna's shoulder. "Okay. Go home, man. Just go home and think about what we said, and I'll call you sometime tomorrow."

"Call me Wednesday or Thursday."

"Okay. Wednesday or Thursday."

Sberna nodded several times, turned, and walked from the restaurant out onto Rush Street.

On Wednesday, Owen needed to call Sberna again, but right then he couldn't bear listening to Sberna's on-the-fence bullshit. It was almost time to go home. He'd been putting off the call all day.

Owen decided on another call instead, for an entirely different case, and leafed through the Calvin Franklin file, looking for the number of Larry Longwood, the public defender assigned to the case.

Calvin Franklin had killed his roommate of five years, Melvin Prescott. That much was beyond dispute. They'd argued before, but that time, they'd both been seriously drunk.

Prescott had stashed some money in a bureau drawer in his room and accused Franklin of stealing it.

Franklin was outraged. He told Prescott to go fuck himself.

Prescott took up a poker from their fireplace instead, clutched it in his fist, aimed it at Franklin's head, and hurled it like a javelin.

Prescott missed. The poker hit the wall and clattered onto the floorboards. Franklin disappeared into his bedroom and reappeared holding a .32 as Prescott grabbed for the poker again.

Franklin leveled the pistol and fired. Then fired again. And again.

One of the bullets hit Prescott in the back of the head, and he died right there.

The cops came and arrested Franklin for murder and took him away. The case came to Owen's courtroom, and Longwood got involved, and a jury was about to start hearing the arguments.

From Owen's vantage, this wasn't murder. Manslaughter, maybe, but not murder. Franklin hadn't put forethought into it. He hadn't planned on shooting Prescott. Owen felt certain killing hadn't crossed Franklin's mind at all. The two of them had been dead drunk. Prescott would have probably killed Franklin with the poker, and Franklin figured the pistol was a good deterrent.

If a jury heard the case, it was murder or nothing. They didn't have the authority to reduce the charges. They had to decide whether or not Franklin murdered Prescott, and Owen figured that when they considered the cold, undisputed fact that Franklin left the room to get his gun, then came back and used it, the verdict wouldn't go in Franklin's favor.

If a jury heard the case, Owen was duty-bound as a prosecutor to go for broke, and he didn't want to. He'd call Longwood and try to convince him to take a bench trial—no jury, just the judge, who did have the power to make a distinction between cold-blooded and accidental. He couldn't see Longwood saying no.

Owen looked out the window, saw the cityscape with a thin corona of gray haze set against an immaculate blue sky. A gust of wind made the window rattle softly.

He reached for the phone to call Longwood, but it rang before he touched it.

He picked it up.

"Gregg Owen," he said.

"Hey there." It was Goggin's voice. He sounded casual and too upbeat. "Listen, do you have a quick second to come talk to me about something? It's important."

Goggin's tone was a clear put-on. Owen was immediately on alert.

"Be right over." He hung up the phone, stood, and put on his suit jacket.

When Owen got there, the door to Goggin's office was shut. There was a gap between the walls and door and the ceiling, and Owen heard Goggin's voice—calm, easy, soothing—say, "Listen to me. It's all right. Listen. We're going to figure this out, okay?"

Owen knocked.

Goggin opened the door a few inches. He and Owen looked at each other. Their expressions did the speaking.

*What in the hell is going on?*

*You're not going to believe this one.*

Goggin opened the door and stepped out, but before he pulled it closed, Owen saw someone familiar on the small couch inside, bent over, elbows on his knees, face in his hands.

Owen was surprised, baffled. He said, "Is that Terry *Hake*?"

Goggin nodded wearily. "Yeah, that's Hake. And he's pretty fucking upset."

"What about?"

"I think you need to come in and hear this for yourself."

Owen had met Hake through Goggin, who'd met Hake through Mike Ficaro when Ficaro was prosecuting Henry Brisbon for the I-57 Murders. Brisbon and a few accomplices had forced a car off the road on Interstate 57 and dragged the female driver out of the vehicle. Brisbon forced her to strip and then put a shotgun into her crotch and pulled the trigger. Brisbon watched her suffer for several minutes before shooting her through the throat.

A few hours later the crew did it again, this time victimizing an engaged couple.

"Kiss your last kiss," Brisbon told them, then shot each one in the face. He was later given a thousand-year sentence.

Terry Hake was Ficaro's assistant during the trial, and because Ficaro and Goggin were good friends, Goggin periodically dropped by the trial to see how it was going. That was the way Hake got to know him.

Hake was deeply impressed with Goggin, and when Goggin was his supervisor at Branch 66, Hake sought out his advice and approval. After he met Owen, Hake paid a lot of attention to the way Goggin and Owen worked during a trial and often watched them try cases.

Owen liked Hake well enough. Their relationship wasn't a deep one—they were friendly and collegial. Hake was reasonable, coolheaded, a decent lawyer. Like Owen, Hake rose through the ranks pretty quickly. Like Owen, he was sometimes referred to as a "golden boy" by other ASAs who thought that rise was *too* quick.

*Golden boy* wasn't meant as a compliment.

But right now, Owen was looking at a different Terry Hake.

The flesh around Hake's eyes was swollen. His eyes were glassy and bloodshot. His face was pale and bloodless.

"Terry, man," Owen said. "What's going on?"

Hake didn't answer at first. He kept his eyes on the floor.

Owen sat down next to him on the couch.

He felt bad for Hake's upset—whatever the cause—because it must have been big to bring him here to Goggin's office, where, it appeared to Owen, Hake might be on the verge of falling apart.

It was off-putting at the same time, for precisely the same reason: Hake looked like he was coming undone, and while that was one thing if it happened in private, it was different making two of your colleagues watch. Owen was feeling a strange tension between pity and discomfort.

"Come on, Terry, what's up? What's going on?" Owen clapped a reassuring hand on Hake's shoulder.

"I can't take it anymore," Hake said. "I *can't take it anymore.*"

"Take what?"

"I never wanted to do this. I never wanted to be a lawyer." He didn't look at Owen, just turned his head in Owen's direction, kept his eyes looking downward. "I wanted to be an FBI agent. Law school was my father's idea. He wanted me to be a lawyer. I did it for him. I wish I'd never listened to him."

Hake trailed off, put his face in his hands.

Owen took his own hand from Hake's shoulder. Was Hake actually trembling?

Owen looked toward Goggin, who was standing nearby, watching. Goggin lifted his chin a tiny bit, as if saying to Owen, *keep going*.

Owen said, "What are you talking about, Terry?"

"I'm sick of it. I can't take it. I can't take the scumbags. The slimeballs. The thieves. The crooks." Hake was talking to the floor. Then he reared his head and looked Owen right in the eyes, enraged. "And I can't take 'Lucius in the fucking box.'"

Hake looked down again. His anger had an almost physical force. Owen sighed to himself. He wasn't sure how to proceed.

"It makes me *sick*," Hake said.

"Terry, we've all seen it. We all see it now. I mean, Mike and I, we've both worked in … and you, too—didn't you work in gun court? Auto theft court? With Judge Devine? You knew what was going on. You knew about Dollars Devine."

Hake buried his face in his hands.

Judge Devine was known among the ASAs as *Dollars Devine*. It was in his courtroom that Owen was first made fully aware of regular, routine corruption. What happened in his courtroom was the same thing happening in courtrooms all over Cook County.

It started daily, around 7:30 in the morning. The clerk arrived and found upward of 125 case files bundled and waiting.

The clerk went through the files and culled any case where the defendant posted bond but did not have a lawyer. Most of the accused didn't have representation. They had a hard enough time affording bond, let alone a defense.

At 8:30, the same small group of lawyers as yesterday, last week, and the week before that—the same small group, going back months—walked into the courtroom to where the clerk was sitting up front with his reorganized files and, a few moments later, walked out with a stack of ten, twelve files.

These were always shit lawyers, lacking the smarts or skills to take their legal careers very far. They became known as *the Miracle Workers*.

Once they had their files, the Miracle Workers hit the hallways outside the courtroom, where the defendants queued up. Every defendant posted a hundred-dollar bond. That was the standard for inconsequential crimes.

They might have been arrested for graffiti, for a bar fight, for shoplifting baby formula or a silk scarf, for holding an illegal gun. Pissant stuff, usually.

When the accused arrived for trial, the city of Chicago returned the hundred-dollar bond, withholding a ten-dollar fee and giving ninety dollars back. Then the Miracle Workers swept in, calling the names in the files, promising every defendant an ace defense—charges dropped, or at least a seriously favorable outcome, guaranteed.

The Miracle Worker approached the accused and told them Judge Devine had assigned him to their case.

Dollars Devine had done no such thing—hadn't even taken the bench yet—but he'd play along, browbeating the ASA's into making deals, maybe dismissing the case altogether.

For Devine's trouble, a Miracle Worker paid the judge a thirty-dollar referral. The clerk got a ten-dollar consideration. The lawyers put the remaining fifty dollars in their pockets.

The Bar Association provided different private attorneys every day, but they got very few cases. New lawyers couldn't make much headway unless they got themselves dirty too. They couldn't earn a solid reputation as a defense lawyer, which meant that later on, they couldn't earn anything close to decent money. They'd have to do corporate law or maybe become litigators instead.

The scam was easy and everywhere. Everyone knew about it.

One time Owen was passing Devine's courtroom at the end of the day, and he recognized the bar attorney who was just coming out—a young guy, who right then looked almost venomous. Owen couldn't recall his name.

"How'd it go today?" Owen asked.

"It sucked. Like usual. A waste of time."

"What do you mea—"

"I got one bond slip. One. I need to make some money, man. One bond slip isn't enough to make a goddamn *car* payment."

The guy stalked away. It was a familiar story that Owen had heard from a lot of different people. He'd talked about this with Goggin. What bothered them most was that these up-and-coming defense lawyers were essentially screwed. The choice was between becoming dirty or staying broke.

It was different for Owen and Goggin. They were prosecutors.

Owen knew there wasn't any way to stop corrupt people from doing corrupt things. But he knew not to let it eat at him. He knew the only thing to do was prosecute his cases as best he could and give the graft a wide berth.

But they came for him eventually, testing him, checking his reaction.

Owen was in the men's room, washing his hands. He'd just had Devine rule against him, and an absolutely guilty shoplifter walked away. The shoplifter's guilt was never in doubt, but Owen could tell the outcome right from the start. He didn't waste his resources sparring against the inevitable.

Then Jim the clerk was right there at his side as Owen stood in front of the sink.

"About that shoplifter," Jim said. "We really appreciate you taking it easy on the poor goof."

Jim held something toward Owen, and out of blind reflex, Owen reached to take it.

Jim was holding a fifty-dollar bill, and he let it go just as Owen pulled his hand back.

The money hit the floor.

Owen felt his hands shake.

"Fucking moron," he said. "You stupid fucking asshole. Who do you think you are? What the fuck do you think I am? Shove that money up your ass. Don't you ever pull that shit with me again. Do you hear me?"

Owen was enraged. Jim was trying to be stoic. The two of them glared at each other, wordless.

A moment passed.

The door opened. The bailiff came in, heading for the urinal, hands already working his belt. Jim stepped around him, walked out and away.

The bailiff stopped.

He knew he'd come in on something.

His eyes caught the money lying on the tiles.

"What's that?" he said to Owen.

Owen offered the barest shrug. "Don't know. Don't know where it came from, but I do know it isn't mine."

The bailiff reached down and picked the bill up. Owen turned and gave his hands another quick wash.

"I'll hold on to this just in case someone comes looking," the bailiff said as Owen dried his hands.

"That's a good idea," Owen said. "But I bet no one will."

The bailiff slid the bill into his pocket. He stepped in front of the urinal, undid his belt, started pissing. Owen went back to his office, beginning to understand what had just happened was only the first time. He wondered how long before someone else came and tried again.

And *Lucius in the box*? It was another scam, this one in the courtroom of Judge Maurice Pompey, worse than Devine by far because it involved payoffs for getting murder charges dropped. Lucius Robinson, a one-time bodyguard for Muhammed Ali, was Pompey's bailiff and acted as Pompey's bagman. To signal someone had paid them off, Lucius would come out and sit in the jury box while that person was being arraigned. When anyone said Lucius was in the box, it meant the case was fixed.

Goggin and Owen both had a little experience with the judge and the bailiff.

In the future, Robinson and Pompey would become a very big deal for Goggin, Owen, and every ASA in Cook County. And an especially big deal for Terry Hake.

Hake lifted his face from his hands. "Yeah, I worked in Devine's court. And it made me sick then too."

Owen felt himself becoming irritated. *Get a grip, Terry. Be a grown-up.*

Goggin cut in. "Terry, we all hate it. *Hate it.* But there's nothing we can do except do our jobs the best we can. Owen and I have been there. We know how you're feeling. We'll help you any way we can, but this is the job we've chosen."

Hake shook his head and went back to looking at the floor. He said, "But it's not the job I signed up for. I can't do it anymore. I *won't* do it anymore."

Things went silent. Owen was thinking, *You 'won't do it anymore'? What does that mean? What are you up to?*

The silence stretched. Finally, Goggin cleared his throat.

"I have an idea," he said. "Gregg, I was thinking, Terry should talk with Ficaro. He'll figure something out."

Owen felt relieved. "I think that's a great idea."

"Terry?"

Hake considered it. Finally, he nodded. "I'm fine with that."

Goggin picked up the phone and dialed. After a moment he said, "Mikey? Goggin. I'm good. You?

"Okay, so, I'm here in my office with Owen and Terry Hake. Owen and I both think it might be a good idea for you to hear what Terry has to say. Okay if I bring him over? Great. See you in a sec."

He hung up. "Owen, you going to be around for a few? If you want to go back to your office, I'll give you a call after we're set with Ficaro."

Owen said, "Yeah, I need to finish up a few things. I'll be here."

Goggin turned to Hake. "Okay. Let's go have a talk with Ficaro."

Hake nodded and stood up. Goggin opened the door. Hake went through it without another word. Owen left and headed back to his office.

About thirty minutes later, Goggin called Owen's desk.

"Jesus," he said. "I don't know what the hell that was. I mean, it just came out of *nowhere*. I mean, I'm just sitting there at my desk. There's a knock, and then there's Hake."

"What did Ficaro say?"

"Nothing much. He just listened. Then I left."

"Did Hake stay?"

"Yeah, Ficaro asked him to stick around."

"Let me ask you," Owen said. "Am I wrong for being a little … "

Goggin gave a sharp laugh. Owen heard him sit heavily in his chair.

"For being freaked the fuck out?" Goggin said. "No, you're not wrong. That blindsided me. Completely. I've seen people break like that at funerals but at work? In someone's office? And over something so … obvious? Where in hell has he been? He's worked here for *years*. It's just hitting him now?"

"I feel for him. I guess. Sort of. But … I mean, keep it together, man. I'll tell you exactly what I was thinking after he left, though."

"I bet you it was the same thing I was thinking."

"I was thinking, no way I can work with him again. Not a chance. Anyone who goes to pieces like that when he's feeling pressured ... who knows what he's liable to say? I'm never going to trust he can keep a confidence. Is that what you were thinking?"

"Yeah, that's precisely what I was thinking," Goggin said. "Word for word."

It wasn't the last they, or anyone, would hear of Terry Hake.

## Chapter 29
*Friday, December 28, 1979*

Owen figured he'd give diplomacy one last serious try.

He reasoned that for this case, for Jay, for Tony Messina, he could fake an interest in a non-work rapport with Sberna, of smoothing over a bumpy start, even a semblance of friendship. Whatever worked.

As he was picking up his phone, he paused and asked himself if he was positive he could stomach the effort. He thought he could. He was pretty sure of it.

He told Sberna to forget the trial, the coke, the murder, the law. Forget subpoenas and forget the Fifth Amendment. "Cedric, I think we got off on the wrong foot. Let's go out," he said. "Hit some clubs, meet some girls. Let's get to know each other a little better. It's on me."

Sberna agreed almost immediately. Owen guessed Sberna wouldn't be able to resist high times out on the town.

At Sberna's suggestion, they met at Faces, on Rush Street. The club wasn't exclusive but it was technically private, and you had to buy a membership. Sberna had paid fifty dollars to be a member for life.

As Owen walked in with Sberna, he fleetingly wondered if Gio had been a member—it seemed likely enough—and then a stray thought arced across his mind that if Gio had been a lifetime member, probably only a dollar's worth of the fee had paid for itself.

It was very dim, the way most clubs were, and lit with rows of vanity bulbs and strips of red and blue and green neon that made corners and alcoves into small lightless zones set off from the dance floor and the bar.

"Don't Leave Me This Way" was roaring over the sound system.

It might have been more crowded than it seemed because most of the people looked like phantoms and shadows in contrast to the light.

What patrons were visible danced in pairs on the dance floor—an elderly couple was in the middle of it all, dancing slowly, one in the other's arms, oblivious to everyone, everything else—or moving to and from the bar. Toward the back of the club, strong white light glared at regular intervals as customers went into or left the restrooms.

As Sberna led them through the club, Owen saw women walking past and checking the two of them out. One woman wearing a scarlet, double-knit pantsuit, her dark hair in an artfully rugged shag, stepped in front of Sberna. He took her hand and raised it over her head and, after she did a single pirouette, leaned in toward her ear to say something that made her laugh. Then she went away.

Owen and Sberna took a booth in the back corner of the club, where it was quiet enough to hear each other. A waitress materialized and Sberna asked for a double Johnny Walker Black on the rocks. Owen asked for seltzer with lime.

The Blondie song "Heart of Glass" started up. Sberna said, "Not drinking much tonight?"

"I'm not much of a drinker any night," Owen said.

"Are you, like, a Mormon or in Synanon or something?"

"No, not at all. I just hate the way it tastes. I have a hard time getting it down."

Sberna seemed to consider it and nodded. Then he shifted in his seat and reached into his coat pocket, removing a rectangle of wood slightly smaller than a credit card, and maybe ¼ inch thick. Sberna started prising the top open.

He asked Owen. "Want a bump?"

"What are you doing? Put it away." Cedric put it out of sight. Owen said, "You carry it around in that?"

Sberna said with some pride, "Yeah. There's always moisture in cocaine, and if whatever you're storing it in is glass or plastic, the moisture doesn't go anywhere, so the coke can clump up. That thing is wood, so it draws the moisture out. It's Honduran mahogany. And the hinges are pretty tight too, so it won't just open and spill all over the place."

Owen said, "Don't ever show me anything, okay? If anyone makes any trouble, it could cause me a lot of problems."

"No one's going to cause a problem," Sberna said, absently. He watched the dance floor for a long moment. "See that old couple dancing? That's the owner."

Owen turned. The music changed to "More Than a Woman," but the couple kept on at the same tempo. When he turned back, Sberna was looking at him.

"How'd you get into all this? Being a lawyer, I mean. A prosecutor."

Owen picked at a piece of lime pulp stuck to the rim of his glass. "It's a long, long story. It doesn't matter."

"It's early, man. We got all night."

Owen put his glass down and pushed it away, then he folded his hands. "Before this, I was in bands for my whole life. I was a keyboard player. And then something happened. It involved a girl."

Sberna pointed his finger. "Hold on. Did you get in trouble with some groupie?"

Owen said, "Pretty much."

"What bands were you in? Would I have heard of you?"

Another song had started, "Disco Inferno." Sberna listened for a moment, bobbing his head, and then sang along, "I can't stop when my spunk gets hot." He laughed and looked at Owen meaningfully—as if to say, *Yeah, here we are, two men, out on the town in Chicago, their spunk hot, looking for chicks.*

Owen didn't think those were the right lyrics.

"You may have heard of my second band. Shady Daze."

Sberna looked incredulous.

"No shit? For real?"

"I joined the American Breed—" here, Sberna made quiet cry of amazement "—and then I was in this band called Jerico."

Sberna slapped his palm against the table. "This is unbelievable."

Owen could see Sberna was genuinely excited.

Sberna said, "I saw you at Rush Up, I saw you at Mothers, I saw you at—" Sberna went on to list a dozen venues, dates, and the other bands on the various bills. They sounded correct. "I loved Jerico. Loved them. Fucking-A. And the band broke up?"

"Well, I quit—because of a chick—but the band broke up a year or so after that. Most of them are in other groups now."

Sberna must have signaled for another round without Owen knowing because the waitress was back. She put Sberna's scotch down first, then Owen's seltzer, smiled, and walked away.

Owen saw Sberna was still watching him. Owen could see in Sberna's face that he, Owen, had instantly taken on new depths and dimensions in Sberna's estimation. Then Sberna looked off into the distance. A minute passed, then another. Owen sipped and sipped at his seltzer. He suspected something significant was about to be said. He saw Sberna take a deep inhale.

"All right, Gregg. Let me think about this." Sberna exhaled noisily. His eyes looked past Owen, at something on the other side of the room. Owen saw an oily smile break over Sberna's face. Sberna nodded and held up a finger.

"I'll be back in a minute," Sberna said. He stood, picked his tumbler up, drained it, and put it back down. He walked away.

The music changed over. Marvin Gaye's "Got to Give It Up" started, and Owen watched a dozen couples hurry to the dance floor.

*No more standin' there against the walls, finally got myself together, baby …*

Owen watched one woman in a vivid, electric-blue dress as she danced. Her partner was a slight, nervous-looking man, awkwardly trying to keep pace with her. She had her eyes shut, hands up, shaking her hips, swaying. She didn't look like Sheri, but something there reminded him of her. He sipped the last of his seltzer.

*All the young ladies are so fine, movin' your body, easy, with no doubts…*

When he looked again, Owen saw the woman's partner was gone. She remained on the dance floor. She was really getting into it, dancing by herself. A few strands of hair stuck to her perspiring forehead.

*Keep on dancin', baby, like a lady …*

Marvin Gaye was singing to her alone.

It was a long song. When he looked at his watch, he realized with some irritation Sberna had been gone for about ten minutes.

The Sugar Hill Gang replaced Marvin Gaye. Owen absently tapped his fingers against the tabletop. Sberna's absence was making him angry.

"Rapper's Delight" was a long song too. Owen tried following the torrent of words, but Sberna was really pissing him off. He turned to watch the area nearest the bathrooms.

*Bust you out with my super sperm …*

Owen was about to walk to the bathroom, barge in, and ask Sberna what the fuck he was doing, but he saw the door open and Sberna come out. Sberna let the door start closing, but it opened again, and the woman who'd spoken with Sberna earlier, the one in the scarlet pantsuit, followed him. The door opened again, and the slight, nervous man emerged. He watched Sberna and the woman walk away. His expression was shocked, incredulous, mildly disgusted.

Sberna nodded at Owen as he came back to the booth. When Sberna got close, Owen saw his lips looked mashed and swollen. There was a distinct white streak on Sberna's mustache, right under his nostrils. With a little revulsion, Owen saw a large wet spot on the front of Sberna's pants and that his zipper was half down.

Sberna smirked at Owen. "Well, I gotta tell you. I feel a whole lot better now. You know what I mean, right?"

*I do*, Owen thought. *You mean you're an asshole.* Instead, he said, "Your fly's down."

"Made you look," Sberna said, tugging the zipper up. He sat down. He turned his gaze on Owen. "You sure you won't give me immunity?"

"That's not going to happen," Owen said. "But we really want you testifying."

Sberna stared at the table for a while, then started nodding his head, slowly, again and again. Finally, he said, "Okay. Let's see where this takes us."

Owen held up his glass in the gesture of a toast. "Cedric, man, thank you. I mean it. Thank you very much."

Owen hoped he'd sounded sincere.

Sberna leaned in. "Listen, though. I need to tell you two things. Are you listening? I am not a drug dealer."

"Okay," Owen said. "And?"

"I loaned Gio $3,000. I've got expenses, man. I could really use that money, you know?"

For a second Owen wondered if he'd misheard.

*Are you* serious? Owen thought. He tried to keep his expression from betraying him.

He said, "We're not bankers, Cedric. There's no savings account with that money waiting for you. You want to pursue it, you need to take it up with Tony Messina."

Sberna seemed to consider it. "Do you have his number? Never mind. Forget it. I think I still have it."

"You'd really do that to him?"

Sberna looked offended. "Come on, man, it's been four years. It's not like it's the day after Gio got killed." He paused. "Ahh. I'll wait till after the trial, I guess."

## CHAPTER 30

A few nights later, Owen and Goggin stayed late at the office, reading Steve Glassman's police report about his friend Mitchell Weinger. It was compelling and significant because of the quickness with which Glassman folded—and actually, he'd barely tried keeping up the lie that Weinger was with him the night of the murders. According to Toenings, the effort was nothing more than a long hesitation. This looked weird, obviously, and could actually help them.

They decided they'd call Glassman right then with the option of going over his police statement at their office or his home. Goggin placed the call, while Owen leaned back in his chair, listening to Goggin's side of the conversation and looking at the ceiling. Owen could tell Glassman was protesting that four years had passed and his recall of what he'd said had mostly passed with it and on and on. Owen had to hand it to Goggin: he had a way of getting people on board that didn't involve sticky chairs in scuzzy nightclubs.

Jocular and expansive, flattering and familiar, Goggin told Steve he'd be shocked by what came flooding back with the right kind of help, so where would he like to meet?

"Uh-huh," Goggin said. "Gotcha." Then he put his hand over the mouthpiece and asked Owen, "Tomorrow night at his place good for you? Six thirty?"

Owen nodded. He went back to staring at the water damage on the ceiling, jiggling his foot, periodically running his fingers through his hair.

He'd hoped Glassman would want to get it over with and tell them to come over tonight.

Owen couldn't tell if the crack running through the cloud-shaped brown stains, up at the seam between wall and ceiling, had lengthened. Had the ceiling even been damaged that first day he'd sat at this desk back when ... ?

Since he'd become a lawyer, Owen had become impatient with loose ends, couldn't tolerate lags and dead time. Time mattered, every second of it. Loose ends could turn into a snare, get you tangled up. Between now and an interview tomorrow evening, a million things could happen.. A wave of tension ran down his back like a claw.

Goggin turned to Owen again. "He says he wants his brother to be there."

"Is his brother a lawyer?" Owen groaned. Having an attorney there could foul up the dynamic . Maybe Glassman was withholding something.

But then again, if a lawyer was there, they'd *know* Glassman was withholding something.

"No. He says, 'moral support.'" Goggin whispered, rolling his eyes and making scare quotes with the fingers of his right hand.

Owen relaxed and shrugged.

Goggin said, "That's fine if you want your brother there, Mr. Glassman. Whatever makes you most comfortable."

The crack on the ceiling was starting to really piss Owen off.

When Goggin hung up, he slugged some cold coffee and scribbled on his notepad After looking at Owen for a moment, Goggin leaned way back in his chair and gazed at the same spot overhead. "What's your problem, Disco? You've got that worried hippie face."

"Disco" referred to a profile the *Chicago Tribune* had done of Owen nine months earlier. It ran on a Sunday, above the fold of the third page, under the title "The Disco D.A. wows 'em in the courtroom" in one edition, "The Disco D.A. rocks around the docket" in another. The article featured two photos. One was a shot of Jerico, with a long-haired Owen front and center, wearing a deadly serious expression and a medieval-looking linen V-neck shirt. The other was a current picture of a short-haired Owen in a suit.

*"They call him the John Travolta of the State's Attorney's Office,"* the article said, right at the top. *"He's a full-time prosecutor, a weekend dancer, and a former rock music star. He's a splash of showbiz dazzle in a world of dark blue suits."*

Owen took a good-humored approach to the story, figuring it was a solid bit of PR for the State's Attorney's Office, and it would be forgotten by Tuesday. He took a good-humored approach to the ribbing from his colleagues.

But he underestimated how many people read the *Tribune* and never guessed the wires would pick it up and give it to seventy-plus papers around the country. When the *Enquirer* sent a reporter so the magazine could do a profile of its own, Owen knew the jokes wouldn't stop anytime soon.

Goggin called him Disco constantly, and Owen didn't bother trying to stop him anymore. In fact, he barely noticed.

Owen started telling Goggin there was no problem, but the words fell apart. "I don't like this."

"Don't like what?"

"The brother being there. Glassman telling us his recall is bad ... "

"Oh, for fuck's sake. The nebbishy little man gave us his half-assed stab at getting out of it, and I shut him down."

"I don't know. It feels off." Owen looked over at Goggin now.

Goggin laughed. "Why the fuck am I reassuring you? If this case is such a dog, why did you drag me into it? Go home, Disco. Go home, get your hookah out, and smoke your marijuana grass."

"Are you picking up a case of Old Style on your way home?"

"No, motherfucker. Bushmills. And then I'm going to eat with the family and get in bed with my wife. So go enjoy your hashish."

The next day involved other matters than the Weinger case alone, although all of it involved murder. Matters of murder, in volume big enough that the start of the day seemed to race immediately toward its end. Owen looked up from his work. The afternoon had quickened into dusk, and the whole office was quieter and emptier, and it was already quarter to six.

"We need to get out of here," Owen said to Goggin.

They hurried out and took a roundabout way to Glassman's that kept them out of Chicago's legendary rush-hour traffic but still got them there four minutes late. A few years of working on tight trial schedules, dealing in evidence where crucial matters concerning people's lives could turn on differences of a minute or two made them think about time in precise, exact ways and gave them a horror of being anything but right on time. There was no parking nearby, so they left the car dangerously close to a hydrant, put the State's Attorney ID so it was clearly visible through the windshield, and buzzed Glassman at 6:35. He didn't seem to notice they were late.

Glassman's was a nice apartment, uncluttered and fastidiously clean. There were real paintings and drawings on the wall—not just prints—and Owen sensed they'd been chosen out of appreciation rather than reasons of status or statement. Owen's tenure working with Tom Breen had given him an awareness of how potent small, barely recognized perceptions were. Owen couldn't look at the length of a pant cuff or the knot of a tie without reading what it said about the person wearing them. Breen made him realize why so many of the older-school guys loved reading Sherlock Holmes stories. It was a complex world out there—complex and multileveled. But not boring. Not when you had your eyes trained to notice.

Things had been too busy for Owen to dwell too much on his misgivings about the strength of the case, but he and Goggin had agreed that Goggin would take the lead with the questions. "You're getting that thing in your voice," Goggin told him. "I'd better do this."

Glassman's brother, Marv, was present but, after a greeting and a handshake, sat back and faded into the décor.

Goggin and Owen each had a copy of the statement and gave a third to Glassman. He read it over carefully. Owen and Goggin waited. It took Glassman several minutes.

When they finished, Glassman looked at them and nodded.

"So, is it coming back to you?" Goggin said.

"Yes, it's coming back," Glassman said with, Owen thought, a little reluctance.

"And what's here is accurate?"

Glassman turned a few pages, as if rereading it.

"Yes," he said. "It's accurate."

"Have you spoken to Mr. Weinger since the night he called you on the phone?"

"No, that was the last time."

"Because you were upset at what he asked you to do?"

"To lie for him? Yes, that was upsetting. It was a weird thing."

"You work in a business where everything's got to be on the up and up, right? So it must have struck you as a real violation—"

Glassman cut him off. "It was a weird thing to do to a good friend. To your best friend."

"You two were that close?"

"Yeah. I've known him for years and years. I called him all the time. We hung out a lot. I was at his wedding."

"Were you in the wedding? Best man?"

"No."

"Groomsman?"

"No, just a guest."

Owen and Goggin exchanged a look.

"Were you best friends when he got married?"

"Sure."

It struck Owen that Glassman sounded a little defiant.

Goggin continued. "And he didn't try and get in touch with you afterward and explain anything? Apologize?"

"No, he didn't." A little defiant. Indignant, wounded too. "You just don't do that to a friend."

"So you were angry?"

Glassman nodded. "But you know who was even more angry? My parents. My dad flipped. 'How could you have been so stupid?' God." Glassman shook his head. "I mean, my dad asked if maybe I misunderstood what Mitchell was asking me to do, but ... " He trailed off.

Goggin sat up straighter. "Did you think you misunderstood?"

Glassman thought for a second. Owen felt dismayed.

Glassman said, "No, I don't think that's the case."

"You don't think so?" Goggin tapped the statement. "You were very clear about what happened in here. Didn't you just tell me it was all coming back?"

"Yeah, what I told the police—all of that came back."

For the only time, Marv emerged from the background. He shifted uneasily in his seat. He didn't say anything. Owen watched him, and Marv watched his brother.

"What you told the police is all that concerns us."

"Sure," Glassman said. "I just want to be sure I'm accurate."

There was a long pause. Then Glassman turned to Owen and asked, "It's really absolutely necessary for me to testify?"

On the way back, Owen was agitated. "Godammit. If we put him on, I bet he'll fuck us. I bet he'll fuck us really hard. And we *have* to put him on."

"What are you talking about? Get a grip."

"He's hedging his bets all of a sudden."

"He's not hedging shit."

"Bullshit he's not," Owen said. "The small, little man seems more bent out of shape about losing a friend than anything else. The shit about his dad asking if he misunderstood? He was just seeing how we'd react."

"You are a paranoid motherfucker."

"It's not paranoia," Owen said. "He didn't once mention the fact two people were dead. He didn't mention his 'best friend' murdered them."

"Yeah, I will say, Weinger might be Glassman's best friend, but Weinger probably feels differently." Goggin thought for a moment. "I'm trying to figure your thinking out. What's the worst possibility here?"

"Worst possibility? Follow my logic here: the case gets transferred to the Daley Center. Weinger gets bond. He has Pat Tuite handling his case. Fischer okays the motion to suppress—"

"I see where you're going. They might have approached Glassman to say maybe he misunderstood, maybe Johnny Toenings got a little too insistent. But ... no, I don't see it. If Glassman tried it, it wouldn't be credible."

Gregg Owen and Mike Goggin

The evening edition of the *Chicago Tribune* (above). The first story about the murders of Delphine "Tinker" Moore and Gio Messina.

The March 7 Sunday edition (below), reporting Mitchell Weinger's arraignment.

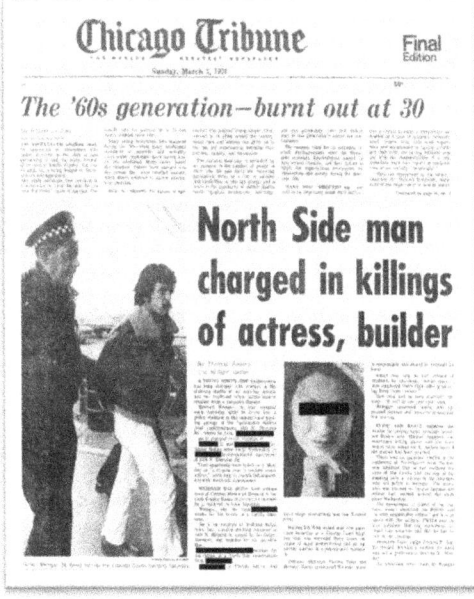

Forrest Haverland, Gregg Owen's grandfather, in Minnesota, ca. 1951. (above) Gregg Owen and his first plane. (below)

Courtroom sketch of Mike Goggin (L) and Gregg Owen (R)

The *Chicago Tribune* "Disco D.A." article, with a photo inset of Gregg Owen's band, Jerico.

Jay Owen, Gregg Owen's younger brother and close friend of Gio Messina, ca. 1980.

The front entrance of Tinker Moore's apartment building, at 2970 N. Sheridan (above); and Moore's first-floor window where Cedric Sberna looked in hours after the murders (below).

## CHAPTER 31

On some days—in the late afternoon more often than not but sometimes on waking and occasionally while falling asleep—Gregg Owen nearly believed Sandy at the Daley Center hadn't been lying, and the Weinger case was cursed. The proof lay in the small matters and details Owen couldn't discover or verify, people or explanations he couldn't find, and questions he couldn't answer: the tenants living adjacent to Apartment 131 had vanished, the building's super was dead. He didn't know when evidence recovered from Weinger's apartment had disappeared and who had helped push it into the void.

Who paid off whom? How much did it cost? How many people got dirty?

By Sandy's reckoning, a cursed case meant it was corrupted by graft or bribes or both and tainted by bad luck. Owen was aware of the graft and bribes and the difficulties they posed for the Weinger case. But his trouble finding Mary "Mickey" Carlyle was probably just bad luck.

He'd called and called Carlyle for several days, but no one answered. She lived in the same place she had in 1976 but had quit the Ritz-Carlton years before. No one presently employed at the bar had worked with Carlyle. No one knew anything about her or where she was. No one had heard of her.

Owen dialed her number at 7:00 in the morning, when most professionals would be readying for work, at 1:00 in the afternoon, when second shift employees hadn't left for their jobs yet, at 7:00 in the evening, when nine-to-fivers were back at home, then again at 10:30. The phone would ring and ring and ring each time.

One midmorning, Owen was on the first floor of Twenty-Sixth and California waiting for an elevator. When the door opened, Johnny Philbin was among those coming out. Owen greeted him and they stepped aside. People streamed past—cops, fellow ASAs, a few public defenders, jurors. The two of them occasionally nodded to someone they knew. Philbin told Owen he was there to testify in a case he'd investigated where one drug dealer had shot another.

"It was confusing as shit," Philbin said. "It got hard to tell who the bad guy was. I couldn't be sure who I was testifying for. What are you working?"

"It's funny—I'm prepping for trial, and the case involves you."

"No shit? What was it?"

"Mitchell Weinger. Stabbed two people in an apartment on North Sheridan."

Philbin thought for a moment. "I don't think I remember. Wait, wait. Was that four or five years ago?"

"Yeah. It was Teddy O'Connor's."

"Yes. I remember. I just helped out on that one. I was neck-deep in another case at the time. You're doing that now?"

"It was about to get tossed, so ... "

"I recall two things. One, the evidence got suppressed and Teddy was pissed off, man. Second, I was there when we picked up a girl at the Ritz who was involved in it, and we brought her here and questioned her, and she was just *gorgeous*. Teddy pretended to flip out on her so badly, she got terrified. She was your type, Disco."

"What do you mean, my type?"

"As dazed as she is beautiful."

Owen laughed a little, incredulous. "How do you know what my type is, Johnny?"

"How many times have I run into you on Rush Street and you've been arm in arm with someone who probably couldn't find her way back to her apartment on her own? Or remember that chick who almost got kicked in the face because she spooked my horse?"

For a while now, Philbin had somehow contrived annual breaks from the homicide squad and spent his summers detailed to the CPD Mounted Patrol. As a kid, he'd passed significant time on his grandparents' farm in southern Illinois, where they'd bred and trained quarter horses, and he'd become a skilled rider.

He passed significant time now riding up and down the beach in jodhpurs and black leather equestrian boots, with a wide-brimmed park ranger's campaign hat as protection against the sun. Philbin had his CPD shirt tailored so the short sleeves accented his biceps. He made a pass at every eligible woman who approached to ask if she could pet his horse. Most of them flirted back.

Owen and a date—Alexis? Stephanie? Connie? Vicki?—had been out walking along the shoreline one Saturday afternoon when they saw Philbin. The woman didn't know him but she rushed over to pet the horse, and the sudden motion along with the excited noise she made caused the horse to prime itself for a kick. Philbin kept it from doing so, and the woman exclaimed over the horse as she petted it, never realizing how close she'd come to having her maxilla and jawbone shattered.

"Anyway," Owen said, changing topic. "That's exactly who I'm trying to track down."

"Who? The one who almost got kicked or the one we brought down here to question?"

"The one you brought here. Mary Carlyle."

"That name is ringing a bell. Obviously, you called Area 6?"

"Uh-huh. But I don't need anyone's help there. I know where she lives; I know what her number is. I just can't reach her. She lives in Newberry Plaza over near Rush Street. I called the management company for the number of the front desk and talked to a couple of the doormen. One of them says he's seen her coming in within the last week. Said he'd leave a message, but whether he did or not, I don't know. She hasn't called back."

"Do you want us to pay a visit?" Owen could tell Philbin hoped the answer was negative.

"No. Thanks, though. I'm going to get a couple of investigators from state's to sit on her front door. I don't know how long I can get them for, so I was holding out, hoping I'd get her before I had to make the request."

Philbin held his hand out, and Owen shook it.

Then Philbin said, "Good luck. Let me know if we can help you out. Am I going to be testifying in this?"

"If we get rock-bottom, hail-Mary desperate, maybe. So don't call us, we'll call you."

"Good. That's what I was hoping to hear."

Two sets of investigators took a twelve-hour shift each and stationed themselves at the front door of Newberry Plaza. Newberry was fifty-six stories tall—unmissable on the Chicago skyline—and had some 525 units. It had been finished a couple of years before Gio and Tinker had died and was an expensive place to live. Owen started the watch on a Wednesday, figuring a weekday was more likely to find Carlyle going in or walking out. The investigators came up empty.

It was probably too late to be calling, but Owen dialed anyway, just in case.

Ted O'Connor answered before the first ring ended. Ted's late presence at his desk was one of the main reasons Owen liked him. O'Connor sounded genuinely pleased to get the call.

He said, "Man, I knew I'd be getting a call from you. I heard you and Mike Goggin were taking a bottom-of-the-ninth, two-strikes, three-balls swing at that Weinger case, and I knew."

"You're kidding," Owen said. "How'd you hear that?"

It had been only a few days.

"I've got my confidential informants. So, I dug through the Area 6 file for a refresher. It's amazing what comes back to you."

"I have some names I wanted to run by you, just get your read on them."

"Okay. Shoot."

"Let's start with the star: Mitchell Weinger."

"Lying piece of shit."

"Can you elaborate?"

"Sure. Lying piece of psychopathic shit." O'Connor laughed. "But seriously—we nailed him lying. We nailed him lying, and we nailed the Glassman kid for lying for him. Then, John Toenings was part of the investigation at the time, and he turned up some pretty decent evidence when he tossed Weinger's place. Most of which, I understand, is no longer available."

"Yeah, that's about the size of it. I'll put Toenings on my call sheet."

"Do you know Toenings?" O'Connor's tone had turned serious.

"A little. In passing. Here and there."

"I wouldn't bet the farm on the quality of his memory."

"Meaning … ?"

O'Connor seemed to consider how to put it. "He wasn't ever really one of us."

Owen said nothing. O'Connor continued. "So, no question—Weinger was good for it. I'm just giving you the bare bones here. I'll be more than happy to sit down with you and go over the report, give you some of my impressions. I predict you're getting ready to ask about Glassman since the name just came up. About as sturdy as wet paper. Fell apart within half a second. And sold Weinger out a half-second after that."

"Axe to grind?"

"No, too weak to even lift an axe. Plus, his brother and a lawyer were there. I don't remember their names, but I do remember neither one seemed inclined to lie. As far as I can see, Glassman's your linchpin."

"Keller?"

"Jesus, yeah. Honestly—my memory with Keller is a little foggy, at least with the particulars. It was getting really late. Everything should be in the report. But a couple of things stick out. He dropped the girl right away, left her stranded—"

"The girl, meaning Carlyle?"

"Right. Then, he told Cedric Sberna to ditch the Messina kid's gun."

"Was the gun legal?"

"Yeah, he had a license. But leaving Carlyle vulnerable like that ... throwing the gun away ... that might be all anyone needs to know about Keller." O'Connor thought for a second. "One thing—not related to Keller. We couldn't make much of a connection between Weinger and Gio Messina. Just that they had each other's numbers. But obviously, that won't get you much traction. Some people at the time figured it was a coke deal gone bad, but I never bought that."

"The number won't get us any traction because it's gone from the evidence locker."

O'Connor scoffed. "Of course it is. Of course it's gone. But as far as connections go, it was a pretty tenuous one anyway."

"I've heard Sberna is really something else."

"Arrogant and cowardly. Vain as hell. Took two rounds with me and Richie Morask going at him, but he cracked. And when he cracked, he broke. Keller told him not to talk, but Sberna talked a whole lot."

"How full of shit was he?"

"You know, I don't think he was that full of shit. We told him he was the prime suspect—I don't remember if we really thought that or not—and he seemed to sense this was his shot. Bottom line, though, his story and Carlyle's story were a perfect match. And that proved to be pretty valuable."

"Did Carlyle break right away? I've been trying to find her."

"We had a hard time getting her too. But no, actually, she didn't fold right away. We picked her up, took her to Twenty-Sixth Street, and gave her a seat outside the grand jury room—"

"Psy-ops."

"You got it. So, I come in, do the mad bull act. She had a can of pop on the table that I batted so hard it dented. Got Coca-Cola everywhere. I still feel bad about leaving that mess for someone. Anyway, she held out for a lot longer than I would have given her credit for."

"How about Tony Messina?"

"Oh, God. That poor guy. When you talk to him—"

"I did. Day before yesterday."

"Yeah? What was your read?"

"Really made me want to … "

"Go the distance for him?" O'Connor suggested.

"Precisely."

"I remember him trying really hard to keep himself together. He wanted to make sure he could help. He wouldn't leave until he did. My heart went out to him."

"Was he a help?"

"Yeah. A big one. You know, there was something that never made it into the report. Tony Messina, Richie, and the maintenance guy went down to the basement. The guy wanted to show Richie something. They were under the bathroom of the Moore girl's apartment, and there was a puddle of blood on the basement floor. It had seeped down through the ceiling. Now, that place wasn't built like Fort Knox, but it wasn't flimsy either. That's a lot of fucking blood. Listen, Gregg, I've got to get home, but I'm here anytime. Anything you need, you let me know. I'm going to give you my home number."

"Thank you, Teddy. Really."

"One last thing. If you find out, you've got to tell me: I never understood what the motive was. Why did the guy do it? I had no idea. None. It made no sense. That's why I remembered the case. I've seen worse, but most of them made sense, at least in the end. This one made no sense at all. Okay. Good luck. I know I'll be talking to you soon."

## CHAPTER 32

Two nights later, Owen and Goggin were getting ready to leave the office for the weekend. Owen said he was going to try Carlyle one more time that day and reached for the phone.

Goggin watched him pick it up and start dialing. Goggin said, "You got the number memorized, huh?"

"I've called it a lot, so yeah, I do."

"If we don't get her, it's not the end of the world."

"Maybe not the end of the world but pretty catastrophic." Owen dialed the last two numbers and sat back, his feet on the desk.

"Anything in this case that isn't catastrophic?"

Carlyle's phone rang and rang, like it had every other time he'd called. Owen said, "No, not really."

"Hello?"

Owen put his feet down and sat up. Goggin stopped writing and looked at Owen.

Owen thought for a moment he'd misdialed.

"Hello. May I speak with Mary Carlyle, please?"

"Yes. Hello. This is she. Can I help you?" The voice had an accent he'd never heard before. More of an affect, really, than an accent, something equal parts Canadian-British and high-toned Boston, both of them high on ether. It sounded like a put-on.

"My name is Gregg Owen, I'm a state's attorney here in Chicago." He waited for a reaction. "The State's Attorney's Office is pursuing a conviction against Mitchell Weinger for the murders of Gio Messina and Delphine Moore in March of 1976. You were brought in by the Area 6 Homicide Squad to answer a few questions. You recall the case?"

There was a pause. A long one. Long enough that he suspected they'd gotten disconnected. Then, "Yes, of course."

The question had been rhetorical, and the pause was alarming. Owen thought it would have been incredible if she hadn't recalled it. In fact, he thought, he probably didn't want to live in a world where someone could forget.

And yet it felt sometimes as if that's where the world was arriving. Just the hesitation he kept encountering, just that alone, had him faintly dumbfounded. Faintly dumbfounded—but still probably not as much as it should.

He couldn't stop reminding himself that these were his peers.

Before his own pause went for too long, he came back to the moment.

"You'll be asked to testify on behalf of the people of Illinois against Mr. Weinger, and I wanted to make an appointment with you to go over the statement you gave the homicide detectives a few years ago. When would it be convenient to meet?"

"Oh, well, Mr. ... Owen, was it? I'm very afraid it won't be convenient at all to meet."

He tried placing the accent. British Canadian, maybe, by way of rich Boston, after huffing ether, trying to do an absurd, appalling imitation of a stereotypical gay man. It irritated him. He was about to tell her, but she went on. Owen motioned for Goggin to lean in. Goggin got close enough to the earpiece so that he and Owen could both hear.

"I appreciate your calling, Mr. Owen, but I'm going to have to say no to you. This just doesn't sound like something I'm interested in doing. The detective I spoke to at that time had let me know that if I answered his questions, I wouldn't have to appear in court or have anything more to do with this entire incident."

Goggin's eyes lit up. He mouthed to Owen, *What the fuck?* and Owen figured he meant both the voice and the sentiment. Goggin made Carlyle strike Owen as funny, but she still pushed his irritation into anger. More, now that he was pissed off, her indifference to the fact of two murdered bodies was like something electrified that Owen had just put his fingers on. It jolted him past mere anger into something blacker, more acute. And threaded through it, fueling and shaping it, was a fierce, indignant feeling that these people were assholes, irredeemable assholes, whose whims risked losing him the case. Tony Messina's face—grief-stricken, furrowed with tragedy, teary—came to mind yet again. And from there, flashes of the crime scene photos and lines and phrases from the toxicology report that he heard in his inner ear almost like someone was narrating them. He had another flash, of the crime scene photo he'd imagined in the Daley Center, of himself dead, in a wide corona of blood. Then the bitterest parts of the moment went to dust, and a little of the ridiculousness came back, and the moment seemed slightly funny again.

"Mr. Owen? Are you still there? Hello?"

Goggin, amused, disbelieving, nudged him.

Owen pursed his lips so he wouldn't laugh, then spoke into the headset and kept up a level tone, making his voice stern. "Miss Carlyle, I think you might misunderstand how this works. This isn't optional. Whether you're interested in testifying or not interested in testifying, either way, you'll be testifying."

There was an edge to the way she responded. "I guess we'll have to agree to disagree. Maybe you should talk to … whatever that detective's name was. Something Irish."

Owen decided that a friendly tone would better put Carlyle in her place than a vicious one. "No, I think I'll have to disagree with our agreeing to disagree. If you refuse, gosh, that means we have to compel you to come in. And if we have to compel you, things get harder for everyone. If you still don't accept you have no choice in the matter, we have to move to next steps."

"What are those?"

"Oh, no, no—let's leave lawyers and bail and contempt of court out of this for now."

"I see."

"That's great. I'm glad you do. And by the way, the Irish name you're trying to think of was and still is O'Connor. Detective Ted O'Connor." Owen's voice was still light. "And I'm fairly certain he didn't tell you your obligations ended with a statement. He's one of our best. He knows what he's talking about."

All the affect dropped out of her voice. She just sounded like some girl from Chicago. "Ted O'Connor was one of the biggest assholes I've ever met in my life. No one has ever been that rude to me."

"Be that as it may," Owen said, "can you meet tomorrow? It's a weekend so we can speak privately because the office will be empty."

A pause, lengthy. Then, the affect was back. "Why don't we meet at one o'clock? Except, let's get lunch, instead of our meeting in a depressing, empty—where would we be meeting?"

"The Criminal Courts building, at Twenty-Sixth and California."

"Instead of a depressing, empty office in the courthouse at Twenty-Sixth and California. Do you know the Water Tower Plaza? Of course you know it. There's a restaurant on the third floor whose name I can't remember right now, but I do recall it was quite good. It's the only one with 'outside' seating. Let's meet there. And so you can recognize me, I'll be wearing a red hat."

## Chapter 33
*February 22, 1980*

Owen got to the Water Tower Plaza and took the elevator to the third floor. Stepping out, he saw a row of restaurants and the outside-the-entry seating Carlyle had talked about. Most obvious, though, was a woman seated with her back to him, at a table by herself, set off from the other tables and the diners at them, wearing an enormous-brimmed red hat. The crown was small and boxy, but the brim looked like the rings of Saturn, except red and far wider.

Owen approached the table but didn't want to startle Carlyle, so he looped around to stop and stand in front of her. The face that looked up from under the red shade of the hat was one of the most beautiful he had ever seen. Maybe one of the most beautiful he'd ever imagined.

She cocked her head and smiled inconsequentially and held her hand out.

He took it and said, "Miss Carlyle? I'm Gregg Owen; we spoke on the phone yesterday."

Owen wondered if she'd say *Charmed* to him.

She did and then broadened the empty smile.

His next immediate impression was of a preposterously beautiful woman dressed in her grandmother's best clothes that she'd found in an attic trunk.

The emptiness was hard to read. Was it a forced smile designed to hide the fact that she very much wanted not to be here, or was she simply not that bright?

A waiter in a white shirt paired with a black vest and black tie came over and laid two menus down, then stepped away, came back with a pitcher, and poured ice water into the glasses sitting on their placemats.

"Please don't call me Miss Carlyle, though. Call me Mickey. Can I call you Gregg? Okay, Gregg—can you tell me what you want from me because I really don't want to do this, and honestly, I resent being bullied."

It was hard to concentrate under the gaze of the face. It was exquisite.

"Just to be clear: I'm not bullying you, Mickey. I'm just telling you how it is. You're a material witness, and you have to testify in the trial;

otherwise, we serve you with a material witness warrant, and the police will bring you in."

"What do I want from you? I want what you're obligated by law to give: truthful testimony about what you told the police. So I want to go over the statement you gave them about what you and your boyfriend did and said that night. We need to corroborate his story."

Her voice turned sharp. "He's not my boyfriend. I don't even want to hear his name. He's a disgusting pig."

She sat up straight and leaned back. She crossed her arms over her chest and fumed for a moment. Then she asked him, "What does *corroborate* mean?"

"Cedric Sberna—sorry—is going to testify that he showed up at the bar where you worked, that he told you what had happened, that you called a doctor or medical student of your acquaintance, and then he called 911. After that, the two of you went back to the apartment where the murder occurred. After he looked in through the window, you returned to your place and called a lawyer, a Mr.—" Owen flipped through his notes "—Jerry Keller, and—"

"It's Jeremy. Jeremy Keller."

"Okay. You called Jeremy Keller, who came over and conferred with Cedric Sberna. Subsequently, you were approached at your workplace and brought to the Area 6 precinct house. Is that about right? That's what happened?"

"Yes. That's what happened. I remember it really well."

"I need you to back his story up. That's what *corroborate* means. That your story essentially matches his."

"I didn't know them at all."

"Know who?"

"The victims. They were Cedric's friends. I met them a couple times—several, I guess. I mean we hung out, I was at Gio's house one night, but I worked nights, so I didn't hang out with them very much."

"Okay. You'll be asked about that too." He couldn't tell how much remorse she had for the fact of their deaths or if she had any. He couldn't tell if she was sorry to have been involved at all, beyond the necessity of appearing in court.

For a few minutes, she asked questions about the processes of a court appearance, and Owen answered patiently. Finally, she sat and watched him for a while. He looked away because he didn't want his resolve to waver. She was so beautiful she might be able to tempt him into a bad place. Owen broke the silence.

"How long have you lived at the Newbury?"

"How long have I lived at the Newbury? I moved in right after it opened, so almost seven years."

"It's a nice building. I had a friend who lived there. I spent quite a few nights at her place."

"A friend? Really? Did you live far from the city then?"

"Not that far, but I'd get done working at three thirty, four thirty."

That working was on purpose. Owen felt it might be better to keep quiet about the bands, although he was curious how'd she react.

"Where were you working?"

He'd steered the conversation in this direction. It was too late to change the subject.

"At the Rush Up, the Gap. At Mother's."

"Up on Rush Street? So you were a bartender."

"I was a musician. My band played at those places a lot."

"What band were you in?"

"It was named Jerico."

Her eyes widened. She looked at him for a few seconds. She looked away. Her expression changed, seemed to soften—prideful and dismissive to respectful and impressed, a smile whispering at the corners of her mouth. He often got that reaction when he mentioned the band, although he never meant to.

She angled her chair a few degrees and faced him directly.

"I saw you guys. It was a while ago, but I saw you." Carlyle's eyes moved aslant of his, like she was watching a snippet of memory play over his shoulder.

Owen didn't believe her. He'd found that when he talked about being in the band, a lot of people claimed to have seen Jerico play. If everyone who said so actually had, he'd be a lot wealthier and more famous than he was.

"It's possible. We did play a lot of gigs."

"It was on Rush Street," she said, angling her eyes up, trying to remember the place she saw them. "It wasn't the Gap. Oh, I know—Mother's. Really late. Like, two in the morning."

Owen guessed maybe she actually had seen them. "Then you probably did."

She was showing a little deference now. "You were fantastic."

The affect in her voice was gone.

"Thank you. I appreciate it." He had unconsciously slipped into the voice he used to use when thanking a fan. He removed his hand and picked up his water glass. The waiter, sensing an opportunity, came over with his pad out.

Carlyle lifted the enormous red circle of hat from her head and laid it on the table. She twirled an index finger in her hair. She touched her left hand to Owen's right forearm, and he flinched mildly, like her fingers held a static charge.

"Tell me again why I should do this?"

"Because it's the right thing to do."

"That usually doesn't convince me."

"It should this time."

She sounded a lot less dazed to him now.

He glanced down, then back up quickly: perfect, ideal legs. He looked at her face. No one should be this beautiful.

Then he felt ashamed. It was unpleasant and got more so. Like heat pulsing outward from the point of a sting.

*What am I doing?*

*You're not doing anything yet, but the thought's bad enough.*

"Okay," she said. "All right. What's next then?"

"Thank you. I really appreciate it," he said.

She waved a dismissive hand.

"The next step is to sit down and go over the statement, point by point," Owen told her. "We'll want to be sure everything is accurate and that you didn't misremember anything then or now."

"It would be a pleasure, Gregg." All her reluctance was gone away. She took her napkin from her lap, folded it, placed it on the tabletop. "Whatever I can do to help."

*An amazing change of heart*, he thought. Quick, total, like she'd never protested at all and certainly like he'd never had to invoke the specter of a subpoena. He wondered what she could be playing at because it was difficult believing she didn't want something.

A server came and cleared Carlyle's plate and utensils, then Owen's, and their waiter appeared and laid the check on the table and then vanished. Carlyle didn't glance at the check or acknowledge it. Owen had assumed the meal would end that way. He doubted she picked up a check very often.

He tried thinking more charitably. She was doing the right thing. No one was expendable. Everyone's testimony mattered. Carlyle's mattered a lot.

After paying, Owen watched Carlyle as she gathered her things.

Not for the first time, he recognized how open and available trouble made itself. It was subtle and had you entrapped before you even knew what happened. When she stood up, he saw with conflicted eyes the way her dress—tight to the point of confining—asserted her shape.

*No one should be this beautiful,* he thought again. And then: desire—acrid, reflexive, dull—spoke to him the way money might speak to someone bribable or heroin to someone who wanted to get royally fucked up. The struggle here set immediate present against possible futures. It factored in his ambitions as a lawyer, which were pitched to the same intensity of desire he felt for her, and the outcome of the wrong choice was clear: inevitably, catastrophically bad.

He wasn't being presumptuous. Right now, she had her hand on his forearm, again, saying, "I was thinking we should meet for dinner to go over everything. Don't you think that would be a good idea?"

*No, it's a really, really terrible idea,* he thought. He understood Carlyle had to be angling for something. He couldn't hazard a guess what that might be. Her transformation had been too quick and too total.

He was enjoying her attention, her flirting, but he didn't trust himself to leave it there. Owen decided to lie.

He said, "We have pretty strict rules around that. When we discuss the statement and your testimony, we can do it wherever we want, but sitting down with the documents is something we have to do in the offices."

Her fingertips lingered on his forearm, and it was pleasant and aggravating at the same time. They agreed on a Monday afternoon meeting, the day after tomorrow. He promised he'd have a car bring her to Twenty-Sixth and California and then back home, and they parted ways. He noticed she didn't thank him for lunch.

## CHAPTER 34
*March 10, 1980*

Two calls to New York City so far, four or five calls to numbers in and around Chicago. One to Boston, one to Colorado, one to Florida. No luck at all.

Owen had started calling the numbers Tony copied from Gio's address book years ago—and recently given to Owen—right after his meeting with Carlyle and had five West Coast numbers remaining, but he'd wait on those until a little later, when he felt less like telling the people he spoke with *fuck you.*

It was, admittedly, a tough lead-in, using the words *state's attorney, prosecuting,* and *double murder.* Follow that by asking if they'd answer a few questions, and no one could end the call fast enough. Could tell the call suggested, if not direct involvement, then some sort of complicity, and in the inquiry alone they seemed to hear a judgment about their choices in friends and acquaintances.

Each conversation followed the same tack, more or less. Owen made his voice easy, inquisitive, just someone calling to clear up a simple puzzle.

People never acted more strangely than around those representing God or the law. But knowing that did nothing for the case.

He explained, "We're trying to establish a connection between Gio Messina and the defendant, Mitchell Weinger ... "

*No, Gio never mentioned a Mitchell Weinger.*

They all said that.

Owen told them, "Okay. Thank you for your time."

But thinking, *Fuck you.*

And the way they said it, too. So quick, reactive.

*No, really—fuck you.*

The sudden off-hook tone rang loud and shrill. His fingers ached. Owen realized he'd picked the phone up, got lost in thought, hadn't dialed, and he was gripping the handset too hard. He leaned over and replaced it in the cradle. The files for the Weinger case lay open across his desk, arranged according to a system no sooner followed than forgotten. It was a good time for a break. Owen stood and shook the pain from his hand and decided to turn in his chits.

Any assistant still working during the dinner hour was entitled to three dollars to cover the cost of a meal. Goggin and Owen, like most of the assistants at Twenty-Sixth and California, were almost always working during the dinner hour and usually long past it. Periodically, one or the other would bring their "dinner chits" to Helen Kasinski's office for reimbursement. Owen usually volunteered so he could spend time talking with the ladies in the steno pool.

Owen had dropped his chits off, socialized, and was almost back to his office when he saw Joe Hein walking out of it. Joe Hein and Greg Bedoe had helped Bill Kunkle prosecute John Wayne Gacy, and when the trial ended, Kunkle had them working as investigators on the Weinger case.

From the expression on Hein's face, Owen knew he was about to hear something big.

Owen stopped just outside the office door.

"What's up, Joe?" Owen said.

"Question for you. That folded piece of paper on top of the Weinger file? It says 'Bill Wright, pilot, TK Aviation Services, Midway Airport.' Is that part of the case?"

Owen thought for a second. Then he remembered he'd found the paper stuffed into the file and had no idea what it referred to. He said, "I wish I knew. Maybe? Maybe not?"

"The guy in charge of TK Aviation Services? Buddy of mine from high school."

"That's a definite coincidence. How close a buddy are we talking?"

"Close enough to ask a favor from."

"Likely as not it doesn't get us anything, but ... " Owen didn't want to finish the sentence. Hein finished for him.

"There's not much of anything you do have."

"*We have*, Joe. Not much of anything *we* have."

Hein told Owen that it had been fourteen or fifteen years since he'd seen Patrick Rice, the owner of TK Aviation Services, the last time being the summer following high school, before it was college for Hein and Vietnam for Rice.

"What I heard, Rice was spraying Agent Orange, and he got sick from it. But I heard he was dropping bombs on Cambodia too, so who knows? What I do know is TK Aviation is one of those businesses that has a rep for 'money, right or wrong.' It's that kind of enterprise."

In the distance, a passenger jet angled up off a runway, the engine roar audible even inside the car, and passed over the rows of apartments. It looked like anyone standing on the roofs could reach up and touch the plane's underside.

Hein saw it too. "It's weird how close that plane looks."

Owen said, "I don't think it just *looks* close. Not as close as it looks from here, but inside, you're going to know when a plane flies overhead."

"I imagine it's a real drag living in one of those," Hein said. "I don't know how you'd stand it. Me, I'd go crazy."

"You tell yourself that someday you'll live somewhere else."

Hein sighed. "Yeah, hope springs eternal."

Owen turned and looked at Hein. The word *hope* had been ringing loudly since yesterday's lunch.

Their own momentum dragged as they neared the airport entrance and hit sudden traffic. Hein put his signal on, edged his car left. Most of the other cars were headed toward the commercial terminals. The slowdown had no obvious cause, but a number of drivers leaned on their horns anyway, as if the noise might force a resolution.

Hein remarked on the pointlessness. "What do they think honking's going to do?" He answered with a few honks of his own. "Every problem in the world comes down to one jagoff doing stupid shit."

It wasn't a bad observation, Owen thought.

"Oh no you don't," Hein told a car trying to edge in front of him. He inched forward, blocking the gap.

"Just let him go," Owen said. "We'll be here all day."

"Start giving an inch," Hein said, "and you'll never get to stop."

A moment later, they veered off from the main artery of traffic. Owen looked out on an immensity of blacktop. Hein drove past trailers and garages with small troops of apron buses and deicers. The hangars were made from corrugated steel, and the farther away they got from the terminals, the more the hangars were rusted and ramshackle.

"So, TK Aviation is pretty remote," Owen said.

"I guess this far out, no one can see what you're doing."

The air outside looked cold and brittle, and the several orange wind socks were full and shaking. When Hein parked and killed the engine, Owen could hear the steel panels' low rattling, pushed and then released by the wind. There were no buildings to break the currents. Everything was low to the ground, built on isolated footprints.

The big hangar door was opened wide enough to admit one person at a time. Owen and Hein stepped out of the car.

Hein said, "Hey, Gregg—before we go in there, I just wanted to let you know, this guy has some unrelated businesses going on here."

"Unrelated, meaning what?"

"Nothing important. Don't worry about it. I just wanted to make sure it didn't throw you."

The frigid wind shouted at them with surprising force. When they stepped inside, the temperature was at least fifty degrees hotter, but the air was as dry as the outdoors, and there was a loud, burring groan from industrial-size heaters, some suspended from the ceiling, others—cannon-shaped, yellow, pocked with rust—pointed from different spots on the floor.

A corridor formed by stacked shipping crates led away from the entrance and toward the left. On the right, there was a shorter passageway that terminated in a row of rooms like storage spaces, with canvas tarps hung over two of the doorways and a threadbare stage curtain over the third.

Owen heard sounds he recognized immediately. At first, he thought they might be noise from something mechanical because one of them came as a series of low squeaks. But then another noise joined in with a long, stretched guttural quality. He walked closer to the cubicles and, coming up toward them, heard long, loud exhales.

One of the exhalations said something—a name, maybe, Owen thought—and then the squeaking stopped abruptly. Only the guttural noise kept on. He heard a long extended grunt.

Owen turned again to the cubicles, and then back to Hein, who was looking past Owen. Hein began laughing. When Owen faced the cubicles, he saw a man in an airline pilot's uniform stepping from behind one of the curtains. He stopped short when he saw Hein and Owen.

Hein called out, "Your fly, sir. It's all the way down."

The pilot disappeared behind the curtain. No sound came from the other two cubicles. Owen thought he and Hein probably looked like some kind of cops. Working in law must get into a person's posture. If not the appearance of detective or agent, then at least the bearing of someone who could cause a lot of hassles for someone else.

Owen found the thought wasn't unpleasant.

The heaters kicked back on, and Owen followed Hein to the main office.

In Owen's experience most people turned indignant when asked for evidence or information that usually required a warrant. Patrick Rice—whether out of trust for Hein, a sense of being insulated, or simply not caring—wasn't one of them.

Rice and Hein fell into old friendship, and Rice treated Owen warmly, without wariness or distrust. He asked Hein what had brought them out to the airport and merely nodded when Hein told him, "Homicide." Rice invited them to sit. He sat at his desk—a jumble of papers, catalogs, and mechanical parts. Owen and Rice found dirty metal folding chairs.

Experience had taught Owen that when civilians heard the words *homicide* or *murder*, it pricked their escape instincts and stoked a wisp of panic. Rice was unperturbed. He sounded genuinely curious when he asked, "How does this involve me?"

Owen spoke. "It probably doesn't. But you may be able to help us find someone who is involved."

"Okay," Rice said, waiting for more.

"We found a name in our files. It was 'Bill Wright' with the word *pilot* underneath, and *TK Aviation*, and *Midway Airport*."

"Shit, yeah. I know Bill. He used to work for me. And we flew together in Vietnam."

Rice stopped there. He was mild-eyed, face full of inscrutable good humor. Owen could tell Rice had talked to the law before. That was usually true of people who only answered with a bare minimum of information.

"What I'm trying to figure out," Owen told him, "is why his name is in our files."

There was a long silence. Rice smiled vaguely. He drummed his fingers on the desk, stopped to pointlessly move a stack of aerial maps a few inches to the left, and started drumming again.

"I've learned not to say never, but I'd have a real hard time believing Billy was involved in a murder."

Rice's eyes were steady, a little uncertain, but not yet contentious.

Owen made a depreciative face, dismissing the idea of Wright's involvement. "I don't think he was. If he had bloody hands, we'd have heard about him. And there'd be more than just a name in our files."

Rice leaned far back in his chair, hands behind his head, feet on his desk.

"So, you're thinking ... what, exactly?"

"He knew someone who was mixed up in it."

Owen and Rice were both paying out minimal line, but Owen sensed Rice wasn't evasive. Just cautious.

Rice asked, "Who is mixed up in it? I don't mean names. What sort of person are we talking about?"

"Bunch of rich kids." *Kids.* It sounded strange. After a second it struck Owen that the victims, suspects, and most of the witnesses were his own age. It wasn't that Gio and Tinker had a stop put to them at a young age and they were fixed there in memory. All of them were aimless, drifting, even hapless, and so they seemed to lack gravitas and maturity.

Rice said, "I see. When was this?"

"Early 1976."

"Well, Bill did a lot of courier flights, a lot of charters. How about this: let's take a look at his manifests from around then."

Rice brought his feet to the floor and stood up.

"You have them?" Owen was impressed and surprised. "And you're okay with us having a look?"

Rice made a gesture suggesting the question was unnecessary. He withdrew behind his bulwark of charts and manuals. Owen heard first one file drawer, then another open and close. He heard a cardboard box being dragged across the floor, Rice muttering to himself, and finally, Rice's cry of triumph.

Hein said, "What sort of courier are we talking?"

Rice's smile was enigmatic and private. "The expensive kind. Bill always believed he was somehow immune to trouble, so he took more chances than most. Chances most people wouldn't take. But sometimes a courier is just a courier, and a charter is just a charter."

Hein said in a broad, jovial voice, "Patrick Rice—are you saying Bill Wright played loose with federal regulations, and you knew it?"

"There's knowing, and then there's knowing, if you get my drift."

"Which kind were you?"

"I don't know."

After a moment, Rice pulled out a thick sheaf of papers. He said, "Are we off the record?"

"We were never on the record," Owen said. "But sure."

"After the war, a lot of guys didn't have an easy time getting readjusted. I did. I was lucky that way.

"Now, I mean it when I say, I admire people with principles. So all those antiwar folks—I respected the commitment of anyone who followed their conscience. Anyone who really put it all on the line. Those people were generally not the shit stains who were screaming at us that we murdered babies. If you're already freaked out about what happened to you over there, someone spitting on you isn't going to help. Plus, I'll tell you from personal experience, when you get back, you find the volume's been turned down real low. So I gave people a chance to get themselves set up and maybe, possibly, an occasional opportunity to turn the volume back up for a minute."

Owen said, "I want to be clear: we don't care about anything but murder. We're not concerned about anything that isn't life or death."

Rice held up the pages.

"I know, I know. I can tell you're someone with principles. Give me a date."

"Let's start with late February 1976, through that March."

Rice went back and forth through the stack and withdrew two sheets of paper. "Not sure if this will help or not. But Bill only made two flights around then. That first page, I know the person. Bill was taking him up to a fishing cabin, hunting cabin, something like that."

Owen looked and found the name and cargo meaningless.

When he looked at the second sheet, he stopped breathing. It read: *Passengers: Gio Messina, Marie (?) Moore, Mitchell Weinger.*

Owen turned to Hein with a wide, elated smile. He pointed to the passenger list and handed it over. Hein took it, read it for a second, and whooped. "Fuck yeah," he said.

"I'm assuming you found that helpful?" Rice said. "I enjoy doing small favors for good people, so glad I could be of service."

"You want to make my entire year? Tell me where I can find Bill Wright. And please don't tell me he's dead."

Rice said, "I won't because he's not. I mean, I hate to piss on your parade here, but Bill is in Tennessee. And that's where your problem starts."

The elation drained out of Owen's blood. "Okay. Drop the other shoe."

"The other shoe is that Bill was flying a particularly heavy load of cargo from ... I think it was Honduras. And he had some trouble. The plane went down. Bill walked away, thank God, but the sheriff arrested him and now Bill's looking at a life bid in Tennessee for trafficking. That's why I wanted to hire people like Billy. Give them decent pay so incidents like this one didn't have to happen. But, shit, look around—it's not like I've gotten wealthy doing this."

Hein said, "I guess that explains the moans and groans from the back of the hangar?"

Rice didn't miss a beat. "No, not really. I mean, I have nothing to do with that. But if someone wants to trade a cut of the action for use of the space, I'm happy to take it."

"We saw a pilot coming out of one of those rooms."

"Stick around for a day and you'll see a lot of pilots coming out of those rooms. But look at it this way: would you rather have someone in the cockpit who's relaxed, clear in his mind, and focused? Or someone who can't get pussy off the brain?"

Hein said, "So you could say you're helping to provide a public service."

Rice thought for a moment. "That's exactly how I'd put it. Here at TK Aviation Services, we're doing God's work."

## CHAPTER 35
*March 20, 1980*

They'd landed in Nashville an hour ago. The charter plane they'd hired was thirty minutes late for takeoff. The pilot was inspecting it now.

A few moments earlier, Owen had seen a tremor in the pilot's hand and tried to forget it as the old man kept on writing in the flight log. Then—actually, just now—he'd seen the hand shake again and made eye contact with the pilot, the only one available to fly them from Nashville International to Tri-City Airport.

Before they realized who he was, they assumed the pilot was just some nice elderly guy—some administrator or supervisor who'd stayed overlong in his job, pitching in to help speed up takeoff. Retirement didn't suit everyone. For all Owen knew, he could have been the owner, founder, or longest-term employee. It spoke well of the company to keep one of their elders on, and this one was clearly competent and thorough, if a bit labored and slow.

But there wasn't anyone else around—not in the hangar or the office, which is where the guy had been sitting, or anywhere nearby.

The more Owen watched him prod, turn, and shake the outer, movable parts of the plane with his jittered fingers, the older the man seemed.

Taciturn at first but still rushing through the preflight, the pilot had probably seen Owen notice the tremor because the old man suddenly started talking about problems—licenses and annual renewals and expensive insurance—and talked rapidly through the rest of the paperwork and halfway through his inspection of the rudders and stabilizers and the edges of the wings, in an agitated voice that sounded both put-upon and confused.

Owen and Goggin hadn't had to say anything. They watched the sky and only half-listened.

At one point, the man moved past Goggin, who signaled Owen over as the inspection continued.

"Does he have a cataract?" Goggin said. "I swear to God Almighty, I saw a cataract."

"Easy. Easy. Don't get tense." Owen used his calmest speaking voice. "Listen to me—hey, are you listening? Okay, listen—I've been around a lot of pilots, and I can tell this guy knows what he's doing."

The winds rushed and slackened. It had turned cloudy, the blue sky turning a darker and darker gray over the span of just a few minutes.

Owen wondered if Goggin saw the tremor but supposed he hadn't. If Goggin had noticed, he wouldn't keep it to himself.

Sheriff Jimmy Strickland had been friendly, polite, helpful, even sympathetic when Owen called to inquire about Bill Wright. His accent had been pitch-perfect, almost too good to be real. It brought to Owen's mind old boys with big bellies and sunburnt faces, lips sticky with tobacco juice.

"Well, whatever help you might need, we'd be pleased to give it," Strickland said. "You want to talk to Billy, then you are welcome to come talk to Billy. And we'd be glad to get you to and from the airport."

As soon as he'd hung up with Strickland, Owen had secured two tickets to Nashville and a guarantee of plentiful charters from there to Johnson City. Within a few minutes, he was hit by a sense of the absurdity of the trip. A lot of money and time. Four hundred and some-odd miles of travel for a conversation that might prove pointless. For a conversation that might not happen.

Strickland could have been toying with him. What if he arrived and Wright was suddenly unavailable?

Or if Bill Wright slowly shook his head and said, "I'm sorry you came all this way, but I just don't remember."

Owen didn't want to have to justify throwing good money and valuable time at a bad case.

Outside by the Cessna, Owen strained to hear the pilot's brittle voice in the gusting wind but learned more anyway about the indignity of yearly physicals and ridiculously tough vision tests and the grifting hands of the Feds, always wanting more and bigger money. Owen could have recited the wingnut's liturgy for him, it was so universal, hackneyed. He turned his attention back skyward.

The pilot kept talking.

All that government nonsense, according to his eccentric logic, almost demanded of him that he cut corners.

Owen's focus jumped back to the pilot. The line about cutting corners had got him. But then he found himself fixating on the way the pilot left off speaking and stood with the wind riffling his sparse white hair, using his left hand to hold his right hand firmly against his waist.

He stood that way for a moment. When the bluster got quiet, he said, "The upside is, with tailwinds like this, we'll shave twenty minutes off the flight time." The pilot looked up. "We may have a little weather up there, but it shouldn't be a problem."

Forty-five minutes into the flight, just above Sparta, Owen saw the sky flash a vivid, pale, electrified blue, and the glare still hung brightly black on his retina when the thunder cracked a second later. Then the rain began.

The Cessna's windscreen was a blur of twisting water.

Two flashes, one right on top of the other. Then a third. Neither Owen nor Goggin had ever heard anything like the sound the thunder made.

"Holy shit," Goggin said. "Holy fucking shit."

There was nothing else to say.

You could look at Goggin's eyes and the way they were taut and shivering, like twinned, cornered animals, and see that terror had taken him over and made itself at home. Owen wondered briefly, uncomfortably—just for a second—if Goggin might be seeing more of the full scope of the situation, more, anyway, than he was, and whether it might be time to shit a few bricks.

But ingrained habit took command. *Don't panic, break down, fall apart*, Owen ordered himself. *If there's a problem, figure it out and fix it.*

About a decade earlier, Owen had gotten his pilot's license at Grandpa Forrest and Uncle Delly's insistence.

His grandfather, uncle, and father were all wartime pilots—Forrest had flown in Europe in 1917, late in the war. Delly in the European Theater against the Reich, his father in one of the first-ever jet fighters over Korea. When the wars ended, Forrest and Delly each paid the military $200 for surplus J3 Piper Cubs and made a living dusting crops, flying charters, and performing in air circuses. Up in Minnesota, Delly had done a loop with a one-year-old Owen as a passenger. They believed good pilots gained skills that made them better men. The second Owen turned eighteen, they rode him until they got his license.

In these circumstances, Owen thought it might serve him, Goggin, and the pilot well.

Owen moved toward the cockpit, unbalanced by the pitching of the plane as it was shoved and battered by the wind.

He said to the pilot, "Everything under control? Anything I can help with?"

Without looking at him, the pilot said, "No. No, don't worry. I'm pretty sure this is going to let up soon."

Owen went back to his seat.

Goggin was muttering: *Oh my God. Oh my God. Oh my God.*

Then he was quiet.

After a few moments, he looked at Owen with a nauseated face and panicked eyes. He was about to speak but then seemed to think better of opening his mouth at all.

Another flash, another seismic crack, and then turbulence grabbed the plane and throttled it.

Goggin said, "This is terrifying."

He sounded outraged, infuriated.

"I know," Owen said. "I know. But trust me, this looks way worse than it actually is."

"I really want a drink."

"I know."

"I think it might be time for a novena," Goggin said.

"It couldn't hurt." Owen was joking but looking at Goggin, he wished he hadn't said it.

"We're going to die." Goggin was insistent.

"I swear to you, Mike, you're not. It's not as bad as you think," Owen said.

The wind roared and the plane shook.

Goggin closed his eyes. He swallowed. He opened his eyes again. He said, "If that old man drops dead of a stroke, can you land this thing?"

"Mike, man, it's okay. It's all going to be fine." Owen tried to say it as if he believed it was true. He'd logged—what?—seven hundred hours of flight time? More? But he was scared shitless too. "If anything happens, I can get this thing to the ground."

Owen left it at that. He could get it to the ground. Whether anyone would walk away was a different story.

"Okay," Goggin said. "Okay. Okay."

The plane went into convulsions.

Goggin started muttering again. *Oh my God. Oh my God. Oh my God.*

Owen watched the pilot seesaw the steering back and forth. Looking at the attitude indicator's white horizon line, he saw the plane kept tilting downward, like its face was being rubbed into the weather.

"My God," Goggin said. He sounded amazed, full of wonder. "Your hair."

The air around them felt as if it was seething, and the hair on Owen's arms rose straight and rigid. Goggin's hair was standing up off his head, and Owen knew his hair was doing the same.

"Shit," the pilot said, and the Cessna made a sharp dive and then leveled off. The seething stopped and the air went dull, and their hair lay back down.

The sky lit up again, but this time there were a few heartbeats between the flash and the thunder, then a few more after the next flash and several more after that.

The wind kept gusting but seemed less committed to killing them. The rain eased, slackened, then disappeared altogether, and when they saw seams of blue between the clouds up ahead, the pilot turned a gray face and weak victor's smile toward Owen and Goggin, and he laughed a little. It was humorless and sounded like gravel rattling in his throat.

The Cessna landed at around 2:30.

They passed a bar on the drive to Johnson City, a square, squat, windowless place painted white. Despite the daylight, a green neon Dixie beer sign burned near the bar's front door. Goggin stared and touched his fingers to the car window as they drove past.

A county deputy had been waiting for them at the airport. He was unfailingly courteous and so brightly hospitable that Owen couldn't quite bring himself to trust it. Owen sensed Goggin felt the same way. The deputy put questions to them about Chicago, prosecuting, the trip down, and their families and reacted with an outsized fascination to each answer. Neither Owen nor Goggin said anything about their flight to Johnson City. The nature of it seemed unsayable.

"Hey, Deputy," Goggin said. "What's a Saturday night like around here?"

He and Owen were in the back seat of the roller, behind the partition. They saw the deputy eye them in the rearview, probably looking for any hint of ridicule. Owen could tell Goggin was genuinely curious.

"I can tell you about last Saturday. Late afternoon, little girl's doing the laundry for her mother in the basement, and swear to God, somehow a cottonmouth got in there, and it was all coiled up by the washing machine, and she didn't see it, and it gets her in the ankle. I got that call." He paused there.

Outside, it was heavily wooded. From time to time they passed a car coming in the opposite direction. Occasionally, Owen saw small, slouching houses right up against the shoulder of the road.

"Damn," Goggin said after a moment. "She okay? What happened?"

"So, the ambulance was out already—old woman, bad heart, way, way out in the hills. The hospital's a ways away, so it's not getting to that little girl anytime soon, and I'm right nearby. I get there, her mama was with her on the porch. Little girl is screaming—and I mean screaming—and her ankle is swelled up bigger than a softball. Right then, the bulkhead flies open, her daddy comes running out of the cellar holding a shovel, and the head of the shovel is all bloody. He's all wild-eyed, shouting at me, 'The thing won't die.'

"Lot of people don't know this, but most snakebites won't kill you if you're a grown-up. They hurt like hell, though, and you get bit on an extremity? Stand a good chance of losing it, you don't act quick. It's different with kids, though. The girl and her mama pile in back, and I must've hit eighty-five getting her to the ER."

"Did she make it?" Owen said.

"Yeah. Seven bags of anti-venom. She's still in the ICU. But I speed back to the house because the doctor wanted to know what kind of snake bit her, and her daddy's out on the porch, shovel at his feet, smoking himself a cigarette. 'It's dead now,' he says. I go to the basement and, I assume it came in through that bulkhead but it tried a different way out, and it got stuck there in the rock walls. The guy smashed at it with the shovel, over and over until it just split open. What was left I pulled out with a rake, and sure enough, it was a cottonmouth. I radioed the hospital to tell them that while I drove fast as I could to the McDonald's, which we're about to pass up ahead, because two peckerwoods got into it over a milkshake or some shit—pardon me—and one stabbed the other one in the neck. Again with the ambulance. This time, it's at a wreck on the highway, so the village cops take the one did the stabbing with them, and I wind up doing eighty again to the hospital. The guy's screaming too, the whole way there. You'd think you get stabbed in the neck, maybe you'd shut the hell up for a few minutes. Blood everywhere back there."

Owen and Goggin looked down at the vinyl seat.

"No, don't worry. Next morning, I took the car over to the guy's place—the stabbed guy—and made his little brother clean it up."

"So, you knew the guy?" Goggin said.

"Everyone knows everyone. Everyone grew up with everyone else. Now, the next call—I didn't know him. Colored kid in a Parks Department shed. Too much drugs. We think he had company that ran when he dropped dead. He was the quietest one all night."

"It's got to get difficult, though, knowing everyone."

"Is it easier in Chicago, then, not knowing anyone?"

"Fair enough."

"Once upon a time, I thought about maybe going to Nashville. Being a cop there would be a little more like being a cop in Chicago, I suppose. But I knew everyone here, so it was too late."

Owen said, "What do you mean, 'too late'?"

They'd passed a number of churches on the way and were just now passing Antioch Baptist. The deputy gestured toward it. "Cain hits Abel, Abel tries to hit him back, and I'm the last line of defense between the two of them."

Goggin said, "That's some responsibility."

"Sure is," the deputy said. "But here, Nashville, Knoxville, New York, Chicago—at the end of the day, we all want to work ourselves out of a job, right?"

Right then, the trees vanished and they were coming into something like a town. Owen saw a mechanic's shop, a bank, a McDonald's, a school in the distance.

When Goggin and Owen didn't answer, the deputy said, "I mean, we want to be obsolete, right? You're a cop, then the best nights are going to be the most boring nights."

Owen reflected on that. It wasn't a thought he'd had before. It was unpleasant to realize that for him, it might not be true. "Is it boring here?"

"Eighty miles an hour with a girl and her mama screaming like the damned in your ear isn't exactly boring." The deputy's voice got bright again and a bit louder. "But let me tell you what. That n— friend of yours? When he crashed landed on us, that was hands down the biggest damn thing that ever happened here. No question about it. Peckerwood with a knife is a dime a dozen. Black boy and all that marijuana pot falling out the firmament? That's one in a million."

Sheriff Jimmy Strickland had his feet up on his desk when Owen and Goggin came into the station. When he saw them, he brought his feet down noisily to the floor. He stood up and extended a hand.

"Are you the two boys from Chicago?"

He had same bright and brash voice as the deputy had at the start and finish of the ride over.

Owen said, "I'm Gregg Owen, assistant state's attorney, and this is my partner, Assistant State's Attorney Mike Goggin, and yes, I guess we are the boys from Chicago."

"I'm Jimmy Strickland, Washington County sheriff. Now, I just want to be sure I've got this straight. You're here to have a little talk with one and only Bill Wright, one of the county's more famous guests, about some information he might have, right? And I'm sure I mentioned his trial would be starting soon."

"And you advised us he's facing some serious charges."

"That boy's looking at life. For what we caught him with? Seven tons of marijuana and who-all-knows how much cocaine. Shit. Pardon me. Life, maybe parole in twenty, if he plays the game right."

Owen whistled. "Seven pounds and he's up for life?"

"No, not seven pounds. I said tons. Seven tons. That's about fourteen thousand pounds. Considerable more than seven pounds."

"Plus cocaine," Goggin said.

"Yeah. That burned up, but while it did, you sure could smell it."

"I guess that's hard to mistake for anything else."

"Sweet, burnt rubbery kind of smell. But I tell you, half the town got high off that pot." Strickland put his hands in his pocket and rocked back and forth on the worn heels of his boots. "Now, you mentioned something about a murder. Did that n— kill someone?"

Goggin and Owen eyed each other. Owen said, "No, he didn't kill anybody. But I've got a double murder, and I need to connect the victim and the killer. I don't have anything solid there."

"And that boy does? Has something solid?"

"Seems that way." Owen laid his briefcase on the seat of an empty chair, opened it, and rummaged through. He pulled out a copy of the manifest Rice had given them. He held it so Strickland could see it. He pointed. "There's Wright's name. And these are the two victim's names. And there—that one is the killer."

"*Mitchell. Weinger.*" Strickland intoned the name. "Did this Weinger kill those two on this same flight that Billy took 'em on?"

Owen couldn't tell if maybe Strickland was putting an antisemitic spin on the way he said *Weinger*. He thought not. Strickland had pronounced the name correctly—with the hard *G*—and on quick reflection, Owen heard something solemn rather than scornful in Strickland's voice.

Strickland said, "How'd he do it?"

"Excuse me?" Owen said.

"Weinger. How'd he kill them?"

"Stabbed them a number of times each."

"A lot of times?"

"Enough times."

"They have it coming?"

"No one has that coming."

"Would it be all right with you if I looked through that file?"

Owen hesitated. Strickland saw it and held a hand up. "No, never mind. It's fine. Don't worry."

*Did that n— kill someone?* Owen glanced around the office with private distaste. It took a moment to remember he'd heard even worse in Chicago squad rooms.

"Sorry," Owen said, handing the file to Strickland. "Habit."

After a moment, Strickland found Tinker's picture—a headshot of the type actors use for auditions—and lingered over it for a moment.

"Pretty girl," he said.

Owen listened for a hint of something condemning or lascivious, but all he caught was a hint of something sorrowful. When Strickland got to the crime scene photos, Owen heard a sharp intake of breath.

"Well," Strickland said, handing the file back to Owen. He didn't say more for a moment. Then, offhanded: "If you get a guilty, you going to kill him?"

The question took Owen off guard. It was a chilly way to put it. He sensed Goggin watching, waiting for Owen to answer. He wondered if he was wrong to take the question as a provocation, with his answer setting the tone for the rest of his time here. He sensed Strickland wanted to hear that not only would Owen—on behalf of Illinois—kill Weinger himself, but it would all be done publicly.

Goggin saved him and stepped in. "Wow. That's a hell of a way to put it, Sheriff."

The answer was its own provocation. As if to mitigate the moment, Goggin added, "It's not up to us, anyway."

Strickland leaned back in his chair. "Don't misunderstand me. I know there's a big difference between Washington County and Cook's County. A world of difference. And I hope it's ever thus. But there's not any difference when it comes to bad men. Just the fact you came all the way here tells me so."

Another deputy had come into the room during the conversation. Strickland looked at him. "Deputy Castor, you spoke to these gentlemen—yes, go ahead, everyone shake hands—so will you escort them to Billy's cell?"

Castor beckoned. "You all want to come with me?"

He led them out of the office, down a flight of stairs, and through a corridor with cracked green linoleum and the scent of a very potent cleaner. Then he took them through another door, up another flight of stairs, and led them into a courtroom. It was vast, with room for a hundred people and a spectator's gallery up above them that might accommodate a few dozen more.

The thing was so out of place and incongruous that for a few seconds neither Goggin nor Owen registered what it was. It was right in the middle of the floor, between the tables for the prosecution and defense, a dozen or so feet from the bench—a cage, with bars, such as might hold something big and feral.

Owen stepped closer and saw a metal chair bolted to the floor.

Now, Goggin's voice was bright and brash. "Deputy, what have we here?"

Owen turned to Goggin and said, "They've got a chair bolted to the floor in there."

Castor said, "What was that?"

"I said, you've got a chair bolted to the floor in that thing. What is that?"

Castor crossed his arms tight over his chest. He looked uneasy. "Well. Well. Now, I don't necessarily call it this, but some of the old-timers refer to the cage as the Johnson City Monkey House. They's only a handful of us here, and we gotta be safe, you know? So … we don't have to keep guard over the prisoner this way. But I admit, calling it the Monkey House is maybe a bit much."

Goggin, still genial, said, "Did a Washington County Grand Jury indict J. Fred Muggs?"

Now Castor was defensive. "I don't know who that is. Listen, I like Billy. I like Billy a lot."

Goggin and Owen exchanged looks back and forth. Castor said, "Let's go see how the boy's doing."

He led them up a flight of stairs and at the top, in a large and otherwise empty small room, they saw a single jail cell, one side against the wall, the other three open-barred. They saw someone lying on a bed inside, reading a book.

When Bill Wright saw them, he sat immediately upright, rigid on the edge of his cot. His face was a studied neutral, but it was clear Owen and Goggin hadn't been expected. Wright was trim and radiated strong, good health. He was unusually good-looking. There was a presence about him that extended beyond the bars.

Castor said, "Billy, you have some visitors. These gentleman are prosecutors from Chicago, flown all the way out here to talk to you."

At this Wright stood up. He started rolling his paperback into a tight curl. For a moment, he had the look of someone ambushed, caught out, but then he was neutral again. He sounded weary. "FBI, DEA, IRS, or Treasury?" Wright said.

"None of the above," Owen said. "Nothing federal. Tell you the truth, we probably feel the same about the Feds as you do."

Wright laughed to himself, bitter. "Okay. Who's *we*?"

"I'm Gregg Owen. This is my trial partner, Mike Goggin. We're assistant state's attorney's from Cook County."

Wright laughed again, louder this time. "That doesn't sound much better."

"We wanted to talk to you about a double murder that occurred about four years ago—" Owen saw Wright start "—a double murder you had nothing to do with. But in your capacity as a pilot, you might have done a charter for someone who *did* have something to do with it."

Wright relaxed a little.

Owen said, "But before I get into that, let me ask you something. How the hell did you fly a DC6 by yourself? I mean, that is a *lot* of airplane to fly without a copilot. I'm a pilot too. Not on your level but enough to know that must have been a tough thing to pull off. Where were you flying from?"

Wright regarded him for a moment. Then he nodded. He said, "What's your name again?"

"Gregg Owen."

"Okay, Gregg. you know I can't talk about *where* I was flying from. But to answer your other question, I guess I *didn't* quite pull it off."

"What happened?"

"I've had a decent amount of time to think about that. I'd say I got tangled up by a bad fuel gauge indicator. I've plotted a lot of flights. A *lot*. I was absolutely, 100 percent positive I had enough fuel to get where I was going. More than enough. Apparently not. The nearest I can figure, someone tampered with the instruments or screwed around with the mixture I put in the tank. The guys I was working for ... you could say they weren't my best friends. We'd had a run-in or two. We didn't see eye to eye over a couple of matters."

"You had a disagreement with your employers, so they sabotaged the flight? With a cargo like the one you had?"

"I didn't say they were very bright. Anyway, I'm flying along, doing fine, no problems. Then I'm over eastern Tennessee, and I'm having problems. The plane starts dragging. I look out the windows. The right engines are okay, but the left engines had stopped working. I knew there was no way I could control this thing by myself, and it's dark at this point, so I start looking pretty hard for a field or something to land in. I see the perfect place, and I start taking it in, and then it feels like all the power's gone, and when I look, the right engines are no longer okay.

"I did my best to hold it steady, keep from falling, but it wouldn't respond. Next thing I know, it dropped on the ground and the rear portion of fuselage broke off. Once it hit, I knew I had to get out of that plane. I kicked the pilot's side window and crawled out. I started running fast as I could manage, and I got about fifty yards away. But I found out—I wasn't completely out of fuel. There was *just* enough left to catch fire and when it did ... all hell broke loose. It was like the Fourth of July on the farm. That fucker caught fire, and then the rednecks showed up, and I've been sitting in this shithole ever since."

Owen marveled. "That's some skill."

Wright made a slight bowing motion. He said, "Now, you mentioned something about murder?"

The travel and hazards of getting to Wright sharpened a sense in Owen that this might avail him nothing. That things could very easily go completely, irredeemably south. He considered just how to ask Wright the crucial questions, as if wrong phrasing might get him a wrong answer.

*Bullshit. Ridiculous*, he thought. Regardless, he couldn't quash the feeling. Right now, he didn't want to ask Wright anything because without a definite answer he still had hope, and the hope felt exquisite.

*Screw it*, he thought.

He said, "I want to ask you about a charter you piloted. This is February 1976. There's a record of you taking three passengers to Lake Geneva."

Wright was watching the floor.

"The passengers were Gio Messina, Delphine Moore, and Mitchell Weinger."

Wright's eyes shot back to Owen.

"Do you recall that trip?"

Wright said, "Yeah, I remember. I remember it very well."

Owen experienced a surge of almost opiate relief. His eyes nearly brimmed with gratitude. For one second he couldn't feel his fingertips.

"Can I ask why that trip is so memorable?"

"I remember when Gio was killed. I was waiting for you guys to come find me. I read all about it. I read about … Is it *Weinger*? Okay, I read about Weinger basically walking away. Eventually, I figured no one was coming to talk to me. But I remember this: when we landed in Lake Geneva, Gio went into some outbuilding to … "

"To buy cocaine."

Wright nodded. "Yeah, to buy cocaine. And five minutes after Gio went in, the other two were all over each other."

"What do you mean, 'all over each other'?"

"I mean, Weinger had his tongue down her throat, had his hand up her skirt; she was grabbing his dick."

Wright stood and took a step up to the bars.

"Did you say anything?"

"Like what? I just sank down in the seat and pretended I wasn't there." Wright gripped the bars with both hands. "But—wait, sorry to cut you off, but this is important—I have felt so bad … so guilty since then. If I had told Gio what I saw … if I'd told him, he'd probably be alive. If I said, 'Hey, your girl was grabbing your friend's cock, and he was fingering her,' do you think Gio would have let that motherfucker into his place? No. No, he would not. He wouldn't have given Weinger a chance to kill him."

Owen waited a moment. Then, he pulled Weinger's photo from his briefcase. "Is this the guy?"

"Yes. That's the guy."

"Will you be a witness in Weinger's trial?"

"What trial is this?"

"He's going on trial in late April, early May. For Gio's murder."

Wright said softly, "Fuck, yes, I'd be a witness."

"I want to bring you to Chicago for the trial."

Wright shook his head. "Good luck. That isn't going to happen."

"Let me see what I can do."

"I guarantee it won't be much. You know, I'm something of a cash cow here?"

"What does that mean?"

Wright affected a broad, acrid grin. "You mean, Castor there didn't charge you two bucks?"

"What?"

"Come on, now. A n— and a few tons of weed don't come falling out of the sky every day. Castor here fancies himself an entrepreneur, so he charges curious hilljacks two bucks to take a look."

Owen held his hands up, signaling he was at a loss for words. Finally, he said again, "Let me see what I can do."

Strickland looked up when Owen and Goggin walked back in. He was instantly cordial and smiling. "Gentlemen. Tell me, did that boy give you anything useful?"

Owen felt everything hinged on his next few words. Everything often hinged on a next few words. His success in persuading judges and juries over to his side laid in having the right words ready.

So, where were they now?

Owen never liked asking for anything because uncertainty could knock a lawyer down dead. On the job, he'd had it drilled into him: never pose a question if you don't know the answer. He was about to ask the sheriff for an enormous favor, and there was no telling how he would answer. He knew what answer he wanted, but on the way here, the weather nearly had him tangled up in a nasty death, and the place he landed was one where people sat for trial in cages. Sense and process were all messed up.

All this came to him at the speed of thought.

Owen noticed a wedding ring on Strickland's finger. The flesh rising over the ring's edges told Owen it had been there a long time.

He said, "I know I mentioned I was here about a double murder. A young man, young woman just heading into their prime. And some psychopath hacked them to death with a butcher's knife. That guy is the son of someone so rich he believes the laws were written for everybody else on earth but him. And not only does this killer have no remorse, does not in the least feel bad—" Owen took Weinger's photo out, Weinger with his boredom-dulled eyes and expression of vague impatience, and held it up for Strickland "—but he looks like the whole thing is just an inconvenience."

"Incidentally, the father of the young man who was killed, he's the one who found his son and his son's girlfriend lying in their own blood. He said when he opened the door, he remembered the smell from Europe in 1944 and knew exactly what he was about to find."

Owen gave the picture a shake. He dropped his voice. "This son of a bitch is about to walk away, never have to answer for it, never have to think about it again. He gets to enjoy his seven-million-dollar trust fund, gets to inherit his daddy's fortune later on. And the guy you've got upstairs is the person who can keep that from happening. Without him, we're probably going to lose."

When Strickland grinned at him, Owen thought the sheriff was about to give him the spoken equivalent of a sharp kick to the balls. But then Owen saw there was nothing malign in the smile.

Strickland said, "Is that the facts?"

It took Owen a second to realize the question wasn't rhetorical. He nodded.

"Shit," Strickland said mildly. He chewed his lower lip for a while. Then he said, "Why don't you fellows make yourselves comfortable for a moment?"

He picked the phone up and began dialing, and then put it to his ear. After a moment, he said, "Marietta? Well, Marietta, darling, it's Jimmy Strickland. Why, I'm just fine. And you? How's everything by you? What? Come again? Why now, darling, I hadn't heard a word about that. That's great. Good for him. I am pleased to hear it but not at all surprised. Listen, I hate to bother y'all, but is my cousin there? Oh, well, I know he is. I know, and I wouldn't be interrupting if it wasn't pretty important. Well, yes, you could say it was urgent. Of course I'll hold. And thank you very much, Marietta."

Castor said, "Jimmy—it's Mary Ellen, not Marietta."
Strickland winced. "Goddammit."

Strickland sat holding the phone against his ear, staring at some private matter of interest at the far end of the ceiling. From time to time the keys on Castor's belt jangled when he shifted from foot to foot. The silence went on for a couple of minutes, stretching toward interminable.

"Cousin!" Strickland cried out. He swung his feet from the desk and sat up straight. "Couldn't be better. How's everything by you, out there in grand old Nashville? ... Now listen—before I get to why I called, I got a bone to pick with you, sir. ... Yes, that's exactly right. The reunion. I know you're a busy man but—wait now. Hold on—I know you're busy, and that's why we didn't disown you for not showing your face. ... Yes. ... Yes. Consider yourself duly warned, cousin. ... Yes, she did make it. She made extra just for you, and her heart broke that you weren't there to have some. ... Yes, of course I'm trying to make you feel guilty. ... Okay, fair enough, fair enough. ... Yes, sir. ... July 19.

"So, I got two old boys from Chicago here. Two prosecutors. Now, you remember that colored boy, crashed his plane here? ... Well, turns out, that boy can help our Chicago friends convict a killer. ... Well, I'll let them give you the details, but as far as I understand, they need to put the killer and the victims together, and our pilot is the one can do it. ... Yes, victims, plural. Young man and a young woman. Stabbed to death. I saw the photos. ... Yes, it was. It was indeed. ... But it sounds like, this boy don't testify, the killer walks away."

Strickland listened for a bit, nodding occasionally. Then he looked straight at Goggin and Owen. "Yes, I believe so. ... Yes. ... I do, yes. ... That's sort of what I was thinking. ... Hold on one moment."

He held the phone toward Goggin. "The coverer says he'd like a word."

Goggin waved his hands and stepped away. Owen took the receiver. He had no idea who or what *the coverer* was, but as far as sobriquets went, it had ominous overtones.

Owen said, "This is Gregg Owen, assistant state's attorney from Chicago, Illinois."

"This is the governor. Gregg, my cousin tells me we may be able to help you out with a case you're working on. Is that about right?"

*Coverer, governor.* The accent was hard to decode.

Owen said, "Yes, Mr. Governor, that's exactly right."

Strickland stage whispered, "Tell him what you told me."

Owen laid the story out for the governor just as he had for Strickland.

After a pause, the governor cleared his throat and said, "Gregg, you know why that boy's in stir, correct?"

"I do, Governor. I appreciate the gravity of it, I assure you. But ... I don't know how to ask, but we'd like to have Mr. Wright come testify in Chicago."

"Okay. Let me make sure I've got it. Without that boy's testimony, there's every likelihood that a man who killed two people will walk away."

"In a word, yes."

"Is that the facts?"

This time it did sound rhetorical. He didn't answer.

"I'll tell you what, Gregg. Someone takes the life from two of God's children, to me that trumps just about everything else. You say you appreciate the gravity of my situation; I appreciate the gravity of yours. When's your trial?"

"About two months."

"We've been holding that boy for some time."

There was a pause, long enough to make Owen uneasy.

The silence stretched.

Then, in a bright voice, the governor said, "Now, in Tennessee, the penalty for possession is a minimum of two years. So, if in two months he pleads guilty to possession, and then after the trial, you bring him back for a couple more months—and he promises never to pull some stupid stunt like that again—well, we'll call the whole thing even."

It wasn't that Owen didn't know the right words. At that moment he didn't know any words. Finally, he said, "I really don't know how to thank you."

"Get the conviction, son. That'll do her. Would you kindly put Jimmy back on?"

When Strickland hung up, he handed Owen a paper with the direct line to his cousin's office.

"Don't lose it," Strickland said. "The governor says go ahead and give him a call back by end of week. Should we see about getting you back to the airport?"

Owen said, "Before we go back, do you mind if I just let Mr. Wright know what the governor told me?"

"Not at all," Strickland said. "Can you find your way back there? Good. We'll be waiting here for you."

When Owen and Goggin got to Wright, it was very late in the afternoon. The light was just now failing outside. Only a little came through the three windows, and even less reached Wright on his bunk, where he sat holding his book up to catch the last few beams of it.

When he heard Owen and Goggin coming in, Wright closed the book and laid it down, and his face was that of someone resigned to hearing bad news. Wright was still, except for the index finger of the hand resting on his book. It picked furiously at a chip on the spine.

"See? I told you," Wright said. He smiled without any levity.

"Did you?" Owen said. "Probably good I didn't listen, then. Here's what's going to happen. You're going to plead guilty to possession. Then you're coming to Chicago. After you testify there, you come back here. Now, possession means two years minimum in Tennessee. But they've agreed they're going to count the time you've been here already, so when you get back to Johnson City, you'll serve a couple more months, then you're free."

A long silence held.

"Bullshit," Wright said finally. His tone was angry. He lay back down on the bunk and, though it was too dark to read, opened his book again.

"I'm not bullshitting you. This is for real. We're getting it in writing."

"How? How in the hell did you do that?" From where Owen stood, it looked like Wright was trembling.

He said, "I talked to the governor."

"I don't understand this," Wright said. "Things don't work this way."

"Until they do," Owen said.

Later, as the pilot reinspected the plane, going over every inch, Owen and Goggin stood off to the side.

Owen said, "I think I'm more scared now than when we came."

Goggin looked up. No clouds. No threat of rain. Just the sun declining west. He said, "Meaning what?"

Tiny depressions in the blacktop still held thin puddles of water from the storm, the surfaces iridescent with oil sheens.

"Everything's going right. Everything's going our way," Owen said. "Luck this good doesn't go unpunished."

## CHAPTER 36
*May 5, 1980*

Right before the trial started and Tony was scheduled to testify, he and Owen met at Villa Marconi for what had become semi-regular lunches. This was a new situation for Owen. He'd never sat down to dinner with the family of a victim, let alone multiple dinners. No one had ever invited him before.

When Owen arrived, he saw Tony was already seated.

*He's always early*, Owen thought. *Every time. It's not a bad way to be.*

When he got to the table, Tony greeted him warmly, but as soon as Owen sat, he could sense Tony was uneasy. It wasn't an unreasonable reaction, given how close they were to the first day.

After the waiter came and they ordered, Tony said, "How's your mother, Gregg?"

When Jay Owen and Gio Messina were friends, Gio had met Jay and Gregg Owen's mother on a few occasions, and Gio had made a good impression. She thought Gio was a polite, very smart kid, and a good friend for Jay. At Christmastime, she'd baked extra cookies for the Messina family. Whenever Owen and Tony met, Tony asked after Owen's mother.

"She's doing well. I told her we were meeting for lunch, and she asked me to say hello."

"Well, say hello for me too." Tony became quiet. He kept smoothing the folds of his napkin. Finally, he said, "Gregg, I really appreciate that you take the time to keep me in the loop. I was glad you could find the time today because I had a couple things I wanted to talk about, and I just thought it would be better to do it face-to-face.

"But before anything else, I wanted to say this: Evie and I, the girls too—I can't tell you how happy we are that we met you. You and Mike both. I never thought we'd see Gio and Tinker get any kind of justice. We didn't even think there'd ever be a trial. And no matter what happens, it feels … it feels really good to have a little hope again. Because what's made all this even harder … "

Tony's eyes welled. It took a moment to get himself under control. After a few deep breaths, he continued. "Did you know the Weingers live pretty close to us? Right near our house. All this time—these past four years—we'd be in town and we'd see Mr. and Mrs.

Weinger fairly often. They'll be shopping, coming out of the library. We've never said anything to them. They've never said anything to us. I think we all pretend not to notice each other. Gina ... somehow, she winds up seeing Mitchell Weinger all over the place. In Walgreens. There's a restaurant she and her friends like, in Glenville, and she's seen Mitchell in there a few times. It just guts her every time, seeing the person who murdered her brother. Just walking around. Alive. Free. Laughing like nothing in the world matters."

"All I can tell you is that we're doing everything possible to make sure he gets locked up for a long, long time. It's not an easy case, but God willing, I genuinely believe he doesn't have too many more days of freedom. You have my word, and Mike's word too, that Gio and Tinker are going to get represented in the way they deserve. They're going to have a voice."

There was a long pause.

Tony said, "You didn't see me, but I saw you the other day."

"What do you mean?"

"I was in the area; I wanted to see what the courthouse was like—what to expect, you know? And I walked into a couple of different courtrooms and sat in the back rows. And there you were."

"When was this?" Owen felt genuine surprise.

"What's today? Wednesday? It was this past Monday."

"No kidding? Wow. That was the domestic case ... "

"I was only there for a few minutes, but it sounded pretty ugly. And you're going right from that case to Gio and Tinker's? No break."

"No, no break." He laughed. "I don't need a break, Tony."

"You were fierce. It was surprising. You were *good*."

"I felt pretty good about it."

"What are you thinking about when you're up there?"

"About the jury. I was taught that during a trial, the *only* thing that counts is the jury. That's all that matters. A lot of times you see some lawyers trying to impress the judge, or show off for the press. But I learned that every bit of your attention goes on the jury."

"'Learned' as in, you took classes in that sort of thing?"

"No. I mean, we had a trial techniques class but ... " Owen waved dismissively. "The real stuff you get taught on the job.

"I had a mentor. A guy named Tom Breen. He was a year, two years older, but oh, man, he was something to watch. When he tried a case? He *owned* the courtroom. In law school, I kept hearing his name, kept hearing other people say, 'You've got to go see Tom Breen try a case.' So I went and watched him, and right then, I said 'I want to work with that guy.'"

"And you did," Tony said.

"I did. That's where I learned. Breen had it all down. Everything was planned out. Everything was for a reason. He called it 'the choreography of the courtroom.' And that's just what it was.

"One of the first things he taught you was never wear jewelry. No watch. No ring. Nothing. You don't want any distractions. You don't want any class resentment. No judgment calls—like, you don't want a juror saying, 'I don't like his watch, so I don't like him.' He told me to always wear a nice, plain, simple black suit. He said we should look like undertakers. No distractions. Nothing to take the focus off my voice."

"Did he tell you how to move around? About hand gestures? Stuff like that?"

"Of course. Absolutely. When a witness is on the stand, he taught me to go to the far side of the jury box, so when the witness answers my question, it seems like they're speaking right to the jury. If you've got a witness you don't like, you stand opposite the jury box, as far away as you can, because then the witness isn't looking at the jury and there's a sense they have something to hide. Though, sometimes that backfired. Expert witnesses? They know to look right at the jury. So if you're standing on the opposite side of the room and the expert witness is addressing the jury, you look like a moron. The one time I did that, afterward, when I sat down, Breen gripped my leg so hard it left a bruise, and he said in my ear, 'Are you fucking stupid? Don't ever do that again.'"

"With other lawyers—the opposition—like on TV, they're screaming *objection* every two seconds, and I've never understood that."

"That's TV. But, sure, sometimes it happens. Breen made us weigh objections really carefully. You run a risk if you do it too much. When people are just constantly like, 'objection, objection, objection,' they do it to break your rhythm. Screw up your cadence. And it will. But you can irritate the judge. You can piss the jury off. You don't want to piss the jury off. When someone does that to me, I might ask for a sidebar. I'll keep cool, but once we're back in chambers, I'll say, 'Judge, this is ridiculous, it's interfering with my ability to try the case,' etcetera. Chances are, if it's enough to call for a sidebar, the judge will agree with me. Then it makes the objector self-conscious, a little overcautious, maybe. Plus, they run the risk of contempt if they keep it up.

"I'll tell you one thing that was hard to get down was the voice. You want to modulate. You don't want to be shouting all the time. You want to keep it even as much as you can because then when you raise it, it has a hell of a lot more impact."

"You had a hard time with that?"

"Oh, yeah. I was ... let's just say I was pretty animated. I was everywhere, running all over, screaming. Breen finally told me he'd break my kneecap if I kept it up."

Owen trailed off.

Tony waited for a moment, then said, "Keep going. This is really interesting."

"Let me save some of the magic." Owen drummed his fingers. "You're going to be part of the magic act pretty soon. You'll see it firsthand."

"Fair enough." Tony laughed quietly, then lapsed into silence. After a moment, he continued. "Look, I asked you here because I want to talk about this life-and-death witness thing you mentioned. Can you talk me through it again?"

"Okay, it seems ridiculous, but we need to get it on record that Gio was alive one day, then he was dead the next. So, a life-and-death witness says, 'I saw him on Monday, and then the following day, he was gone.'"

"You need this?"

"It's almost always a really emotional moment, and the jury is really affected by it." Owen stopped and looked away, his face pained. "I really don't want you thinking we take this lightly. It's not some gimmicky, melodramatic trick."

"It's fine. I know you don't take this lightly." Tony reached over and patted Owen's hand, then sat back. "Go ahead."

"We like putting life-and-death witnesses on before lunchtime. We want that to be what the jury is thinking about. We want them ... We want to make it real for them. Make it so we're not just having a back-and-forth about some abstract name. And, I hate saying it, but if the circumstances are really awful, that's what they'll have in their heads while they eat."

Tony nodded, eyes on the table. When he looked at Owen again, he had a hint of a bitter smile. "Who goes on after lunch?"

Owen exhaled. "Usually, we'll put a dynamic witness on. A lot of people get drowsy after eating, so we want someone who keeps them from drifting off."

"Who's the dynamic witness for this trial?"

"The medical examiner, for one. I recommend you skip his testimony."

Tony shook his head. "I already know what happened to Gio. No one's going to tell me anything new. But, back to the life-and-death witness … "

"Right. We prefer when a mother testifies. That's the person who always hits the jury the hardest."

"If you're saying you want to put Maria on the stand, we're not doing that. No. I can't put her through it. I won't. If the girls want to testify, that's their choice. If they're compelled to testify, I won't object. But not Maria."

Owen was dismayed but didn't want Tony to see it. He figured correctly that would be Tony's response, so he had made a point of not asking. Still, he hoped Tony might suggest it himself. Everything counted now. Every element.

"I'm having a hard time with the pace in here," Tony said. "There's a lot of commotion."

Tony fussed with the fold of his napkin. His fork fell noiselessly onto the table. He kneaded the napkin between his thumb and index finger, with more and more force. Then he stopped abruptly, spread his fingers wide above it, and gently brushing the cloth smooth again, replacing the fork where it had been.

Tony looked up. His eyelids fluttered. He had a just-discernible tremble to his lip. He closed his eyes and shook his head.

"Oh my God," he said. Owen wasn't sure what it was in reference to. Tony didn't elaborate.

The waiter came, carrying two pasta bowls that he laid at each place. Tony took up the napkin again but this time put it over his lap.

"If I order pasta at lunch," Tony said, "I always get shells instead of noodles."

Owen said, "So you don't spatter sauce all over the front of your shirt?"

Tony looked slightly surprised, then nodded approvingly.

"Yeah. Exactly." He speared a few penne. "The little things, Gregg. The small details."

"Ninety-nine percent of my job is small details. Small details are everything."

Tony pointed his fork at Owen. "That's why we're going to win."

Tony addressed himself to his pasta. Owen, fork poised over his bowl, watched him. He didn't quite understand the connection between details and winning.

*That's why we're going to win.*

Owen wondered if, once again, he should try to recalibrate Tony's expectations. But at this point, what possible safeguards were there against a potential disappointment that big? A disappointment, Owen knew, Tony could never get out from under.

They ate in silence for a while.

"But about Maria," Tony said, "she wouldn't be able to stand it. I'll do it. I'll testify. She didn't see him. She hasn't even looked at the pictures. She saw him at the funeral, but that wasn't Gio. That was a likeness. I'll do it. I'm going to be firm with this. She's never seen him, but if she had to testify, whether or not she heard it described, or saw pictures, it doesn't matter. She'll see him anyway, and it will be worse than anything anyone can show her."

## CHAPTER 37
*May 7, 1980*

There were pages of notes Goggin and Owen had written about their witnesses and how to use them. They weighed lines of questioning, speculated about who to coax, whose arms to twist, who'd respond best to gentle pressure, whose experience made coaching unnecessary.

It was 11:30 in the morning, and Owen had been at it for hours already. The sentences had started seeming like random arrangements of words, and the longer he stared at them the less sense they made. He wanted a break. He needed a break. But he wouldn't take one. At some point later today, Goggin was coming down and going over trial strategy, and Owen thought if he stopped, he'd lose the thread. There could be a key to the whole case, and whatever that key was, it might be about to reveal itself.

Right then, though, all sense and logic had fled, and his head felt heavy, and he couldn't keep his toes from tapping against the floor, and he couldn't keep from shifting in his seat. When the phone rang, he welcomed the interruption. He suspected it was Goggin calling and he was right,

"Disco, what have you got going in two hours? Are you open?"

"I'm free all day. I'm open now if you want."

"Nah, I need a little time. One o'clock, okay? So we can get logistics under control? Yeah? Great. I'll come by at one."

When Goggin came by, he suggested they move to the conference room with the chalkboard, if it was empty.

At the height of Vietnam, Goggin had a bad draft number and probably would have been called up. He would have gone too, despite never quite knowing what was really at stake over there and never fully believing the official reasons for getting involved. So, for four years he taught kids with disabilities in a Chicago public school and went to law school at night. It earned him an exemption.

That had been a long time ago, and he still felt good with a piece of chalk in his hand.

He picked one up when he and Owen walked in and stood shaking it in his cupped hand and rocking back and forth a little bit on his heels. He always had an organic command in a group or in front of a jury. Owen considered Goggin a great speaker, easygoing yet full of gravitas, and a great presence. He was a good leader because he was a bad tyrant. A lifetime of sports made him more comfortable as part of a team, someone integral rather than completely in charge. Owen also felt Goggin had a gift for strategic thinking, while he—Owen—was a stronger tactician. Goggin saw the goals and possibilities; Owen saw the best practical ways of making them happen.

"So, first of all, I just found out about the defense," Goggin said. "You want to hear about Weinger's 'dream team'?"

He gave *dream team* several air quotes.

Owen pushed his chair from his desk and put his hands behind his head. "Am I going to hate this?"

"Yeah, you're probably going to hate this."

"Just don't tell me it's Harry Busch."

Busch was a Chicago legend, famous for defending crime syndicate figures and serving on Jimmy Hoffa's defense team. Owen and Goggin thought he was insufferable.

"Okay, I won't tell you it's Harry Busch," Goggin said. He took a seat. "Except it is."

Owen groaned. "Come on. I can't handle listening to that jackass all day every day."

"Well, don't worry about it, Disco. You won't have to. Jo-Anne Wolfson is on the team."

Jo-Anne Wolfson had a reputation for being pugnacious and abrasive and became famous when she defended The Janes, a team of women arrested and charged with providing abortion access when it was still illegal.

They respected Wolfson and even liked her in a way, although they agreed her reputation for being abrasive was well-earned.

Owen nodded optimistically. "Okay. Good. That's fine."

"Yeah, I've always thought she did a good job. But that's not all." Goggin gave Owen a wide, malicious grin.

Owen closed his eyes and made a gesture of defeat. "Who? Who else?"

Goggin rose from his chair and assumed a stance like a Roman orator. "As the world turns, we know the bleakness of winter, the promise of—"

"Oh, man, are you serious?" Owen's tone turned flinty. He made a weak, pointless slap at some papers on his desk.

Goggin was talking about Sherwin Magidson, a DePaul law professor, expensive defense lawyer, and periodic scriptwriter for *As the World Turns* and *The Young and the Restless*.

"I really dislike that guy," Owen said.

"He's a blowhard. A pompous ass." Goggin watched him for a moment. "You're not worried, are you? You know we'll put that has-been all the way out to pasture." He sat down again.

Owen stared at the floor. After a moment, he said, "No, I'm not worried. I just really, really dislike that guy."

"Everyone dislikes that guy. Did you know him?"

"I've told you the story about him."

"No, I don't think you have. I didn't know you'd met him."

"As matter of fact, I have. At length. So, yeah, there's a story."

Owen told Goggin the story.

A friend had let Owen know about the Trial Techniques class. It was a good one, his friend said. Useful. Instructive. And a guaranteed B at least. Knowledge of basic law was presumed, but the rest of the class—conducted in mock trials—depended on arguing well in a compelling way, outtalking and outthinking your opponent. Owen was good at that and always had been. Even as a kid, he was especially persuasive. It had helped him keep the bands together. And he hadn't lost the skill: he got good feedback from the other students. He knew he was doing well.

At the end of the course, at the close of the last class, the instructor walked the room, passing each person a sheet of paper, folded in half lengthwise, with their name written on the outside.

He skipped Owen.

He told everyone else, "Your grades are written inside. Let's keep these folded. Open them outside of the room. Enjoy your summer, all of you. Gregg, could you stay back for a second?"

Owen stayed seated. His last in-class argument had gotten him the best critiques from the others he'd gotten all semester. Two times before that, the critique had been almost as good. When he'd finished, the instructor gave him a nod. Owen didn't need the guy's praise, but it wasn't unwelcome, and he felt eager to hear it.

The instructor moved another desk over and turned it to face Owen's. He pushed it so the desks touched.

"Gregg, I've got your grade right here." He held up the paper in his right hand, waving it while he talked. His voice was kindly enough. "As I watched you during the class, I could see that you just don't have what it takes to be a trial lawyer.

"Your demeanor during your presentations … it's just so far off from what it needs to be. It seems like … like … Well, Gregg, it seems like you just didn't get it. And I'll be frank: your appearance will not be received favorably in any courtroom."

*He's joking*, Owen thought. *He can't be serious.*

His instructor continued. "Not everyone is cut out to be a trial lawyer. There are a lot of different areas of law that don't involve a courtroom. I'd suggest that you go into an area of law that's more suited for your abilities."

Owen wanted to protest. He wanted to do it loudly, aggressively.

He thought he had done a good job during the mock trial sessions. In fact, he knew he did. He also knew protesting was a waste of time.

"It should have been a *D*," the instructor said helpfully. "But I gave you a *C-*."

Owen looked at his instructor and said, "Professor, I'm shocked because I really felt that I did a good job. Other people in class seemed to think so too. And it seemed like it came naturally to me. I liked what we did in this class. I liked it quite a bit. So, I'm going to go ahead and disagree. But thank you for weighing in."

There were two strong hands squeezing his lungs. His vision shivered. He had a tremor in his hands.

He got up and left in as calm and relaxed a way as he could manage.

"Wait a fucking second," Goggin said when Owen finished. "Is that instructor … What was his name?"

"You know where this is going. Yes, the instructor was Sherman Magidson."

"You've got to be kidding me," Goggin said. "That's … That's … *unconscionable.*"

Goggin and Owen were still working out strategy several hours later.

"The 'dream team' is going to know who our linchpin is, and they'll try and rip his throat out. They'll suggest he's the one who actually did it. But I don't think they can pull that off. There's no evidence, and who's going to believe Cedric Sberna as a ruthless killer?"

They both understood a lack of evidence was the least of their worries. All the defense needed to do was force a hesitation in the jury's thinking: *Yes, it looks this way, but it just might actually be that way.* Make the jurors pause long enough to think they might not be seeing the real nature of the moment. Admit a possibility, and doubt takes root.

Goggin said, "The odds of putting Weinger on the stand are probably … ?"

"Zero." Owen was convinced of it. "But if they do, you need to question him."

"No. Uh-uh. It's your case, Disco. You know what you're doing."

"I can't," Owen said. "I'm in this up to my neck. It's too personal, and I have no objectivity. I'm not going to hear him. Not really. I'm just going to be wanting to kill him."

Goggin, sitting on the edge of a table, head bowed and arms crossed, stared for quite a long time at the floor tiles. Owen saw the door open in the conference room opposite theirs, and die-hard Marine Kenny Waddas standing in the doorway. He could just see an older woman seated inside.

Waddas said, "Stop me when I'm as far from you as your brother-in-law was when it happened."

His back was almost pressed against the door window. "Was it this far? Farther? No? It was nearer. Okay, what about now?"

Goggin glanced up at the noise, then over at Owen. He said, "Let's make a deal. I'll put li'l Mitch through the ringer, but you take care of Cedric. I don't want to have to look at Cedric Sberna that long."

"Deal," Owen said. "Okay. We need to get the witnesses ordered. Just for my own sanity."

Without hesitating, Goggin said, "Cedric, Carlyle, then … No, that's not right. Forget that. Let me think." He gave it thought. "I'm going to ask you outright: do you think there's any chance—any chance at all—Glassman will flip on us?"

"What does that mean?"

"That he'll all of a sudden say, 'Oh, shit—I wasn't honest. Those mean detectives forced me to say something that wasn't true.'"

"Well, I hadn't thought that before now. Damn it. Shit."

"He's weak, man."

"We ask Machala to rule that he's a hostile witness. Then, we prove he's lying, and there we go. Plus, we already have him telling the same story to O'Connor and us, both."

"And you're certain Machala would rule that way?"

Owen was silent.

"Here's what I'm thinking," Goggin said. "We put O'Connor on first. He goes into all his Ted O'Connor detail, and everything else corroborates his testimony."

"I might not be saying this clearly, but if Ted goes first, it's like he's the narrator, and everything has to corroborate his story. We're going to have to go through it chronologically; he's going to tell it in his own way. He presents all the cold, hard facts, and that's going to force us to put people on the stand in an order we might not want, asking questions that maybe we'd rather not ask. We have to set the story and have Ted corroborate that. Does that make sense?"

"Maybe," Goggin said, considering. "I think so. Yeah."

"Tony goes first?"

"No, we don't want to start with a crescendo. Listen. Let's put Glassman first. Think about it—he's the man who's taking Mitchell Weinger down. In one way or another, he's a target. Get him up there and then out of the building; that way no one can get to him. Knock on wood." Goggin knocked on wood. "The longer we wait to put him on, the more chance they have to bribe him. Plus, if we have Glassman saying Weinger is a liar right off the bat, then everything the defense does after that is suspect."

"I'm honestly not sure that he has the balls to perjure himself."

"Enough money can make someone pretty brave."

"Okay, then, by the same logic, let's get Cedric Sberna in right after Glassman. Same day if we can. Minimize the chances anyone will get to him."

"He might not even show." Goggin waved a derisive hand.

"He'll show, Mike. One thing. Cedric says he's willing to waive attorney-client privilege. Keller says he needs it in writing. And it has to be notarized. I haven't been able to find him the past few days. But before you even say anything, no, I'm not worried. We'll get it done."

"By the way, you talked to Pommerich?"

"Yes. She's cool. She is not a fan of Cedric's, or Carlyle, from what I can tell. But she said the same thing now that she said then: Cedric didn't come to the bar looking all fucked-up or covered with blood."

"Tony should go last. Or close to last."

"Why?"

"Because I just have a gut hunch that Maria Messina might not be up to being the life-and-death witness. If she can handle it, great. If not, let's have Tony prepared. I don't especially want to put a mother through that."

Owen said, "I want to close with Stein. For one thing, I want the jury to get a cold, clinical view of what two butchered people look like. But more importantly, there's something he's going to say that we can use. It sounds small, but actually, it's huge."

"What's so huge?"

"The coke. Where it was found."

"The report says there was coke all over the place."

"In her vagina."

"What about it? I'm waiting to be blown away."

"It's way more significant than anyone thinks. Just keep going. I'll explain it later."

Goggin rolled his eyes. "Open with Glassman, then Cedric. We have Carlyle corroborate Cedric, Pommerich corroborate both of them."

"Then ... O'Connor and Dick Morask. O'Connor sat through—how many? Two? Three?—interrogations with Keller in the room. Morask was around too. So, after that, then we put Keller on."

Goggin was quiet for a moment. "By the time they're done, I think the jury's going to be feeling a little fatigued. So, let's liven things up, get their attention back with Wright. I mean, between him and Glassman, those are the two biggest bangs."

"So, what have we got?" Owen picked up a pen.

Goggin ticked the names off on his fingers. "Glassman. Cedric. Carlyle. Pommerich. O'Connor. Morask. Keller. Wright. Tony. Stein."

"I feel like we're forgetting something."

They both tried to remember. Then Goggin said, "What's his name? The dispatcher—we forgot him. You were going to get a subpoena, right?"

"Took care of it already. He's been served. Did you get a list from Magidson of witnesses they're going to call?"

"No because there's no such list. They aren't calling anyone." After a moment, Goggin grinned. He said, "Their whole case is about poking holes in ours. And I'll tell you, Disco, their arrogance offends me."

## Chapter 38

Several things Glassman had said at his apartment stayed with Owen. More accurately, what stuck with him had less to do with what Glassman said than how he'd said it. Too fleeting to touch or label but definitely concerning. Owen couldn't shake a feeling that Glassman's commitment was fragile.

*I want a subpoena*, Glassman had said. *I don't want Mitchell thinking I wanted to testify.*

They'd gotten Glassman what he asked for.

*My dad asked if I misunderstood what Mitchell was asking me to do.*

Goggin got a little confrontational when Glassman had said it. Owen sensed Glassman was just floating it, trying it out, a possible easy exit.

Back in '76 when he questioned Glassman, O'Connor noted Glassman seemed pissed off, indignant over Weinger involving him. O'Connor had told Owen a few weeks ago that was just what he'd wanted to hear coming from Glassman—a retaliatory note chiming through.

When Goggin and Owen talked to Glassman, it seemed like the four years had cooled and soothed any urge at all to strike back.

Glassman had seemed distant from it, like they were all discussing someone else's story. Like they were discussing some abstract hypothetical.

Glassman might not think too hard about taking the convenient way out of something distant, hypothetical. He might not worry overmuch about bending the truth, if that was the most expedient thing to do.

The way Owen's mind was working, it was just a few too-short steps from *might not* to *definitely will*. He tried keeping any worries to himself, but the evening before the trial started, Owen couldn't corral them anymore, and at that point he reached for the phone.

"I don't think Gregg is totally off-base here," Bill Kunkle told Goggin. He'd been at his desk, almost finished for the day, when Owen called and said there was something important that needed talking about. Kunkle told Owen to come by his office and bring Goggin along. "We've all seen stranger shit."

Kunkle thumbed through the statement and a few other pages from the file. He said, "I'm shocked Judge Fischer gave the motion the nod, but at the same time, I'm not shocked at all."

"You too?" Goggin said. He laughed. "Now I'm starting to second-guess myself. 'Paranoia strikes deep.'"

"Look," Kunkle said. "Why not cover your asses? I'll send a prover in the morning Glassman testifies. So, you guys go over the statement with Glassman, and if he deviates, you can call bullshit—the prover was right there. When's Glassman on?"

"First," Owen said. "Get him to repeat what he told Area 6—"

Goggin cut in. "—make Weinger a liar right off the bat."

"Good," Kunkle said. "That's smart. Am I remembering right— that you guys worked in Machala's court for a while?"

"About a year, more or less," Goggin said.

"How was he?"

Owen and Goggin looked at each other, a bit hesitant, searching for the exact right description of how he was.

"Machala? Maybe not an incredibly nuanced thinker," Owen ventured. "Nice enough, fair enough, not an ambitious legal mind. The thing I noticed is you could always tell when Machala was impressed with someone, and once he was impressed with that person, they weren't ever wrong. You'd have to do something pretty egregious to have him say you were out of bounds."

"Was he impressed with you?"

"He liked us," Goggin said. He pointed to Owen. "Machala might have gotten a little irritated with the Doberman, here, but when we kept things in low gear, we did fine."

Owen occasionally got vocal when he shouldn't have. It wasn't just Machala's courtroom. During a recent trial, as he began his cross-examination, he commented on a witness's testimony, "If we believe what we just heard, well, then, we are every bit as stupid as the defense believes us to be."

When those kinds of moments happened, the judge always admonished the jury to disregard what they'd just heard, but while disregarding something was possible, forgetting it wasn't.

"Busch, though," Kunkle said, referring to one of Weinger's defense team. "He's due to be put out to pasture any day now, but the guy is such a character, I get enthralled despite myself."

"Similar thoughts have occurred to us," Owen said.

Kunkle thought for a second. "Okay, say Glassman does flip on you. Give me your best guess: What's Machala going to do? Hostile witness or not?"

"All things being equal, declaring him a hostile witness should be a foregone conclusion," Owen said. "But with this case, reality gets a little different. Rod Serling–different."

"And the likelihood of Glassman fucking us? I'm genuinely asking both of you."

Goggin considered the question long enough that Kunkle and Owen knew he was giving it serious thought. Finally, he said, "Unlikely. If he does, it's not going to convince anyone."

Kunkle looked at Owen.

"It doesn't matter if it's convincing or not. If Machala says Glassman's testimony is no good, that's it. There's the ball game. We know it, defense knows it. But here's why I think it's pretty likely. Weinger's dad is richer than God and the Rockefellers together, so why wouldn't you throw a million dollars at Glassman, get him to tell the jury, 'No, what I said wasn't true. That cop—the only one in the room when I was questioned, incidentally—intimidated me into lying.'"

Goggin said, "Disco, I'm not arguing the logic. I'm saying we have no reason to suspect that's happened. Or is about to happen. And if Glassman does get cute? We fuck him up bad."

"How do we fuck him up when our case is shot?"

Kunkle cut in. "We want to make sure we know what flipping looks like here. We've been thinking in terms of Glassman completely reversing himself. I agree—that would be a tough sell. But what if Glassman says he misremembered, and when Weinger asked it was a different night? Or he says Toenings gaslighted him into thinking it had been the wrong night? Or, even simpler, 'I was tired, hungry, scared, freaked-out, and I got confused.' That's pretty believable. It'd be hard for that to make Glassman a hostile.

"And Gregg, for the record, I don't think it's so outrageous that he could get paid off. A million bucks to say 'I wasn't thinking clearly.' I get why you're nervous. All we can do is be ready. Be prepared. Figure out every possible way they'll come at you. And they will come at you. You think Busch has been doing this for two centuries because he gives it up to state's time after time? Putting Glassman on first is good strategy, but one of the three of them—one at least—is going to figure out why you're doing it."

# Part III

# The Trial

## CHAPTER 39
*May 13, 1980*

Owen watched as Frank Machala brought the gavel down once and then a second time and then even harder the third and fourth times before the murmurs in the courtroom died. Machala looked out from the bench and saw the gallery was full, without a single empty seat. Two sketch artists had managed to claim spots right up front, and for a moment Owen watched them looking up at Machala, then back at their pads, eyes jumping back and forth between the bench and their sketching. He couldn't recall their names, but the woman in the aisle seat to his right was very talented. She'd given him one of the sketches she'd done, and he thought she'd captured his essence pretty well. She'd given Machala one too. The way she'd drawn Machala's profile and angled the cigar in his mouth made him look like General Patton. The sketch hung in his office. She always got a good seat because she arrived so early, but she seemed to believe Machala had pulled a string or put in a word to someone on her behalf, and she always gave him a small, furtive wave when she was in his courtroom.

It had gotten quiet. Machala laid the gavel down, looked at the defense table, watched the defendant stare at the tabletop. It looked like Machala was fixating on Mitchell Weinger's handmade suit, a beautiful bit of work that looked obscenely expensive. The expression on Weinger's face was self-conscious and a little awkward, making it clear he knew he was being watched. Machala looked over several times at Weinger's three lawyers. The day before, Owen had been waiting outside Machala's door to be called in and overheard Machala say that that someone in Weinger's situation was lucky to have them. He'd met everyone on the team a few times over the years and found each of them impressive. Fierce, quick-thinking, articulate, persuasive. He'd sat at a Bar Association event several years back with Joanne Wolfson and her husband, Warren, a fellow judge. It had been a tipsy, pessimistic evening, but they'd all avoided any talk about pending cases.

During that dinner he'd learned the sort of fees they charged, and looking at them seated next to Weinger, he guessed the cost of their defense was stunning.

Outside, the sky was dark in a way that brought to mind wet ashes. Occasional rain blatted against the windows. Machala made eye contact with Busch first, then Magidson. All three nodded at one another. Then he turned and looked at the prosecution. Machala addressed the jury. "Ladies and gentlemen, at this time we have what we call 'opening statements.' Each side has the opportunity to address you, which they'll do now. The State will have the opportunity to speak first."

He gave Owen and Goggin a nod.

Goggin almost imperceptibly cleared his throat, squared his shoulders, took a breath, gathered himself. Owen tapped the tip of his shoe against the bottom of Goggin's chair leg, a silent signal of encouragement.

Goggin stood. He put a hand on one of the manila files on the table and then tapped it several times, as if he was encouraging himself. Owen had written—in huge block-printed capital letters, visible from a distance—*DOUBLE MURDER*. This was another Breen-inspired move. They wanted the jury to see it.

Busch shuffled a few papers and started drumming the eraser end of his pencil against the tabletop. Wolfson sat still, silent. Magidson cleared his own throat loudly—on purpose, Owen thought. The sort of sound one makes to break an awkward stretch of silence or suggest such a silence was occurring. Very little was ever done accidentally in a courtroom. If it was at the threshold of perception, everything visual or auditory was by design.

From the gallery, there was the rustle of watchers shifting in their seats, a few onlookers getting a last cough out of their system, a murmur that stopped abruptly when Machala gave out a sharp look.

Goggin spoke to the bench. "May it please the Court, counsel for the defense."

He stepped out from behind the table, moved onto the stage between the tables and bench, and turned to face the jury. "Ladies and gentlemen, I'd like to introduce myself and my partner. My name is Mike Goggin. My partner is Gregg Owen. We are both assistant state's attorneys. We represent the People of the State of Illinois in this criminal lawsuit."

Goggin carried himself in an unperturbable, steady-footed way. He favored pinstriped suits and wing-tipped oxfords—a conservative style with a long lineage. His physical presence was a significant part of his success with juries. He had an athletic musculature and linebacker's center of gravity. People tended to listen more closely when a person giving every appearance of being able to fuck someone else up didn't use their bearing in any intimidating, menacing way—such a person didn't need to be cool, nice, courteous, and when they were, it landed with greater impact. Jurors seemed to take it as a sign of humility, and Goggin appeared sincere, serious-minded.

Of the two of them, Owen was the more lunging, full-bore figure in court—an aggressive presence when aggression was needed. There were a number of occasions when Goggin had to grip Owen's wrist or kneecap under the prosecutor's table and tell him, "Disco, calm yourself. Get it together."

Mike Goggin continued. "A lawsuit. I'd like to emphasize that that is exactly what this is before you today. Not a television show, not an instant replay. It's a criminal lawsuit brought by the grand jury of Cook County in March of 1976.

"The People of the State of Illinois have charged the defendant through the grand jury with a criminal offense. There are two sides to this lawsuit. Each side deserves a fair trial before an impartial jury, such as you. And that's all we're looking for here. Impartiality by you ladies and gentlemen in this jury."

He spoke with a gentle, faintly grave tone that sounded as if he was asking the jury for their consideration, not demanding it.

"Each victim is the cause of two different counts of murder, and I will explain those to you.

"On March 2, 1976, the defendant, Mitchell Weinger, committed the offense of murder in that he knowingly stabbed and killed Delphine Moore, with a knife, without legal justification. He is also charged with having committed the offense of murder in that he stabbed Gio Messina and Delphine Moore with a knife, knowing that such an act created a strong probability of death or great bodily injury."

Goggin half turned toward the defense table and gestured toward it. "And there, ladies and gentlemen of the jury, is the defendant. Mitchell Weinger. This man. This man seated right here. This man seated right here in the brown suit, with a mustache.

"We will present evidence from the witnesses.

"We'll present you with unimpeachable expert testimony.

"We will show you exhibits. We will show you photographs.

"And then we will rest our case."

Later that afternoon, Goggin and Owen called their first witness, Steve Glassman, to the stand.

After Glassman took the oath, he glanced over at Owen, then gave Weinger a longer look, took a quick scan of the jury, then fixed his attention on Goggin.

Owen scrutinized Glassman for any tell, any hint that he might flip. Glassman seemed jarred, uncomfortable. He wasn't sweating but his skin looked dank, and the tip of his tongue kept darting out to lick his lips. He shifted around in his seat with the awkward motion of a windup toy fallen over.

Glassman had just made eye contact with Owen but looked right through him, with no sign of familiarity or recognition.

Owen eyed the jury and saw each of them intent on what would be Goggin's first question. Just five or six seconds had elapsed since the bailiff had finished swearing Glassman in.

Goggin's unfailing, steadfast calm was baffling.

Owen found it harder to breathe than a moment before.

"Could you please state your name?" Goggin said.

"Steve Glassman."

"Spell your last name for the court reporter."

"*G-l-a-s-s-m-a-n.*"

Goggin said, "Sir, what is your occupation?"

"I am a commodities broker at the Chicago Mercantile Exchange. I buy and sell currencies."

"Could you tell me where you were living in March of 1976?"

"I was living with my parents on West Pratt Street, in the city of Chicago."

"I'd like to ask you if you know an individual by the name of Mitchell Weinger?" Goggin said.

Owen didn't dare to look over at the defense. After a minute, though, he couldn't fight the impulse. Busch and Magidson watched Goggin and Glassman. Joanne Wolfson was watching Owen. When their eyes met, she looked away.

Glassman's show of nerves, his quality of dampness, his pink, flitting tongue—it all had a distasteful effect, Owen thought.

There had been nothing in Wolfson's mien that struck Owen as significant.

Glassman said, "Yes, I do, sir."

Goggin said, "I'd like to again direct your attention to the first week in March, specifically, after March 2, which was Tuesday, 1976. Did you talk to the defendant, Mitchell Weinger on the second?"

"Yes, I did."

"Do you recall the exact day it was that you talked to him?"

Owen peered at Machala's cigar, but there was nothing to read right then in the judge's face.

Glassman said, "I believe it was either a Wednesday or Thursday."

Glassman told his story, in essence the same story he'd told Ted O'Connor but with more detail this time around:

He'd been a close friend of Mitchell Weinger's—close enough that he'd attended Weinger's wedding to Marilyn Weiss in 1975, spoke often with Weinger on the phone, and spent significant time together at bars, clubs, and at each other's houses.

Close enough that Glassman was Weinger's alibi for the night of March 1.

On the night of March 2nd, right before dinner Weinger called Glassman at home.

"This is important," Weinger said. "Marilyn's out and she's coming back any second. Listen, Steve, man, I need a favor. And no questions right this second, okay? This is serious."

Weinger's voice was low, clipped. Urgent, if not frantic. It made Glassman vaguely wary, but he didn't let on. "Okay, what's the favor?"

"If anyone asks, I need you to tell them that I was with you last night. Tell them that we were in the basement together playing cards."

"Like who?" Glassman asked.

Weinger was testy. "Like who? Like anyone. I just said, 'If anyone asks ... '" His voice became suddenly reasonable again. "Okay, like Marilyn. If she asks, I was with you. But if anyone else asks, I need you to tell them the same thing. We were playing cards. Five-card stud. Ace and joker were wild, and you took me for forty-three dollars. I was there from ten o'clock at night until five in the morning."

"But like who? Who's asking? I'm trying to understand here."

Weinger had an outburst. "Are you being deliberately fucking dense? Anyone. Any-fucking-body. Please. Can you do this for me?"

"Fine," Glassman said.

Glassman sat in his room later, thinking about Weinger's call.

He wasn't as shocked as he should have been. No, *shocked* was the wrong word. He wasn't shocked at all. Not as surprised as he figured he should have been. Not at Weinger screwing up again and doing something requiring an alibi. That wasn't the surprising thing. The surprise was that Glassman found himself unfazed.

It irritated Glassman to be involved, irritated him that he might need to lie to Marilyn. He liked her, even if she kept him at a polite, cordial distance. It served to remind him he was Mitchell's friend, not hers. Whenever he went to their apartment and knocked, if Marilyn opened the door, she gave him an obligatory, friendly smile without true warmth. But she was pretty enough that any acknowledgment from her felt like a compliment.

That Weinger had called to ask this favor meant it was more likely than not Glassman would be pressed to answer for him.

Glassman came from a well-off family, but Weinger came from a rich one. Weinger conducted himself like he was always on the other side of a *but*. Glassman wanted to move out on his own to a nice place, but Weinger lived in a great place already. Glassman made decent money selling currencies, but Weinger made better money doing something involving insurance, though whatever it was he didn't do much of it.

Weinger's wife was enviably good-looking, and so were the girlfriends Mitchell guiltlessly stepped out with. He judged Weinger unfavorably because he had girlfriends. It seemed to him excessive and entitled. But if Glassman was straight with himself, some part of him wished he had the same opportunities as Weinger. He wished he had the same opportunities with women and the balls to take full advantage of those opportunities. He didn't have either. It nettled him, just a little.

Weinger had been born into great expectations that he didn't seem to appreciate. He expected Glassman's help in safeguarding them. That nettled Glassman too, and more than just a little.

Goggin looked at Glassman in the witness stand, then pivoted toward the jury box and said, "Would you tell the ladies and gentlemen of the jury under what circumstances you were woken at approximately four to five o'clock in the morning, on March 6, 1976?"

Glassman kept going.

When the doorbell rang, he leapt out of bed because he didn't want his parents disturbed and ran to the front door. He thought it might actually be Weinger, drunk or high or both, too fucked up to appreciate the hour, or maybe in trouble with Marilyn. Glassman flicked the foyer light on so whoever it was could see they'd been heard and acknowledged, then pulled it open.

It wasn't Weinger.

An hour later, Glassman followed Detective Toenings through Area 6 and looked around himself at the desks and the men seated at them, and he heard the snap of typewriters, the drone of voices speaking into the phone, and louder voices yelling across the squad room for someone's attention. It wasn't even 6:30 yet.

All the noise, the action, the activity—Glassman felt impressed and intimidated. All these guys were serious people doing serious work. They made Glassman feel like a lightweight. They'd grind you into nothing if you got in their way and he started thinking that if they pulled him out of bed like that, this early in the morning, and dragged him down here—well, that meant he might be getting in someone's way.

You were always hearing rumors that Chicago cops weren't necessarily opposed to forcing information out of people, but Glassman figured that was a last resort, after everything else had failed. Only the worst of the worst would hold out against that. The icy looks the detectives fixed on him said they'd use whatever means they had to, whenever they deemed it necessary. None of these faces looked as if they were bluffing.

This unsettled him the way any suspension of standards will.

Turning from the jury back to Glassman, Goggin asked, "Did you know Mitchell Weinger in the month of March 1976?"

"Yes, I did."

"And did you see anybody else at Area 6 that you knew?"

"Yes, I did."

"And who was that?"

Following Toenings back even farther through Area 6, Glassman passed a room and happened to look inside. Mitchell Weinger sat in there, looking as if he was handcuffed to the table, hunched over. Maybe from the cuffs, Glassman thought, but it looked more like Weinger was slumped in defeat. Glassman wondered if he might even be praying.

But then Glassman saw Weinger wasn't praying. He seemed to be resting, as if tired or bored, and either way, he was imperturbable. Handcuffed to a table in an interview room, in the homicide squad's offices, and he was imperturbable. Right then he looked like the worst of the worst.

His first thoughts were outraged. Then they changed over to confused. Then, finally, he felt he understood that this is the way things were supposed to be. Weinger was unconcerned because he had no reason to be otherwise. Weinger had pressed Glassman to tell a fib because the detectives were in error. They wrongly believed his friend had gotten mixed up in something, and their evidence, though circumstantial, was damning. He was willing to help his friend out.

Glassman kept company with those thoughts for a few steps, but then he was led into an oppressively drab interview room, with a two-way mirror, a table, a few chairs, shrill fluorescent light, and a poster bearing the Miranda Warning.

When the detective seated him, his conclusions suddenly sat less well. Glassman's brother Marv had called a friend of his, Bob Tarnoff, who had agreed to act as Glassman's counsel. He came into the room now and sat down next to Glassman.

Tarnoff leaned in and whispered, "Do you know why you're here?"

He motioned at the two-way mirror, to indicate Glassman should speak quietly.

"No," Glassman said. "Not really. As much as I can tell, this is some misunderstanding."

"As far as that goes, I know it involves your friend, Mitchell. And that we're here in a homicide squad interview room. Did anything happen that could have gotten you here?"

"No."

"Okay. If I nudge you, stop talking. I know this involves Mitchell, but my impression is that this is just establishing a timeline or something," Tarnoff said.

Glassman whispered, "They dragged me in here at five in the morning. It couldn't wait? Did they tell you anything?"

"Nothing more than I just told you. But look, if you aren't involved with anything, don't worry. Tell the truth. But keep your answers short. Yes, no, basic clarification."

There was a quick rap at the door, and it swung open, and John Toenings stepped in. Toenings seemed cordial but Glassman knew it was formal and perfunctory.

Toenings said, "Mr. Glassman, sorry to bring you down so early, but it's important we spoke to you right away."

"What is it we're speaking about?"

"About this past Monday night. Could you tell me where you were on that night?"

Toenings gave him an expectant look.

"Am I being accused of something?" Glassman said.

"I just need to know where you were that night."

Glassman shocked himself by saying, "Playing cards at home" before he even had a chance to think it through.

Toenings affected a look of surprise. "All night?"

Glassman turned to Tarnoff, whose face was neutral.

"All night, Mr. Glassman? You were playing cards all night?"

"No," Glassman said.

Toenings said, "Did anyone ask you to say that you were?"

Glassman hesitated. "Yes, they did."

## Chapter 40

Goggin took a pause and let Glassman's story resonate.

Owen wondered who was seated in the gallery behind him. Maybe Jay, although his brother hadn't said if he'd be there the first day or not. He'd heard that Chuck Moore, a Chicago musician and brother of Tinker Moore, would be present. Less press than he anticipated. John Wayne Gacy's trial had left everyone murder-fatigued, but that was fine with Owen right then. It meant fewer eyes on what might happen when—

What might be happening right-fucking-now: Goggin had just glanced over, and Owen knew the question was about to get asked.

It seemed to Owen everyone was leaning in, waiting, but no one other than he and Goggin and Kunkle knew what was at stake right that second.

Owen felt sick. He'd eaten almost nothing, but his stomach seemed as if it might try to empty itself anyway.

He mastered a small ripple of nausea. He saw Goggin put his hands in his pants pockets. He saw Goggin taking a deep breath, trying not to show it, trying to look casual and unperturbed.

Goggin gave Owen the faintest nod, then turned back toward the witness stand and paced in front of Glassman.

He said, "Now, was Mr. Weinger with you on Monday night, March 1st, playing cards at your house?"

Owen saw Goggin brace himself.

He saw Glassman steel himself.

Owen drew himself up. He was sitting perfectly, rigidly straight in his chair. He laid his palms flat against the tabletop. He was taut, barely breathing.

"No, he was not," Glassman said.

The tension in Owen's body evaporated. The tension in the room disappeared.

Owen closed his eyes.

*Thank God. Thank God. Thank God.*

Goggin continued. "Mr. Weinger was *not* with you Monday night, March 1st, at your house playing cards?"

"No, he was not."

Owen peeked at the opposition. The three defense lawyers were impassive. Weinger was trying to be impassive, but anger streamed off of him, hot and bright.

Goggin said to Machala, "No more questions at this time, Your Honor."

As Goggin walked back to the table, he shot a quick, triumphant smile at Owen, so brief it was barely liminal. Owen worked to keep his expression neutral.

When Goggin sat, Wolfson rose and slowly made her way toward Glassman. Then she did something strange.

Wolfson said, "Mr. Glassman, while you were there, at Area 6, you saw Mitchell Weinger in handcuffs?"

"Yes, I did."

"He wasn't around when you were giving this statement, was he?"

"No, he was not."

"Now, after you left the police station, do you know whether or not you had a copy of the statement with you?"

"No, I don't know." Glassman sounded apologetic.

Wolfson smiled. "But sometime thereafter, between then and now, in this past four years, you saw Mr. Goggin with the statement?"

"Yes."

"Where was that?"

"At my apartment."

"When?"

"Sometime—I believe it was sometime near early March of this year."

"Was that the first time you met this prosecutor?"

"Yes, the very first time."

"Did he come with a subpoena?"

"No, not then."

"Did he call you before he came over?"

"Yes, he told me who he was, and I said, you know, 'Okay.'"

"Where did he call you?"

"He called me at my apartment."

"Between March of '76 and March of 1980, you moved to a new home, is that correct?"

"Yes, I moved in June of '76."

Owen noticed Goggin beginning to stir in his chair.

"In June of 1976. Did you notify a prosecutor of where you were moving to?"

"No, I did not, not that I recall, Ma'am, no."

"Now, you came without having somebody come out and get you to do it, right?"

"Well, I was told that—I have talked to a couple of people, and they told me—I have never obviously been through anything like that before, and I was a little confused. I was told that if you're served a subpoena, you better respond."

"Then once again, today, this morning, you went over the statement with this prosecutor?"

"Yes."

"Between the time you talked with Mr. Goggin in your apartment and today, you didn't have a copy of it, did you, the statement?"

"No, I did not."

"Now, when you met him, when he came over with the statement, did he come with identification?"

Goggin shot an incredulous look at Owen. Owen could feel it.

Glassman said, "Yes. Identification and everything else."

Owen couldn't see the point—was she trying to derail the momentum of Glassman's admission? An inept stab at casting doubt on whether Owen and Goggin had played by the book?

*Probably*, Owen thought, she figures enough questions, *even if they're pointless*—and her questions definitely were—*makes it seem like there's something there to be uncovered*—and there definitely wasn't. Plus, it was being done at Goggin's expense.

Goggin was pissed and Machala was visibly impatient. Whatever her intention, Wolfson had misstepped. Among the jurors too—Owen could see it. They were always a good barometer of whether you'd gotten under their skin.

Wolfson continued. "You said he explained to you and told you he's a state's attorney and he's got to prosecute this case. He's got to file—"

Goggin stood up so quickly his chair teetered back.

"Objection to this nonsense." Goggin struggled to keep himself even. "This is nonsense."

"Sustained," Machala said.

"Well, I object to your statement," Wolfson said. She affected outrage. "I don't think it's nonsense. I don't think it's nonsense at all."

"The prosecution's objection has been sustained."

Wolfson offered Machala and Glassman a forced smile. She said, "No further questions."

At that point, Busch stood up. "I have a motion at sidebar, Your Honor."

Machala sighed, gave a shake of his head. He took the cigar from his mouth, rolled the ashes into his ashtray. He looked back and forth between the bailiff and the jury. "We'll give the jury about five minutes recess. Ladies and gentlemen, you can step out, please."

The sergeant directed the jury out of the courtroom.

"Okay," Machala said. "The jury has left the courtroom. What's your motion?"

Busch said, "Defense moves for mistrial, Your Honor. Based upon the Court's ruling in connection with remarks of the state's attorney that Ms. Wolfson's questions were nonsense."

Machala nodded. "Anything else?"

"It's unnecessary and prejudicial," Busch added.

Machala smiled. "Denied. Motion denied. All right. I think we're finished for the day. Court recessed until ten tomorrow morning."

## Chapter 41

Most working days, Goggin and Owen walked to and from the courtroom behind their metal cart, with its erratic and noisy wheel, and no one said hello or asked how they were or how the trial was going. No one said anything, and most didn't even nod when they passed in the lobby or hallway.

This wasn't unique to Goggin and Owen—any team trying a case got identical latitude from their coworkers. A team on trial was seen almost like monks in meditation—any intrusions were understood as bad form and bad luck.

The wheel on their cart squeaked and rattled as Goggin pushed it back toward their office.

Immediately after Machala recessed, Glassman bolted. Owen couldn't blame him.

"It bothers me when someone is that weak." Goggin was referring to Glassman. "He says he'll stick up for his friend because his friend strong-arms him. Then his dad gets mad at him, and he folds. And Teddy O'Connor gets him in, and after two questions, Glassman breaks."

"Sure, but in another sense, so what? It proves he's a bad liar." Owen was listening but not fully invested. Thoughts concerning Cedric Sberna were distracting him.

The elevator arrived and they got on.

"Okay, but it also shows he can get bullied into doing whatever a bully wants."

Owen had arranged for Sberna to spend the night at the Drake Hotel, with a couple of investigators watching him. He'd told Sberna it was a safety precaution, figuring correctly that it would make Sberna feel important or pivotal—enough so it outpaced his being afraid.

In reality, Owen had worried that the drive between Lake Forest and the city gave Sberna too much time to think about what he was doing and too many chances to bolt. Giving him a nice room and a pair of babysitters cut risks to a minimum. Owen had been feeling a grudging but real gratitude to Sberna for, so far, keeping his story consistent—and keeping his promise to testify.

The elevator opened to the twelfth floor, and they got off and walked to their office.

Plus, Sberna might actually be at some risk. It was possible. Wealth like Caleb Weinger's could get a lot accomplished and quite a bit eliminated. Money like that—money that didn't just make someone rich by contemporary community standards but almost robber baron rich—money like that could remake the world.

In a way, it bothered Owen that no one had tried bribing Sberna. It hinted there might be other solutions in play. It bothered him to the point that—

"No comments here?" Goggin asked. "You got nothing?"

Owen hadn't really come to a conclusion about Glassman's testimony. He had a feeling Goggin had just wondered aloud if Glassman's weakness might taint his credibility with the jury.

"No, I don't think they'll discount anything," Owen said.

Goggin made an impatient noise. "That's not what I said. I said it bothered me at first, but then I could see jurors six and ten looking at Mitchell like … like he did it."

Goggin and Owen each sat down behind their desks.

"I'm sorry, man. I've got Cedric on the brain," Owen said. He'd arranged for the investigators to bring Sberna to the office to prep him for his testimony. "I'm listening. Really. I saw the same thing. And that alternate juror too. Did you see him? The mean-looking Chicago Heights guy?"

"Yeah, that guy. Yeah. If that really wimpy-looking teacher begged off so he could get back to his classroom and Mr. Chicago Heights stepped in? He's with us. No question. He's on our team."

Goggin said, "So what is it about Cedric?"

Owen considered his answer and then shook his head. "Nothing. It's just … last-minute worrying."

"You're worried he's going to fuck us and take the Fifth?"

"I'm not worried about that. I was, but now I'm not."

"Why not?" Goggin said.

Owen stopped.

"Because if he does," Goggin said, "we can't win. It blows the whole thing to shit."

"He won't," Owen said. He was suddenly certain of it. Or mostly certain. "He waived attorney-client privilege. He signed off on it. And signed off literally—Keller wanted things notarized. He's come too far. What's he going to do? Change his mind? He's not going to do that. He can't do that."

Goggin looked incredulous. "Are you joking? Why can't he? He can just say Keller's lying, and it's Cedric's word against the word of a lawyer who's been fucking suspended, who had his client get rid of evidence, who … do I need to keep going?"

"He's not going to do it. You're going to have to take my word."

"No thanks."

"—take my word for it, but I've spent a lot of time around the guy. Enough to know that, believe it or not, he'll do the right thing."

Goggin shook his head once, then turned and looked out the window for a while.

Owen had had to quell some of Cedric's anxiety about going to court and being dragged into the public eye by the press. He told Cedric—truthfully—that yes, there was some press watching the trial but not much press. Certainly a lot less than Cedric anticipated.

The thing was, Owen explained, everyone was tired of John Wayne Gacy. Gacy had worn everyone out.

Day after day, from one news cycle to the next, article after piece after segment: gruesome descriptions of victims and killings, grieving parents, legal analysis, person-on-the-street opinions. Everyone had gorged on murder.

People paid short attention right now if a murder wasn't as bloody and spectacular as those Gacy committed.

Privately, Owen wasn't certain whether it was a good thing.

Gacy was a guaranteed win for the prosecution. The evidence was under Gacy's house. All those dozens of bodies lying right there below Gacy's feet.

But Owen didn't see as clear a path to a guilty verdict in the Weinger case, and if things didn't go Owen's way, better it happen outside the spotlight.

On the other hand, if the press swarmed the trial, it would send an important message: It doesn't matter who you are, what family you're from, or when you did it—you're going to get caught. No amount of money will keep you out of court. No amount of money will stay any sort of punishment or penalty.

For his part, Owen wanted Gio's and Tinker's family and friends to feel vindicated, to feel something had been accomplished in their interests. That feeling would be greater, the message would have more impact, if it all happened loudly and in public.

He had heard Kunkle more than once say, "The absolute worst thing is to lose a case you're supposed to win." The corollary, as Owen saw it, was "The best thing is to win a case that's unwinnable."

And again, you hope one happens in private, beyond anyone's notice, and one happens in full view of the world.

He didn't mention Gacy much when he spoke with Tony Messina because Owen wanted to stay off the topic of murder fatigue. The idea of that discussion was objectionable, he thought. And on the night he'd brought Cedric Sberna to the courtroom, several weeks prior to the trial, just so Sberna could get a feel for what it was like to be in court and sitting in the witness chair, he wished he hadn't even mentioned Gacy's name because now Sberna wouldn't shut up about it.

Sberna, enthralled, amazed, gripping Owen's arm: "Are you shitting me? Are you fucking serious?"

The two of them stood in the middle of the empty courtroom, Sberna's voice carrying to the walls and rebounding. Even with no one around, Owen shushed him, just out of reflex. Empty or full, there was a right way to comport yourself.

They'd walked in a few minutes earlier, coming in to take a look, spend some time because Owen figured that showing Sberna around would make him relaxed. The more relaxed the witness, the smoother their testimony, and a preview of the courtroom always made it less imposing. At least a little less. Or so Owen had been told.

"I'm serious," Owen said. "Those doors you saw when we got out of the elevator? Right in there. It's the penalty phase now."

He wanted Sberna to focus. It was a wasted effort if Sberna was too distracted to register the courtroom experience.

"Have you been in there?"

"Sure." Owen shrugged.

Sberna, rapt: "What was it like?"

Owen considered the board Kunkle had brought out during the trial, with photos of every one of the victims, or at least the thirty-three they knew about, and the way just seeing it in front of you was a hard punch to the solar plexus. Gacy's lawyer, Sam Amirante, in his dark blue suit and lavender shirt and matching tie, leapt up yelling, "Object! Object!" When Amirante rose, the pocket watch chain on his vest bounced and reflected a brief, sharp pinpoint of light.

Instead, Owen told Sberna, "If you were a lawyer, it was fascinating. For everyone else, it was probably dull as shit. Things move really slow in there."

"Did you see him?"

"Who? Gacy?"

"Yes. When you went into the court did you see him?"

"Well ... I mean he was on trial. So yeah, I saw him. At a distance."

Actually, one of the times Owen had gone in was to ask Kunkle a question, and when Owen got to the prosecution table, he glanced over at Gacy, sitting with Amirante a few feet away. Gacy made eye contact, held it, offered a lewd smile that made Owen's skin shiver.

"What was he like? Did he look ... " Sberna gestured, searching for the right word.

"He looked like a pudgy, sweaty, pathetic, fat dude." Owen couldn't tell if Sberna found this compelling or disappointing. He took the opportunity to move the moment back on track. "So, Cedric, sit. Sit in the witness chair. Just sit up straight—no, not rigid. Relax a little. Not that much. Don't slouch. Right there. Good.

"Now, I'll be asking most of the questions. I'm going to ask you a lot of detailed questions. Most of them are going to require a yes or no or just a few words. We're going to go over this again before the trial, but you absolutely do not want to say more than the answer requires. If you drove to Elgin on April 3, and the car you drive is a blue Volkswagen—

"I own a Porsche."

"Okay, so, if the car you drive is a blue Porsche, and I ask you if you drove to Elgin on April 3, all you need to say is yes. Not, 'Yes, I drove to Elgin in my blue Porsche.' Just say yes."

"I know. I get it."

As if he hadn't heard, Owen said, "The more you say, the more opportunity they have to try to tear you apart when they cross-examine you. They're probably going to be pretty brutal. They'll be rude. Insulting. They're going to come off nice, at first, then they'll turn on you."

"Turn on me how?"

"Turn on you as in make it look like you killed Gio and Tinker."

Sberna was horrified. He opened his mouth to speak but closed it. Then his brow knitted, and he stared at the floor. When he looked back up, Owen thought Sberna was about to say, "I'm not doing this. I'm taking the Fifth." But before Sberna said anything, Owen told him, "We're not letting that happen. It will not happen. And just to be clear, they wouldn't ever say, Cedric Sberna's the one who killed them.

They'll just try to make it sound like you're a fucking liar and plant the suggestion in the jury's minds. But we're not even going to let it get that far."

Sberna was quiet. Then, "How long will I have to be up here for?"

Owen didn't know what the right answer was. He went for the honest one.

"A while. Probably a few hours. It won't feel that long. You won't be bored."

Sberna said, "I don't care about that. He's going to be there, right? Weinger's going to be staring at me the whole time."

"You'll be looking at me or looking at his lawyers. Whoever's talking to you."

"He'll have his eyes on me the whole time."

Owen thought for a second. He affected a private smile. "It's funny. When you said *eyes* just now, it made me think of Gio's dad, when he was inside the apartment you … escaped from. But when he was there, he said Tinker's eyes were closed, and it looked like she was asleep. But Gio—his eyes were wide open. I mean, that's some staring."

Sberna didn't look at Owen, didn't respond.

Finally, Owen said, "Come on. Let's go upstairs. You need to meet my partner, Mike Goggin."

Goggin's reaction to Sberna was immediate, comprehensive, and entirely unfavorable.

So far, at every point during their trial prep, Owen had watched Goggin get more and more irate with everyone involved in the case who was under the age of thirty-five.

Irate at first—astounded, bewildered too—then disdaining, and ultimately landing somewhere near aloof. Not to the case and not to the crime, though. Failing to prosecute without bringing one's full resources to bear was almost like a boxer throwing a fight. Goggin was no Sonny Liston.

Still, he saw Glassman, Carlyle, even Gio and Tinker, as if they were softly tainted. That they were mostly rich kids who snorted cocaine kept him from getting personally overinvested. Goggin planned on screwing Weinger to the wall as hard and ferociously as he could because Weinger was a killer. But he felt like it could have been otherwise. Weinger wasn't the killer here by necessity—the role of murderer and murderee were essentially interchangeable. They were the product of a different Chicago than the one he knew. Maybe a different America altogether, like there was an alien world within the world and one he was content leaving unexplored.

But Sberna ... Goggin was having a tough time with Sberna. A tough time talking to him, looking at him. A tough time sitting in the same room.

Sberna had been oblivious, but when he and Goggin first shook hands, Owen felt the air in the room go bad. Who knew what it was, what had catalyzed it. Maybe it was the way Sberna looked Goggin up and down, assessing him as someone lesser. Or the way Sberna's crowing made it seem like he occupied more than his share of space. Maybe the semi-shrewd calculations Sberna seemed to be running in his head before he answered a question. It could have been any or all of that. But Owen did know the exact moment Goggin's scorn became irrevocable.

It was at the end of that first meeting, after Owen had shown Sberna the courtroom and brought him back to talk in the office, after Sberna's handshake made Goggin's face pucker, like he was holding a moist, greasy bone.

Sberna was putting on his shearling coat and said to Owen, "Can I ask you a favor? That $3,000 I gave Gio—I know you said the police weren't going to give it up, but is there anyone you could call and double check?"

Goggin's face got tight and filled with an ersatz goodwill. He had a viper's smile.

"What money is this?" he said, his voice a little too loud.

"I loaned Gio Messina money," Sberna told him. "I'd like to get it back. It's been four years."

Goggin was silent for a moment. Then, "Is this the money you loaned him for your cocaine deal?"

Sberna's face turned murky. Owen watched carefully, waiting to see what reaction would resolve from it. If he was pissed, it might bode well for Sberna's testimony—a signal he'd stand up—or at least try standing up—to the defense's efforts to gut him.

Sberna wasn't pissed. He was defensive and petulant.

"Everyone thinks I'm a drug dealer. What the fuck is that? I'm not. I never have been. I'm never going to be."

His voice dropped to a conspiratorial volume. "Okay, yeah, every once in a while, I like a little coke. Not often. Just once in a while."

His voice rose again. "Jesus, man. I loaned Gio $3,000. That's serious money."

Owen said, "I told you, Cedric, you're going to have to call Tony Messina if you want to try and collect it."

Sberna considered this. Then he glanced around the room, taking it in. Then he looked at Goggin and back around the room. His voice dropped again. "Well … I don't know."

Neither Owen or Goggin knew if he was referring to the phone call or if he was souring again on the idea of testifying.

To Owen, Goggin's disgust was nearly visceral.

Looking hard at Sberna, Goggin said, "There are no problems we need to address, right, Mr. Sberna?"

Sberna stared back.

Owen thought, *Shit, Cedric, can't you tell this isn't the guy you want to pick a fight with?*

Then Sberna folded. "No. Of course not. Gregg said you'd need me to come in before the actual trial. Is that right?"

"Yes, that's right. Mr. Owen and I will be in touch about getting you prepped for trial. Nice meeting you." Goggin turned away, sat down, pretended to address some paperwork.

Owen extended a hand. "Thanks for coming in. Talk soon."

Sberna walked out of the office and down the hall. They heard the elevator open, then close again.

Goggin whipped around. "What the fuck, Disco? I can't believe that guy. What a piece of shit. What a piece of human garbage. That's our key witness? How can you stand the motherfucker?"

"Because I have the good sense and wherewithal not to piss our witness off. Pretend I'm in the CIA. I'm recruiting an operative."

"I don't know how you can be cool to him. I really don't."

"What good is going to come from being an asshole to him?"

Goggin sat down heavily.

He said, "Well, I'll tell you this. You can do your hippie-dippy, smile-on-your-brother bullshit, but keep him away from me."

## Chapter 42

The night before his testimony, Sberna came to the courthouse at Twenty-Sixth and California again, at around 8:00. The building was mostly empty, and Goggin and Owen took him to the courtroom.

"Okay, Mr. Sberna," Goggin said, "what I want to do here is this: I'm going to ask you questions taken straight from the statement you gave to the police. Now, pretend that Weinger's lawyers had asked you to tell them all about the evening Gio was murdered, and all the answers you gave them corresponded with your statement. They went first, and now it's time for us to do our cross-examination. You probably know what it means, but just to make sure, it means we're trying to blow holes in your story and make you look like a liar in the eyes of a jury. Now, make sure you only answer the question I'm asking. You don't need to volunteer any more information than what you're asked for, okay? Just yes or no, because no one's going to ask questions that require much more than that."

"Everything I said in the statement is true. That's the way it happened." Sberna was adamant, tilted his chin up, demonstrating he was set to withstand whatever he needed to.

Owen said, "It doesn't matter. It doesn't matter if it's true or not. It's the way the question gets asked that matters. Okay. Sit there in the witness chair. All right. Here we go. Mike? He's all yours."

Goggin closed his eyes, took a breath, then looked up. His whole demeanor had changed. He seemed affable, almost kind.

"Good afternoon, Mr. Sberna. By the way, is it okay if I call you Cedric? Okay, thank you, Cedric. My name is Mike Goggin, and this is my partner, Gregg Owen. We're assistant state's attorneys. That means we represent the People of the State of Illinois. When I say we represent the People of Illinois, I'm not just talking about being representatives of law enforcement.

"When I say we represent the people, we represent you. We represent Mr. Busch, Ms. Wolfson, and Mr. Magidson. We represent everyone on the jury. We represent Judge Machala. We even represent Mitchell Weinger, the defendant. We represent the interests of justice.

"When we say *justice*, we don't just mean restitution or punishment. We're not talking about an eye for an eye. When we say *justice*, we're talking about a process. A process where everyone, no matter who, no matter what, is treated fairly. Where everyone's voice is given equal weight.

"Now, if I may, I just want to clarify a couple things that came up during your examination by Mr. Busch. Do you mind if we do that? That's great. Thank you."

Owen broke in. "Okay, you know what just happened? Mr. Goggin comes on all polite, nonconfrontational. He's humble, ingratiating, and right there—the jury likes him. They think he's a nice guy. He's not out to screw anyone; he's not out to frame anyone. He just wants to get to the truth of the matter. Just clear up the mystery. Okay? Let's keep going."

Goggin kept going.

"Now, I think I may not have heard you correctly, so just for my benefit, tell me again where you live? Okay, I did hear that correctly, then. That's pretty far north from the city, right? How far away is it? About thirty miles, give or take, from Lake Forest to Chicago city limits. And from city limits to Tinker's apartment, we're talking around another ten miles, right? So that adds up to forty miles. So, at that time, you lived forty miles from Gio and Tinker's place? Okay, and did I hear you right that you live with your family? Okay, thank you.

"If you don't mind me making an observation, by any measure, your suit is really nice. When you dressed to come here this morning, obviously you put some thought into what to wear. Which I, for one, appreciate because it says you take this trial seriously and you respect everyone involved. And I'd bet you put thought into what you wear not just on special occasions like this but for every occasion, special or not, because you seem like a man who takes pride in his appearance. Is that fair?

"Now, your girlfriend at the time was Mary Carlyle, right? Sometimes called Mickey? And just to make sure I have the correct information, she lives in the Newbury Plaza complex? I'm guessing that it takes you about an hour or so, even when there's no traffic?

"An hour's not so bad, but I bet there were times when it got late and you just didn't feel like making that hour trip? So, on the night in question, were—you know what? I don't want to ask you that yet. I want to ask you this first. Certainly, you had stayed over at Ms. Carlyle's apartment a number of times, correct? When it got late? Or if you'd been out at a club and had a few drinks, you didn't want to break the law or put anyone at risk by getting behind the wheel?

"So, just to touch on your clothes again for just a second, you told us a moment ago that you're the type of person who wouldn't want to wear the same dirty clothes for two days in a row, is that right? So, you brought some clothes for the following day, correct? Because you're definitely not someone who's okay with wearing the same socks, short, pants—the same underwear—as you'd worn the day before.

"Wait, you didn't bring clothes? You weren't concerned with how you were going to look the next morning? Okay, I see."

Sberna curled a lip. "I didn't bring clothes because I had clothes there. I have my own drawer."

Owen cleared his throat.

"Then that's what you tell them," he said. "If you don't point it out, you know what? You're going to look like a fucking liar. You're all finicky about what you wear, but you went in planning to stay over and didn't bring clothes? Bullshit. And if you did bring clothes? Then you knew you'd need to change them that night."

"What do you mean," Sberna asked. "'change them that night'?"

"Because they were covered with Gio's and Tinker's blood. That's why you would have had to change."

"Screw that," Sberna said, emphatic, genuinely indignant. "Bullshit. I didn't have any blood on me because I didn't do anything that would get blood on me. They can't just say that."

"They can't say that, and they won't say it," Owen explained. "They'll hint at it. All they need to do is plant the seed. And once they plant it, that's it. There's no coming back. So, let's keep going."

Goggin continued. "Now, when you were speaking with Mr. Busch, you mentioned you'd called Gio Messina several times that Monday, right? And you spoke with his sister at least a couple times? And you also testified that you saw Gio that Saturday, right? At the Sheridan Hotel? And you went to brunch with Gio, Tinker, and Mickey the next day? That Sunday?

"Now, didn't you say that you had loaned Gio $3,000 just a few days before that? You loaned him the money on that Wednesday?

"And so you'd seen him on a Wednesday, then again on Saturday, then the next morning, on Sunday? And then you called several times Monday, and when you didn't get ahold of him, it was so important that you speak to him, you drove forty miles at 10:30 that night? You said it was because you were concerned with how he was acting that Saturday? That you thought he was acting erratically, and it concerned you enough to make that drive?

"And did you mention on Sunday when you saw him that you were concerned with how he was acting? You didn't? And when you spoke to Gio's sister those two times on Monday, you must have mentioned to her that you felt concerned? You didn't? Okay, I see."

Owen stepped in, pointed at Sberna. "You see what just happened there? The jury is going to say, *Yeah, why did he do that?* And then you know what you look like? A liar. Keep going."

Goggin took over again. "Now, I just have a couple more questions, Cedric. You gave Gio $3,000 on Wednesday, and shortly after that, he hosts a party at the Marriott. You had said there was quite a bit of cocaine on offer at that party, correct? The whole time you were there, Gio was offering cocaine to everyone? So, you had given him the $3,000 to buy cocaine, right? And here he was, giving it all away. But the only reason you went down to Gio and Tinker's was you were worried about him?

"And when you were at the apartment that Monday, Gio called someone he knew at 11:30 at night to offer him cocaine? And he said this guy would pay a lot of money for the coke? So, you must have been putting a lot of pressure on Gio, to the point where even though he was drunk and high, he had the wherewithal to grab his address book and make the call. And then you said the person was there within minutes to buy a couple of grams of cocaine?

"Now, you testified that for some reason, Gio went into the bathroom with the man who came over? And a short time later, you heard noise from inside that alarmed you enough so that you opened the door? And when you opened it, you saw that Gio was lying on the floor, bleeding profusely? And the man who'd just showed up was holding a knife in his hand? At that point, you said you turned and told Tinker to get you the gun that had been lying on a coffee table? And she did that? And then you ordered him to come out?

"This is where I get a little confused. You said that when you ordered him to come out, he told you that he was a narcotics officer. Now, I know you've probably watched crime shows on television, seen crime movies, probably even heard some stories about how police operate. Is that true?

"Now, have you ever in your life heard of a police officer using a knife to defuse a confrontation? To use a knife during a struggle and stab that person? I believe you also said that at that time, after being told that he was a narcotics officer, you shortly thereafter left the apartment, with the gun in your hand, and left your friend in the bathroom with this officer? And left his girlfriend?"

Owen came and leaned against the rail of the witness stand. "Do you realize how cockamamie, fucked up that sounds, Cedric? How are you going to answer that?"

Sberna sought an answer, looking frantic. "I know it sounds ridiculous, but that's what happened. That's the way it was."

Owen slapped the rail. "Bullshit, that's the way it was. It sounds completely absurd. You tell the jury that? With a straight face? You know what you're going to look like."

"What am I supposed to say?"

Owen snorted. "I can't tell you what to say. You think I'm allowed to put words in your mouth? But let me suggest something. You also said you were pretty freaked out, right? You were stunned. In shock."

"Yeah," Sberna said. "I was. Wouldn't you be?"

"Probably. Probably I would," Owen said. "When you're in shock, you're not thinking real clearly, are you? No. People in shock don't think logically or rationally or clearly at all. Okay. Mike—let's finish it up."

Goggin continued. "So, Cedric, you came downtown, didn't bring any clothes with you, planned on staying the night, sought out Gio for the entire day, then went to his place at 10:30, and out of nowhere a guy shows up and stabs your friend and tells you he's a narcotics officer, and you believe him and then immediately flee the scene? Is that correct?"

Sberna stared at his hands for a long time. "Okay."

"Okay what?" Goggin made a gesture signaling he was puzzled.

"Okay, I get it. I understand."

Goggin turned away and as he did, he said, "I'm sure you do. I hope you do."

Later, after Cedric left, Goggin looked at Owen. He said, "Well, Disco, I guess you can safely assume we're fucked."

## CHAPTER 43
*May 14, 1980*

The next morning, Gregg Owen watched Cedric Sberna's few steps to the witness stand, and the expression on his face as he declared, so help him God, he'd tell the truth, and he watched as Sberna relaxed into the chair, crossing his legs, intertwining his fingers, and letting his hands lie in his lap.

More than he had at any point so far, Owen listened to Sberna's voice and the way it sounded: very faintly bored, almost as if the time spent speaking it was a gift to the hearer. Though the voice was slack—not just bored but unhurried and unworried—there was a current of something tart, something subtly at work criticizing the hearer for demanding Sberna's time to begin with.

Years ago, Owen had been driving his compact east on Belmont Avenue. It was dusk and there was an ember-red sunset sinking behind him. It draped everything in front of him in a soft pink luminescence. His eyes chanced on his rearview, and the molten light burning there in the mirror's rectangular frame was overwhelming.

At an intersection, he had the left-turn right-of-way, but a hulking Buick coming west was too light-blinded to see it and barreled through.

Owen put all his weight against the brake, and his tires screamed, and the cars didn't crash.

On the other side of the moment, Owen found that the adrenaline screwed with his equilibrium and made his limbs ache miserably.

In Courtroom 606, he felt like that now.

No one would have guessed. He hid it perfectly. To Machala, Sberna, the defense, and everyone in the courtroom, Owen just looked eager.

He said, "Could you tell the ladies and gentlemen of the jury what your name is?"

"Cedric Charles Sberna."

"Cedric, in the month of February 1976, did you know a person named Gio Messina?"

"Yes, I did," Sberna said.

"And during that time did you also know a person by the name of Delphine Moore who had the nickname of Tinker or Tinkerbell?"

"Yes, I did."

"How long prior to March the first of 1976 did you know Gio Messina?"

"Approximately a month and a half."

"And during that time that you knew Gio Messina, how would you characterize your relationship with him?" Owen asked.

"Close friends. Good friends."

Owen's questions from there elicited an account closely matching the one he'd given the police four years ago, retold to Owen a couple of months before now and to Goggin a few nights prior. Owen focused particularly on one point of fact—the coke he saw Tinker stuff into her underwear—and he asked Sberna about it several times, in several different ways.

In their opening statements, Owen recognized the defense would say that Sberna was the killer and try to smear his hands in Gio's blood. Owen knew he could undermine them with two simple assertions: duress and shock had gotten Sberna out of sorts, so much so that he couldn't possibly have changed his clothes and disposed of them without a trace between the time he left Tinker's and arrived at the Ritz-Carlton, nor would he have thought to do so. When he got to the Ritz—and he was seen by a number of people there—his clothes were unbloodied, and he was clearly, profoundly upset.

Sberna had just finished telling the jury his story. Owen was about to posit the facts about Sberna's appearance and demeanor. Magidson didn't want to let him.

"When you left Tinker's and drove to your girlfriend's place of work, were you wearing the same clothes?" Owen asked. He thought he saw movement at the defense table.

"Yes, I was," Sberna said.

Owen said, "What was the first thing you did after you went to where your girlfriend was working? Did you say something? What did you do?"

"I went to the bar and ordered a brandy and waited until I saw her."

"And did you eventually see her?"

"Yes, I did."

"Did you speak with her?"

"Yes."

"Do you recall what you said to her?"

Magidson leapt in. "Well, Your Honor, if he's asking whether he recalls, I don't object, but if he's asking for the conversation, word for word—"

"What was the question?" Machala said.

Owen said, "I asked, 'do you remember what you said to your girlfriend when you got there?'"

"He may answer," Machala said. "Does he recall?"

"I told her—" Cedric began.

Magidson cut in again. "I don't think the witness understands."

"Do you recall?" Machala said to Sberna.

"Yes, I do," Sberna said.

"What did you say to her?" Owen said.

Magidson called out, "Objection."

"Sustain that objection," Machala said.

Owen felt frustration begin to throw off a little heat. "Well, did you tell her what you just told the jury?"

Magidson sounded pissed. "Object. If the Court please, I move the question be stricken and counsel admonished."

Machala agreed. "We'll strike that."

Owen knew he shouldn't, but he asked again. Even if it wasn't in the record, the jury wouldn't forget it.

"Well, that's what you did, isn't it, sir?"

Magidson was visibly angry. "May we be heard, please?"

"Sustained," Machala said, putting emphasis on the word. "Let's proceed."

Owen composed himself. Then, "Well, you had a conversation with her, didn't you, sir?"

"Yes," Sberna said. He seemed glad to be allowed to answer.

Owen wondered if Sberna could tell what Owen was trying do and Magidson wanted to keep him from doing.

"Did you relate certain facts to her at that time?"

"Yes, I did."

Magidson, again: "Object, if the Court please."

It was a yes-or-no question. Owen was pleased Magidson had tripped up. It demonstrated Magidson felt a need to protect himself.

Machala told Magidson, "That answer may stand."

"And did she say something to you at that time?" Owen asked.

"Yes."

"And did you and your girlfriend go somewhere at that very moment when you spoke to her?"

Sberna described the call to the medical student whom Carlyle knew.

"And after talking to that person," Owen said, "did you call someone else?"

"Yes, I did."

"Did you call the police at that time?"

"I did."

"And did you have a conversation with someone at the Chicago Police Department?"

"Yes, I did."

"And do you recall the very words you used?"

"Not exactly, I'm afraid."

Owen said, to Machala and Sberna in turn, "I'm going to mark this cassette tape for identification and show it to counsel. Mr. Sberna, I'm going to play a tape for you—"

Magidson and Wolfson both stood up.

"Object to a statement, and I'd like to be heard, if the Court please," Magidson said, clearly agitated. "We request a sidebar."

Machala nodded. "Okay. Let's retire to my office."

In Machala's chambers, Magidson was livid. Owen thought Magidson's reaction was out of proportion and assumed Machala would see it too.

Magidson pulled his Zippo out and lit a cigarette. He drew hard. The ember lengthened and began to droop. He exhaled violently.

"That tape is not in evidence and saying that he's going to play it before it is in evidence or before it's even qualified as evidence—well, I object to that. And we haven't even covered whether the tape is even admissible."

Machala was about to speak, but Magidson kept on, the words flooding out and not, to Owen's ears, very sensibly.

"There are ways to qualify it, and there are ways that you can't qualify it, and just simply saying in front of the jury, 'I'm going to—I'm going to play a tape for you,' without ever seeking to introduce it in evidence or qualify it … Well, I think this is worthy of a motion for mistrial, and I make that motion, Judge."

Machala shook his head. "Denied."

Wolfson spoke up, sounding reasonable. "There are some additional objections I'd like to make. Right now, actually."

She glanced over at Goggin and Owen, and from her face they could tell she'd anticipated what they'd intended with the tape.

Magidson drew on his cigarette again, and the length of the ember doubled. He exhaled.

She continued. "I think there are some further questions to ask the witness, what words did he use, how long did he take, who did he talk to, and if his recollection is exhausted. There is a way to do this, but just to play it and say, a-ha, here it is—no, that's not the way to do this."

Goggin said, "If I may add, at this point we want the exact words. We don't want to poke around at what the essence of it is. We want the exact wording. That's what Mr. Owens asked. We are asking at this point to have this played before the Court to refresh this witness's recollection as to exactly what was said."

Harry Busch put his hand up. "He hasn't exhausted his recollection."

Magidson ground his cigarette out in the brimming ashtray on Machala's desk.

Goggin shook his head. "We just asked him if he knew exactly what he said, and he told us, 'No.' So, I'm sorry. I disagree, Mr. Busch. We'll disagree a number of times."

Magidson lit another cigarette.

Busch scoffed. "Quite probably. But don't be fooled: that doesn't mean you're right."

Goggin smiled grandly. Owen could see a hint of loathing percolating under it.

"I anticipate that, and I welcome it," Goggin said.

"I want to hear the tape," Machala said.

Within a few minutes, the sheriff was back in Machala's chambers, setting up the court's tape player. They listened to the call and could hear the dispatcher disregard Sberna at every point.

Magidson said, "This is ridiculous. It's hearsay. I know what you're trying to do. You're going to try and say it's excited utterance. You want the jury to think this is an accurate reflection of Cedric Sberna's frame of mind. It's not. He doesn't sound agitated. He sounds like he's reciting a story he made up. Therefore, it's hearsay. Maybe it's accurate, but almost certainly it isn't. He had a chance to think about what he wanted to say, how to say it, what would sound best. If he's saying this is what happened and it isn't, then the hearsay rule—"

Owen thought this was so wrongheaded, it was as if they were arguing evidence from another case entirely.

Goggin was losing patience. "Mr. Sberna had just witnessed a trauma — he had just seen one of his friends brutally murdered. He had left another friend of his at an apartment, and when he contacts the police, it's an outcry. This is absolutely an excited utterance."

Wolfson rebuffed it. "This is certainly not excited utterance. Gio Messina is killed. Then Mr. Sberna had a conversation with Moore. He then put on his coat and took the gun and left and went to his car. We don't know where his car was parked. But he went to his car. He drove to a nearby tavern or gas station or whatever he claims it was. He stopped, and he made a phone call. He then went around the block and came back and took a look at the place. We are now at 2970 Sheridan Road. From there, he went down to Water Tower Place. We assume he was obeying traffic signals. Maybe he was. He parked the car at Water Tower Place, went to a lobby where there were lights and people. He saw the people there. He went to the bar, and he sat down at the bar, and he ordered a brandy, and he waited until the girl came to him."

She looked at Machala triumphantly. "I don't think that this is, in any realm of the imagination, by any stretch of the imagination, an excited utterance."

Machala shook his head. "I just heard this, right now, and he's excited."

"He doesn't get excited until the second sentence," Wolfson said.

"Well, he sounds excited to me."

Goggin looked at Owen, and his expression said, *They misjudged us pretty badly. They misjudged themselves pretty badly.*

Owen looked back. *They're getting panicky. They're tipping their hand.*

*They know—*

*If the jury hears it—*

*Yes, if the jury hears it, they're going to know—*

*He's not faking.*

*He's not faking at all.*

They nodded.

Owen considered the vulnerability they'd just seen. He thought Wolfson and Magidson knew, or at least sensed clearly, that their defense—piss-poor so far and unavailing—was weaker than they'd believed it to be when the trial started. Busch, on the other hand, who'd essentially come out of retirement for this one, had arrogance enough not to see it, not to even consider they'd done an inadequate job. His exorbitant suit, the hint of the smug grin telling everyone he had all the confidence in the world, and that each time he opened his mouth, it was a generosity of legal wisdom and juridical truth.

He thought about Caleb Weinger, that the man hadn't reached his station by making bad investments. But this was a million-dollar defense team, giving only a $10,000 return.

Defense lawyers, Owen thought, obviously had some small leeways, but if the prosecution misstepped, then everyone could just go home.

Owen hoped, not for the first time, he never lost his fear of fucking up.

## Chapter 44

A little later, back in the courtroom, in front of the jury, Magidson had steered testimony toward the phone calls between Sberna and Tony. He made no secret of what he wanted to accomplish.

"Had you socialized with these senior Messina's, that is Mr. Messina and Mrs. Messina?"

"Yes, I had."

"And was this all during this period of a month and a half during your good, close friendship with Mr. Messina?"

"Yes."

"You had been there twice?"

"Yes."

"You had dinner there?"

"Yes."

"Mr. Messina senior called you on Wednesday morning at your home, did he not?"

"I believe he did."

Magidson had been subdued but now became more animated, pacing back and forth in front of the witness stand, retreating toward the defense table, returning to stand in front of Sberna. He gave Sberna a raptor smile he'd probably intended to be benign.

"Early in the morning sometime before 8:30 a.m., wasn't it?"

"I believe so."

"And he told you at that time that he had been looking for Gio, did he not?"

"Yes, he did."

"He told you that he hadn't heard from Gio since early Monday. Isn't that correct?"

"Yes, it is."

"He told you that Gio had asked that he be called at Delphine Moore's apartment early Tuesday morning to be awakened to go to work, isn't that correct? He had tried to telephone and reach Gio for the past twenty-four hours?"

"I don't remember."

Magidson made a small show of perplexity.

"Well, he had told you that he had tried to reach Gio and had been unsuccessful at some time, didn't he?"

"Yes, he did."

"The man was concerned about his son, wasn't he?"

"Yes, he was."

"And he asked you if you knew where his son was, didn't he?"

"Yes, he did."

"And when Mr. Messina told you that he couldn't find his son and asked if you knew where his son was, you told Mr. Messina you didn't know where Gio was, didn't you?"

"Yes, I did."

"You told Mr. Messina that you had tried to contact Gio Monday evening on the telephone, didn't you?"

"Yes."

"And you told him that you just didn't get an answer and so you ceased calling Gio, didn't you?"

"Yes."

In a voice full of sadness, Magidson said, "You were lying to him, weren't you?"

"Yes."

"That wasn't the truth."

"No."

"All right." Magidson nodded benevolently. "Now, before you left for the police station, did you make a call to Mr. Messina senior?"

All right ... Owen thought it a slick, devious little move, those two words—as if Magidson had finally gotten it settled that Cedric Sberna was an irremediable liar.

"I believe I might have."

"And did you tell Mr. Messina senior that the police had called you and told you that Gio was dead?"

"That is possible. I don't remember."

"Did you express sympathy to Mr. Messina?"

"I don't remember."

"I see," Magidson said, looking at the jury.

The thing was, Sberna looked like he actually didn't remember. Owen knew that right then it would be impossible for the jury not to see someone who didn't express sympathy to the father of a murdered son as a particularly terrible person.

Sberna's sudden shift in his chair said he realized it too.

"And did you tell Mr. Messina that upon learning of this news, you wanted to find out the details from him?"

"I don't remember." Sberna seemed to regret his answer.

"Did you ask Mr. Messina who it was that discovered Gio was dead?"

"I don't think I did. I don't remember."

"Did you ask him how he died?"

"I don't think I did. I don't remember."

"Did you ask him anything at all about the circumstances of Gio's death or the discovery of his death?"

"I don't remember."

"Did you ask Mr. Messina where Gio was?"

"I don't remember the conversation very well."

"How long was that conversation with Mr. Messina?"

"I have no idea."

Magidson shook his head, smiling, as if incredulous. He looked over at the jury and then back at Sberna.

"I'd like to ask about your going to the Area 6 police station. You weren't served with any subpoena or summons at that point, were you?"

"No."

"You had gone there in response to a telephone call from the officer, is that correct?" Magidson emphasized every question with his forefinger.

"That is correct." Sberna twisted in his seat.

"Now, at that time did you tell them that you had last seen Gio Messina and Delphine Moore on Sunday, February 29?"

"That is possible." Twist.

"That was a lie, wasn't it?"

Twist. "That is possible."

Emphasis. "You mean, it's possible it wasn't a lie?"

Owen couldn't help admiring Magidson's deft maneuvering. Sberna struggled to salvage himself.

"I mean, it's possible because I am not exactly sure what day I told them."

"You didn't tell the police that you had been to Delphine's apartment on March 1, did you?"

"No, I did not."

"You didn't tell the police that you had been to Delphine's apartment on March 2, did you?"

"No, I did not."

"Did the police ask you when you had last seen them?"

"I believe they did."

"And did you tell them that it was at brunch on Sunday, February 29?"

"I may have."

"Did you tell them you had seen them at any later time than Sunday, February 29?"

"Under the advice of counsel, we didn't answer those question."

"You mean, you refused to tell the police when you had seen Gio and Delphine Moore after Sunday, February 29."

"Yes."

"Did you tell those two police officers in the evening of March 3, Wednesday, in response to their question about whether you went to Delphine Moore's apartment on Monday evening, March 1, 1976, that you did not go to Delphine Moore's apartment on that night?"

"I believe we didn't answer that question."

"And after you said, 'No, I did not go to Delphine Moore's apartment—'"

Owen and Goggin spoke in near unison.

"Objection, Judge—"

"Objection, Judge—"

Owen was infuriated, but he tried sounding otherwise. "He didn't say that. He didn't say that at all."

Magidson appeared pleased with himself, but when he looked over, Owen saw a few of the jurors showing disapproval.

Magidson affected surprise. "Well, now, Judge, the case law requires that I ask the question."

Owen realized Magidson knew Sberna could send Weinger to jail or keep him out. The strategy was clearly to defend Weinger by maligning Sberna.

"Counsel needs to restate the question properly," Owen said.

Magidson asked, "Judge, may I come to sidebar?"

Machala held his hand up. "We will strike that question. I will sustain the objection."

"Well, Judge, I'm asking for a sidebar because I don't want to argue the law in front of the jury."

"I don't see we need to argue anything right now," Machala said. "Let's proceed."

Magidson turned back to Sberna. "Do you remember the attorney advising you not to answer those questions after you told the police, 'No, I had not been to Delphine Moore's apartment on Monday, March 1'?"

Owen made a gesture of exasperation. "Objection, Judge. He never said that to the police. Same objection."

"Sustained." Machala's displeasure was clear.

Magidson seemed not to notice. "Now, when you talked to the police on Wednesday, March 3, at Area 6, did you tell them at that time and place that you knew of no illegal activities in which Gio and Delphine were involved?"

"I did tell them that."

"That was a lie, wasn't it?"

"Yes, it was."

"You knew that Mr. Messina possessed, used, and dealt in cocaine, did you not?"

"Yes, I did."

"You knew that Gio Messina at times had access to rather large quantities of cocaine?"

"I'm not sure what you mean by 'large.'"

"You saw Gio Messina with cocaine from time to time, did you not?"

"I did."

"Did you ever use any?"

"Yes."

"Did Gio ever sell cocaine to any other individuals while in your presence?"

"I told Gio in no uncertain terms that I did not want to be present for any drug deals whatsoever."

"What about when he told you Mr. Weinger was on his way to Delphine Moore's apartment? Before he made any calls, did he warn you it would be an opportune time to leave?"

"He did not."

"And what about after the call? Did he warn you then?"

"No. He didn't warn me."

"And after you say Mr. Weinger arrived, Gio didn't tell you, 'Get out of here, my good friend Cedric. I don't want you involved in any deals,' did he?"

"He did not."

"You testified earlier that Gio measured out two small packages of cocaine from a larger package and handed you the larger package back before Mr. Sberna made a phone call?"

Sberna hesitated. He looked puzzled.

"No. I am Mr. Sberna."

"Yes, correct, thank you. So, you got the package back before you made the phone call—"

"I am Mr. Sberna, and I did not make a phone call." His anger was genuine. "And if you're trying to catch me in something, you will have to redirect the question."

Magidson was trying to demonstrate a certain incoherence to Sberna's answers. Owen reflected that Sberna's arrogance was, at the moment, a good thing. Sberna wasn't going to let Magidson succeed.

Magidson didn't pause. "Mr. Sberna, is it your testimony that Mr. Messina gave you the main bag back for a second time before making a phone call?"

"No. He gave me the bag after the phone call."

"When this person whom you say is the defendant, when this person arrived, did he ask Gio who you were?"

"No."

"No statements were made to the effect that you were Gio's friend, that you were all right. Your presence was no cause for concern?"

"No. It would be understood that if someone objected to my presence, Gio wouldn't bring them near me."

"You mean you and Gio had an understanding that he wouldn't deal cocaine in your presence, but if he did, he would do it with somebody who was all right?"

Owen was about to object, but Sberna did it for him.

"No. No, Mr. Magidson." Sberna's anger hadn't dimmed, and now he looked offended. "That is not what I said."

"All right. What is it that you say?"

"He wouldn't bring anyone objectionable into my presence, for any reason."

"Do you encounter objectionable people often?"

"More than I'd like."

"What do you do when it happens?"

"I try to get away. Any way I can."

After Sberna was done testifying, Machala called a break. Sberna walked over to where Owen sat and leaned in.

"How'd I do?" he asked.

"You were great. It was perfect. You kept your cool when a lot of people would have lost it. What you said was true, and it was important. So, thank you. Really."

"You're welcome." Sberna looked around. His glance rested on Weinger and the defense lawyers, then it returned to Owen. "You're welcome. And I'm out of here."

"Okay, cool. I can't see any reason why anyone would call you again, but if they do, we know where to find you."

Owen held his hand out. Sberna looked at it, seemed about to say something. Then he took Owen's hand and gave it a perfunctory shake.

"You don't know where to find me."

Owen looked at him. Sberna seemed resolute, almost defiant.

"Oh. I get it. Okay. You don't need to worry. We're not telling anyone where you may or may not be."

"No, man, you *don't* get it. You don't know where to find me unless you have my number in Palermo. I'm flying out of Chicago tomorrow morning."

Owen stared. "No. Don't tell me that. You need to be around, man. We might need you again. It wouldn't be for anything—"

"No. No. No way You're not going to need me. You can't have me."

"Cedric, come on. You can't stick around for two days? We're coming up on it. We're just about done."

"No, Gregg. No, I can't." Sberna seemed agitated, like he'd been when Owen first met him. His voice dropped to above a whisper. "You don't think someone like Caleb Weinger would hesitate to punish me, do you? Or make sure that if this drags out, I won't get a chance to testify again? Don't think I'm being dramatic. He can make things happen. So I'm out of here. I did what you asked me."

"Two days. Please."

"No. I did what you needed me to do. I'm doing what I need to do." Sberna turned on his heel and walked away.

After lunch, Goggin called a James McNichols, formerly a 911 dispatcher, to the stand. McNichols took his time standing up.

He took hesitant steps to the front of the room.

He took the stand, raised his hand, and took the oath.

Then he took his seat.

He sat slumping, with his shoulders hunched and his head bowed. His eyes were closed. His posture said it plainly: he'd be anywhere but here if he could be, preferably as many miles away as anyone could get.

Owen had wondered if McNichols might turn defiant when the questions started. Try to keep his dignity. Try to save his reputation.

*He might*, Owen thought. *He might have some fight in him yet*. He might not let himself fall down disgraced this easily, passively, without doing something to prevent it.

Owen watched McNichols wiping and re-wiping his palms on the knees of his pants, inhaling deeply and exhaling raggedly, withering by the second inside his suit and its mismatched pieces in two different shades of black. Owen knew McNichols wouldn't turn defiant. Most of the fight had been bled out of him. And any bit of fight remaining wouldn't remain much longer.

He'd retired in November of 1979, after thirty-one years with the Chicago Police Department. He worked as a security guard now, but his old job wasn't completely behind him. McNichols was about to answer for his part in letting the life bleed out of Gio Messina. McNichols had answered the 911 call Cedric Sberna made from the late-night quiet of the Ritz-Carlton.

Sberna told McNichols about the stabbing, and McNichols figured Sberna was bullshitting. He ignored the call and forgot about it until the evening news jogged his memory a few nights later. At this point, the notion that Gio might have lived if McNichols had listened to Sberna wasn't particularly controversial.

A moment earlier the bailiff had set up a speaker on the prosecutor's table, right near the jury box, wired to a reel-to-reel player, so the jury and everyone in the courtroom could hear audio of Sberna's call. He tested it, and the first few words—*City of Chicago Police* and then Sberna saying, *There has been a murder*—issued out clearly. The bailiff turned it off.

Wolfson, Magidson, and Busch had fought to keep the jury from hearing this at all.

The bailiff nodded toward Owen and then toward Goggin and walked away. Owen slid over, got ready to turn the tape on, and Goggin got ready to examine McNichols.

"Would you tell the ladies and gentlemen of the jury what your functions and duties were at the time of March 1 and 2 of 1976," Goggin asked.

McNichols said, "To receive complaint calls from citizens and dispatch cars to troubled areas when required."

"How many other operators work with you during normal hours of a tour of duty?"

"Fifty-two."

"Sir, did you receive a phone call at approximately 12:30 in the morning on March 2, 1976?"

"Yes, sir."

"Do you recall if the voice on the other end of the call was male or female?"

"Male." McNichols's answers came slowly, sounded deflated. He shifted uneasily after each one.

"Mr. McNichols, at this time, I'm going to play for you a tape recording. We have played the recording for you prior to today and affirmed that it was a correct and proper and exact recording of the conversation you had on March 2, 1976."

Goggin nodded at Owen. Owen turned on the machine.

*"City of Chicago Police."*

*"There's been a murder. I witnessed it and I was forced to leave the apartment. The man threatened my life. I had to leave the apartment. Okay. The address is 2970 North Sheridan. It's under ... I don't even know the apartment name or number. The apartment is under the name D. Moore. M-o-o-r-e."*

*"What is it you seen?"* McNichols's voice was gruff, heavy with a Chicago accent.

*"Pardon?"*

*"What is it you seen?"*

*"The man had an eleven-inch knife ... and my friend laying on the bathroom floor with blood all over."*

*"Your son?"*

*"No. A friend of mine."*

"There at 2970 North Sheridan?"

"Correct."

"And you want us to go up and see a Mr. Moore?"

"No. The apartment is under an D. Moore."

"That is not necessarily the man that did all this, right?"

"No. It's not. It's a chick's apartment. I don't even know the chick. I just— I was just told to go there, you know, with … we were there for a drink. I don't even know what the hell is going on here, but this guy is nuts. He is nuts."

"Where are you calling from?"

"I'm calling from the Sheraton—from the Ritz, I mean—"

"From the what?"

"The Ritz."

"Whereabouts?"

"The Carlton. The Ritz-Carlton. Just … just please get there. Thank you very much."

"But who are you, sir? You are a witness?"

There was no answer. On the tape, McNichols ended the call. Owen turned the tape off.

It seemed to Owen a quieter silence than he usually heard in court. The silence held. Then the jurors were craning their necks, looking at one another, and there were a first few murmurs, a couple of loud-whispered exclamations of *Oh my God* from the gallery.

There was a quick ripple of protest and indignation, and McNichols withered that much more on the stand, in his suit. He shut his eyes again, bowed his head again briefly.

Machala rapped his gavel once.

Goggin said, "Mr. McNichols, was that the call you received around 12:30 on March 2, 1976?"

"Yes, sir."

"And that was your voice on the line, speaking to the caller?"

"Yes, sir."

"Did you send a squad car to North Sheridan Road?"

"No, sir."

"Did you notify any of the homicide headquarters that night?"

"No, sir, I did not."

"Did you contact any other police personnel on March 2, 1976?"

"No, sir." McNichols was just this side of audible, now.

Goggin said, "Did you send any squad cars to the Ritz-Carlton Hotel?"

"No, sir."

"Why did you not notify anyone?"

Words seemed to be slippery for McNichols: "Well, at the … at the time, the time … the type of call, and where the call was coming from … from the Ritz-Carlton Hotel … I just figured it was a prank."

McNichols's answer just hung there.

Owen heard rustling noise in the gallery and a familiar voice saying, "Excuse me, excuse me," and when he glanced he saw Tony, looking half stricken, half violent, picking his way to the aisle and walking to the door, pulling it open, moving through it, letting it shut.

Goggin saw it too. He turned back to McNichols. He said, "I guess it turned out to *not* be a prank, did it not?"

Wolfson was on her feet. She called out, "Objection."

"Sustained," Machala said. He looked over at the jury. "The jury is to disregard that."

Goggin was looking at McNichols when he told Machala, "Nothing further, Your Honor, at this time."

## CHAPTER 45

Carlyle would be taking the stand first thing in the morning, and Owen had asked her to come in for prep later that evening.

At 6:00 p.m., the Cook County security guard assigned to their floor tapped at their door.

"Gregg, there's a woman out front says she has an appointment to see you. A very nice-looking woman. And by 'nice-looking,' I mean *really* beautiful."

Owen looked over his shoulder. "Okay, thanks, Jimmy. Could you please send her back here?"

A few moments later, he heard the sharp snap of high heels against the tiles, clacking louder and louder as they got closer, and when the noise stopped, he looked up and saw Carlyle poised in the doorway, with an airy, *pleased-to-meet-me-aren't-you?* semi-smile. She wore a soft-patterned skirt, with a teal blazer and white blouse, more modest and conservative than the sheath she'd worn on Saturday. Owen had a fleeting thought that looking like a well-to-do Sunday school teacher wasn't any less alluring.

She said, "Hi, Gregg. I told you I'd be here."

Goggin's back had been to the door, but he turned around now, and after glancing at Carlyle for a moment, he turned to Owen and then looked back and forth between them. He wore a faint expression of distaste.

Owen said, "Mickey, thank you for coming. It's really a pleasure seeing you again. This isn't too inconvenient, I hope."

"Not at all, Gregg. And the pleasure is mine."

Owen heard Goggin mutter, *Good Christ*, and when he looked over, Goggin was looking back. A little incredulous. Relieved that she'd shown up. Amused. Irritated.

Owen continued, "This is my partner, Mike Goggin."

Goggin held his hand out. His voice was flat. "Very nice to meet you."

"May I call you Mike?" she said, but Goggin didn't answer. Owen broke back in before the pause got too awkward. He gestured at the chair placed by the side of his desk. "Please, sit."

She sat down. Goggin swiveled around so he was facing Owen's desk. Owen thought he might have detected a slight shaking of Goggin's head. Owen handed Carlyle a copy of her statement and a red pen. "If you see any errors as we're going through, just make a mark, and we can address them."

An hour later Carlyle hadn't found any mistakes, and then she left. Owen closed the office door behind her. He sat and turned to the agitated expression on Goggin's face.

"Wow," Goggin said. His tone was caustic. "Wow. She seems a little ... dingbatty"

"But we need her," Owen said.

"That's true. We do need her." Goggin laughed quietly. "God help us."

Owen had tasked two investigators—Patton and Keyser—with picking Mickey Carlyle up at 7:30 a.m. in front of her apartment and getting her to Twenty-Sixth Street by 8:15. It allowed Carlyle a few minutes to get acclimated and settled in before Machala called the court to order at 9:30.

At 8:45, they still hadn't arrived.

Traffic, Owen figured. Had to be traffic. It was plausible, even likely, but he still felt profoundly uneasy.

Once his eyes had locked onto the clock, Owen was immediately conscious of the time and the way it seemed to be sprinting and freezing simultaneously. His left eyelid started twitching, and he pressed his fingers against it to keep it still.

Goggin was at his desk, writing notes to himself, crossing them out, writing new ones. Owen felt Goggin watching. Goggin's glance had weight.

Owen exhaled noisily and cracked his knuckles at 8:49. His eyelid was still twitching.

At 8:50, Goggin dropped his pen on his desk. Owen knew he was angry. In court, meetings, around the office, Goggin wrote constantly, compulsively, until something pissed him off, which was when he'd drop his pen.

"You left her unsatisfied, didn't you?" Goggin said.

Owen looked over at him. Goggin was seething. "What are you talking about?" Owen said.

"I'm saying, when you slept with our Ms. Carlyle, I guess you probably didn't help her finish. Right? And now she's got it in for you? And that's why your girlfriend isn't here? She's not coming. 'Hell hath no fury ... '"

Owen's voice was steady and quiet but poisonous.

"I did *not* sleep with her. That's it. End of story. I did not sleep with her. I'm going to say it one more time. *I. Did. Not. Sleep. With. Her.*"

Goggin picked up his pen and started writing again.

It was 8:53.

At 8:59, Goggin's writing had slowed. He said to Owen, in a singsong whisper, "What the fuck, Disco? What the fuck?"

Owen mastered an urge to vent nerves and fury. He remained quiet. The crawling minutes gained on him. It was 9:04.

At 9:06, in his most even voice, Goggin said, "I think it's time for a plan B. We can ask for a little time, get Pommerich in here, and put her on instead. Who knows? Maybe that's all the corroboration we need. Maybe she's enough."

"She's not enough," Owen said.

"No," Goggin agreed. "She's not enough."

At 9:10, Owen was almost overpowered by a need to break things. He stood and put the papers he needed into his briefcase, then got his suit jacket on. He looked at Goggin and shook his head.

"Oh my God," Owen said. "How is this happening?"

Debbie Culotta, one of the secretaries on the twelfth floor, young and sharp-tongued, leaned into their office.

"Gregg? There's a girl here to see you."

Goggin *tsk-tsk*'ed. "Oh, Disco. Must you?"

"Aren't you in the middle of a trial?" Debbie said. "Is this you trying to impress some young thing?" She deepened her voice into a parody of Barry White. "Want to come watch me try a case?"

Debbie was the only secretary who bantered with them.

Goggin laughed. His persistence in gleefully spreading wild rumors and fabrications had most of the building believing Owen would try making it with anything and everything that moved. Owen usually endured it, but today he couldn't.

"Just send her away, Deb," Owen snapped at her. "I really don't need anyone's shit right this second."

He regretted it immediately. Owen expected her to be hurt or offended, but instead, she looked faintly amused.

The slow steps of very high heels echoed in the hallway.

"Too late." Debbie feigned dismay. She went back into the hall. Goggin and Owen heard her say, "That's Mr. Owen's office on your right."

Then Mickey Carlyle was standing in the doorway.

"Oh, hiiii, Gregg." She said it in a sultry way, stretching the *hi* out for too long. "I'm so sorry I'm late, but I waited outside for almost thirty minutes, and no one ever came. I took a cab here. It was three dollars. Here's the receipt."

Owen gave Goggin a fleeting, bitter smile.

Goggin shrugged, almost imperceptibly. He stood up and took her receipt.

## CHAPTER 46
*May 15, 1980*

When she took the stand and was sworn in, Owen noticed most of the courtroom was especially fixed on Carlyle, and she seemed to relish it.

Owen had walked over to the far corner of the jury box, just the way he'd described to Tony months ago.

From his spot at the jury box, Owen asked, "Now, since, say, approximately April of 1976, have you dated or gone out with Cedric Sberna in any way shape or form?"

"Not at all," Carlyle said.

"Since April of 1976 have you seen Cedric Sberna at any time?"

"Yes, I have."

"When was the first time after April of 1976 that you saw Cedric Sberna?"

Wolfson called out, "Objection."

"She may answer," Machala said.

Wolfson said, "What's that got to do with the case on trial?"

Machala, flat-voiced, on the way to perceptibly impatient, said, "She may answer."

Carlyle fixed her attention back on Owen. "The first time was February 18, 1980."

"And were you with someone that particular day?"

"I was with my boyfriend. It was the night of his birthday. That's why I remember the date."

"Did you speak to Mr. Sberna on February 18, 1980, at all concerning this case—" Owen was saying.

Wolfson leapt in. "Object."

"—on that date?" Owen continued.

Machala didn't wait for Wolfson to elaborate. "She may answer."

Carlyle said, "Pertaining to the case? No, not at all."

Owen asked, "Did you see Mr. Sberna at any time after February 18, 1980?"

Wolfson, leaping in again: "Object."

Machala took a breath. "She may answer."

Carlyle said, "Yes, once."

"And did you have any conversation with him when you saw him after February 18, 1980?"

"Object."

Carlyle answered anyway. "No."

Machala had a thin, humorless smile. "The answer may stand."

Each time the defense slammed a brake on his momentum, Owen felt frustration stinging him. For a second he thought his temper might come loose, but then he intuited that the objections were becoming grating for the jury to sit through, and pretty soon the defense would do itself damage. It was only intuition, nothing concrete. Just a sense. But it relaxed him a little.

He said, "Do you recall where you were when you saw him after February 18, 1980?"

"Object."

*Knock yourself out, Jo-Anne*, Owen thought.

Speaking to Carlyle, Machala's tone was kind. "You may answer."

Carlyle said, "It was in a restaurant."

"And were you alone or with someone on that date?"

"I was having dinner with someone."

"And did you have any conversation with him on that date?"

"No, not at all. He was —"

"Object to the conversation with him after February 1980," Wolfson said.

*Oh for fuck's sake*, Owen thought.

"The answer may stand. You may proceed."

"Now, have you seen him or spoken with Cedric Sberna," Owen said, "since the meeting at that restaurant in which you were with someone and you didn't speak with him?"

"No, not at all."

Owen took a line of questioning that eventually brought testimony back to the night Sberna came in a panic to the Ritz-Carlton.

He asked, "Now, when you saw him, did you notice anything unusual about him at that time?"

"No."

"Did he say anything to you at that time?"

Carlyle said, "When he first came up to me? Oh, yeah. Well, he was extremely upset and—"

It was Magidson's turn to derail Owen's rhythm. He called out, "Object."

Machala's response was immediate. "That answer may stand."

Owen said, "And did he say anything to you at that time?"

Carlyle was firm. "Yes, he did."

"Object," Magidson said.

Machala drummed his fingers, looked over at Magidson. "The answer again may stand."

"What did he say to you at that time?" Owen said.

"Object."

Machala addressed Owen. "That I will sustain."

Owen sensed where the objections would lead. He was introducing what Sberna said to Carlyle as "excited utterance," something said out of shock or panic or another heightened, stress-soaked state of mind. The defense would try to call it hearsay. While hearsay wasn't admissible because it was a secondhand account of what was said, excited utterance was admissible because what had been said was treated as if it was an event. Owen decided he'd neuter the objections before they got out of hand. "Ask for a sidebar, Judge."

Machala sighed. He'd have preferred to stay seated. He picked up his cold cigar from the ashtray and motioned with his hand. Goggin, Owen, and all three defense attorneys, along with a stenographer, followed Machala out of the courtroom into his chambers.

When they were all in, Owen turned to Machala. "Judge, I am not certain, but I believe Mr. Magidson's objection would be to hearsay."

Magidson made his tone acerbic. "It would."

Owen said, "To my belief, Judge, there is no better example of excited utterance than the statement Mr. Sberna would have made to this young lady at that time. She has already testified—"

"Wait a second," Machala said. "What do you anticipate her answer would be at this moment? What did he say to her?"

Owen said, "He told her, 'Gio has been stabbed; I don't know what to do; what should we do?' And she made certain statements to him as to what she thought should be done.

"Now, first of all, her statements are not hearsay in that she is on the witness stand. She can be cross-examined as to what she said. But, as to his statements, they qualify as an exception to the hearsay rule in that they are definitely excited utterances. In fact, he spoke to no one from the time he left to the time he got to the bar, and this was the first conversation he had with anybody."

As Machala considered it, he opened his Zippo, sparked the flint, and stoked his cigar again. He blew out a tremendous gray billow. "No, Sherman, I'm going to allow it."

Wolfson curled her lip, Busch *tsk*'ed, and Magidson threw his hand up in a pantomime of exasperation.

They all removed themselves back to the courtroom.

Machala said to the room, "I will permit this witness to answer the question. So perhaps the question should be read back to her."

The stenographer read out Owen's last question.

Carlyle nodded. "Upon our first meeting at the bar, yes. He told me that Gio had been stabbed, and he didn't know what to do."

Owen's questions moved Carlyle's testimony through the events of that night. At one point, he approached the defense table and in a low voice said to Goggin, "Hand me the picture—the exterior shot."

Carlyle was describing the moment when she sat in the car while Sberna had gotten out and stood on a twin-nozzle hydrant and looked into Tinker's apartment. The picture Goggin handed to Owen was a wide shot of the outside of the building. Someone had circled the hydrant with a grease pencil. Prior to the start of the trial, defense and prosecution shared the evidence they'd be admitting, so the defense knew which picture Owen would show to Carlyle.

Before Owen had even turned away from Goggin, Magidson asked for another sidebar. Machala affected an expression of indulgence, good-natured defeat. He stood and motioned everyone back to his chambers.

Owen looked at Goggin and was a little surprised to see him fuming. Goggin's neck was flushed, vivid against the white of his shirt collar.

In the chambers, Magidson said to Machala, "I stopped Mr. Owen, and I apologize for interrupting like that, Your Honor. But he is going to show her a photograph that is already marked by another witness, and I object to that. I don't mind if he shows her a plain photograph if he has a copy of it."

Owen was about to speak, but Goggin, angry, cut in. "Can I ask what the basis of that objection is?"

"Yes. He is going to show her a marked photograph—" Goggin tried interrupting, but Magidson put his hand up. "You asked me a question. I am trying to answer it."

"Right," Goggin said. "So let me just make sure you understood the question: what possible basis is there for that objection?"

Magidson seemed to relish Goggin's irritation. He spoke like an adult to an unreasonable child. "Because, when you mark a photograph, it is a photographic reproduction of testimony. And what he is doing is showing her another witness's testimony with the mark on it."

Goggin's face seethed red, and his expression was disbelieving, but his voice was still on the near side of calm. "Judge, I have never heard that one."

Magidson, condescending, said, "You may never have heard of it, but—"

Busch, condescending too but also contemptuous, broke in. "There are many things you have never heard of."

Goggin snapped at him. "Oh, just shut the fuck up, you pathetic old man."

Busch drew himself up, pointing in outrage at Goggin, but Machala shouted, "Enough. Enough. I'm serious. Good Lord. Everyone shut up. Show me the picture."

Owen handed it to him. After a little scrutiny, Machala said, "There is a circle around what seems to be—"

Magidson, emphasizing the qualification, said, "Again, I don't care if he shows her a plain photograph."

Machala looked at Owen and Goggin. "You have no other copies of this?"

"No," Owen said.

Machala looked at the photo again, then handed it back to Owen. He addressed Magidson. "Your objection will be overruled. He may use that."

They all returned to the courtroom. Carlyle answered a few more minutes of questions—finer-point details of her previous testimony—without significant interruption. When she was done, Machala thanked her, asked the court sergeant to show her out through the back exit, and called a recess. When the courtroom broke into murmur and movement, a bailiff approached the prosecutor's and defendant's tables and told them Machala wanted to see everyone in chambers to talk about scheduling.

Carlyle was just then making her way over toward Goggin and Owen.

They both looked up. Goggin gave her a nod and perfunctory social smile and continued collecting his papers and notes.

"Miss Carlyle," Owen said. "Thank you for your time this morning—"

She cut him off and treated him to a broad smile that might have been half sincere.

*It almost works*, Owen thought. He took a sidelong glance and saw Goggin with an air of distaste.

"How did I do, Gregg?" she said.

*It really did almost work.* Quietly, he told her, "You were perfect. We couldn't have asked for anything better."

"Well, would you be up for a drink to celebrate?"

Owen heard Goggin exhale heavily.

"I would love to." Owen said it to keep her appeased. He figured that was the smart move. She might feel slighted. She might see it as a small takedown. She might be less cooperative. It was possible. People pulled some weird shit. They might not mean to, they might not know it, but they pulled some weird shit.

And at the same time, he wasn't just flattering her—he was serious. He meant it.

Not now, he figured. Definitely not now. But the trial was over soon, and at that point…

Owen scaled the right and wrong of it, weighed the ethics of sleeping with her, considered the pros and cons of—

No way. A horrible, horrible idea.

"I'd love to, but let's wait for a conviction," Owen said. Goggin stood and gestured toward Machala's chambers. "And then after that…"

She said, "I look forward to it. Is it a promise?"

"Absolutely."

A horrible idea he couldn't quite push all the way out of his head.

Goggin motioned toward chambers again. Owen walked away with him.

"Did you … " Goggin started to say.

"Did I what?"

"Sleep with her."

"How can you even ask that? Are you serious?"

"I don't know," Goggin said. He had a grim cast around his mouth. "Am I? I swear to God, if I find out anything happened … "

"I should be insulted, you know. But I'll tell you. No. I didn't. Absolutely not. Why would you think that?"

"Because you'll do pretty much anything to win."

## Chapter 47

After a recess, Goggin and Owen called Mary Pommerich to the stand to corroborate what Carlyle had sworn to: that Cedric Sberna was visibly upset but had no noticeable signs of blood anywhere on him. She didn't testify for long.

After a few minutes, Owen asked his last question.

"You didn't see any blood on his clothes; did you, ma'am?" Owen asked.

"No," Pommerich said.

Owen sat down. Joanne Wolfson got up immediately to cross.

She asked Pommerich, "He wasn't eating an ice cream cone either, was he?"

Pommerich said, "Ummm … no."

"He wasn't waving a gun, was he?"

"No."

"He didn't have a bag full of a white substance that he was waving around, did he?"

For a moment, Pommerich was baffled. She turned and looked at Owen and then back to Wolfson.

"A what?" Pommerich asked.

"Strike that," Wolfson said. "Did he have a knife in his hand?"

"No."

Wolfson turned away.

"Nothing further," she said.

Later, back in their office, Goggin was seething. "I cannot believe that shit. It's goddamned outrageous. Thirty-two times. I counted. One hour of testimony, thirty-two objections."

"And six sidebars," Owen added.

"And six sidebars," Goggin agreed. "I kept thinking—the whole time—how amazing it would be to feel my fingers sinking into the flesh of Magidson's throat."

"But Carlyle—she kept it together. She was good."

"She was very good," Goggin said.

"And so was Pommerich. When Jo-Anne pulled that bullshit? Pommerich looked like she thought Jo-Anne was out of her mind."

"Yeah." Goggin's face was losing its angry color. "And the dream team isn't scoring points with the jury. All of them looked irritated."

"Actually, they looked pretty pissed at times. Even Machala was gritting his teeth."

Goggin said, "So what? He sustained enough of their objections. The thing that really galls me is that when Magidson and Busch pull that crap, they're smirking. It's like they feel they're getting one over on us and we're too fucking pathetic to know what it is."

"Sure, but still—they pissed the jury off. I think it's going to cost them."

Then the office secretary was in the doorway. She said, "Hi, guys—I didn't hear you come back. I got a message for you."

"Mike or me?"

"Either. Or both. A flight from Tennessee arrived at Midway at 3:00. I guess one of you had arranged for a Mr. Wright to be taken to the jail? Anyway, he's there now and they can bring him up whenever you'd like. Do you want me to call and get him over here?"

"Would you, please?" Owen said. He looked at his watch. "Actually, just so Mike and I have a little extra time to get ready for him, would you be able to call over when you're done for the day?"

"That's going to be in about thirty minutes. Is that enough time?"

"We'll make it enough time."

It was just about 8:00 in the evening. A few hours earlier, two marshals had escorted Bill Wright, without cuffs or restraints, to Goggin and Owen's office. They'd spent the time since prepping Wright for his testimony in the morning. Owen had mentioned to Goggin that it was important that Wright keep his cool and remain levelheaded, because Magidson, Busch, Wolfson—someone was going to try and get Wright rattled.

Goggin said, "I think if you're a combat pilot, levelheadedness is assumed."

Now, they were going over some of the questions they expected the defense would ask Wright on cross-examination.

Owen was saying, "When they're hammering at you—and they will hammer at you—pretend you're back in the Air Force, okay? You're back in the Air Force, you've had to parachute out, you've gotten captured, and now you're being interrogated. Name, rank, serial number. That's all you're required to give, right? So, here, it's the same principle. *Yes, no.* Just keep it basic. No narrative, no elaboration, no stories. Yes and no. No and yes."

Wright said, "Let me see if I understand. You want me to pretend I've crashed, been captured, and then interrogated. I think somehow, I can pull that one off. Okay. So, what do you mean 'hammer' me?"

Owen said, "Mr. Wright, how long have you been a pilot?"

"Fifteen years."

"So quite a bit of experience. Where did you learn to fly?"

"I was trained in the Air Force."

"Is it true you were flying a DC6 when you crashed in Tennessee?"

"Yes, sir."

"Doesn't a DC6 require a copilot?"

"It does."

"Did you have a copilot?"

"I did not."

"Were you taught to disregard safety rules in the Air Force?"

"No, sir."

"When you crashed the plane, had that been a part of your Air Force training?"

Wright's face cast off quick sparks of friction, then was impassive again. He said, "Actually, sir, I was awarded—"

"Stop right there," Goggin said. He was playing the antagonist now, and he turned on Wright. "Let me ask again. Was crashing part of your training, Mr. Wright?"

"No, sir."

Goggin's voice relaxed. "All right, good. Now I've asked those asshole questions, you've given your short-as-hell answers, and now, on redirect, Gregg can ask … "

Owen said, "Were you awarded any commendations while you were in the service?"

"Yes, sir."

"What were you awarded?"

"I was awarded the Distinguished Service Cross."

"And the Distinguished Service Cross is awarded to those who demonstrate extraordinary heroism and bravery in battle?"

"Yes, sir."

Goggin said, "Good. You, see?"

"Yes, sir," Wright said.

"We're not pretending now."

"Got it. What do want me to tell them as far as the pot goes?"

Owen and Goggin looked at each other and their eyes conveyed mute alarm.

Owen, emphatic, his voice clear of any ambiguity, said, "Mr. Wright—I can't stress this enough—but we do not want, and we aren't asking for, anything except the truth."

The formality of Mr. Wright and the volume at which he spoke was as if someone was eavesdropping and he wanted to set a record straight. He continued, "We can suggest a way of answering. Or, maybe it's better to say, we can suggest a way of phrasing your answers, but if anyone thinks we're putting words in your mouth, that's it. We're done."

Wright nodded. Owen continued. "You didn't have any reason to bullshit me when we met. You had no idea this deal—any deal—was possible. What you told us that day ... it's the truth? There wasn't anything you omitted? Nothing you might have added? There wasn't a single detail that isn't true? It's fair for me to say that, right?"

It was almost like Wright took offense. "Yes, it was true. Every word. Every word I said was the truth."

"So, we didn't tell you what to say, is that correct?"

"Well, you told me to tell the truth. And no one told me what that truth was. I told you what the truth was."

"Great. Excellent," Goggin said. Then he turned adversarial again. "Is it true you were charged with smuggling drugs?"

"Yes, sir."

"What quantity of drugs were you smuggling?"

Wright closed his eyes. "Around seven tons."

The weight had been discussed before, but hearing it again on the eve of the trial made it sound more incredible.

"Is it true you were facing a life sentence?"

"Yes, sir. That's true."

"And Mr. Owen and Mr. Goggin offered you a deal, correct?"

"No, sir, it isn't."

"They didn't make a deal that if you came here and said my client was there in the plane with you and Mr. Messina and Ms. Moore, your life sentence would be significantly reduced?"

"No, sir. They did not."

"I'm confused. Could you clarify?" Goggin feigned disbelief. "What deal did they make?"

"Mr. Owen and Mr. Goggin only asked if I'd testify as to what happened."

"Then who made the deal with you?"

"The governor of Tennessee. That's what I was told. He offered a deal, which was conveyed to me by Mr. Owen and Mr. Goggin. Now, if I understand how this goes, after cross-examination, there's redirect examination, and one of you two will be asking me what the deal was. So, I can say, 'I was offered a deal by the governor, if I came here and told the truth because it was more important to stop a murderer than to punish someone for drugs. And what I told you was the truth, that Mr. Weinger was on that plane."

"Yes. Great. That's great. 'He offered a deal' rather than 'He offered me a deal' is a lot better. He didn't actually come and offer it to you," Owen said. "They'll object, but we'll get it in. So, now, let's go over what you saw in the plane."

Goggin interrupted. "Actually, Gregg, can I talk to you outside?"

Owen was about to decline and suggest they speak later, but Goggin's mien was insistent. "Sure."

They stepped into the hallway and closed the door.

Goggin's voice was hushed. "We're not going to ask about Weinger and Tinker putting their tongues down each other's throats."

Owen was incredulous. "What are you talking about? Bullshit we're not asking. *That's* the motive."

"Then that's what our motive sounds like: bullshit. It sounds made up."

"Mike, come on—you can't be serious."

"Owen, think about it for a second—"

"We have to ask—"

"Listen, if we—"

"We have to ask."

"Shut the fuck up for two goddamn seconds."

Owen crossed his arms and looked at the floor.

Goggin said, "It's too much. Too much, too perfect, too neat. Too convenient. I'm not going to introduce it. You have to trust me on this one, Disco."

Goggin turned, signaling it was all he wanted to say on the matter, and walked back into the office, leaving the door open. After a moment, Owen followed him through it. Wright was sitting stoically in his chair, looking like he hadn't moved at all. He said, "Just so you know, I heard that whole thing."

Owen didn't say anything. He still had his arms crossed.

"Okay, let's do one more quick round of questions," Goggin said. "I think you know exactly what you're doing, but let's make sure we do, then we can call it a night."

## Chapter 48
*May 16, 1980*

On the morning of Bill Wright's testimony, Gregg Owen got to the courthouse at a little after 7:00 in the morning. He'd planned a final, meticulous run-through of the redirect questions they'd ask if the defense tried smearing shit over Wright's credibility.

Owen figured maligning Wright was a risky strategy for them. It was bad form to go after a war hero, but Wright was a damning witness. He also thought that in this case the truth served as good armor: a well-educated, decorated pilot returns from Vietnam and can't get hired anywhere. What's left for him but breaking the law to earn his bread? Still, the worth of the argument depended on the jury valuing service to the country more than any unease attendant on dark skin.

Wright's testimony was precisely the same account he'd given to Owen and Goggin in Tennessee, and it didn't deviate from what he'd told them during the previous night's preparations.

Magidson made three objections, none of them significant, all of them overruled, and each one seeming almost reflexive, compulsive. It made proceedings move quicker, but it also put Owen and Goggin on guard. If the defense wasn't attacking, there was a reason for it. Owen and Goggin steeled themselves for what was coming.

When Goggin said he had no further questions and sat down, Magidson stood and leisurely approached Wright on the witness stand.

Magidson asked, "What time did you leave Midway Airport to pick up Mr. Messina in Palwaukee, before taking him to Lake Geneva?"

Wright answered, "Approximately 11:00, 11:30."

"I take it the reason you say *approximately* is because you weren't required to make a flight plan for that kind of flight."

"Yes, sir, correct."

"Now, you say you left at approximately 11:00, 11:30. Approximately. So you don't remember exactly when. But you do remember it was late morning?"

"Yes, sir."

"How long does it take to fly to Palwaukee?"

"Ten or fifteen minutes, at most."

"How long did you wait around Palwaukee?"

"Mr. Messina was there on my arrival, so maybe five or ten minutes."

"Did you see his car?"

"I believe so. But the parking lot was full."

Magidson nodded thoughtfully. After a stretch, he asked, "Did you see him in his car?"

Wright was suddenly cautious. "No, sir."

"How did you know you saw his car, then?"

"When we returned, I walked the three passengers to the fence by the parking lot."

"And all three of them got into the same car?"

"I don't recall, sir."

"Well, now. Did this fella that you've identified as Mitchell Weinger and the woman, Ms. Moore, did they get into one car and Mr. Messina get into another?"

"I don't recall that, either, sir."

"And what time was it you left for Lake Geneva?"

"Approximately 12:30. In the area of 12:30."

"You're being approximate because you have no means of literally specifying the time?"

"Correct."

"What time did you land at Lake Geneva, again?"

"Sometime between 1:00, 1:15."

Magidson affected a look of surprise. He turned directly toward Wright. "One o'clock, 1:15. Could it possibly have been 1:30?"

"It might have been."

"How long did you have to wait there while Mr. Messina was conducting his business?"

"I'd say, twenty or twenty-five minutes."

"Do you have any way—a log or any other specific way—of computing the time?"

Without looking up, Goggin drew a question mark on the corner of a sheet of paper. Owen answered with a question mark of his own.

"No, sir," Wright said.

Magidson continued. "What time did you get back to Palwaukee?"

"Two thirty. Somewhere around there."

"Two thirty. Is it possible, Mr. Wright, is it possible, sir, that it could have been 1:30?"

"No, sir, I doubt that."

"Could it have been as early as 2:00?"

"Possibly."

"Possibly?"

"Possibly."

"How long did you spend on the ground at Palwaukee talking to your passengers?"

"Five or ten minutes."

It went on like that for a long time, maybe twenty interminable minutes, Magidson asking again and again about specific times, revisiting the sequence of events in the morning, the flights to and from Lake Geneva, and then—almost minute by minute—the remainder of Wright's day. Owen thought back to Wolfson's endless questions to Steve Glassman concerning exactly when Goggin identified himself as a state's attorney. Both Owen and Goggin had thought Wolfson was circling around something. They waited for her revelation, but it never came. Owen and Goggin knew, however, it would come today. Wright needed to be seen as dodgy, suspect, with a vested interest in lying through his teeth. That was the obvious strategy. It wasn't difficult guessing which angle they'd hammer hardest. They'd torch him with the drugs. A drug smuggler carrying tons of product—anyone in that position would say anything he was asked to.

Magidson, after pinning down the particulars of Wright's movements in the evening, commenced nodding again, hands clasped behind his back. He turned and looked at Owen and Goggin, then the jury.

*And here it comes*, Owen thought.

"No further questions." Magidson sat back down in his seat.

Owen looked at Wright, and Wright was very obliquely looking back at him. Owen could see Wright understood something unexpected had occurred and also that he shouldn't give any indication that there was a rapport between the two of them.

"The witness is excused," Machala said. "We'll have a recess for lunch."

As the marshals escorted him out, Wright barely looked at Owen and Goggin, giving just a faint nod. Owen and Goggin went back to their office.

After they closed the door, Goggin said, "What the fuck just happened?"

"What were they doing? They didn't mention drugs. At all. Not once. It made no sense."

There was a knock. Goggin said to come in, and Bill Kunkle opened the door, stepped through, and closed it behind him. He said, "Hey—I poked my head in for Wright's testimony. I figured with a deal like he got, it was going to get ugly in there. What was that?"

Owen held his hands out in a gesture communicating *Who knows?* He said, "They have to have somebody in their pockets. A juror, probably. I've wondered once in a while if maybe Machala had gotten bought, but even he looked confused today. No one—no one—sucks that bad. Unless it's on purpose. And if it's on purpose, then they have something going on where they don't even feel like they need to bother."

"But wouldn't you at least try to disguise the fact something's bent?" Goggin seemed almost angry, as if Magidson's failure to cover a wrong was worse than the wrong being committed at all. "Would you make it obvious? No, of course not. I think they didn't want to dirty Weinger up."

"I had the same thought," Kunkle said. "Keeping company with wannabe cocaine sellers and marijuana smugglers? Shit."

They all considered the potential toll of bad company. Then Kunkle said, "So, what's next? Who's next?"

"Tony Messina," Owen said. "The victim's father. They are definitely going to leave him alone too. But at some point ... they've got to have something, right?"

## Chapter 49

Tony began his testimony looking drawn, nervous, like he wished he could be anywhere else. They hadn't drilled Tony on what he was going to say. It was clear to Goggin and Owen both he was prepared.

Right before Machala called the court to order, Mitchell Weinger stood up and turned around to face his father, who'd been sitting in the first row of the gallery from the first day. The motion caught Owen's attention. Caleb Weinger gave his son a long, tight hug of support. When Owen saw it, he looked at Tony, sitting farther back in the gallery. Tony seemed to have his attention trained on something else. But when they broke the embrace, the elder Weinger clapped his son hard on the back, and it made enough noise to draw attention. Owen saw something ripple across Tony's face, something that hinted at both horror and impossible anguish. Quick, flickering, gone in an instant, but Owen couldn't forget it.

He and Goggin had decided Owen was the better choice to conduct Tony's direct examination. The morning of the testimony, Tony and Owen had met in Owen's office. He'd gone over everything with Tony beforehand, but Owen wanted to touch on a few quick points and remind Tony of the sorts of questions he'd ask and some best guesses about Magidson's cross.

Tony had said little, mostly nodding in response.

Owen was telling Tony to try to remember to look at the jury while he was being questioned.

He saw a single pearl of sweat roll from Tony's temple down his cheek.

When Tony went to wipe it away, his hand was shaking. Owen didn't call attention to it, but Tony had noticed and pushed his hand between his leg and the seat of his chair.

On the stand, Tony was calm and poised and answered questions in a consistently steady voice. Owen prompted him through what was essentially the same story he'd told years ago and many times since.

But then Magidson misstepped.

"When you got to the apartment on North Sheridan," Owen asked, "what did you first do?"

Owen was standing near the jury box, so it seemed more as if Tony was speaking to the jury than to Owen.

"It's a difficult area to park in, so the first thing I did, I drove around the block to find a spot, and while I was doing that, I saw Gio's car. And when I saw it, I ... I just had a terrible feeling."

Magidson stood. "Excuse me. I object to any personal conclusion."

Owen turned on him. "You object to him having a terrible feeling?"

Machala sighed. "Strike the phrase 'terrible feeling.'"

Magidson said, "Judge, may I be heard please?"

"No," Machala said.

"I have a motion to make, if the Court please."

"I would ask you to hold it. Mr. Owen—you may continue."

Owen said, "Now, when you saw your son's car, you felt what you felt. What did you do?"

Magidson leapt up again. "Judge, look what he does. Now, I'm sorry, but may I please be heard?"

Machala rubbed his eyes. "Will the court reporter read back that last question?"

"It's not a question," Magidson said.

"It goes to his state of mind, Judge," Owen said. "And counsel knows it."

"Perhaps you should rephrase your question, then" Machala told Owen.

Owen was irritated on Tony's behalf, but it made Magidson look like he was trying to shield something big and damning behind a small, formal point of procedure.

Eventually, it was the defense's time to cross-examine.

Magidson exhibited an air of patience with Tony that at first struck Owen as the sort of stance you'd take with a young kid if you were trying not to spook him—indulging him, almost, until he was at ease and comfortable. Then Owen started seeing it as if Magidson was handling Tony.

Magidson was courteous enough, but it had the effect of casting Tony as a fragile man who knew something crucial, and Magidson as wary of digging too deep. It left the jury to infer that some truth was going unspoken.

Magidson kept harping, as he had with almost every witness, on specific times, and what—precisely—was said during those times.

When Tony, like almost every witness, couldn't recall something or remembered it out of sequence, Magidson returned to it again and again, poking and worrying the error until it bled. His relentlessness over picayune splinters of data did him no favors with the jury.

Toward the end of his cross, when his demand for exact particulars verged on a provocation, Tony answered a sixth question about the hour and minute of a phone call by telling Magidson for the sixth time, "I don't remember."

It was clear he was telling the truth.

Magidson feigned exasperation and was about to speak, when Tony simply said, "Sir, please. That was a very bad week."

Too late, Magidson recognized he appeared officious, unreasonable. He backed off.

"I don't doubt that, sir," he said quietly.

As soon as Magidson said he had no more questions, Owen stood.

"Your Honor," he said, "we would request that Gio Messina's father be allowed to stay in the courtroom."

Keeping witnesses out of the courtroom, both before and after they testified, was standard. It kept them from being influenced by other testimony prior to their own, or depending on the nature and quality of the testimony, influencing the jurors one way or another. Any exceptions required a request, and the request required a sidebar. But Owen had told himself, *screw it*. He figured that if Tony stayed, "Gio Messina's father"—that was a deliberate move, meant to humanize Tony and Gio both—would keep drawing on the jury's sympathies. If the defense objected, which was their right, they'd look like callous assholes.

When he said it, Owen saw Busch stir in his seat, clearly about to object. Magidson put his hand and Busch's arm and said, "The defense has no objection."

"How are you feeling about tomorrow?" Goggin asked Owen after court recessed for the day.

"With Ted O'Connor and Dick Morask? I'm feeling pretty good. No problem. Keller, though—whenever I think about that guy, my mind feels dirty afterward. By the way, did I ever tell you about him?"

"Tell me about Keller? Tell me what? I don't think you told me anything."

"All right, then. We were at DePaul around the same time. And guess who his Trial Techniques professor was?"

Goggin thought about it for a moment. Then it seemed to dawn on him. "No. No way."

"Yes—Sherman Magidson."

Goggin grinned broadly. "That's perfect. That explains so much. No way I'm leaving that alone. I'm going to bring that up for sure." Goggin paused. "Let's not forget, Magidson was your teacher too."

"Yes, he was. Motherfucker gave me a *C-*."

"If we lose, I'm bringing that up too."

"The other thing, I remembered Keller's name from somewhere. Back at school. Then it hit me: there was this rumor about him going around at the time. Allegedly, he and a buddy had a system worked out where they could tell each other the answers on tests by tapping their pencils. Supposedly, they got caught. But I don't know if it's true because they didn't get expelled. Suspended for a while, I believe."

Goggin's moral outrage could surge without much provocation. The notion of cheating got him suddenly livid. "What an asshole. What a piece of shit."

Goggin's angry color was rising up his neck. That was all he had to say on the subject of Keller and cheating.

## Chapter 50
*May 19, 1980*

On May 13, when the trial began, they'd wanted to be prepared to the fullest extent. Invulnerable.

By the second day, it seemed like they needn't have bothered.

Anticipating a full-throated attack on Sberna's credibility, and knowing Sberna had lied to the cops, they'd assembled witnesses to back up the things he'd been truthful about.

After using Glassman for an opening salvo, after building their foundation on Sberna and putting Bill Wright on to snare Weinger in a bad lie, everything else was corroboration.

Except the defense didn't try very hard, if at all, to undermine the corroborative evidence.

They'd gone after Sberna, just like Owen and Goggin figured they would, but the point the defense latched on to—whether or not Sberna had sounded sufficiently frantic—had struck Owen as a wasted opportunity on their part. But the rest of the time, Magidson followed Wolfson's example from the day Glassman testified and targeted their cross-examination on bullshit.

When Jeremy Keller testified, Owen had to hand it to him. He never deviated from his original statements, and even when he'd been humiliated by the defense and prosecution both, he kept his cool. Magidson, however, had a hard time keeping his. During direct, Goggin drew attention to every stupid decision Keller had made during the first few days after the murders. He hit at Keller again and again for telling Sberna and Carlyle to wait for the cops to find them, to say nothing when they were questioned, and for advising Sberna to throw the gun away. Goggin made a point of asking who had taught Keller's Trial Techniques class at DePaul, and Keller pointed to Magidson.

Magidson was furious. But in the middle of his anger, something seemed to occur to him, and he pivoted to his left to look at Owen.

Owen realized Magidson had just made the connection to the Trial Techniques class that had ended the semester with Magidson sitting across from Owen, telling him to reconsider the path he was on.

Still, the one thing Magidson concentrated on during his cross-examination was whether or not Keller smelled vomit on Sberna's breath when they conferred in Carlyle's bathroom. After a lot of prodding, a bewildered Keller answered "No." Owen knew this was meant to speak directly to whether Sberna had been in a panic, but the defense never picked it up again.

Amazingly, they'd failed to ask Bill Wright a thing pertaining to drugs.

During Ted O'Connor's testimony—which wavered not at all from before—Wolfson and Magidson ignored everything else he said to ask repeatedly whether or not O'Connor had given Weinger his Miranda warning from memory. O'Connor told them he had read the warning to Weinger. They pressed him several times on it, until O'Connor removed the actual card from his wallet and showed it to them.

Owen had it entered as People's Exhibit 29.

When Ron Hale took the stand, Owen showed the jury photographs Hale had taken of the lobby outside the bar at the Ritz-Carlton. Owen wanted to make it clear that if Sberna had come in covered in blood, no one could have missed it. He'd assumed Magidson would make visibility into a sticking point, but Magidson just asked three or four questions about film and camera filters.

The State's last witness was Cook County medical examiner Robert Stein.

Goggin and Owen both believed that few people were as suited to their work as Dr. Stein. There was something uneasy-making about the guy, maybe an excess of enthusiasm for his work. Almost no one living could bring the same energy and passion for the dead.

Owen wanted Stein to tell the jury about lividity, mortification, the difference between cuts and stabs, and how it all played out in the killing of Gio and Tinker. But Owen especially wanted Stein's account of what he'd found during the course of Tinker's autopsy. He'd brought Stein into his office for an interview a few days earlier, just to make sure Owen had his facts right.

During the interview, Stein had said, "It's really a shame, Gregg. What a beautiful face she had. And then I examined her further, and I saw just how attractive she was … *elsewhere.*"

Now, in the courtroom, Stein had just been sworn in.

"Doctor," Owen asked, "in performing the autopsy on the body of Ms. Moore, did you find any unusual substances or anything at all unusual within the body area of Ms. Moore?"

"I did," Stein said.

"Where was it you found something of an unusual nature?"

"An examination of her vagina revealed the presence of a plastic-like transparent baggie, which upon subsequent examination revealed the presence of a white, powdery substance. The toxicology analysis identified it as cocaine."

No one seemed to understand the significance of the plastic-like, transparent baggie. When Magidson cross-examined Stein, he asked just two questions: how tall was Gio Messina? And how much did he weigh?

The trial had run against the grain of their expectations.

While they'd been preparing, Goggin and Owen had probed their arguments for anything fragile or inadequate, tried anticipating and answering in advance every counterargument the defense might make. They broke each argument like a bone, then reset it, then tried to break it again.

"*Why?* It's the most basic question," Owen had said to Goggin one night around 9:30, sitting in their office, right as the trial was getting underway. "What are they going to wonder about? They're going to wonder about *why* this happened at all. And it's a valid question. Even if we don't have to have the answer … I mean, if no one can make sense of it, not having motive is pretty likely going to be a problem."

He was referring to the jury, trying to predict which gaps in the case against Weinger might leave them doubting when deliberations began.

"And then," Owen had continued, "they are going to shove that up our ass."

He was referring to the defense, now.

"No," Goggin said. "*Why?* isn't our responsibility. It's not our problem. We just *prove*. We don't have to explain. It's Sberna—that's what's going to get shoved up our ass."

Owen assumed Goggin was set to enumerate all the things about Cedric that he couldn't stomach.

He said, "Please. Enough about Sberna—"

Goggin shook his head. "No, shut up for a second. I'm not even talking how much of a prick he is. And, honestly, it's not the fact that he lied a few times that scares me shitless. It's the call to Tony. Fishing for info. No condolence. No commiserating. That's cold."

"Yeah, I've thought about that too."

"Bill Wright?"

"Before he testified, I thought, 'Okay, they're going to do exactly what I would and make him look pretty bad. Drug-dealer, saving-his-own-ass-from-a-life-sentence bad. But I figured, we've got the manifest, if nothing else. And then nothing from them. Not a sound."

"It's not sitting right. I've got this sense … "

"I do too. But feelings aren't facts."

"What about your intuition? Hmm? Your never-wrong gut?" Goggin asked.

"Intuition and nerves aren't the same thing."

## Chapter 51

Owen had met Miles Rothstein seven, maybe eight years ago when they were both studying law at DePaul. It might have been in class, at a party, through a mutual friend—Owen didn't recall how they became acquaintances, but they weren't ever more than that.

Rothstein didn't invite anything more, anyway. He was full of jittery, low-grade aggression. He looked outworn before he hit thirty. He got thick and bald too early, resenting it way too much.

Owen didn't mind him as much as many did, but he'd always been good at looking a little further in than most.

Both men worked for the State's Attorney's Office, hired right out of law school.

After a couple of years, Owen made it to Twenty-Sixth and California.

Rothstein didn't.

On occasion, they'd encounter each other for work reasons. When they did, they spoke in a cordial, polite, collegial way about the paths of former classmates and certain notorious Chicago crimes. It didn't get much deeper than that.

Definitely not deep enough for the five While You Were Out messages Rothstein left him in less than a day. Owen found them in a pile on his desk after court adjourned at 4:30.

Getting them at all was strange. But what they said—*VERY important, Urgent, Please call back ASAP, Need to speak right away, Call tonight ANY time*—what they said baffled him. Baffled him and didn't sit well.

Owen asked himself, What did Miles Rothstein want that's so burning and serious?

He tried thinking it through for a few moments but came up empty. It might be dire. It might be nothing. He didn't know.

Owen dialed Rothstein's number with a reluctant finger. Rothstein said hello before the first ring ended.

Owen sat way back in his chair and put his feet up on his desk.

He said, "Miles, it's Gregg Owen. What's going on? I got your messages. Sounded like it couldn't wait. What can I do for you?"

Rothstein's voice got clearer over the handset even as its volume dropped too confidential. He obviously didn't want anyone hearing him. He said, "Could you meet me somewhere? I need to pass some information on, and I can't do it over the phone. Could you do that for me?"

"Can't you just give me—"

"I can't do it over the phone, Gregg. Just trust me. I wouldn't reach out if it wasn't absolutely important. I know this is bad timing. I know you've got your rebuttal tomorrow, but ... "

"This is something I need to know?" Owen figured it must involve the trial directly.

"It's something you absolutely need to know. But you'll have to find out in person. I'm not going into it on the phone."

Owen sighed silently, rubbed his eyes. It sounded too important, and Rothstein came on too insistent. If it concerned the case, Owen was duty-bound to pay attention.

"Okay. I can meet you. Where and what time?"

All the worry left Rothstein's voice. "Excellent. How about Gino's? Seven? Seven thirty? I'm buying."

Rothstein sounded immediately brighter, jovial. Owen thought his shift in tone was the strangest part of the call so far—as if whatever Rothstein wanted, the greater part of it and biggest obstacle lay in arranging the meet at all.

Owen felt the weight of work. He begrudged the quantity of time dinner with Rothstein required. He wasn't all-the-way convinced he'd hear something—anything—as important as Rothstein made it sound.

"Yeah, all right," Owen said. "I've got a little to do here, but I'll be at Gino's at seven."

Owen got to Gino's pizzeria on East Superior ten minutes early. A line was just then forming under the awning at the door. Owen went inside, explained to the hostess he was meeting someone, and began looking around.

The dining room was dim and cavernous, loud with conversation and music echoing off graffiti-choked brick walls. Customers had been writing in chalk on the walls since the place had opened in the '60s, and the names and declarations written there survived in perpetuity. It was difficult, apparently, effacing chalk from brick. Somewhere in the scrawled disarray of words were the band names American Breed and Jerico.

There were tables arranged on the floor of the dining room, all of them full, and a row of booths along one wall, each one occupied. Owen saw Rothstein stand and signal him from a booth in the center of the row.

When he reached the booth, Owen saw Rothstein sitting next to his briefcase, coat, and a blue-and-white canvas duffel bag. On the side, the bag read, *Suffolk Downs, Boston, MA* over the stylized outline of a sprinting greyhound. There was a paper coffee cup on the table in front of him, close to empty.

Rothstein gave Owen a firm handshake. He sat. "Hey. Hey there. It's Gregg Owen. The Disco DA. Ladies and gentlemen, I am pleased to be dining tonight with the pride of Chicago prosecutors citywide, the one and only Disco DA."

Owen sat down across from Rothstein. "Hey, Miles, nice to see you. How's everything?"

"Everything's good now that the Disco DA is here."

"Jesus." Owen's irritation spiked. "Okay, that's enough."

"No, there's never enough when it's the Disco DA. How'd you get Jane Fritsch to write that article about you?" Rothstein lifted his coffee cup and sipped loudly. There were a few drops of coffee pearled in his mustache. Then his tongue snaked out and licked them away.

"You saw it?" It sounded like Rothstein was doing a little glad-handing. A lot of glad-handing, actually. He was excessive with it, and Owen wanted to leave.

"Of course I saw it. Everybody saw it." Rothstein sipped again, put the cup down, looked up at Owen. He said, "How's everything going? How's the trial?"

Owen didn't sense anything urgent in Rothstein. Nothing dire, burning. Something seemed off. Owen felt his patience thinning. "It's going really well, Miles. We're pretty happy with the testimony we got."

He was suddenly wary of giving much away.

"Hey. Good for you, man. That's surprising because the way I heard it? There wasn't much there at all."

"What do you mean? With the witnesses? No, we had solid witnesses. You heard wrong."

"No, I'm talking overall. I heard the case was real thin. No substance."

Owen thought for a second that might be some sort of gambit or lead-in, but Rothstein's tone wasn't right for confiding. It came off almost like a bit of a gloat.

"Then you absolutely heard wrong." Owen wanted to push back at him. He made his voice broad, sardonic. "There was a lot there, Miles. It just had to be dug up. And that's my specialty. I'm really good at digging stuff up."

Rothstein let it go unacknowledged.

He said, "You guys are wrapping it up tomorrow?"

"Yeah, we are."

Rothstein leaned in. "That's what I want to talk about."

A waitress arrived at the booth carrying a cast-iron pan on a tray, holding it steady with a dish towel folded over several times. She placed the pan on the table, along with two white plates and a spatula. "Enjoy your meal," she said and started walking away. She stopped and warned, "That pan is very, very hot."

"Understood," Rothstein said. He took the spatula and lifted a piece of the pizza onto one plate, sliding it over to Owen, then gave himself a piece.

Rothstein cut his pizza and took a bite. Then another.

Owen had felt hungry on his way over, but a growing, pulsing rage suddenly overtook his appetite. He pushed the plate away.

"All right. I'm going," Owen said. He meant it. He started gathering his things.

Rothstein pointed at Owen with his fork. "So, did you know I go to the same synagogue as the Weingers?"

Owen was visibly surprised. "Really?"

"Is it surprising that I go to the same synagogue they do, or that I go to synagogue, period?"

Owen laughed a little. "I'm embarrassed to say it's the latter."

"Well," said Rothstein. He smiled to himself. The smile was acrid, unpleasant. "Well. I just wanted to tell you, the Weingers? They are wonderful people. The most kind, generous folks you're going to meet. Down to earth. Humble. Very generous."

"There's absolutely no reason you need to vouch for Caleb Weinger, Miles."

"Yeah. Yeah, of course. I know that. But I've also known Mitch since we were kids. He's all right. Really. Can he be a bit of an asshole? Sure. But deep down, he's all right. He's not a bad guy."

Owen looked at the table, examined his fingernails, trying to keep his voice even. He waited a couple of beats. "Well, Miles, I'm going to have to disagree with you here. He's not a bad guy? He's bad enough to stab two people dead. He's bad enough to leave them bleeding out on the floor. How is he all right?"

"I don't believe he did any of that. And deep down, neither do you. But I do believe you probably want this over and done. You want to put it behind you."

Owen's steady disposition fell apart. He had a feverish urge to reach over, grab Rothstein's ears and try to twist them off his head. "What the fuck do you know about what I believe? What's that even supposed to mean? You think I'm that much of a piece of shit that I'm going to convict someone just because I'm supposed to? We took the same oaths, right? I wasn't kidding when I took mine."

"Oh, come on, Gregg. Let's talk straight here. Let's get real. Yes, I know we're serving the interests of the People of the State of Illinois and faithfully discharging the duties of the office and no one's above the law. Yeah, yeah, yeah, yeah, yeah. Well and good and fine, Gregg, but there's no noble fight here. One druggie got into a little tiff with another druggie. Things went sideways. That's it. One piece of shit killed another piece of shit."

"One piece of shit killed two innocent people of the state of Illinois."

Rothstein threw a hand up. "Yeah, okay. Okay. Fine. Except, only half of that's true. You've got the wrong person on trial. Period. End of story. You've got the wrong person."

Owen picked up his coat. "I don't like this conversation, Miles. This was a waste of my time."

Rothstein reached his hand. "Hey, come on. Come on. Would you just sit down and hear me out? Do me that courtesy. You know this case was fucked from the start, right? Everyone knows this case was just bullshit fuckery. And no one ever—not for one second—considered that maybe, when everyone's crying about how it's dirty, it's toxic, it's whatever—maybe it's not dirty or toxic in the way they think it is. Someone's got to answer for this, right? That's what this whole thing's about isn't it? Bringing this dead fucking case back from the grave? Someone has to answer for two bodies. Well, friend, you've got the wrong answer. The wrong answer, and none of you care. As long as someone swings."

"Are you serious with that shit? Please. Don't insult me. You think I'm that much of an idiot?"

"No. Not in the least. I think you're smart enough to see the bigger picture. A father is on the brink of losing his son. His innocent son." Rothstein pounded the table and the plates jumped. "That family needs someone to stand up, do the right thing. People close to the family want that, too. Generous people. People who know how to show appreciation."

Rothstein reached over and undid the duffel bag's zipper.

The bag bulged with money.

When Owen didn't say anything, Rothstein said, "Don't tell me you're not curious."

"Not the least. What the *fuck* are you doing, Rothstein?"

"There's $50,000 here, Gregg, and it can be yours. All of it. And no one's asking that much of you. Honestly. All that's being asked here is that tomorrow, when you're doing your rebuttal, just tone it down. That's it. Just a little bit."

"Tone it down."

"Just a little."

Owen could feel his pulse throb in his temples. His arms were shaking now too.

"Fuck you, Miles," he said quietly.

Rothstein looked as if he hadn't heard correctly. "What?"

Owen stood up, raised his voice. He was loud. "I said, 'Fuck you, Miles.'"

Rothstein looked horrified. "What the fucking hell are you doing? Sit down."

"You crooked motherfucker," Owen said.

Other people turned to watch. Rothstein looked outraged. He pulled the zipper shut. It took a few tries. He said, "What the fuck is wrong with you? Fucking asshole."

"Let me say it again. Fuck you. Fuck you for wasting my time. Fuck you for thinking I'm the kind of person who'd take your fucking money. Don't ever, ever fucking contact me again. If you see me, you turn the other fucking way."

Owen rose and walked away. He didn't turn to check Rothstein's reaction. His hands still shook fiercely. He jammed them into his pocket, out of everyone's sight.

Later, Owen was standing in Goggin's living room, on the phone with Bill Kunkle. He'd called Goggin from a pay phone after leaving Rothstein and then driven over.

Goggin stood close by so he could listen.

"I'm trying to get my mind around this," Kunkle said. "Now, you're telling me that this guy offered you fifty grand? And told you—outright—that he wanted you to take it easy when you rebut tomorrow? He said it like that, 'You can have this in exchange for that'?"

"Yeah. That's exactly right."

"You tell Mikey yet?"

"I'm calling from his kitchen."

"Brazen little bastard. How do you know Miles Rothstein?"

"We were briefly in school together. We've bumped into each other here and there since then. He's getting moved out of the Daley Center over to gun court."

"Jesus," Kunkle said.

Goggin thought for a moment, then said, "Don't you think it probably takes a little effort to get fifty grand together?"

"Sure," Kunkle said.

"So, he had it all ready, right? That means they knew in advance they were going to try and pay Gregg off. All this time, we've been asking—did they get to a juror or something? Did they bribe Machala? They've done such an absolute shit job, that's the only thing we could think of, that they bought someone. What if they were counting on Gregg here to be a kink?"

They thought about it.

Then Goggin asked, "So, Bill, what do you want to do?"

Kunkle was silent for a time.

"Goddammit," he whispered. "*Goddammit.*"

"What was that?" Goggin asked.

"We're not going to do anything. Not now. We wait until after the trial. Do *not* say a word about this to anyone. Understood? Not a word. You understand, Gregg?"

"Understood."

After hanging up with Bill Kunkle, Owen and Goggin didn't say much. Owen put his coat on and reached for his briefcase. Goggin bit at his lower lip, interlaced his fingers, and rested both hands on his head. He puffed his cheeks and exhaled loudly. Owen turned and walked toward the front door. Goggin followed. There was everything and nothing to say about a fifty-thousand-dollar bid for a weak close to the trial.

Owen stepped onto the stoop. The nighttime air had lately lost its cold bite, and tonight was merely chilly.

"Well," said Goggin. He was fed-up, pissed off, yet still disbelieving. Owen was in precisely the same state. Goggin said to Owen, "Wow. I guess they're worried. Panicked to the tune of fifty grand."

"Rothstein's eyes bugged out when I told him, 'Go fuck yourself.' He couldn't believe I wasn't even considering it." He shook his head, as if dislodging a stuck thought. "Okay, man. I'll see you in the morning."

"Good night." Goggin thought for a moment, then called after Owen. "Hey, Disco—what do you think the going rate is for a bribe?"

Owen thought for a second. "You know, that's a good question. I have no idea. I guess it would depend."

"I keep wondering: should you feel insulted or flattered?"

"What the hell are you talking about?"

"Is fifty grand a lot or a little to throw away a murder case?"

Owen gave a wearied laugh. "You tell me, Mike."

"How much do you think it's costing to pay those nitwits?"

"Which? The defense? A million. At least a million."

"You could say that offering you … what? Point-zero-five percent? They think you can be bought off that cheap? That's an insult. Right?"

"Under the right circumstances, I think most people could probably tolerate the insult. Maybe that's just the standard fee. Or maybe it's generous. Who knows? But from our vantage—yours and mine—it's a lot of money. Rothstein's paper bag was pretty full, at any rate."

"The other thing I thought of was what if you had taken it?"

"Fuck you. Come on."

"I'm not saying you would. I'm saying 'if.' If you had taken it … I'd bet my right nut someone was there with a camera ready to document the moment. But I'll bet you something else." Goggin pointed at Owen. "You turning it down? If they were panicked before, now they must be shitting themselves."

## Chapter 52

Back at home, Owen prepared his rebuttal to the defense team's closing statement. He was almost certain Magidson would close, but not of exactly what Magidson might say. Since the first day, their strategy, such as it was—if it even was at all—had been opaque. It seemed like the whole of it hinged on interrupting Goggin and Owen at every possible opportunity and occasionally petitioning for a mistrial. Magidson, for the most part, made it his show. Joanne Wolfson had cross-examined Steve Glassman but was otherwise silent. Harry Busch simply sat in his chair, being old.

Owen had entertained an idea that Busch, because of his storied, showy career in the courts, had been hired to lead the defense. Of course he'd lead it. He wouldn't take part unless he took charge. His arrogance gave him an outsized confidence that blinded him to the fact that Goggin and Owen were getting the better of the defense. It had probably never occurred to Busch—or to Magidson either—that they needed to do much more than show up and negate the prosecution.

*Sherna. That's the angle that makes the most sense.*

Owen opened his closet door and took out his black suit. He owned six others of different patterns and colors that he cycled through during the workweek, but he saved the black one for closing arguments. This was a practical superstition he'd picked up from Tom Breen, who always closed his trials wearing the same black suit and always won. Breen would have his black suit cleaned but never mended or altered, and he repaired any frays or splits with a Swingline stapler. Doing any more might have weakened its accumulated magic.

Breen and Owen both knew this was the courtroom equivalent to whistling while passing a graveyard, but they also knew wearing an austere black suit—looking like an undertaker, as Breen had put it—worked a subtle psychology on jurors. It didn't distract, and it said next to nothing about the relative affluence of the person wearing it.

Breen pointed out to Owen that most defense lawyers—or at least the monied ones in nice suits—buttoned their jackets when they stood up in court. Breen made sure his was open. He usually addressed the jury as "folks" rather than "ladies and gentlemen." He did what he could to close the distance between himself and the people listening to him.

Owen considered the way Magidson had gone after Sberna. Magidson hadn't gone for the throat with anyone else, but he was relentless with Sberna, trying over and over to trip Sberna up. When Sberna finally snapped back at Magidson, Owen had very much enjoyed the moment. But he was probably correct in assessing Sberna as the key to Magidson's defense.

Owen laid the suit on his bed and inspected it for spots or stains. Finding none, he returned the suit to his closet, made sure his white shirt was pristine, and looked down at his row of shoes, checking for scuffs. He began walking back and forth across his room, mentally addressing the jury, gesturing with his hands, listening to himself with his inner ear, constructing his arguments. He jotted down anything that leapt out and declared itself shrewd or astute, although once its novelty palled, he usually saw it as weak or illogical. Epiphanies and sudden insights flared and faded quickly and tended to be of negligible value. Irrefutable arguments felt like things remembered or rediscovered, rooted deeply, hard to forget. That was why Owen never needed or used notes when he addressed the court.

Owen knew he was right. Sberna was the key. Magidson would do his level best to convince everyone Sberna was full of shit. Which was true—Sberna was full of shit. Narcissistic, cowardly, selfish, and brimming with bullshit.

But not about everything.

## Chapter 53
*May 20, 1980*

On the morning he drove to Twenty-Sixth and California for the last day of the trial, Owen thought about the strength of their case and the merits of their evidence. He didn't question Weinger's guilt, and he didn't second-guess the evidence they'd presented—it was solid enough, he felt, to negate any doubts. But when he'd looked at one of the jurors the other day, during Wright's testimony, he thought that the rigidity of her posture and tightness of her lips betrayed a certain skepticism, and since then he'd been unable to rid himself of her image for very long.

Naturally, his thinking turned to what Wright had told them about Weinger and Tinker and their interlude in the back of the plane.

Goggin was wrong. It was a mistake not to ask Wright about it.

Did it sound fantastical? Yes, it did. But it was indefensible too. How could they answer it? What refutation could they give, especially when one of the three people in the plane at that moment was dead and the other was—wisely—not speaking on his own behalf? It would be Wright's assertion against Weinger's denial.

Maybe that would have been pushing their luck.

Magidson had defied expectation and chose not to leverage Wright's drug bust.

Owen thought, if it had been Goggin and him doing the defending, they would have exploited the shit out of that. They would have gotten Weinger off too.

But it was possible tying Gio and Weinger together via the plane wasn't as damning as Owen thought.

For whatever unknowable reason, Magidson didn't think gutting Wright was worth the trouble. Maybe he would have thought differently if they'd introduced a motive as neat and convenient as raw animal jealousy. But Owen couldn't deny it—a motive that neat and convenient sounded a little ... fantastical. Magidson wouldn't have had any choice but to demolish Wright. Animal jealousy would be too damning.

But it assumed that Wright could be demolished. That wasn't a sure thing. The way he'd cheerfully withstood Magidson's pompous, graceless nonsense about where Wright had been at precisely which time ...

He thought of Tony and what it would do to him if the jury foreman read out "not guilty."

The thought of Tony enduring the wounds and sadness again sent a pulse of nausea through Owen's gut.

He had to consider that Goggin may have been right when he suggested that Owen was too personally invested.

They had a sort of unspoken pact: if either of them insisted on something, if either of them was prepared to go all in, then the other would concede.

So far, that deference had paid off every time.

Goggin's insistence that they leave Weinger and Tinker's moment out was mild on its face, but Owen could see he absolutely meant it. He conceded. He had to trust Goggin.

He had to, but he was choosing to trust him. He wanted to trust him. That choice felt liberating, in its way. If he felt differently about the trust, it would indicate that his instincts were trying to tell him something, and Owen had never known his instincts to fail. Somehow his capacity to make the choice and feel good about it was the clearest sign yet they'd win the case.

Wolfson was walking away from her car when Owen pulled into the garage. Her expression struck him as troubled. Resigned. He might have been wrong. Maybe that was what he wanted to see on Jo-Anne Wolfson's face on the morning of closing arguments. After all, we saw what we looked for.

When Owen closed and locked his door and Wolfson looked over and saw him, her demeanor changed instantly, and she favored him with a broad, friendly smile and a wave. He waved back.

It seemed gracious to him, like an acknowledgment. Like they'd held their own against her and Magidson and Busch. Like he and Goggin had bested them.

The hallways were empty, but when he got to his office, he found Goggin was already there. He was seated, looking meditative, restive. But more than that he looked ... if not assured, then definitely unworried.

"You good?" Owen asked.

"Hell yes, I'm good. I'm set. I'm ready. We're going to ream the motherfuckers." The way he said it was even, almost laconic. "Weinger is going to see the rest of his miserable life fall apart in there. I'm going to run them over, then you take the wheel and run them over again."

## CHAPTER 54

Machala called the court to order and, when the room settled, told Goggin to present his closing argument. Goggin rose and walked in front of the jury. He didn't rush, he didn't lag, there was no show to it. Just a regular guy stepping up to address a small crowd of regular people.

He seemed a little worn out but at the same time like he wanted to be certain the jury was at ease. It was a good tactic. It told the jurors they mattered, that their opinions were important.

"Ladies and gentlemen, I'd like to speak about responsibilities. Each and every individual in the courtroom today has a responsibility. The court reporter has a responsibility to record what's said. The clerk is responsible for the files and swearing in witnesses. "

He gestured toward different people around the front of the room.

"The sheriffs have a responsibility to take care of you, to make sure you aren't bothered and that no one tries to influence you. The judge has the responsibility to conduct a fair and impartial trial.

"Mr. Owen and I have a responsibility to the People of the State of Illinois to prosecute this case to its fullest.

"I believe we've done that."

Goggin glanced at the defense and then turned back to the jury with a polite, tight smile.

"The defense counsel has a responsibility to this man here, to Mitchell Weinger, to him alone and to no one else."

He dropped his voice. "And you have the responsibility of deciding the facts in this case. You've heard the evidence. And you, twelve different people, from twelve different walks of life, will come together in a moment to make that decision. You'll base that decision on evidence and the law. And just as crucially, you'll base it on your experiences of life and on your common sense. You're God-given common sense."

He paused for a moment.

"I want to talk about corroboration, about how one witness confirms the testimony of another. How each witness we called was here for a special, specific purpose. Each witness bolstered or corroborated the testimony of other witnesses, and I'd like to review those witnesses.

"Mr. Messina testified to finding his only son brutally murdered and to finding his son's girlfriend lying dead nearby, murdered just as brutally. He testified to seeing his son Gio, Delphine Moore, known also as Tinker, and Cedric Sberna at the Messina residence on a Friday and then again the following day. On Sunday, the day after that, he is with Gio in the afternoon. On that Monday, he sees Gio at midday. This will be the last time he ever sees his son alive. On that Tuesday, Gio is nowhere to be found. No one can tell him anything about where Gio might be.

"And on Wednesday, that awful day, at Tinker's apartment building, Mr. Messina has to enlist the help of the superintendent to open Tinker's door so he can find Gio and Tinker, each lying in a pool of their own blood."

Goggin's face turned almost mournful, and his voice thickened.

"I want you to realize what it is we're talking about here, ladies and gentlemen. We're talking about murder. About two dead people. We're talking about Gio Messina and Delphine Moore, who were alive one moment and then dead the next because Mitchell Weinger murdered them—and murdered them brutally."

And now, talking faster, indignant.

"I want to talk about how Cedric Sberna called the Messina home on Monday night, at 9:30, asking Gina Messina where Gio was and being told Gio was at Tinker's. You heard that Gio called later that night, that Gina told him about Cedric's call and about how Gio told her, 'I am high. I am cool. Everything is nice.'

"I want to talk about Cedric Sberna and his testimony. He described his friendship with Gio and what he and Gio did together that weekend and when. He talks about a party Gio hosted at the Sheridan North Hotel, where he entertained four or five other couples, offering drinks and cocaine to everyone. Cocaine that he'd borrowed money from Cedric Sberna to buy. Cocaine that Gio and Cedric Sberna were planning on selling. He spoke about going to see Gio on Monday night, at Tinker's, and finding him well into their supply of cocaine. Cedric tells Gio he's concerned, that Gio needs to cool it, settle down, that he's blowing the money Cedric had given him, and he'd better start taking care of himself."

He stopped as if taking a moment to steady his emotions. When he spoke again, he spoke slowly, deliberately.

"Everything that Cedric Sberna says during his testimony can be corroborated and, in fact, has been corroborated.

"When Cedric gets to Tinker's, he sees Gio is high as a kite. There's cocaine lying out. Gio is drunk. And when Cedric Sberna confronts him, Gio says, 'I'll show you. I can make money. I've got a guy who will buy cocaine for way more than it's worth.'"

He became animated again.

"Gio calls this person, and fifteen minutes later, Mitchell Weinger arrives. Right after Mitchell Weinger arrives, he picks up Gio's gun and starts recklessly waving it around. Mitchell and Gio go into the bathroom to conduct the sale of cocaine. During that time, Cedric hears a gurgling sound.

"Cedric asks, 'What's going on?' and the defendant tells him, 'Nothing, we had an argument, but everything is fine.' When Cedric grabs the gun and tries to press the defendant to come out, going so far as to push the door open. Cedric gets a brief look at Gio, bleeding profusely, lying on the floor, the defendant standing over him with a butcher's knife. The defendant then claims that he's an undercover narcotics officer and that there are three other officers on the way. He warns Cedric to leave.

"Cedric does leave. And he tries convincing Tinker to come with him, but for whatever reason she decides to stay. I wish that Cedric had forced her to go. I'm sure Cedric wishes the same thing."

Goggin paused, closed his eyes, inhaled deeply, opened his eyes, and regarded the jury.

"We know what happens next, how Cedric—who still has Gio's gun—goes to Mickey Carlyle's workplace, how they call the police. You've heard that call. You heard one of the worst examples of irresponsibility I've ever encountered in my ten years as a prosecutor, when Officer Nichols ignores the call. You heard the fright and excitement in Cedric's voice on that tape. There's been some suggestion that it isn't genuine, but you have to decide whether or not that's true. You alone. No one else.

"We know that Cedric and Ms. Carlyle seek the advice of a lawyer, one Jeremy Keller, who commits one of the other most egregious acts of irresponsibility I've heard, when he tells Cedric to ditch the gun and directs Cedric and Ms. Carlyle not to make any more contact with the police, to wait until the police find them, and even then not to say anything.

"When the police do find them, Cedric does say something. He says a number of things. And those things have been corroborated. There's a Dr. Christopher, he's the medical examiner's toxicologist, he can corroborate that Gio was very, very high. His blood alcohol content showed Gio had in excess of fifteen drinks in his system. He had taken cocaine, which is an upper, and quaaludes, which are downers. Dr. Christopher determined that Gio's reflexes would have been so compromised, it wouldn't be possible he could have defended himself."

He nodded faintly, as if reluctant. He spoke slowly again.

"Dr. Stein corroborates Cedric, as well, in confirming Gio's cause of death—which is necessary in a murder case—and Tinker's too. He confirmed that Cedric would have heard a gurgling noise because of the stab wound that perforated Gio's lung, allowing an emission or ingression of all the air in that lung. That caused the sound Cedric described. He said that when Tinker died, she had wounds on her hands and an abrasion on her chin. These were defensive wounds, inflicted when she was fighting off her attacker. A man she knows. A man whose name she knows. A man whose name she screams out several times. *Mitchell.*

"We can tie the defendant to this case through a witness like Ted O'Connor, who arrested the defendant at the parking garage under his place of residence. The defendant is warned of his rights, but later, he says several important things, regardless.

"He says he knows Gio Messina but doesn't know Gio's girlfriend's name. The newspaper clipping from the *Tribune* found in the defendant's home, with Tinker's picture and name, undermines that claim.

"The defendant claimed that the night of the murders, he was at his friend Steve Glassman's house, playing poker. Mr. Glassman, however, says differently. Mr. Glassman says that not only wasn't the defendant there, but the defendant asked Mr. Glassman to lie and say he was. Now, the defense suggested the defendant, who is married, might have been with another woman and just wanted Mr. Glassman to act as a 'beard' as Ms. Wolfson called it."

Goggin gave the jury a rueful smile, shaking his head.

"I have to say that if I was arrested for murdering two people, but I had actually been with another woman, I wouldn't care what my wife or anyone else thought. I wouldn't waste time lying; I'd tell the police right up front who I was with, when I was with her, and where we were together."

Then he was serious.

"Suggesting the defendant might have been with another woman is a good example of the trickery that is sometimes used during cross-examinations, trying to make you think about something that is not in evidence.

"But there is no evidence that the defendant was anywhere else but Tinker's apartment, at 2970 North Sheridan. There is no evidence of that. There's evidence that directly contradicts that. You've been told that the defendant had been read his rights and that there was no lawyer present because the defendant declined to call one.

"But when Detective O'Connor caught him in a lie, he sure as hell called one quick.

"We can tie the defendant to this case through a witness like Bill Wright, the pilot. Mr. Wright said, 'Yes, I flew Tinker, Gio, and someone introduced to me as Mitch to Lake Geneva. And Mitch is sitting right there at the defense table with his lawyers.'

"That, ladies and gentlemen, is the evidence in the case. As I said, the evidence is complete."

He paused for a few moments, looking a little wide of the jury, like he was weighing the best possible words. Then he held his hands out, palms up.

"We've had a fair and impartial trial. You will, in a moment, go to the jury room to impartially decide the facts in this case. When you do, remember that Gio and Tinker didn't get a trial. They were doing cocaine, yes, and that is against the law, but it was not proper that they be executed for it."

Goggin put his hands back down, made his posture formal, dignified.

"The absolute worst crime a person can commit in our society is murder. The defendant has no rights—none whatsoever—to take anyone's life. The buck stops with him.

"Time stopped for Gio Messina and Delphine Moore and for both their families on March 2 and 3 of 1976. Mitchell Weinger stopped it when he murdered Gio and Tinker, and it is time that he be held accountable for what he did."

He nodded at the jury once, then, keeping his eyes down, walked back to his seat, without rushing or lagging.

## CHAPTER 55

Magidson rose from his seat at the defense table and buttoned his suit jacket. He put a hand on Weinger's shoulder and gripped it, stood that way for a moment, guardian and protector, and then stepped to the front of the courtroom. He put his left hand in his pocket, took a deep, measured breath. Turning and silently regarding the jury, for a long moment he didn't speak.

He had his hands behind his back, his face grave, his chin tilted up. After another few seconds, Magidson began. His voice was even and solemn.

"Ladies and gentlemen of the jury. I want to thank you. I want to thank you for being attentive. I want to thank you for your impartiality. I want to thank you for your service."

Magidson raised his hand, extending his index finger, as if emphasizing a point. He was near enough so Owen noticed that Magidson's chain-smoking had stained the finger the color of jaundice.

"I am here to talk about this case; to talk about evidence, and the lack of it; to talk about claims and proof, theories and possibilities, and conjecture. I hope to do so in as calm and as dispassionate a voice as I can because God forbid that you folks should make your decision based on finger-pointing or voice raising or dramatics or cute phrases or anything else.

"A spectacle is not evidence. Dramatics are not evidence, and finger-pointing and showcasing doesn't really help you folks do your job, which is what is so important right now.

"Let's go back to some things that have been said that you really should consider here. An awful lot has been made of the fact that Cedric Sberna says he'd never seen Mitchell before—" he gestured toward Weinger "—and, yet, he picked him out of a lineup."

Owen made a mental note to demolish that point. He was surprised Magidson left an opening, a vulnerability like that. As if you wouldn't recognize someone who'd murdered your friend.

Magidson continued. His hands were together behind his back, and he paced a few steps back and forth. He had the aspect of someone thinking deeply, carefully. "Now, let's think for a minute about the evening of the murder and, most importantly, what Cedric did after the murder.

"He made a phone call.

"What did Cedric Sberna accomplish that Monday evening with his phone call? Or rather, what didn't he accomplish? Cedric failed to give a description of the person he said was in Gio Messina's and Delphine Moore's apartment. He did not give a description of the person who was on the street free as a bird. Which is what Cedric was—free as a bird. He could go as he wanted and do as he wanted to do, to learn what he could or see what would happen in the wake of this crime for four full days.

"Now, here's Cedric, free to go where he wants, and all the time in the world to put his story together. Let's look at what this story is."

Magidson said the word *story* in voice rich with contempt, with his eyes shut. When he opened them again, he appeared incensed, aggrieved. He steepled his fingers against his chest, a gesture of confidence.

"Cedric says he was not in business with Gio Messina. But Gio wants to borrow $3,000. Cedric knows not why. That's what he tells you. That was his sworn testimony to you. Now, you heard that the $3,000 was known by Cedric Sberna at the time to be part of a coke deal. Those are the words that counsel said.

"But Cedric tells you he did not know what that $3,000 was for. He did just what any other ordinary normal human being would do. 'My friend wanted to borrow $3,000, so I wrote myself a check for cash, took the check to the bank, and carry the $3,000 around in my jeans until I saw my friend the next time, so I could give it to him in cash. So, there would be no evidence of any money transaction between my friend and me.'

"Perfectly normal, happens every day, right? That is your experiences in life, isn't it?"

Owen wondered, absurdly, if behind him, Caleb Weinger was nodding, as if saying, *Yes, yes, it's true. It is my experience.* He glanced at the jury. Two of the jurors in the front row, a man and a woman, had their arms crossed tightly against their chests, seeming almost defiant. Their reaction cheered him. When he looked at Machala, he saw Machala looking back, then they both looked away. Next to him, Goggin sat looking at a piece of paper on the table in front of him, pen poised just slightly above it, like he was waiting for a cue.

"He tells you at some later time he learned that Gio Messina had spent part of this money, or maybe all of this money, for cocaine. I should pause here. Please criticize me if you get the slightest impression that I am asking you to justify anything because people were using cocaine or quaaludes or drinking excessive amounts of alcohol.

"There was murder here. There was a double murder here." Magidson looked at the floor, shaking his head, incredulous, dismayed. "Two people were stabbed to death, and there is absolutely no justifying that because they were using cocaine or they were selling cocaine. But calling the murders what they are is not proof that this defendant did it or that Cedric did not.

"Now, Cedric says, 'I had no plans to meet Gio that night, March 1, none whatsoever. I just happened to call his home and look for him. I just happened to place two or three calls to his home looking for him, and then, when I talked to him at ten o'clock in the evening, I decided to get in my car and drive thirty miles to see him. Thirty miles, at ten o'clock at night.'

"That's what he tells you. Just happened, folks, no big thing, it was a nice bitter cold winter's evening.

"That's what he told you. Just coincidence. He says he gets to Delphine Moore's apartment around eleven o'clock in the evening. Now, folks, he had to say that. He had to say it. The whole Messina family knew he was looking for Gio. The whole Messina family knew that he had been told that Gio was with Delphine Moore. The whole Messina family knew that he had been told that Gio was going to spend the evening at Delphine Moore's or at least would be there late that night.

"So, Cedric had to say he went there. He couldn't say, 'I didn't go.' That didn't occur to him at first, as you saw, but he eventually had to say they all knew he was looking for him."

For quite a long time, Magidson detailed all the calls that came into the Messina house that night, how long they lasted, what was said. He made it so convoluted and was so particular with every detail that Owen began losing the thread of Magidson's narrative. He glanced at the jury box. Several jurors looked miserable.

"Now, we get deeper and deeper into Cedric's story. Let's see how it works out. Let's talk about narcotic agents. Cedric tells us his conduct, what was motivated by a belief that the person in the bathroom, the person he claims was in the bathroom, the person who had stabbed his friend with an eleven-inch butcher knife, was a narcotics agent and that he learned all about narcotics agents from television and from the movies."

Magidson was laughing in derision. "Is there a five-year-old in this world who by reason of television, movies, comic books—I don't care what source—honestly believes that narcotic agents carry eleven-inch butcher knives and go around stabbing people to death in bathrooms? As part of their official duties?

"Is there a five-year-old in this entire universe who honestly believes that this is the conduct of a narcotics officer? Next, Cedric shows his utter contempt and disregard for the law. Utter and complete. He tells you because he's now made a track—an error, a slip-up—and he's got to corroborate it, see. He made a track, and he's got to cover it. And here's what he does. He slipped. Just a little slip. Oh, but make no mistake—it's there.

"He told you that when he made that telephone call, he did not tell the officer at the other end that this was a narcotics agent. He did not say that a narcotics agent is in my friend's apartment with an eleven-inch butcher knife. He said some nut is in there because by that time—and, folks, this was just right during his cross-examination because by that time—he had come to the realization that it was not a narcotics agent in Delphine Moore's apartment.

"And then he turns around, and he tells you, folks, that Wednesday night—" Magidson paused. He breathed deeply as if trying to master charged emotion. "I apologize, ladies and gentlemen. Excuse me for raising my voice. He tells you that Wednesday night, when he went to the police station at Area 6, he did not tell the police what had happened because he was concerned about the narcotics agent involved."

Magidson threw his hands up. "So we have *Yes, I believe that was a narcotics agent. No, I don't believe it was a narcotics agent. Yes, I did believe it was a narcotics agent.*"

Magidson affected an expression of disorientation. "Well, Cedric used that narcotics agent business with you as a shield and a crutch in the hope that he could convince you of the good nature of his conduct."

At that, Goggin wrote on the paper in front him. He'd scrawled a question mark. Owen answered with a barely perceptible shrug.

Magidson moved on, describing Sberna's movements after leaving Tinker's apartment. Magidson hammered over and over at the fact that Sberna hadn't changed his clothes, not because Sberna hadn't stabbed Gio and Tinker but because he hadn't done so very savagely. He held up a single picture and referred to it in a way that suggested there were no others.

"You've seen one picture of blood on a wall in that apartment. That's all. That's it. And look at where I'm pointing—that, right there—that's supposedly a spatter effect on the front door. Looks more like a fingerprint smudge than anything else. You decide what it is. You look at it. You look at those pictures. Wherever they are. And you decide whether blood spattered anywhere.

"This photograph is not proof that blood spattered or blood got all over somebody, as counsel claims. That is just proof that somebody bled. Now, why do I raise this? Because you are being shown shadows, and you are being asked to believe a shadow is enough to implicate Mitch. A shadow is not proof. So counsel tries to make the shadow more than what it is by offering corroboration. The sad, sad thing is that what counsel for the State calls corroboration—remember Ms. Carlyle and her coworker?—well, that is no more 'corroboration' than—please excuse the mixed metaphor—than the fancy chimneys or the fancy gables or the front doors on a gingerbread house. Corroboration? Their corroboration is nothing more than candy on gingerbread.

"When you go to buy a real home, if the salesman shows you how good the doors are, and how well-wrought the grill work over the windows is, and how nice the landscaping is, and what a great intercom system it has throughout, and how nice the marble is in the bathroom, and you say to the salesman, tell me about the foundation. Well, I believe we have offered a solid foundation that proves Mitch had nothing to do with the murders of Gio Messina and Delphine Moore."

He walked directly behind Weinger and put a hand on each shoulder and squeezed. His face took on the expression of someone moved nearly to tears.

Magidson took another deep breath and closed his eyes. He opened them and said, "Now, when you retire to the jury room, I pray that you give that foundation, and the whole of this case, the greatest attention and the greatest thought you have ever given anything in your whole lives.

"It's important. Every case is important. Whether it's a bicycle theft or a double murder. Every single one is what separates us from beasts in the jungle. It's the only instrument to sanity and civilization we have to hang on to, and in these times, God knows we need it. When you go into that jury room, consider, please, the things I have said, and if I have omitted to say things or forgotten to say them, blame me. Don't hold them against Mitchell."

Magidson bowed his head in the attitude of someone praying. Then, he looked up, nodded once to the jurors, and clapped Weinger's shoulders. He took his seat without looking at Goggin or Owen.

Machala called for a break and left the bench for his chambers. The jury rose and followed the marshal out of the courtroom. Hushed conversation started between onlookers seated in the gallery.

Owen took a covert look around.

Jo-Anne Wolfson was leaning in, speaking to Weinger, whose parents, relatives, and friends had come for the last of the trial in a show of encouragement and reassurance.

Caleb Weinger stood waiting for a word with his son, in the stance of someone who still retained some hope, even if his confidence was ebbing.

During the trial, Owen had wondered once in a while which would be worse: being father to a son who'd been snatched out of life or father to a murderer who'd spend his life in prison. At first it had seemed obvious, but the lunch he'd had with Tony—when they considered whether Caleb Weinger believed his son was innocent—caused Owen to reconsider. Tony had remarked he'd had a tough time imagining a father's sense of failure when his kid is proved a killer. Owen took him to mean, in more than one sense of the word, that it was an unbearable loss of innocence.

He turned around a little more and saw Weinger's wife; the chair where Caleb Weinger had been sitting; and next to that, Owen's mother. She never told him she was coming, but he always saw her when it was time for closing arguments.

Still, he was surprised. In a courtroom this crowded, it was half miraculous that she'd gotten a seat so close to the front and next to a principal player. She met his eyes and offered a quiet smile.

Back at the defense table, Busch appeared to be praising and congratulating Magidson. Magidson was beaming.

The old guard, Owen thought, the prior generation of lawyers—those guys prized showmanship, gave their arguments and examinations a theatrical flair. Breen had taught Owen the same thing. But Busch and Magidson's idea of theatrical derived from a time when actors hadn't shaken off the legacy of silent movies, when everyone was expressive in broad, exaggerated, almost vaudevillian ways. Harry Busch looked like he'd stepped out of a monochrome gray world. Magidson had learned drama from people like Busch. Tom Breen was more subtle, nuanced. Kodachrome, colored.

Goggin leaned in.

"I don't want you to feel pressured. I don't want you to lose your composure. But swear to God, Disco, if you mess this up, I'll leave you bleeding wherever I find you." He paused for a second, then tipped his chin toward Busch and Magidson. "Look at those two. Convinced they and their reputations are fucking bulletproof. Like they could come in, piss on my shoes, shake off on my pant leg, and not come out any worse for it."

"But that's true. That's the thing—it's true. I almost feel bad for Jo-Anne, though."

"Why? Because she's probably been a nonentity since day one?"

"Precisely. I'm sure she was like, 'Okay. To hell with both of you. I've got my head down; I'm just going to do my job, collect my fee.' But if this ever gets written up, she and Busch probably won't even be footnotes. This is the Sherman Show. Star of his own soap opera. And right now, the credits are about to roll."

"Maybe someday he'll write us into a script. On *The Restless Days of our Young Lives* or whatever the hell it is. Two lawyers—Spike Cogman and Reg Bowen—trying to railroad the young heir of a ... a zinc fortune. I'll feel like I've truly made it." Goggin looked again at the defense. "Okay—Busch, Magidson, little Mitch; how much do you think one of those suits costs? I bet each one is worth more than my mortgage. Honestly—wouldn't you feel a little embarrassed wearing one of those?"

"Yeah. And that's why we're on this side of the aisle."

Owen had thought a bit about his history last night. The previous morning, Machala had stood in the chamber doorway making small talk with Wolfson, Goggin, and Owen. They'd all arrived very early. Machala had told them in detail about a performance of Mussorgsky's *Pictures at an Exhibition* he and his wife had attended over the weekend at the Medinah Temple.

The title had Owen recalling the Emerson, Lake, and Palmer show he'd seen—they'd encored with *Pictures*—and the leaden dismay he'd felt watching Keith Emerson in total command of his instrument. Owen had realized—inarguable, sudden—that his own musical talent had limits. That realization was a significant part of the reason he was on this side of the aisle. But the most he could say against the decision to quit the band was that it had left him wistful. But that was it, and just once in a while. He didn't have any regrets about it.

Now, Owen looked over at the defense. He'd never wanted to wear one of those suits. At the same time, he never played any of his ELP albums anymore.

Right then, Machala's door opened and he emerged from a blue haze of cigar smoke. He closed his door and stepped to the bench. He signaled the marshal to bring the jury back in. Under the table, Goggin kicked Owen's shoe, and whispered, "Bury them."

## CHAPTER 56

Owen rose and walked in front of the jury box. His jacket was unbuttoned—one of those barely liminal moves Breen had taught him to make.

"Good morning, folks. I'm not going to thank you for your time. I'm not going to thank you for sitting in your seats and paying as close attention as you did because what you did was your duty. As Americans, as citizens, we're asked to do our duty, and we do it. You did your duty. I appreciate that you did it to the best of your abilities. But you did what we're all supposed to do when asked to fulfill a duty, and I confess, I've always thought that thanking a jury was really a little bit of glad-handing, kissing up. So, I won't thank you, but I will tell you I respect each of you for answering the call of duty and carrying it out so ably. I respect the way you did your duty very much."

It was always *folks*, according to Breen. Be like one of them because you *are* one of them. Don't say "Thanks for your service" because every juror knows you don't mean it. It sounds hollow.

Owen continued.

"I'm going to speak with you for just a few short minutes, and I'll tell you in advance—I'm not here to defend anyone. I'm not going to defend Cedric Sberna because he's not on trial here, despite Mr. Magidson's heroic efforts to make it seem otherwise. He's not on trial because he didn't do anything, and there's no evidence to even hint that he did anything. If there was, believe me, he would be on trial. There's one suspect here and the evidence we do have, evidence that has gone uncontradicted and undenied—"

"Objection!"

"Sustained."

Breen's rule of three: attack the defendant, attack evidence, attack the lawyer.

He hadn't gotten to all three there, he thought, but it was worth a try. Owen looked at the jury, rolled his eyes a little.

"The judge, when I'm done, will almost certainly tell you to consider your verdict using your 'common experience.' I'm pretty sure that simply means 'common sense.' Now that you've heard all the evidence and had all the facts presented to you, common experience, common sense, is going to tell you, unequivocally, that the evidence and facts lead to a single conclusion: during this trial, only one killer—one double murderer—has been present in this courtroom, and there—that's him. That's the double murderer. Mitchell Weinger."

He'd learned to speak a defendant's given name as infrequently as possible. Stick to *the killer, the murderer* instead.

"The facts don't point anywhere else. He's why we're all here. He's why you've been called on to do your duty as citizens. Because he stabbed Gio Messina and Delphine Moore until he'd murdered them both. The evidence tells you that. Common sense corroborates it.

"*Corroborates*. Mr. Magidson sure had a lot to say about corroboration, and I think we heard every bit of it. At least it felt that way to me. Actually, folks, there's very little to say about corroboration. It confirms what we know. It removes any doubt over what a witness says and what evidence says. Why did we ask Steve Glassman to testify? Why did Mary Pommerich, Mary Carlyle, Jeremy Keller, Ron Hale, Dr. Stein, and Detective Morask take the stand? To corroborate what the evidence told us, what Cedric Sberna told us. Here's evidence, and here's testimony. Here's the corroboration. Now, after we look at it using our God-given common sense, we can say, beyond any doubt, here are the facts.

"Mr. Magidson says differently. He claims that what we've heard and seen add up to something other than the truth. But common sense doesn't corroborate what Mr. Magidson says is true—or to be blunt, what he desperately wishes was true. And this is because he's not telling you everything. One of the most important facts of this case was something Mr. Magidson saw fit not to speak about for the hour he addressed you. A quiet fact, easy to miss. In fact, Mr. Magidson was counting on it being easy to miss. It may seem tawdry, or it might be sickening, but it shows I don't have to defend Cedric Sberna, and neither does Mike Goggin.

"Our last witness—Dr. Stein—do you remember what he told you? He told you something that wasn't in the report he originally made following his autopsy of Delphine Moore. He told us that he found a package of cocaine within the interior of her vaginal canal. And Cedric Sberna—remember?—he told us that she had taken the package of cocaine and, in a panic, pushed it into her leotard to hide it.

"Now, are you going to tell me that while Gio was in the bathroom, busy not being stabbed to death by the defendant—because remember, Mr. Magidson insists our murderer here," he gestured toward Weinger, "wasn't there with Gio, Cedric, or Delphine—that while Ms. Moore was sitting by herself, she picked up a small bag of cocaine, pulled the waistband of her leotard open, and dropped it in and somehow—mysteriously, inexplicably—Cedric just knew?"

Owen tossed the question out and turned his back on it, walking off to the side. He feigned deep consideration.

"How did he know where it was? How could he have known? The only way he could have known was if he'd seen her do it when he was making his cowardly escape. I say *cowardly* because he's a coward. No doubt about that. But unfortunately for Mr. Magidson's argument, cowardice isn't a crime in the state of Illinois.

"Let's set the scene. There's Cedric, with a loaded gun. Some guy yells, 'I'm a narc!' and Cedric thinks, 'Hell, no. I'm not getting involved with this. It might make me a rotten friend, but I need to look out for number one, and I am getting out of here.'

"Cedric says to Delphine Moore, 'I'm leaving. You want to come with me?' But Ms. Moore tells him no. Now, Cedric testified that he wanted as little to do with cocaine as possible. So, what does he do? Brave hero that he is, he tosses the cocaine to her. And what does Ms. Moore do? He says she stuffed it into her leotard. No one else could have known she did it. And when else could she have done it, except for when Cedric Sberna, the coward, was backing out of that apartment with a loaded gun in his hand? And while we're talking about guns, does anyone else find it significant that these people were stabbed to death?

"A woman running around an apartment, screaming as loud as she can, is going to be a lot louder than grabbing one of the pillows lying around, putting it over that woman's head, and pulling the trigger. When Cedric left, he had the gun to protect himself. He didn't have anything else. He didn't have the $700 or the valuable gold watch. He didn't have the cocaine. This man that Mr. Magidson is pleading with you to believe is there and committing acts of murder because of money, leaves with nothing but the gun. Which, by the way, he tells the police about. Tells them he has it. And after he ditches it in the sewer, he tells the police where it is. A person hoping they can avoid suspicion isn't going to tell them anything about having a gun. I mean, come on. That's ridiculous.

"You know what else is ridiculous? Mr. Magidson's claim that there are no blood spatters anywhere." There was no fucking way Owen was going to let Magidson even try to minimize that blood. "And even more absurd, that there are no pictures of blood spatters. Well, I guess then I don't actually have these pictures in my hand right now. I don't have a picture of the bathroom door with blood all over it. I don't have these pictures of blood spattered on the walls."

Owen showed the pictures to the jury, one after another.

"What do you think that is? Where do think that came from? It's blood, and it came spurting out of Gio Messina when he was stabbed in his heart and in his lungs. Mr. Magidson, though, insists I don't have them and that they don't exist. Well, he insists on a lot of things.

"But you know what corroborates the blood spatter beyond having the actual pictures of it? Detective Morask's testimony. Now, Detective Morask doesn't have any interest in this case beyond simply wanting to catch who did it. He just wants to catch the killer, and he doesn't care if it's Cedric or if it's the defendant. But he told us there was blood all over the place, just like in the pictures.

"Now, you'd be correct in thinking that if someone stabbed a person to death so that blood spattered onto every surface of a room, they'd get at least a little on them. Cedric didn't have any on him. And believe me, the forensics team checked. That's why Mr. Magidson is crossing his fingers and hoping against hope that you'll believe that what killed Gio and Tinker was a gentle stab wound that didn't create any spattering and that's why Cedric didn't have any blood on him.

"Well, so sorry to ruin his fantasy, but they weren't gentle stab wounds. They were brutal. There is no way Cedric didn't get blood on himself. And there's no way that anybody with blood on them is going to go into the lobby of the Ritz-Carlton, walk around, have a drink, make a call without anyone noticing. That's why I had Ron Hale take pictures: to prove that any blood on Cedric's clothes would have been clearly visible."

Owen gave a surreptitious glance at Magidson. He hoped he'd catch Magidson shooting him a look of coldly smoldering contempt because Owen wouldn't get a better sign he was winning the battle.

Unless it was seeing a juror nod. Get a juror or two nodding in agreement with you and you weren't just winning the battle. You were winning the whole damn war.

And one of the jurors was nodding at him right now. Owen felt charged, buoyed. He pretended not to see it.

"Mr. Magidson went out of his way to make sure we all knew it was very cold out that night. That being the case, Cedric couldn't have changed outside. He'd have to go somewhere with his bloody clothes and change. But he didn't have anything to change into. Remember that? Remember how he testified to that fact? So, he'd have to go somewhere, strip down, scrub all the blood out of his clothes and, by some miracle of science, remove any trace, spot, or stain from the fabric. Then he'd have to go outside in the freezing, bitter cold with wet clothes—and that's not only not believable, but it's also a bit dangerous. A late winter evening in Chicago is cold enough to give someone hypothermia."

Owen started walking off to the side but stopped mid-step and spun back again. He held his index finger up.

"It's a safe assumption that everyone here has been involved in some kind of romantic relationship, right? Now, imagine having a girlfriend or boyfriend for a few weeks, like Cedric and Mary Carlyle. If you have any interest whatsoever in keeping that relationship going or any hopes of not being turned in, are you going to go to your partner after killing two people and say, 'Ignore the blood, ignore the wet clothes, but I just saw a guy murder my two friends, and I don't know what to do'?"

He appeared skeptical, unbelieving.

"No. That's the last thing you're going to do. Just like getting in the car with a murderer and going back to scene would be the last thing Mary Carlyle would ever do.

"Or what about a little later that same night, when Cedric is introduced to Attorney Jeremy Keller, Mr. Magidson's former student? Are we to believe that if he had even an iota of suspicion, Keller would have gone into a bathroom for a conference with a murderer? Or gotten in his car with a murderer?

"What else would a guilty person not do? They definitely wouldn't call the police and tell them about a crazy guy who was in the process of killing two people so they'd better get over there quickly. That's going to be a disaster for a guilty person. And what if someone wasn't dead, as we've heard that Gio wasn't? Then Gio could have identified the person who stabbed him."

He threw a hand up as if the point wasn't worth the mention.

"Let's talk about this business of the narcotics agent. Mr. Magidson was incredulous over this. How could anyone—even a five-year-old—believe that the murderer Mitchell Weinger was a narcotics officer? Have any of us ever seen any narcotics officer behaving like that in a movie or on a television crime show or maybe a soap opera? He asked us to use a television mentality and make a judgment. Let's do that. Anyone seen *Serpico* or *The French Connection*, where a stash of drugs disappears after a crooked narcotics agent makes an arrest? What about a show where the narcotics agent made a big, fatal mistake and needed to cover it up? Someone here must have seen *The Choirboys*, where the cops kill the wrong person and try to lay the blame on someone else. So, if we use our television mentality, it's really not at all ridiculous for Cedric to think something awful was happening. It wasn't a delusional fantasy."

He showed a chain of expressions—thoughtful, distrusting, something dawning on him. Then the look of a person who'd just had the scales fall from their eyes.

"And you know what? In that awful moment, being as shocked and intoxicated as she was, I think Tinker believed the killer was a narc too. Why else would she catch the cocaine Cedric tossed her and stuff it into her tights? No, it wasn't a delusional fantasy.

"But you know what is a delusional fantasy? That we'll buy Weinger, the murderer's claim to have been at Delphine Moore's apartment on Sunday at nine o'clock. We know that's just a lie. We know he was in the plane with Gio and Tinker until two thirty that afternoon. We know Gio was with his dad until nine thirty that night and wouldn't have gotten down to the apartment until well after the killer said he'd left. Gio would have arrived well into the time Weinger was supposed to be playing cards with his friend Steve Glassman. Which is what he told police he was doing and asked Glassman to lie about.

"Why would he lie about being there Sunday? Because he'd been there Monday night, killing Gio and Delphine, and maybe he couldn't remember if he'd taken his gloves off and touched anything—and he knew the police would very likely come up with a fingerprint or two.

"He said he didn't know the name of Gio's girlfriend, even after spending two hours with her in a plane. And even before he was arrested, he called Steve Glassman and said, 'Steve, my long-suffering friend of seven years, if anyone asks where I was Monday night, tell them I was playing cards with you.'"

Owen moved and stood right in front of the jury so he was blocking their view of Weinger.

"This double murderer made up an alibi in advance. He lied about knowing Delphine Moore. He lied about where he was and when. Who lies so consistently?"

He moved far to the left, and the jurors' eyes followed him.

"Who invents a ridiculous alibi far in advance of needing one? A double murderer does."

Owen moved to the far right, and their eyes followed him there.

"A killer does."

He moved so he was standing right in front of them again. Then he turned sideways and gestured toward the defense table.

"Like Mitchell Weinger did."

He remained standing sideways for a while, letting the jury get a long look at Weinger. Then, measured, calmly:

"Folks, Judge Machala will instruct you that neither prejudice nor sympathy should influence your verdict. That's a tough one, I know. Really—I know that. You're being asked to make an enormous and enormously important decision, and in the face of something so enormous, it's only natural that you … or you … or you too … "

Owen had picked that up from Breen too. Go one by one, juror to juror, eye to eye. Look humble.

He touched the knot of his tie, then tilted his head a little to elevate his chin. He held his hands down in front of him, fingers interlaced, both thumbs up.

"It's only natural that any of us would be moved to sympathy. That's to be expected. But we'd ask one thing. If you feel that justice, in this case, should be tempered with sympathy, please be fair. Show Mitchell Weinger the same sympathy he showed Gio Messina and Delphine Moore when he stabbed them over and over and over, until their blood covered the floor, and walls, and ceiling, and they were dead."

Owen looked slowly across the jury box, then nodded.

"Thank you."

He sat down.

The courtroom was, for a second, nearly noiseless.

He'd taken a fast, stealthy look at the defense. Mitchell Weinger was looking back. He had a thousand things happening on his face: uncertainty, outrage, disdain, disbelief, violence, aggression, terror, something spooked and unnamable. A chaos of expressions. His face swarming like a hive.

Owen thought back to the Daley Center, right at the start of this past grueling winter, looking at Weinger's picture, taken aback by it. Startled by the vacancy of it. A person getting their mug shot taken wondering how a person getting their mug shot taken should look.

Weinger wasn't stupid, but his thinking couldn't extend beyond a few next moments and his own immediate self-preservation.

If Owen saw someone like that on the El, it would scare him shitless. Seeing it here in a court was somehow worse, but he understood a little better why he was a prosecutor. It wasn't just keeping the people of the city of Chicago and state of Illinois safe and protected. At least, it wasn't that alone. It involved his own self-preservation because he was a person in the city of Chicago and the state of Illinois too.

Jo-Anne Wolfson, Sherman Magidson, and Harry Busch were pointedly, fixedly regarding their papers and pens and hands on the tabletop.

Then from the jury box, a pair, trio of cleared throats. Rustling and shifting in the gallery.

Owen leaned close to Goggin. "We've got the motherfucker."

"Relax." Goggin exhaled. "The jury's watching."

"He's done."

Goggin kicked his wingtip against Owen's oxford.

Machala turned to the jury. "Ladies and gentlemen, I'm going to give you your instructions concerning how you are to deliberate the innocence or guilt of the defendant. 'A person commits the offense of first-degree murder when he kills an individual, without lawful justification, and if, in performing the acts which cause the death ... '"

## CHAPTER 57

When Goggin and Owen had walked in earlier that morning, the stifle of the room hit them a moment before they saw every seat was taken and a crush of people, three deep, stood along the walls. Owen recognized a number of reporters, detectives, ASAs. A few people from City Hall. Expensively dressed business-types—Owen guessed they were associates of the Weingers'. Other onlookers he couldn't place.

Goggin and Owen had to angle themselves down the center aisle to their table.

Owen pretended not to notice them now, but he found himself aware of everything happening around him all at once.

Machala had finished his instructions, and all the jurors stood and started slowly filing out. Owen watched them closely, wondering what he should read into their miens and postures and bearings or if he should, or could, read anything there at all. All of them moved as if the moment's gravity was especially weighty. Or it might have been reluctance. He predicted, though, they'd have a long deliberation to get through.

He glanced left and saw Goggin gathering notes together neatly, his eyes on the jury too. Glancing right he saw Wolfson, who appeared dismayed and—he might have been over-perceiving it—a little disgusted. Weinger was next to her, and he was sitting perfectly motionless. Wolfson raised her eyes and met Owen's. She mouthed, *Good job, Gregg*, then turned away.

Harry Busch was standing, leaning against the table just a few feet to Owen's right, glassy-eyed and animated, navy-blue suit looking fresh and crisp and newly clean, listening to Magidson, whose hands moved in sharp, truncated, emphatic gestures—one palm open, thrusting at it with the forked fingers of his other hand.

Machala rose from the bench, met Owen's gaze, and offered a single, possibly admiring nod.

Owen heard louder voices to his right, and he turned to see Magidson and Weinger double shaking each other's hands, Magidson's face the very picture of good news. Some ways off, he saw Tony, Maria, and their three daughters, adrift in a current of people moving in different directions around them. Everyone's voices were getting louder and more relaxed, making the courtroom noisy. He knew Tony was waiting for a quieter moment to signal him and Goggin. They'd planned on having a lunch together that Owen knew would be rough with tension.

Coming in that morning, Owen had also seen his mother, sitting right up front next to Caleb Weinger, the two of them talking. He was certain she'd seen him pass, but of course neither acknowledged the other. He'd been wondering ever since what those two could have talked about. Owen had noticed Weinger wasn't distressed or agitated, so his mother must have been discreet while she was sitting next to him, a few feet away from Mitchell Weinger, among the Weinger family and their friends and associates, like a double agent, agreeable, sympathetic, interested. He wanted to check her reaction when he finished his rebuttal but didn't look at all. There was a lot of studied inattention going on. He tried to find her now, but she wasn't anywhere in his lines of sight.

Out from under scrutiny, Goggin ventured a quiet observation. "When you brought up the coke in Tinker's crotch? And how Cedric could have known? Their eyes were glued to you. Four of them were nodding."

It was a universally positive sign for whatever side got the nod.

The bailiff was in front of them. "Hey, Machala's calling you."

Machala's face said he'd called them several times. They rose and walked over.

"Do me a favor," Machala said. "I know it's probably pointless, but just in case: if you're going anywhere other than your office, leave a number where we can get you, okay?"

It was a standard, if in this case unnecessary, request. The jury might want a question answered, but usually none were asked this early, and verdicts never came that fast, at least not in a case like this. Goggin had already written down the number of Villa Marconi, an Italian restaurant just a few blocks away.

Goggin walked to the gallery and waved Tony over. "Gregg and I have to bring our files upstairs. Should we meet in the lobby in, maybe, fifteen minutes or so?"

Tony nodded and went back to standing with his family.

"Just relax, Disco. You're still tense. Nothing more to be done, now. Que sera, sera." Goggin sang the Spanish part. He was pushing the cart again. Owen found the noise of the bad wheel less foreboding but just as obnoxious. Goggin was right—Owen was still tense.

He didn't respond. Goggin drew him out.

"What do you think? I don't see how they can cut him loose after that. I just don't see it."

Owen shrugged, fatalistic, not quite stoic. "I wouldn't think so."

Goggin said, "I'll tell you, though, the one thing here that gets to me. How could those three do such an unbelievably shitty job? It was a travesty. A wreck. It makes me think … "

"Makes you think what?"

"That they know something we don't."

"I'm pretty sure they just never thought we'd actually do a good job. I'm pretty sure they thought we'd be inept. And they wouldn't even have to try."

Goggin pushed for a few more steps. "Too bad for them, then. Too fucking bad."

"Jo-Anne looked over and told me 'Good job.'"

"No shit? Well, I guess I'm glad they kept her on the sidelines. She's one of us. Basically, at least. She's someone to take seriously."

As they walked, Goggin and Owen passed a few other assistants. Everyone made a point of not looking at one another.

The Messinaes and Owen's mother were waiting in the lobby when Goggin and Owen returned. Tony and Maria tried to be jovial, with Tony telling them, "You both were astounding. I was proud to know you. And we can't thank you enough. You brought this thing back from the scrap heap. And no matter what, that means everything."

Goggin and Owen thanked him. Tony shifted from foot to foot. Then, he said, "But how do you think it's going to go? You can be honest with us."

Goggin and Owen exchanged a look.

Goggin said, "Tony, you learn pretty quickly not to assume anything and not to be in too much of a hurry to make predictions. A lot can happen. A lot does happen. But if I was a gambler … " Tony looked chagrined. Goggin continued. "If I was a gambler … put it this way: I don't think a guilty verdict is a long shot."

When they all arrived at Villa Marconi, the lunch rush was underway, and their table wasn't quite ready. Goggin stepped over to the manager's station and asked he be notified if any calls came in for him or Owen.

Then Owen's mother was at his elbow. "When you're in a courtroom, I always forget who you are."

Owen watched two waiters attend the table, arranging napkins and cutlery and glasses with a pace just short of frantic. Yet they were still in control of themselves. They began pulling chairs out for the Messina women and bowed from the shoulders, gesturing to the seats, making a grand show of hospitality.

His mother continued. "You're darting around. So focused. Your voice is rising, getting quiet, rising again. It seems spontaneous but so thought out too. So controlled. The way you were leaning right into the jury ... I had never known you were like that."

She'd seen him in court before but never offered her impressions in so much depth.

"That's a compliment?" It sounded that way to him. When he looked, he saw her eyes were wet.

"It's a compliment. You're amazing. I'm amazed. I'm so, so proud." She leaned in. "I want to tell you something. When you came in earlier, I know you saw me sitting with Caleb Weinger. Well, he pointed to you and Mike and said, 'I hate them. I just hate them. But if someone killed my son, I'd want them to go after whoever did it.'"

Owen looked over at Goggin, who had the same lupine grin on his face he'd given Owen years before. Now, it was filled with good humor.

"Another thing," his mother said. "That Magidson came over at the end and shook Caleb Weinger's hand. Like a politician. And he told Mr. Weinger, 'Your son will be coming home tonight.' I thought, I have no idea which trial he was watching, but it seemed cruel to get a father's hopes up for nothing."

The two of them sat down. A waiter stood at Tony's elbow, and Tony pointed at the menu, ordering calamari and boiled shrimp for the table. When Tony laid the menu down, the waiter turned to Maria. She ordered veal Milanese. Gina asked for risotto, Lisa and Christina for chicken piccata. Goggin asked for veal Parmesan. Owen's mother hadn't decided, and neither had Owen, and the waiter gave them a moment.

The manager came over, leaned in, and whispered to Goggin.

Goggin stood up. "A call from Twenty-Sixth Street. I hope this isn't a ridiculously stupid question."

He walked away. Owen's mother wavered between several choices from the menu. Owen watched Goggin's back as he spoke on the phone. Then Goggin hung the phone up and pivoted around and walked directly to the table. He grabbed Owen's shoulder. "They've got a verdict."

The table went quiet.

"You're kidding," Owen said. "You're joking."

"No. No, I'm not. We have to get back." Goggin looked up at the waiter, and his voice was genuinely apologetic when he said, "I'm so sorry, but we can't stay. I really apologize."

There it was, after months—years—of stress and strain, of griefs scraped raw, time and again. It was all over.

It took one look, and Owen knew the Messina family wasn't ready for this. Their thoughts were coming too fast, pivoting too quickly—it showed on their faces. None of them spoke. They may have thought they were ready, but they weren't.

## CHAPTER 58

"We've got to go," Goggin said. He said it again to Owen. "We've got to go."

"Wait," Tony said. He drew a deep breath, squared his shoulders. "Is it a good sign, Mike? When the jury comes back that quickly?"

"In our experience ... " Goggin searched for the right words. He kept his voice level, low, earnest. "In our experience, this is usually a pretty good sign. We'll see you over there."

Goggin and Owen rushed away. They were still pulling their suit jackets on while they burst out of Villa Marconi's doors.

"No way they're going to let that mother walk, Disco, no way." Goggin said it out loud at least five times on the way back to Twenty-Sixth Street. His voice was no longer level or low. He sounded rabid and his face was flushing red.

Goggin elaborated. "There's no way they're cutting him loose. No way. Not after just two hours. No way. Not when it's quick like that. Not a chance. Not a fucking chance."

Owen considered the jurors—they'd been nodding during his rebuttal. He'd seen them nodding, and he'd taken it as one of the best signs possible because it was one of the best signs possible.

He said, "Of course not. That won't happen. It can't happen."

He thought, *But weirder things do happen. In fact, anything you can imagine is bound to happen sometime.*

*Just don't let it be today.*

The courtroom was still loud and busy when they got back. The defense team was already at their table, and for the first time since the trial began, Magidson and Busch showed unease. They didn't show much—they were too seasoned for that—but it was there, and Owen could see it.

Mitchell Weinger was sitting with his lawyers, rigid, absolutely still. He might as well have been a scarecrow in Armani, stuffed to bursting with large denomination bills. They were going to lose. They were going to lose, and each of his lawyers would take a payday bigger by far than Owen's annual salary.

Owen felt his would be the better payday by far.

Magidson kept stealing looks at Caleb Weinger, who sat staring past the defense table at Machala's bench.

Owen studied Caleb Weinger for a moment. *If the guy didn't know before what a quick verdict usually meant,* Owen thought, *it seems like he's been made aware.*

Owen's feelings fell just short of empathy for Caleb Weinger. Short of empathy but not quite compassion and not quite pity.

And then Jo-Anne Wolfson was arriving, and Owen saw the bailiff see her and go back to let Machala know.

She was clearly sorry to be coming back late and did her best to settle in quietly.

Her partners didn't react. Magidson was leaning back, relaxed, knees crossed, hands together and resting on his belly, fingers steepled.

Magidson, Busch—neither one had lost a single drop of blood doing this. They hadn't bothered breaking a sweat.

Goggin was right. It was probably best Jo-Anne had gotten sidelined. She was worth taking seriously. Owen remembered she'd done relatively quiet pro bono work with the Black Panther Party.

Busch and Magidson? Back in 1966, they helped defend Jimmy Hoffa against charges of defrauding the Teamster Pension Fund to the tune of $20 million.

If it landed their names above the fold, then maybe Busch and Magidson would bother defending a Panther. Magidson could have woven it into a *Young and the Restless* teleplay. Busch could have fallen asleep at night mentally writing and rewriting the episode in the biography he believed someone should be writing.

It was noisy in Owen's mind, noisier still in the courtroom, but then the bailiff was there, calling out, "All rise, all rise," and everyone stood. Talking dropped to murmurs. When Machala appeared, the room went silent altogether.

Machala sat. He asked the bailiff, "Could you please bring the jury in?"

The bailiff went out, and the door swung to.

All along—from the second he'd paged through the scant, near-nothing file at the Daley Center, then building the case, fitting the pieces roughly together, up until now—all along, Owen had asked a question he couldn't answer.

He'd had theories: some seemed plausible, some possible, some half likely once in a while but never anything probable or obvious. Cedric hadn't offered any insight. Ted O'Connor didn't know and didn't want to hazard a guess. Tony as blind to an answer as anyone.

Glassman didn't tell them anything. The shrinks dug in and prodded and found nothing.

Bill Wright came closest, maybe, to something solid, but Goggin didn't want to touch it. Goggin might have seen or sensed something Owen hadn't, but Owen believed then and still believed now, leaving out what Wright saw going on in the back of his plane at Lake Geneva was a big mistake. Because nothing else explained why Mitchell Weinger did it.

Nothing else explained why someone with the world for a birthright, someone well-loved by his family and a beautiful wife would venture out late in the evening, into an assault of bitter cold and biting wind, to go buy cocaine at an insultingly inflated price. Nothing else explained why someone without a record—someone never charged, arrested, fined, or ticketed—would take a butcher knife with him down North Sheridan Road; go to an apartment with at least one unknown person present; arrive and find Gio Messina wasn't necessarily the biggest, broadest, most muscled person there; see a loaded pistol close at hand; and then take his host to the bathroom and kill him. Then kill his host's girlfriend and then leave the two of them bleeding out, leaving behind money, cocaine, a watch worth thousands, and an eyewitness.

What Wright saw—Weinger ramming a tongue down Tinker's throat and a hand down her pants, while Gio was off conducting business ...

Jealousy didn't explain it all either, but nothing else even came that close.

One or several or all the jurors would get hung up on motive. Owen was more and more sure of it.

There was no avoiding catastrophe now. He and Goggin had made a colossal mistake.

A few bumping noises came from behind the courtroom doors—probably the jury, gathering to come back in. Owen wanted to be sick.

He saw Goggin sitting there nervous, tight but unpanicked, unperturbed.

"We'll get around it." Goggin told him that two weeks before, when the question of motive came up, and again the other day before Wright took the stand.

*We'll get around it.* In other words, we don't need the lust/jealousy angle.

In other words, trust me.

Trusting that right then felt like a nigh-on impossible leap of faith, but Owen went ahead and took it.

The courtroom doors opened with a sharp sound of hinges, of air displaced, and then the jurors were walking in.

Goggin and Owen saw it; Machala, also; and Magidson, Busch, and Wolfson saw it too, and even if it was lost on nearly everyone else, the fact was that when the jury came back to the courtroom and filed in, they looked at the judge, the bailiff, the gallery, at Goggin and Owen, at each other—but not one of them looked at Mitchell Weinger.

It was a storied phenomenon. Juries primed to deliver a *guilty* never looked at the accused.

Magidson and Busch craned their necks, as if they might alter things by catching the attention of a few jurors—or any juror—but no one even glanced.

Wolfson laid her pen down on the table.

*Oh my God, I really want to see Mitchell Weinger leave here handcuffed,* Owen thought.

Goggin turned to Owen and whispered, "We got him."

Owen, even more quiet, said, "I know." But Owen still felt his pulse beating, banging, pounding right behind both eyes.

"Mr. Foreman, has the jury reached a verdict?" Machala asked.

"We have, Your Honor."

He could feel Goggin drawing up, inhaling, holding it.

Owen put his hands between his knees, brought his knees together, pressed his hands to the point of pain in his knuckles.

"Would you please hand the verdict to the bailiff?"

The bailiff carried it to Machala, who opened it up, read it.

After a year with him, Goggin and Owen knew about Machala's quirks and habits. On every verdict, all the jurors signed off. A *not guilty*—Machala figured there was no need to count every signature. *Guilty*? Then, you count and recount and make sure all twelve are accounted for.

Machala was using his pen to count the signatures.

"We've got it. We've got it." Goggin sat there smirking.

Owen was nearly inaudible: "Oh hell yes, we do."

Machala handed the verdict to the bailiff, who handed it over to the clerk.

Machala said, "Will the defendant please rise?"

Mitchell Weinger rose.

"The clerk will read the verdict," Machala said. "And let me instruct all those present that there is to be no outbursts or any expressions of emotions of any kind."

The clerk stood. He said, "Mitchell Weinger, on the charge of the first-degree murder of Gio Messina, the jury finds you guilty—"

There were gasps. Machala glared.

The courtroom went quiet again.

"On the charge of the first degree murder of Delphine Moore, the jury finds you guilty."

Owen heard Goggin exhale, go slack.

Owen bowed his head. He fought the need to jump up, pump his fists, whoop, scream. He couldn't do it—wouldn't do it. You didn't show an ecstatic face to a shellshocked family. It was bad form.

Machala asked the jurors to return to the jury room for just a few minutes so he could speak with them. When they were gone, he turned to Owen.

"Mr. Owen do you have a motion to make?"

"I most certainly do, Judge." Owen stood up. "The People of the State of Illinois, after having convicted this defendant of double murder, motion this court to revoke the bond that he's been free on for the last four years and have him taken into custody, instanter."

"The defendant will approach the bench," Machala said.

Weinger tried to stand but couldn't. He sat back down. After a moment, he tried again and made it to his feet. Magidson reached over and touched his arm, but Weinger jerked it away. He approached the bench and passed Owen, who stood next to the defense table. Owen angled to give Weinger space to get by.

Weinger stopped and looked right at Owen. Weinger's face was ashen, but his eyes were scorched and livid.

"Fuck you," he hissed.

"I'm not the one who'll be getting fucked," Owen said. He didn't think Weinger had heard him, but then he realized Weinger had heard him perfectly.

When Weinger stopped and stood in front of the bench, Machala looked down at him and held the look. Then he inhaled deeply.

"Mr. Weinger, the jury having just convicted you of two murders, I'm going to grant the State's motion and order you to be taken into custody. Mr. Bailiff, please take the defendant into custody at this time. I will set a sentencing date thirty days from today to June 23, at 10:30 a.m., in this courtroom."

Machala banged the gavel, stood, came down from the bench, and walked back through the doors toward the jury room.

Two court sergeants approached Weinger holding a pair of handcuffs. Weinger's face twisted and shook, but he managed to keep himself steady.

When the bailiff led him away, Mitchell Weinger's mother and wife both wailed bitterly. Magidson grabbed his briefcase and followed Mitchell Weinger and the bailiff back to the holding cell.

Tears coursed down Caleb Weinger's cheeks as he watched the doors for almost a minute.

Then the Weinger family gathered their things and left the courtroom.

"I need to take a leak," Goggin told Owen. He hadn't said anything since the verdict was announced. "Give me two seconds, and I'll be back."

Goggin hurried off toward chambers to use Machala's bathroom.

Owen heard a noise behind him, and he turned just as Tony grabbed him in a bear hug, squeezing him until Owen's ribs throbbed. Owen embraced Tony back. Maria was right at Tony's shoulder weeping quietly, desperately, reaching a hand toward Owen but too far to touch him.

"Oh my God, my God," Tony sobbed. "Oh my God, I don't know what to say. I don't know how to thank you. Both of you. Oh God. Oh, Gio—we did it."

Owen wondered if maybe Tony had mixed up Gio's name with his and found it bothered him not at all, but then Tony said, "Gregg. Thank you so much. Thank you so much. I'll never forget what you've done. No matter what, I'm never going to forget this."

Owen said, "Tony, I'm not going anywhere. I'd hoped—"

"Promise me, then. Promise you won't vanish."

"I don't need to promise you. I'll just show you."

Tony wept and wept, and Owen stood with his arms around him until Tony was done.

Goggin came back just as Tony was leaving, and Tony embraced him too.

"Tonight. Seven o'clock, okay? Dinner. I reserved the Consort Room at the Drake Hotel. Mike, you'll be there? Bring your wife if you'd like. And Gregg—"

A voice called out, "Mike, Gregg—" It was the bailiff. "Machala's asking for you in the jury room."

"Go, go," Tony said. "I'll see you a little later."

Goggin and Owen made their way over to the bailiff.

"I think the jury wanted to speak with both of you for a minute," he explained.

Several jurors stood up when Owen and Goggin walked in.

"Here they are," Machala said. He clapped Goggin's shoulder as he walked out.

The mood was neither jovial nor disheartened—more relieved, tired.

The oldest of the jurors stepped toward them and shook their hands. "Mr. Goggin, Mr. Owen, you were both very good."

A woman said, "I was really on the fence, and I was thinking you hadn't quite convinced me, but when the Stein fellow talked about where he found the cocaine, I said, 'Hmmm, maybe Cedric isn't lying.'"

"I liked the pilot," another woman said.

Owen waited for more. Peripherally, he saw Goggin shooting him a look.

Another man picked up the thread. "The pilot—that clinched it for me. Like, 'God damn, they did know each other.'"

The older man asked, "How much time will he do?"

"It's hard to say, really," Goggin told him. "But he probably won't be young when he gets out."

"Can we attend the sentencing?"

Goggin was taken aback. "Well … it's an open courtroom, so, yes, you can attend the sentencing."

"What did he say?" one juror asked the others. Someone told her. She nodded. "Oh, good."

The older juror spoke again. "What really bothered me was Mr. Magidson. A guy loses his son—think about how hard that must be—and you're going to be an asshole to him? Pardon my language."

"Not at all," Goggin said. "I'll tell you, sir, Gregg and I have pretty much seen everything, but that was way over the line."

When they walked out, Sherman Magidson was standing near the door to the holding cell, briefcase at his feet, coat draped over one arm, a file open, looking at a document.

Owen stopped.

"Hey, Mr. Magidson," Owen called out.

When Magidson raised his head, he seemed startled. He regarded Owen for a moment. He said nothing.

"Mr. Magidson—not too bad for a *C-* student, right, professor?"

Owen wasn't certain but he thought Magidson may have flinched. Goggin was about to laugh but stifled it in his throat.

Magidson closed his file, picked up his briefcase, turned, and walked away from them.

## Chapter 59

Goggin and Owen waited for the elevator. Goggin had been quiet, but then he laughed sharply and shook his head.

"What is it?" Owen asked.

"'I liked the pilot,'" Goggin said. "Shit, I don't know why I'm laughing because it isn't funny."

Owen shook his head but didn't laugh. "What if we hadn't found Wright?"

"I know," Goggin said. He stopped laughing. "I know."

"I'll tell you what blew my mind. When that woman said she was leaning toward *not guilty* until Stein testified. I mean, seriously—that was really late in the game."

"But they did it. They made the right choice." Goggin was quiet for a moment. "What did Weinger say to you?"

"He told me to fuck off."

"You're kidding."

"When he looked at me, as he said it—his eyes, man. Those were the eyes of someone who murdered two people and didn't care."

Goggin watched him for a second. Then, "So, Disco, how are you feeling?"

*How are you feeling?*

How *was* he feeling?

Owen felt ... felt ...

Felt what?

*Vindicated?*

No, that wasn't it. After hearing the verdict read, even as the words faded, so did his loathing, revilement, derision for Weinger. Those feelings were spent fuel now. Owen was already seeing Weinger dispassionately, impersonally. Like a neutralized threat.

Watching and speaking with Tony had shown Owen how a crime echoes and ripples, how it shakes through everyone who loves the victim and everyone who loves the criminal. Owen had known it before but had never before fully appreciated it. He wasn't inclined toward revenge.

He felt gratified that his path and Tony's had crossed. He was amazed that there had been such an uncanny convergence of time and circumstances that had brought them together, allowed them to get to this point right now, today. But *gratified* wasn't the word he was looking for.

*Pride?* He was proud of what he and Goggin had pulled off but more in the loose way pride is generally understood as being pleased to have won. The right thing to be proud of was in the doing. The process. Owen's mother had planted that seed. Breen had nurtured it. Goggin had brought it into bloom.

Owen had looked at Weinger's mother in the courtroom, sobbing so hard she was noiseless, mouth open, with strings of saliva stretched between her lips. Pride in sending Weinger to prison meant taking pleasure in Weinger's mother's anguish. Owen took none.

Owen understood, too, in a real way, that the fruits of his best efforts were completely inadequate. Tony and his family could never have Gio's death made up to them. Who would ever think it would be otherwise?

That morning, Owen had seen a new file on his desk. He'd opened it and gave a quick scan: gang-related, a little girl killed when someone opened fire on the apartment where she lived with her family. It looked like they had the shooter dead to rights, but there was a complication, of course, and—

Owen had closed it. He didn't want to lose his focus before the rebuttal.

He'd win that case, and there would be another case after that one, indifferent to what had preceded it and unaffected by it.

Owen was doing his best and had done his best today.

It wasn't enough. When there was a homicide, everyone thought *that's it—that's the end of the victim's involvement.* The prosecution took over, and they proved the accused did or didn't do it. That was the job.

But there was more to the job. And that was not it for the victim either. A person still had to speak for them, bear witness on their behalf. At a minimum, you aimed for another kind of convergence, of what was possible and what was required.

It was still not enough. It was never enough.

He couldn't give Goggin the right answer.

"How am I feeling?" Owen said. "How do I feel? This will do, for now."

From the way his eyes gleamed, Owen saw that Goggin understood completely.

The elevator door opened, and the two of them stepped inside.

"You know what?" Goggin said. "I think I actually will see if Katie wants to come. I'm going to go to my office on four and call her. Dinner's at seven, right?"

"Yeah. Dinner's at seven."

The elevator reached the lobby. When the door opened, Goggin and Owen saw a reporter from the *Tribune* and another from the *Sun-Times*, deep in an animated conversation.

The *Tribune* reporter broke off and said, "Supervisor Goggin and the Disco DA. Congratulations, gentlemen. Well done. Any comments?"

"I think the jury just made the best possible comment. What else is there to say?" Goggin said. He turned to Owen. "So, meet you back here at seven?"

# Afterword

On June 27, 1980, a month after a jury found Mitchell Weinger guilty of murdering Delphine Moore and Gio Messina, Judge Frank Machala sentenced Weinger to a 30 – 40-year prison term.

Weinger's defense team appealed the verdict on the grounds of procedural errors on the part of the prosecution during the trial and closing arguments, as well as certain rulings by Judge Machala. In 1981, the Illinois Appellate Court ruled in Weinger's favor and sent the case back to the Cook County Criminal Court for retrial.

The defense had hoped Weinger's conviction would be overturned, but when faced with a second jury who would hear the same evidence, Weinger pleaded guilty to the murders. In exchange for his plea and a public confession of killing Gio and Delphine, his sentence was reduced to 14 years and 1 day—the minimum prison time for murder in the State of Illinois.

We have never been able to establish the motive behind these brutal murders. That has been a bother to me for forty-five years.

—Gregg Owen.

www.ingramcontent.com/pod-product-compliance
Lightning Source LLC
Chambersburg PA
CBHW070608030426
42337CB00020B/3715